BROADCAST ANNOUNCING WORKTEXT

BROADCAST ANNOUNCING WORKTEXT

A Media Performance Guide

Third Edition

Alan R. Stephenson

David E. Reese

Mary E. Beadle

ELSEVIER

AMSTERDAM • BOSTON • HEIDELBERG • LONDON • NEW YORK • OXFORD
PARIS • SAN DIEGO • SAN FRANCISCO • SINGAPORE • SYDNEY • TOKYO
Focal Press is an imprint of Elsevier

Focal Press is an imprint of Elsevier
30 Corporate Drive, Suite 400, Burlington, MA 01803, USA
Linacre House, Jordan Hill, Oxford OX2 8DP, UK

Library of Congress Cataloging-in-Publication Data
Application submitted

British Library Cataloguing-in-Publication Data
A catalogue record for this book is available from the British Library.

ISBN: 978-0-240-81058-4
ISBN: 978-0-240-81059-1 (CD-ROM)

For information on all Focal Press publications
visit our website at www.elsevierdirect.com

09 10 11 12 5 4 3 2 1

Printed in the United States of America

CONTENTS

VIDEO AND AUDIO TRACKS LIST FOR THE CD

VIDEO TRACKS

Track Number	Track Listing
2.1	The Radio Studio
2.3	Hand Microphone
2.4	Microphone Positioning & Distance from Mouth
2.5	Audio Level Proper and Improper
3.1	The Television Facility
3.2	Talley Light
3.3	Eye Contact Poor
3.4	Egg-on-the-Face
3.5	ChromaKey Improper Dress
3.6	Rocking On Camera
3.7	Posture Counts (Even in casual situations)
3.8	Poor Posture: Seated

AUDIO TRACKS

PREFACE

Performance, be it by broadcast, cable, iPod, or Internet remains an attraction to young adults. And, because of the media growth, there are opportunities for those who have talent and are willing to work hard. But the skills and awareness presented in this book are tools to success in many areas far removed from the mass media world. For the beginner, this book lays out the techniques and approaches that will give you an advantage in the competition for that desired job. Many of the individuals whose name and picture you will see within this text have studied the same type of material and it certainly contributed to their success. Hard work, plus knowledge will open many doors.

However, there is another group who will benefit from the study of presentation techniques. Most college graduates will have the opportunity, probably be expected, to lead at some point and level in their career. Whether it is a sales presentation, a meeting with the press, a staff meeting, a job opportunity or even a new personal relationship, the manner in which you speak, the clarity of your voice, the accuracy of delivery, and "life" you put in your voice all will be major factors in determining how successful you will be.

This book lays out the information you will need for success, based on the thinking of many professionals. The challenge to you will be to learn and apply these guidelines, and put in sufficient practice to make them a normal part of your "performance," regardless of the format or circumstance. Professionals regularly record their efforts and critique themselves aggressively, seeking to find a way to be more successful. In many situations in which performance is a major factor, management may use regular recorded evaluation sessions as a means of helping you progress and alerting you to areas where you are not meeting expected goals. We recommend that you regularly record your work and do a tough analysis. Thinking "I did pretty well" accomplishes little. Seek what you can do better.

ACKNOWLEDGMENTS

First, the authors wish to again thank all the professionals who contributed their knowledge and experience to enriching the previous editions. Many even shared recordings of their work. We deeply appreciate all the help.

For the third edition we are indebted to many others, as well as some who have assisted us again. Thanks go to Daniel Anstandig, Vice President/Adult Formats, McVay Media; Bill McGinty, news anchor, KQH-TV Spokane; Chris Schneider, KRLD, Dallas, author of *Starting Your Career in Broadcasting*; Lisa Brooks, news anchor, talk show host and voice-over specialist, KOMO Radio, Seattle; John Dodge, KBPS, Talent Coach and Consultant, Portland, Oregon; Michael Cardamone, Co-Host, *Good Company*, WKYC-TV, Cleveland; Bobbin Beam, Voice Actress for Broadcast and Business; Al Pawlowski, sportscaster for ESPN and Major League Soccer; Nate Tannenbaum, KDWN, Las Vegas; Brooke Spectorsky, General Manager, WKYC-TV, Cleveland; Eric Dionne, KXTE, Las Vegas; Nate Marinchick, WTAM, Cleveland; Amy Caples, Temple University; Clayland H. Waite, Radford University; Jesse Schroeder Northwestern Oklahoma State University; Dr. Jackie Schmidt, John Carroll University; Tom Ryan, Assumption College, Worcester, Massachusetts; Dennis Knowles, WVIZ-TV Producer, Cleveland; Robert Nolls, John Carroll University; Kim Linzy, KUNV, Las Vegas; Darren Toms, Director of News Programs, Clear Channel, Cleveland; Jane Temple, Producer, WVIZ-TV, Cleveland; Joe Madigan, Associate Producer, the Cavaliers Radio Network; Lisa Lewis, John Carroll University; and John Carroll University students Loriann Ace, Robert Duns, Paula Goncz, Meredith Hurst, Erica Miller, and Maura Reilly. It should be noted that all contributors are listed at the station of their employment at the time of the interview.

CHAPTER ONE

INTRODUCTION TO PROFESSIONAL ANNOUNCING

1.1 INTRODUCTION

The thought of professionally announcing—performing in front of a microphone or camera and being paid to do so—attracts many to a career in the radio, television, or cable industries. Now, with satellite radio, Internet podcasting, and various other forms of "broadcasting," new announcing opportunities are being added that didn't exist just a few years ago. Mass media performers provide information, entertainment, and companionship to hundreds, thousands, even millions of listeners and viewers on a daily basis. It's an exciting and rewarding profession, but it's also a challenging and ever-changing business. For example, satellite radio broadcasting has meant increased job opportunities for the announcer, but broadcast station consolidation, along with voice tracking, has meant fewer on-air jobs and less creative opportunities for announcers. Technological changes have also brought new techniques and procedures, such as increased concern about performer make-up in the high-definition, digital television studio or increased attention to audio levels for the announcer working with a digital audio console. This chapter introduces you to the world of media performance. You'll learn what it takes to become a professional announcer, what is expected of you when you do get to be a talent, and what job possibilities exist in this field.

1.2 ANNOUNCER, TALENT, OR PERSONALITY?

The *Merriam-Webster Online Dictionary* (www. m-w.com) defines announcer as "one who announces: as

a: a person who introduces television or radio programs, makes commercial announcements, or gives station identification **b:** a person who describes and comments on the action in a broadcast sports event." The *Chambers Dictionary* notes an announcer is "a person who announces; a person who reads the news and announces other items in the programme (TV and radio)." The *Grolier International Dictionary* says an announcer is "**1** someone who announces **2** a radio or television performer who provides program continuity and delivers commercial and other announcements." You get the idea, don't you?

While we often equate announcers with radio announcers or disc jockeys, in a more general sense and in tune with the above definitions, an announcer is a radio or television (or cable) performer. And considering performance opportunities made possible by the Internet, satellite-delivered programming, and other technological developments, we should now think of the announcer as a media performer.

In the broadcast industry, two other terms—personality and talent—are frequently used to describe a variety of announcing situations. A personality is generally a notable or famous person, often in the entertainment field, such as a radio personality. A talent is someone with a natural aptitude or superior skill, such as a television talent. These labels are often used interchangeably when referring to the same broadcast performer; however, be aware that the term may be used even though the performer isn't nearly as famous or skilled as the person believes him- or herself to be.

We will look at some more narrowly defined announcing situations later in this chapter and text, but for now and throughout much of this book, the term announcer is used in the broadest context possible.

THE WIZARD OF ID

FIGURE 1.1   A forerunner of the modern broadcast announcer. (Artwork by permission of Johnny Hart and Creators Syndicate, Inc.)

1.3   ANNOUNCING: AN HISTORICAL PERSPECTIVE

If you've ever seen the newspaper comic, "The Wizard of Id," you've seen one forerunner of the broadcast announcer. High atop a castle parapet, he's the medieval guy shouting, "One o'clock and all is well!" as shown in Figure 1.1. Of course, if it's the comics, chances are that all is not well, but that's another story. In any case, our "announcer" is speaking to an assembled audience in the castle courtyard, providing them with a time check as well as news of the hour or lack of it. It's probable that other similar messengers can be pulled out of some different historical context, but all will lack one ingredient essential to being a true announcer—they will not have an electronic delivery system. The announcer is a product of the electronic era, specifically that time in its development when voices could be transmitted through the airwaves. In other words, when radio came into being, so did the announcer.

Early radio announcers bore little resemblance to modern disc jockeys or on-air talent. First, we'd probably have to look hard to find a female announcer because a deep, bass voice was considered a basic requirement. Second, almost every announcer utilized a very stylized delivery. The speaking style heard on the radio was unlike the normal speech of most people. You could probably liken it to a British style today—very proper. It was so formal, in fact, that early radio announcers, like the one shown in Figure 1.2, often wore a tuxedo as they did their announcing chores! Today, both male and female announcers are common,

FIGURE 1.2   Early 1920s announcer, Harold W. Arlin, considered by many radio historians to be the first full-time radio announcer. (Photo courtesy of the Library of American Broadcasting, University of Maryland.)

and a wide range of vocal styles can be heard on the air. The old stylized delivery has given way to a modern conversational tone and, except at an awards banquet, there hasn't been a working radio announcer seen in a tux since the golden age of radio.

1.4   ANNOUNCING: AN EMPLOYMENT PERSPECTIVE

Broadcasting, in general, is not a big business, and it becomes even smaller when we consider only the performing area of the industry. In 2004, the broadcasting industry provided around 327,000 total jobs. Since there are about eight times as many radio stations as television stations, it's logical to assume that the majority of announcers will work in the radio industry. According to the U.S. Department of Labor, Bureau of Labor Statistics, the total announcer workforce is approximately 69,000 (2004), with about 57 percent employed directly by radio and television stations. Additions to this workforce would include satellite radio announcers, announcers in the cable industry, and announcing positions that fall into related categories, such as industrial video narrators or Internet announcers.

The compensation for a broadcast announcer varies dramatically, but, in general, is fairly low. In most instances, salaries are higher in television than in radio, while income for cable television performers often falls somewhere in between. Like many aspects of broadcasting, announcer incomes are driven by the size of the market where the announcer is working; salaries are higher in larger markets than in smaller ones. Other compensation variables include whether the announcer is at the local or network level and whether he or she is working in commercial or public broadcasting. Network-level positions in commercial broadcasting would usually command the highest pay. In 2006, the mean annual wage for the radio and television announcer was $36,100; however, beginning small-market performance positions often start in the teens or low-twenties. However, major-market talent can enjoy a six-figure income and network-level announcers often command million-dollar salaries. For example, in 2006, CBS paid Katie Couric a reported $15 million a year when she took over the anchor position for the network's *Evening News*. Labor statistics also note the median hourly wage for broadcast announcers as $11.69 (U.S. Department of Labor, 2006). So as a beginner in the smallest broadcast markets, you'll earn a modest income, but the promise of a larger payday is there for those who are talented enough and willing to work for it. Additional material about employment in this area is covered in Chapter 13, which explores getting that entry-level job as a broadcast announcer.

Broadcast announcers, for the most part, work in a comfortable environment. Studios are usually well-lighted, air conditioned, and ergonomically designed. Broadcast work is generally not hazardous, and occupational illness or injury is below average in the broadcast industry.

1.5 ANNOUNCER SPECIALIZATION

Most announcer work falls within four broad areas: music announcing, news announcing, sports announcing, or specialty announcing as noted in Figure 1.3. Because broadcast staffs are relatively small, especially in radio, it is not unusual for an announcer to work in more than one area. For example, a disc jockey may also be a news anchor for part of his or her workday. In fact, it's to your advantage to be skilled in as many different announcing specializations as possible when you are first trying to find a job in this field.

FIGURE 1.3 Most announcer work falls in four broad areas: music, news, sports, or specialty announcing. Is your future here?

Music announcing mainly refers to the radio disc jockey (DJ), but also includes the position of video jockey (VJ) on cable channels, and announcers for Internet music sites and the satellite radio company, SIRIUS XM radio. These jobs require the announcer to provide the live or ad-lib material between music selections heard during the program. Audio announcers may also present news, sports, weather, commercials, and community announcements. They often interview guests, operate the audio equipment, sell commercial time, and write commercial copy or news scripts.

News announcing includes anchors and reporters. While news has traditionally been delivered on radio, television, and cable stations, the Internet and other content delivery systems have opened the door to additional news announcing possibilities. The anchor is thought of as the lead on-camera (or on-microphone) talent who guides the direction of the newscast by both reading stories and introducing other reports from on-the-scene reporters or pre-produced news packages. The reporter is an announcing position that requires gathering, writing, and reading news stories. Often these stories are taped for broadcast as part of a newscast.

There are three positions usually associated with sports announcing: the **sportscaster**, **play-by-play announcer (PBP)**, and **play analyst**. Sportscasters function similarly to the news anchor except that they deliver sports news. They usually select and write sports stories, interview sports personalities, and provide results of games played. Whereas a sports broadcast usually stands alone on the radio, it is often just a segment of a newscast on television. Play-by-play and play analyst announcers work as a team to describe the action of a sports event. The PBP announcer is the lead announcer and gives the "play-by-play" action (even if there aren't actual "plays") of the sport. The play analyst is also known as a "color" announcer who provides analysis of the event along with insight and background into the game or contest. In today's broadcast climate, most play analysts are neither broadcasters nor someone who has trained for an announcing position, but rather former athletes and coaches who have played that particular sport. Especially on the network level, it may be difficult for the broadcast student to ever become a color announcer.

Specialty announcers are those who work in other announcing positions, such as commercial voice-over announcers, weather forecasters, narrators, talk show hosts, or television staff announcers (who voice station breaks and other program information). Cable television, satellite radio, and other new multimedia platforms have all increased the importance of announcer specialization because they provide programming choices that can include financial news, home shopping, cooking, gardening, and home repair. Most of these areas require special knowledge and, quite possibly, special skills for the broadcast performer. For example, weathercasters gather information from satellite weather services and regional weather bureaus and then relate and forecast weather conditions for their broadcast area. A job position at Sirius XM Radio required not only announcing skills, but a background in the Catholic religion. Individual chapters later in the text will develop each of these announcing areas in greater detail.

1.6 IS A COLLEGE DEGREE NECESSARY FOR AN ANNOUNCER?

Do you need a college degree to be a good announcer? Not always, but in some announcing specializations, such as the news area, it is probably required, and it will very likely be necessary if you have any aspirations to move toward an administrative position in broadcasting. Regardless of what announcing situation you find yourself in, having a degree probably will help you. In most competitive situations, a degree makes it easier to get a job and get promoted once you have a job. There are many excellent two- and four-year schools that offer broadcast or communication programs that will help prepare you for a performance career. You can check the web site of the Broadcast Education Association (BEA) to find some of the schools that offer communication programs. Their site is located at www.beaweb.org.

Regardless of what specific school you attend or even what actual major you pursue, your education for an announcing career should include these elements: a broadcast education, a general education, and a specialized education. Obviously, you should get some education in the mass media field. Introductory and history courses will give you a good grounding in the industry, while performance and production courses will provide you with necessary skills and techniques. Additional courses in writing, programming, and management can help create a solid foundation for your work in the broadcast business. Some would recommend an actual major in broadcasting, but others suggest another major with some course work in media. Both approaches have been successful for numerous broadcasters, so choose the one that appeals to you.

In addition to a broadcast background, you will need a broad, generalized educational background. Almost any college degree program will require you to take some type of core curriculum course work. Don't look at this as just taking courses to earn credits, but as an opportunity to become familiar with a wide array of areas. As any type of media performer, you will be expected to be conversant on any number of topics. For example, radio DJs are expected to be able to ad-lib about almost anything, and cable television news reporters should have an understanding of the history behind today's news stories. Take courses in art, music, drama, literature, political science, psychology, and as many writing courses as you can. A mastery of the English language, especially the principles of grammar and proper spelling, are invaluable to the broadcast performer. Broadcast announcers should also be computer literate because computers are a part of most aspects of modern broadcasting. A well-rounded education will also prove helpful if you ultimately find yourself working outside the broadcast industry.

The final element of your education should be specialized courses: courses that match the announcer specialization you'd like to pursue. For example, if you see yourself as a classical music announcer, a strong foreign language background will be helpful (and probably required). Similarly, a weathercaster is going to want to take courses in meteorology, and a consumer affairs reporter will probably take some specialized courses in the business, legal, and ethical areas. Regardless of the announcing specialization, you should pursue some very specific course work that will help you attain the position you'd like.

Obviously, this text stresses a college education, but another option for entering the broadcast industry is a trade school, such as the Connecticut School of Broadcasting. Many broadcast trade schools are legitimate and will provide you with a background in broadcasting and plenty of hands-on experience working with broadcast equipment. There are many success stories about their graduates, too, but you need to know what you are getting from a trade school. Essentially, through courses that last six months to a year, you will receive a broadcast background, but that's it—no general education, no specialized education, and no degree of any kind. Because more and more college graduates trained in broadcasting want to get into the industry, it has become harder and harder for non-degree graduates to compete. Be cautious before you decide to take the trade school route. Remember, while there are good trade schools, some are more interested in taking your money than in providing you with any serious broadcast training. Be especially cautious if the school's literature claims "hundreds of stations will want you upon graduation" or "huge sums of money await you upon entering the broadcast field." These are not realistic claims and should alert you to the questionable quality of the school. Before enrolling in a broadcasting school, you might want to contact a couple of managers or program directors of area radio and television stations and ask if they feel the school has a good reputation for preparing its students for entry into the broadcasting business.

At one time, many on-air performers, especially in radio, would have had to obtain a license from the Federal Communications Commission (FCC), in addition to any educational background. The license was not required to perform in any manner, but was needed in order to be in charge of the station's transmitter and take meter readings, which was often an additional duty of the announcer. Because of deregulation, the FCC no longer requires such a license.

1.7 KEY PHYSICAL REQUIREMENTS FOR ANNOUNCERS

As noted previously, early radio announcers were expected to have a deep, bass voice.

Today, a greater range of voices is accepted in broadcasting. However, one physical requirement is that you have, at least, a pleasing voice. Certainly, a deeper-sounding voice is advantageous, especially for female announcers, but as long as your voice is not difficult to listen to, you should have no trouble working as a broadcast performer. In general, the broadcast voice is also free from any regional accents. Although there may be exceptions, Standard American English is the accepted form of speech and grammar in broadcasting. Announcers should display outstanding word pronunciation and accurate grammar usage.

For television talent, another physical requirement is an attractive appearance. While attractiveness can have various definitions, most successful television performers are well groomed in a conservative fashion; have straight, nicely spaced teeth; and probably favor contact lenses over glasses. Few television performers are overweight, have facial scars or acne, or have unusual features (such as a large nose or ears that stick out). No, it's not politically correct to put so much emphasis on someone's appearance, but it is a reality of the performance aspect of broadcasting that will come under consideration one way or another. If you are serious about becoming a television talent, then you must take stock of your appearance and correct any "defect" that might keep you from being considered for a position.

Another physical requirement of broadcast performance is stamina. Since many broadcast stations are on-air 24 hours a day, talent is often required to work long hours and frequently be available at odd times. For example, the television newscaster who works the late local news will obviously not work a typical nine-to-five day. A radio announcer may only be on-air for a four-hour shift, but it is four hours of "live" work that happens in real time. If you make a mistake, you can't go back and do it again, and you don't really get any breaks during that shift. Broadcast announcers need to be in good physical condition to maintain the pace of the business and look (or sound) energetic on-air whether it's their first hour of the day or their tenth.

Beginning performers should also be aware that they are most likely to be the ones working holiday and weekend shifts.

A final physical requirement would be having the physical strength to carry the necessary broadcast equipment. A radio performer may have to manipulate nothing more than a microphone and portable recorder, but a cable or television performer, especially in a smaller market, may have to be a one-person crew, handling a camera, tripod, laptop, and other equipment. The experience of one college graduate illustrates this point when she landed a dream job at a major ski resort. Her job? Ski the mountains each day, carrying a video camera, microphone, and so on, while taping the trails, activities, and people who are there. She then edits her tape into a show, which she hosts each afternoon, for the resort's cable system. It's true that audio and video equipment has gotten smaller, lighter, and more portable over the years, but the broadcast performer will still be expected to be an equipment carrier from time to time.

1.8 KEY EMOTIONAL REQUIREMENTS FOR ANNOUNCERS

Broadcasting, in most instances, is a 24-hours-a-day, 7-days-a-week, 365-days-a-year business. Performers are frequently put under tremendous time constraints. One emotional requirement you need to bring to this profession is an ability to handle stress, especially the stress that comes with working under time deadlines. For example, the commercial voice-over announcer is expected to properly emphasize key words and convey the proper emotion within a commercial and read it in exactly 30 seconds. A newscaster may have to finish reading the newscast at exactly five minutes after the hour. Such tight time schedules can be nerve-wracking. In broadcast situations, there is usually no room for error. It's also stressful to perform before a large audience. Even if you can't see them, you know that you are speaking to thousands or maybe millions of listeners or viewers.

Another emotional requirement is a perfectionist attitude. You can't settle for "good enough" in broadcast situations. For example, the audience expects radio DJs, television newscasters, and cable sports announcers to be perfect. On-air performers never make mistakes, never mispronounce words, and never seem flustered or confused—at least, that's what is expected of you. Of course, we are human and even

the most professional announcer will make an occasional slip-up. That's how we get "bloopers." But some media situations are intolerant of such mistakes, and more than one announcer has lost a job because of an on-air miscue. If you're heading into the performing arena, you need to foster a perfectionist attitude from the very beginning.

1.9 IS PRACTICAL EXPERIENCE NECESSARY FOR AN ANNOUNCER?

The broadcast industry looks for entry-level performers who have some form of experience, along with the previously mentioned educational, physical, and emotional requirements. You'll learn more about this in Chapter 13, which deals with landing that first job in the broadcast field. However, it would be to your advantage now to try to gain some type of practical, hands-on experience. An on-air position at a campus radio or television/cable station is one possibility and an internship is another. Many college programs offer course credit for internships at commercial broadcast facilities.

While it's not likely that you'll end up on the air during an internship, you will gain the valuable experience of working within the broadcast environment. Other commercial broadcast stations offer informal internships to students. These jobs are often "go-fer" positions and are frequently in the promotions area of the station, but they can give you experience and they can lead to something better down the road. It should be noted that some stations expect you to have some technical skills such as audio editing, video editing, and uploading content to the web. You should seek to get these while in school. No matter how you accomplish it; it will be important that you have some practical experience to go along with your educational background. If you are able to work at more than one facility, such as the campus radio station and an internship at a local television station, so much the better. In addition to gaining some hands-on training, you'll probably establish some valuable contacts in the industry. Hear more thoughts on getting practical experience from Megan Mosack on Audio Track 1.1.

---

*This CD-ROM icon [shown icon] which you will see in various places throughout the text, indicates that there is supplemental material on the CD-ROM accompanying this book.

PERFORMANCE TIP 1.1

The Importance of an Internship

Dr. Jacqueline J. Schmidt, Professor, John Carroll University

Should I get an internship?

In the electronic media, internships are becoming essential and in many cases have replaced entry-level positions. Why? Because internships let employers know that you are really interested in the profession and can work effectively in the business. An internship is also a great way to expand your experiences. Internships allow you to gain valuable knowledge of how stations operate, put your academic learning into practice, expand your skills, develop confidence in your abilities and get feedback from professionals. Furthermore, internships allow you an opportunity to build a network of contacts for future employment. If you cannot find or do not have time for an internship get some portfolio-building work through co-curriculars, such as the radio station or television /cable facility on your campus or offer to do volunteer media work for nonprofit organizations. It is important that you be able to show future employers you can operate in a professional setting.

What should I expect in an internship?

First, don't anticipate getting paid. Because of the supply of students and sometimes union considerations, most stations do not pay interns. A few nationally competitive internships offer stipends. Second, expect that you will be doing a share of grunt work. Everybody works as a team, and attitude is important. Third, be prepared to use the internship to your advantage. Don't wait to be told what to do, instead ask questions, offer to shadow different positions, and display enthusiasm and a willingness to learn.

How do I find an internship?

Start with local television, radio, or cable organizations. Most have an internship director. Call and ask for the internship director. If there is no director ask to speak to the head of the area in which you want to work (news, sales, promotion, etc.). For national opportunities check out the websites of the major networks and news organizations.

Dr. Schmidt teaches courses in public speaking, interpersonal/organizational Communication, and interviewing. She also directs the department's internship program and is the advisor to Lambda Pi Eta, Eta Eta chapter, the

JCU chapter of the national communications honor society. She received her B.A. (Phi Beta Kappa) from Macalester College in Minnesota and the M.A. and Ph.D. from the University of Iowa. She has done extensive consulting on improving interpersonal and organizational communications for numerous corporations and community groups including BP, Reliance Electric, Kaiser Permanente, Sherwin Williams, and Bowman. She has had articles published in numerous journals, including *Training and Development,* the *Journal of Communication Administration,* and the *Journal of Business and Training Education.*

1.10 ANNOUNCER RESPONSIBILITIES

The job of an announcer comes with a certain number of responsibilities. As a performer, you have a responsibility to entertain, inform, or persuade your audience. Depending on the specific announcing specialty in which you are involved, you will probably think of yourself as more of an entertainer than an informer or more of a persuader than an entertainer. In reality, you'll likely find your responsibility is a combination of all three. Certainly, the disc jockey is expected to entertain his or her audience. Often the DJ is expected to project a certain image that goes with the station's image or format. However, this same disc jockey will often inform the audience, for example, of time and weather information and community events. The television news anchor has a responsibility to inform, and that's certainly the primary duty, but there is a small degree of entertainment responsibility even here. A commercial voice-over announcer would have a responsibility to inform the audience about a product, but also to persuade the listener or viewer to buy that product.

The broadcast performer is also a communicator and must consider the audience—who they are, their likes, and their dislikes. To communicate effectively requires the announcer to understand the meaning of the message and to connect that idea with what interests the audience. This can be extremely important when delivering commercials, public service announcements, and station promotional spots. Most media outlets have a good description of their audience and it is the responsibility of the announcer to understand how to reach them. Such descriptions often include demographic information, such as age, income, and educational background. They may also contain lifestyle information, which could include the types of restaurants people frequent, how many times per week people eat out, how often people travel, and why. Most announcers need to become familiar with reading and interpreting this type of information and then using it in their performance efforts.

An announcer should also feel some sense of social responsibility. That is, performers have a certain obligation to use their position within the broadcast industry to do some good for society. The audience tends to put broadcast performers on a pedestal, giving announcers a certain degree of influence over their audience; this is known as the "status-conferral" function of the mass media. For example, television newscaster Walter Cronkite was often labeled "the most trusted man in television," and the late *Meet the Press* host, Tim Russert, was dubbed "the most influential journalist in Washington, D.C." Even a small-market radio disc jockey or cable television host will enjoy this type of prestige. As a broadcast performer, you should take advantage of your status to do something positive for society. It may be nothing more than calling attention to a social problem like AIDS or drug abuse, and your ability to make this a better world may actually be quite limited, but there will be times when you can make a difference, and as a broadcast performer you should feel an obligation to do so.

Going along with this social responsibility, a broadcast announcer should also feel a responsibility to participate in community activities. The announcer is often the most "visible" person at a broadcast station, and when the general public thinks of that station, they think of the on-air personalities. Announcers are frequently called upon to speak at various civic functions, emcee an event, or just make an appearance somewhere around town. Sometimes they are paid for such services, but a good broadcast announcer should feel an obligation to be active in the community and volunteer to be a part of whatever is happening there. It's good for the station and it's good for building rapport between the announcer and his or her audience.

The broadcast performer is also responsible for not misusing his or her position. Announcers need to be aware of legal and ethical concerns, especially in regard to indecency, libel, and slander laws. Ethical issues may be described in a professional code of ethics or may simply be an understanding between the management of a station and the talent. It is the responsibility of the announcer to know what these legal and ethical guidelines are. In most cases, "I didn't know" will be grounds for dismissal and not accepted as an excuse. A further examination of legal and ethical issues faced by the broadcast performer is presented in Chapter 12.

On a more technical level, an announcer has a responsibility to be able to properly operate any necessary broadcast equipment. Again, this responsibility will vary greatly depending on the announcer's specialty. Most disc jockeys must operate their own CD players, audio recorders, broadcast consoles, and all the other equipment necessary to go on the air. News reporters, especially in smaller markets, will probably shoot some video and edit stories. On the other hand, the television news anchor may not need to operate any equipment as part of his or her job responsibility.

PERFORMANCE TIP 1.2

Announcer Responsibility—Equipment Operation

Daniel Anstandig, McVay Media

"Radio has the distinct advantage over other mediums of accessibility and 'intellectual stage presence'—or theater of the mind. There was once a time in radio when the performer simply performed. Now, the performer must run the spotlight, be his or her own stage crew, coordinate the other actors entering and exiting the stage, and put on the show all at once. Mastery of the studio equipment is essential. The only way to focus sufficient attention on your own performance is to make the mechanical operation of the studio second-nature."

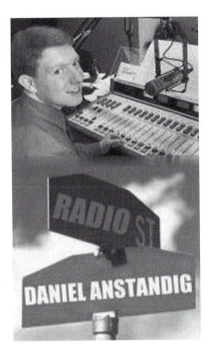

Daniel Anstandig is Vice President/Adult Formats at McVay Media, the world's largest radio consulting firm. Recognized by *Billboard Magazine* as one of the top-five innovators in media, Anstandig oversees new media clients at McVay Media, as well as radio stations in AC, Hot AC, and Christian formats. Among the clients Daniel has consulted for are Clear Channel Radio Interactive, recording artists Jewel and Jim Brickman, TM Century, Legato Café, and various broadcasters around the country. Daniel's experience includes stints as general manager, syndicated program director, and various on-air stops. Daniel is also on the board of directors for Radio Conclave, a 501C(3) serving to grow the radio industry.

Finally, another announcer responsibility is emergency notification. On the national level, most broadcast stations are part of the Emergency Alert System (EAS). In the event of a national emergency, the public would turn to the broadcast stations to find out what was happening. According to the plan, information would be passed along through a network of all the stations. Announcers, especially those on the air, need to know what the emergency procedures are at their particular stations and be ready to act if necessary. More likely, emergency notification will be on a local or regional level. Broadcast stations are often utilized to pass along weather-related emergency information, especially if those areas of the country are subject to flooding, tornadoes, and/or severe winter storms. For many stations, a weathercaster will be involved with such emergency notification, but this duty may fall to a radio disc jockey or newsperson instead. In a serious weather situation, early warning by a broadcast announcer could very well save lives. Again, it is the responsibility of the announcer to know what actions to take and what procedures to follow.

1.11 ROLE MODEL ANNOUNCERS

For anyone just starting in the business today, it wouldn't hurt to look at the careers of some well-known radio, television, and cable performers and use these eminent announcers as role models. While the goal should never be to just copy another announcer, you can learn a lot about performing by seeing what has been successful for others. Adapting some strong, basic techniques to your announcing can only help you develop the unique performance style you want.

Since 1951, Paul Harvey (see Figure 1.4) has been a radio commentator with the ABC network. Over 1200 stations currently carry his *News and Comment* and *The Rest of the Story*, making him today's most listened-to radio announcer. *News and Comment* is also streamed on the Internet twice daily. While Harvey does have a resonant voice, he's best known for his unique delivery style. His staccato, but rhythmic, reading features a mastery of inflection, pacing, and especially dramatic pauses as you can clearly hear in Audio Track 1.2. While he's been broadly labeled a conservative commentator and many of his themes broach the values of God, country, family, and a strong work ethic, his listeners transcend a single political slant. Paul Harvey's exact style may well be difficult to copy, but his skillful use of various delivery

FIGURE 1.4 Paul Harvey is the most listened-to radio personality in America. (Photo courtesy of Paul Harvey News.)

techniques deserves study and makes him a role model for the student of broadcast announcing.

Here are a few other contemporary announcers you might want to study. Jim Rome is one of the nation's leading sports talk performers. His syndicated radio show, *The Jim Rome Show* (which is also known as *The Jungle*), is carried on over 200 stations nationwide. In addition, he is seen on *Jim Rome Is Burning*, a television sports talk program, which airs daily on ESPN. Known for an aggressive, well-informed, rapid-fire delivery, Rome's opinions on the world of sports has gained him respect from athletes, fans, and fellow broadcasters. His unique form of sports commentary and an ability to connect with his listeners and viewers have made Jim Rome one of the most esteemed voices in sports broadcasting.

Katie Couric has been anchor and managing editor of the *CBS Evening News with Katie Couric* since June, 2006. She is also a correspondent for *60 Minutes* and anchor for various *CBS News* primetime specials. She began her journalism career in 1979 as a desk assistant at ABC news in Washington after graduating from the University of Virginia. During the 1980s, she was a news reporter for CNN, WTVJ in Miami, and WRC-TV in Washington. In the early 1990s, she became co-anchor of NBC News' *Today* as well as a contributing anchor for *Dateline NBC*. The *Today* show stint helped her become one of the most recognized and popular TV morning news personalities; however, her straightforward, down-home manner should not be taken as a lack of substance. Couric has a solid newsgathering background, and she has covered numerous major breaking news stories and has conducted a number of newsworthy and award-winning interviews with national and international political leaders, as well as pop culture celebrities. Although she has received some criticism for being more a "celebrity anchor" than a "hard-core journalist," as the first woman to solo-anchor a weekday national network newscast, Couric has already made her mark in the broadcast news arena.

The self-proclaimed "King of All Media," Howard Stern, is a shock jock, best-selling author, moderately successful movie star, and television host. For over 20 years, he was best known for his controversial nationally syndicated radio show that often ran afoul of the FCC because of its lewd banter and sexual topics. In January, 2006 Stern left terrestrial radio and moved to Sirius Satellite Radio (now Sirius XM Radio) with his live radio show and numerous taped features and affiliated programs. His satellite radio show follows a similar format as his old show, but enjoys the greater freedom of less FCC restrictions. Regardless of how you feel about his programming content, listen to Howard Stern interview a guest or ad lib a commercial and you'll hear someone who knows how to use the radio medium to reach an audience.

One of today's top female sports broadcasters is Suzy Kolber. In a field traditionally dominated by men, Kolber has earned the respect of both fans and fellow broadcasters. Her on-air demeanor displays a studied intelligence for the sports she covers, an unending work ethic, and an obvious love of sports. As an ABC Sports and ESPN sports reporter, she is probably best known for her sideline work on NFL games, especially *Monday Night Football*. She has also been an anchor on ESPN's *Sport Center*, and host for *X-Games*, and *NASCAR Countdown*. A 1986 graduate of the University of Miami, Kolber would, by the early 1990s, work her way into being one of the initial anchors for ESPN2. A few years later she joined Fox Sports, but returned to ESPN in 1999.

Al Roker has been called "America's Favorite Weatherman," and watching his congenial on-air style makes it easy to see why. Since 1996, he's been the weather and feature reporter for NBC's *Today*, but has also served as the weekday weathercaster on WNBC-TV,

THE LIBRARY OF AMERICAN BROADCASTING

Located at the University of Maryland in College Park, the Library of American Broadcasting is one of the premier collections of radio and television history in the United States. Formerly called the Broadcast Pioneers Library, it was for many years housed at the headquarters of the National Association of Broadcasters in Washington, DC. The Library traces its lineage back to a history project sponsored by the Broadcast Pioneers organization in 1964. Since then, the Library has grown to include thousands of books, periodicals, pamphlets and photographs (see Figure 1.5 below), and audio and video recordings, as well as hundreds of radio and television scripts, television kinescopes, and programs on film.

FIGURE 1.5 Boys listening to radio station KDKA, Pittsburgh circa 1921. (Photo courtesy of Library of American Broadcasting, University of Maryland.)

The Library also serves as a repository for the papers of numerous individuals whose careers cover every aspect of the broadcasting industry. Several broadcasting-related associations or groups have donated materials to the Library as well. Collections of note include: the National Association of Broadcasters' Library and Historical Archive; the papers and broadcasts of radio and television personality Arthur Godfrey; the papers of radio actress Harriet Foote Underhill (who for many years played the title role on The Romance of Helen Trent); the Sol Taishoff Collection, which documents the career of the publisher of the influential trade journal *Broadcasting & Cable*; and the archives of the Television Information Office, a public relations organization established to burnish TV's image in the wake of the quiz show scandals of the late 1950s. You can visit the Library of American Broadcasting online at www. lib.umd.edu/LAB/.

the network-owned and operated flagship station in New York City. Roker has hosted various holiday specials for NBC, including the annual Christmas at Rockefeller Center and the Macy's Thanksgiving Day Parade. In the mid-1990s, he formed Al Roker Productions, Inc., to produce various video projects for TV, cable, home video, and public broadcasting. He has been recognized by the American Meteorological Society with their prestigious Seal of Approval and noted as a pioneer in utilizing computer graphics in his weathercasts.

These profiles aren't intended to glorify just this handful of broadcast talent, but rather to illustrate the diversity of people who have become successful performers. None of these announcers was born with extraordinary broadcast talent, but they all learned the basic broadcast skills necessary for their position, added their own unique personality, and worked hard to obtain a place of respect and admiration in the broadcast industry.

1.12 CONCLUSIONS

By now you should realize that being a media announcer or performer is not just going before the camera or microphone and talking. It is a true profession that requires some degree of skill, that necessitates an understanding of techniques and procedures, and that carries with it certain responsibilities. A study of contemporary and past radio, television, and cable performers (see insert on The Library of American Broadcasting) can prove beneficial to your future development. Broadcast performance can be one of the most rewarding areas of the industry, both financially and artistically. While it is a small job market, there will always be opportunities for good broadcast performers. But it is the most highly competitive part of the broadcasting field. To be successful takes talent, hard work, and a degree of luck. The rest of this text will continue to prepare you for a career as a radio/TV/cable performer.

Self-Study

■ QUESTIONS

1. One broadcast term often used to describe a variety of announcing situations is "talent."
   a) true
   b) false
2. According to the Bureau of Labor Statistics in 2006, the mean annual salary of the radio-television announcer was about?
   a) $26,000
   b) $36,000
   c) $46,000
   d) $56,000
3. To prepare for a career as a radio disc jockey, you should only be concerned with taking broadcast courses in college or a trade school.
   a) true
   b) false
4. One physical requirement of all broadcast announcers today is a _____.
   a) deep, bass voice
   b) male-sounding voice
   c) pleasing voice
   d) high, treble voice
5. All broadcast performers are highly paid personalities and will have a crew available to operate any equipment necessary to go on-air.
   a) true
   b) false
6. Which of the following people would not be a "role model" broadcast announcer?
   a) Suzy Kolber
   b) Katie Couric
   c) Jim Rome
   d) Alfred E. Neuman
7. Which of the following is not a characteristic that entry-level announcers should display?
   a) stamina to work long hours
   b) willingness to accept inevitable mistakes
   c) ability to handle stress
   d) previous broadcast experience
8. At the network level, the play-by-play announcer is frequently a former athlete or coach.
   a) true
   b) false
9. How large is the total broadcast announcer workforce?
   a) 69,000
   b) 127,000
   c) 269,000
   d) 327,000
10. In sports broadcasting, the term "PBP" stands for _____.
    a) play broadcasting person
    b) play-by-play
    c) players broadcasting plays
    d) panic-button pusher
11. If you are interested in being a television talent in the cable television area, physical attractiveness is not a very important consideration in today's market.
    a) true
    b) false

12. As a media performer, it is not necessary to become a perfectionist. After all, a natural delivery includes mistakes and the "blooper" tapes are an indication of this.
    a) true
    b) false

13. In relation to the broadcast announcer's responsibilities, "EAS" refers to _____
    a) the Emergency Alert System
    b) the call letters of the channel the announcer must tune in to notify the listeners of emergencies
    c) the Eastern Alert System
    d) the government agency responsible for issuing emergency alerts

14. An internship at a commercial broadcast station is an excellent way to fulfill which requirement for a broadcast announcer?
    a) educational
    b) physical
    c) practical experience
    d) emotional

15. Which broadcast announcer is best known for a staccato delivery style that shows a mastery of inflection, pacing, and dramatic pauses?
    a) Howard Stern
    b) Suzy Kolber
    c) Al Roker
    d) Paul Harvey

■ ANSWERS

If You Answered A:

1a. Correct. "Talent," as well as "personality," is a term used to describe a variety of announcing situations, so this is a true statement.

2a. No. Although many small market, entry-level announcing positions pay less than this amount, this is not the correct answer. (Reread 1.4.)

3a. No. Broadcast courses are only part of an education for an announcing career. (Reread 1.6.)

4a. No. While this would help you, it is no longer a requirement. (Reread 1.7.)

5a. Wrong. Many broadcast announcing situations will require the talent to operate their own equipment, for example, most radio disc jockeys do so. (Reread 1.10.)

6a. Wrong. Kolber is one of the top female sports reporters for ABC Sports and ESPN. (Reread 1.11.)

7a. No. Broadcast announcers often work long hours. (Reread 1.7.)

8a. No. You are confusing this with the "color" or analyst announcer. (Reread 1.5.)

9a. Yes. This is correct according to the Bureau of Labor Statistics in 2004.

10a. No. This is just a made-up expression. (Reread 1.5.)

11a. No. Television, both broadcast and cable, is a visual medium and appearance is important so this is a false statement. (Reread 1.7.)

12a. No. This is a false statement. You can't settle for good enough in broadcast situations. The audience expects the broadcast performer to be perfect. While there may be occasional mistakes, it is possible to lose a job if you make a mistake on the air. (Reread 1.8.)

13a. Correct. Announcers are responsible for knowing the procedures of the EAS for notifying the public during an emergency.

14a. No. While you would no doubt learn something from an internship, this isn't the best thing you'll gain from one. (Reread 1.6 through 1.9.)

15a. Wrong. Stern is an excellent announcer, but is best known for his shock jock style. (Reread 1.11.)

If You Answered B:

1b. Wrong. This is a true statement. Both "talent" and "personality" are terms used to describe the broadcast announcer. (Reread 1.2.)

2b. Correct. This was the mean annual wage of the radio-television announcer in 2006 according to the Bureau of Labor.

3b. Correct. This is a false statement because an education for an announcing career should include not just a broadcast education, but also a general education and a specialized education.

4b. No. There are many female voices that are excellent for broadcasting. (Reread 1.7.)

5b. Yes. Many broadcast announcers, such as the radio disc jockey, will have to operate their own equipment, so this is a false statement.

6b. Wrong. Couric is anchor for CBS's "Evening News." (Reread 1.11.)

7b. Yes. While mistakes do happen, broadcasters are expected to be perfect and certainly should foster a perfectionist attitude.

8b. Yes. This is a false statement; while most PBP announcers are broadcasters, frequently the "color" or analyst announcer is a former athlete or coach.

9b. No. This is not correct; the announcer workforce is much smaller. (Reread 1.4.)

10b. Correct. This identifies the announcer who describes the action of a sporting event.

11b. Yes. The demand for attractive people on television has not changed. Broadcast and cable TV is visual and believability is judged, in part, by physical appearance.

12b. Correct. What is expected of a broadcast announcer is to never make mistakes, never mispronounce words, and never seem flustered or confused. Occasional slip-ups may happen, but they are not acceptable and could cost you a job.

13b. No. The letters stand for Emergency Alert System. Broadcast announcers have a responsibility to be aware of the procedures of this system of emergency notification. (Reread 1.10.)

14b. No. You'll experience some of the physical requirements of broadcasting during an internship, but this isn't the best thing you'll gain from one. (Reread 1.6 through 1.9.)

15b. Wrong. Kolber is best known for her intelligence, work ethic, and love of sports. (Reread 1.11.)

If You Answered C:

2c. No. This would more likely be a medium market salary; the mean annual wage was less. (Reread 1.4.)

4c. Yes. While a wide range of voices are acceptable for broadcast announcing, they should at least be pleasing to listen to.

6c. Wrong. Jim Rome is a respected voice in the world of sports broadcasting, heard on both radio and television. (Reread 1.11.)

7c. No. Broadcast announcers often work under deadlines and other stressful conditions. (Reread 1.8.)

9c. No. This is not correct, the announcer workforce is smaller. (Reread 1.4.)

10c. Wrong. This is just a made-up expression. (Reread 1.5.)

13c. No. EAS is the Emergency Alert System. Notification can be given on a regional or local basis, but no special organization like the Eastern Alert System exists. (Reread 1.10.)

14c. Yes. Internships are an excellent way to gain some practical, hands-on experience in the broadcasting field.

15c. Wrong. Roker is best known for his congenial delivery style. (Reread 1.11.)

If You Answered D:

2d. No. This would more likely be a major market salary; the mean annual wage was less. (Reread 1.4.)

4d. No. Many high-pitched voices are difficult to listen to and may be unacceptable for broadcast announcing. (Reread 1.7.)

6d. Correct. Neuman is not a broadcast announcer, as any reader of *Mad* magazine knows.

7d. No. Most beginning broadcast announcers are expected to have gained some experience, even if only through an internship. (Reread 1.9.)

9d. No. This is not the correct answer. You may be getting confused with the total broadcast jobs according to the Bureau of Labor Statistics. (Reread 1.4.)

10d. No. This is just a made-up expression. (Reread 1.5.)

13d. No. EAS is the Emergency Alert System. It is the identification of the affiliation of radio, television, and cable stations that are part of a national system of broadcasters who will inform the public during emergency situations. (Reread 1.10.)

14d. No. You'll experience some of the emotional requirements of broadcasting during an internship, but this isn't the best thing you'll gain from one. (Reread 1.6 through 1.9.)

15d. Correct. Harvey is best known for this delivery style.

Projects

■ PROJECT 1

Interview a local announcer.

Purpose
To give you a chance to learn more about broadcast performing from someone making a living doing just that.

Notes
1. Your instructor may have some guidelines regarding which local announcers you may contact.
2. Be aware that broadcasters can have demanding schedules and even though you have scheduled an appointment to talk with someone, you might find that your appointment gets canceled at the last minute. Make sure you give yourself plenty of time to do this project and be prepared to work a bit to complete the interview.

How to Do the Project
1. Decide which announcer you would like to interview. Use the broadest definition of announcer; that is, you may interview a radio DJ or a TV news anchor or a cable TV play-by-play announcer. In fact, anyone who fits the announcer definition used in this chapter would be a possible interviewee.
2. Call the facility where the announcer is employed and set up an appointment to talk with him or her. Don't be late for your appointment, as broadcast schedules will not allow an announcer to wait for you. You may conduct a phone interview if your instructor approves, but you will get more out of a face-to-face meeting.
3. When talking with the announcer and then writing your paper (see below), try to include the following points:
   a. Describe his or her announcing specialization.
   b. Ask about his or her educational background. Does it follow the requirements mentioned in this chapter?
   c. What were the early positions that this person held in the broadcast field?
   d. Does this announcer seem to meet the physical requirements mentioned in this chapter?
   e. Ask if he or she agrees with the emotional requirements mentioned in the text.
   f. How important does this announcer feel practical experience is?
   g. If this individual could do it all over again, would announcing be his or her career choice again? Why or why not? If the answer is yes, what would he or she do differently?
4. Avoid extremely personal questions, such as "How much money do you make?" and try to conduct your interview in a relatively short period of time.
5. Take good notes as you conduct your interview or record it if your announcer agrees.
6. Write a paper based on your interview.
7. Include a summary page that answers these questions: What did you learn by doing this project? What surprised you? What is your attitude about a broadcast career now?
8. Make sure your paper is a finished, polished project—misspellings or errors in grammar will count against your grade. It should be three to five pages long, typed, and double-spaced.
9. Do not put your paper in plastic binders or covers; rather, put a simple title page at the front that includes your name, the name of the announcer you interviewed, and the title, "Announcer Interview." Put a blank page at the end of the paper for comments from your instructor.
10. Turn in the finished paper to your instructor to receive credit for completing this project.

■ **PROJECT 2**

Profile a renowned announcer.

Purpose
To give you a chance to learn more about someone who has attained the status of a well-known broadcast announcer.

Notes
1. Your instructor may have some guidelines regarding the definition of a "renowned" announcer. Some contemporary broadcasters were mentioned in this chapter that few would disagree are renowned, and there are many more. Some historical announcers certainly have legendary status and would work well for this project.

How to Do the Project
1. Decide which announcer you would like to research.
2. Check several references for information. You might want to start with Current Biography or Who's Who in America, but don't overlook magazine articles or books written about your announcer, and don't forget to check Internet sources.
3. Profile your announcer in a four- to six-page paper. Be sure to include the following points:
    a. Describe his or her early life and education.
    b. Was there any one event or person that pointed this individual toward a broadcasting career?
    c. What were the early positions that this person held in the broadcasting field?
    d. What job or event represents the zenith of this person's career?
    e. Why do you feel this person is a legendary announcer?
4. Make sure your paper is a finished, polished project—misspellings or errors in grammar will count against your grade.
5. Do not put your paper in plastic binders or covers; rather, put a simple title page at the front that includes your name, your legendary announcer's name, and the title, "Announcer Profile." Put a blank page at the end of the paper for comments from your instructor.
6. Include a bibliography.
7. Turn in the finished paper to your instructor to receive credit for completing this project.

■ **PROJECT 3**

Complete a self-evaluation.

Purpose
To give you a chance to appraise yourself in relation to various qualifications of a media performer.

Notes
1. Evaluating yourself is a very difficult task. Be sure to get feedback from someone you trust. An honest appraisal will allow you to work on weaknesses and build on your strengths.
2. Listen and watch local broadcasters when completing your appraisal of your physical qualifications. Try to determine if you fit in with what is currently typical in your market.
3. Your evaluation should be considered just a beginning. Reevaluate yourself from time to time to develop that perfectionist attitude of a top broadcast performer.

How to Do the Project

1. The Self-Evaluation Checklist in Figure 1.6 is a list of qualities that you must consider if you want to be a successful broadcast announcer. Read each statement and indicate how frequently that statement applies to your individual situation.

ANNOUNCER SELF-EVALUATION CHECKLIST

Name: _____   Date: _____

Read each statement and indicate how frequently that statement applies to your individual situation.

	Considerations	5 Always	4 Often	3 Sometimes	2 Seldom	1 Never
1	I speak with a pleasant voice.					
2	I smoke.					
3	I am interested in many things.					
4	I run out of air when I speak.					
5	I utilize correct grammar when I speak.					
6	I speak with a regional accent.					
7	I am a responsible person.					
8	I pronounce words correctly.					
9	I feel I have to strain to produce vocal sounds.					
10	I am able to handle stressful situations.					
11	I get plenty of rest at night.					
12	I speak with vocal variety (don't sound monotone).					
13	I speak utilizing my lower register or pitch.					
14	My voice sounds "creaky" or "dry".					
15	I have a perfectionist attitude.					
16	My voice is "weak" or difficult to understand.					
17	I am in good physical condition or health.					
18	I am able to complete assignments on deadline.					
19	I speak with vocal fillers ("um," "uh," "like," etc.).					
20	I speak with an obvious problem (lisp, stutter, etc.).					
21	I am confident if using broadcast equipment.					
22	My voice is "raspy" or "hoarse".					
23	I have a conservative appearance (hair length, clothing, etc.).					
24	I sound conversational (rather than "reading" or "saying lines").					
25	My voice is "clear" or "resonant".					
26	I have good posture, both sitting and standing.					
27	My voice is "shrill" or "harsh".					
28	I am willing to work "as long as it takes" to complete a project.					
29	I have an attractive appearance (well-groomed, no obvious physical defects, etc.).					
30	When I speak, I seem enthusiastic.					

Scoring: For statements 2, 4, 6, 9, 14, 16, 19, 20, 22, and 27 reverse the numerical score, i.e., "Never" becomes 5, "Seldom" because 4, etc. For all other statements, just add up the numerical score of the column you checked. The higher your total score, the more likely you are to be a good announcer.

FIGURE 1.6 Completing a Self-Evaluation Checklist gives you a chance to appraise yourself in relation to various qualifications of a broadcast performer.

2. It is important that you review your answers with someone you trust. We often see ourselves differently than others see us, so this additional input can be significant.

3. After you have discussed your evaluation with someone else, go back and revise any ratings that you may have reconsidered.

4. Based on your ratings, write a paper that summarizes your self-evaluation. Do you exhibit the qualities that most broadcast performers do? What are your strengths and weaknesses? Include a goal statement that indicates how you plan to improve your performance qualities.

5. Do not put your paper in plastic binders or covers; rather, put a simple title page at the front that includes your name and the title, "Self-Evaluation Checklist."

6. Put a blank page at the end of the paper for comments from your instructor.

7. Your instructor may have you complete another self-evaluation in several weeks and include a statement that summarizes your development rather than a goal statement.

8. Turn in the finished paper/s to your instructor to receive credit for completing this project.

CHAPTER TWO

THE AUDIO PERFORMANCE ENVIRONMENT

2.1 INTRODUCTION

As a broadcast performer, you'll work in many different environments, both in-studio and in the field. How much actual equipment you may be required to operate can also vary widely. For example, a television news anchor may never do more than clip on a microphone and read the script from a teleprompter while the other television equipment is operated by a crew behind the scenes. In contrast to this, in most instances, a radio or Internet announcer will be required to operate all the equipment in the audio studio while he or she is announcing. In any case, every performer will benefit from a basic knowledge of the environment in which he or she works and the equipment being used for their performance.

Don't worry if you don't initially comprehend all the technology; you'll understand it better as you actually use the equipment or perform in various settings. This chapter mainly looks at one environment—the basic audio studio and the equipment normally found there—and focuses on working with the most fundamental piece of equipment the audio performer will use—the microphone. You should also note that, in addition to working with traditional audio equipment, the modern performer may also need to manipulate computer-based equipment, as this has become an integral part of most audio studios.

2.2 THE AUDIO STUDIO

An audio studio is the most formal setting for a broadcast audio performer, such as a radio DJ announcing in a radio studio (see Figure 2.1). While the terms radio studio and audio studio are often used interchangeably, not every broadcast performance in such a studio is for radio. For example, a voiceover announcer may have a recording session at a local radio station to record some commercials or an Internet "broadcaster"

may work in a homemade studio with a minimum amount of actual broadcast equipment. Regardless of the setting, the basic equipment found there will be similar, and the performer working there will follow many of the same procedures.

Radio performers spend a lot of time in the two main audio studios found in most radio stations—the on-air studio and the production studio. As the name implies, the on-air studio is the domain of the **disk jockey (DJ)** or announcer who is broadcasting "live" from that studio. Most of what is done in the on-air studio is simultaneously going out over the air. The production studio is often a similarly equipped room that is used to produce and record material that will eventually be used in the on-air studio, such as commercials or radio station promotional spots. Some stations may also have an announce booth, which is nothing more than a small room or studio that houses a microphone plus a table and chair or stool and counter set-up. The audio **output** from this booth is usually sent to another studio, such as the production studio; however, sometimes an audio recorder in the announce booth records the performance.

Audio studios are designed to house various pieces of audio equipment on top of and underneath counters and in cabinets and racks as shown in Figure 2.1 and Video Clip 2.1. One common arrangement of counters is a U-shape or L-shape because this puts all the equipment within arm's reach of the announcer. This is important when the announcer is **working combo**—announcing and operating the equipment at the same time. In other words, the announcer is both performer and engineer, making an understanding of the equipment in the studio vital to successful announcing.

Some audio performers—such as a podcast host or Internet DJ—may find they're working in a much less formal setting than a professional radio studio. A simple home recording studio (see Figure 2.2)

FIGURE 2.1   The audio studio is one broadcast performance environment. (Copyright Kevin G. Reeves Photographer. Courtesy of Westlake Reed Leskosky.)

FIGURE 2.2   For many audio performers, another performance environment is the home recording studio. (Image courtesy of Bobbin Beam, Voice Actress for Broadcast & Business.)

FIGURE 2.3   A small audio mixer is often part of the home recording studio and performs most of the functions of a larger broadcast console. (Image courtesy of Behringer USA, Inc.)

can make quality recordings using a computer. Most home computer set-ups can handle audio recording, but obviously the faster the CPU, and the more RAM you have, the better. You'll also need a decent sound card and some audio editing software. Audacity is a basic free program and Adobe Audition, which is used

in many home recording studios, offers lots of options at a reasonable cost. To this computer-based equipment, you'll need to add a quality microphone (see Performance Tip 2.1), small **audio mixer** (see Figure 2.3), and headphones or speakers to monitor your recordings. Many home studios are simply set up in a quiet corner of a room; others have built small soundproof enclosures to house the studio, and many fall somewhere in between. No doubt, you're both performer and equipment operator in your home studio, so learn the ins and outs of your equipment to make the best possible recordings.

PERFORMANCE TIP 2.1

Selecting a Microphone

"I've faced many mics though the years, and really like Sennheiser, AKG, and of course, the Neumann U87i. In my own studio I use a Neumann TLM 193, as well as, a Rode NT1A. Both are large-diaphragm condenser microphones and both maintain extended frequency and low self-noise. The Rode is the improved version of the original NT1. It retains the large capsule (25mm) with its gold-sputtered diaphragm along with the internal shock mounting but now uses state-of-the-art surface mount electronics to provide an ultra-low noise level through its transformer less circuitry. The design is rugged and finished with a heavy-duty nickel finish, so it travels well. The Neumann TLM 193 compares well to the U87, and brings me Neumann's long tradition as well as offering high-end technology at an affordable price for my home recording studio. I use this for a "warm, close" sound. Both microphones carry my varied vocal ranges very well, and the Neumann is especially excellent in close-to-the-mic situations. My mic chain runs through a Behringer Zenyx 1204 mixer and the M-Box and I compress or EQ in ProTools if necessary, which is not very often."

Bobbin Beam, voice actress for broadcast and business

Bobbin Beam's professional career began in FM rock radio while she was still in high school. She attended University of Dallas and Carroll College, majoring in theater and mass communications. Her radio career spanned twenty years in major markets, followed by starting her own advertising agency, On the Beam Productions, where she signed new clients, purchased media, created and produced television, radio commercials and non-broadcast videos. Since 1984, she's resided in Escondido, California and records freelance voice-over for clients all over the world.

2.3 MICROPHONES

Because it converts the announcer's voice into an **audio signal**, a **microphone** is one of the key pieces of equipment used in audio performance. Since it is a device that changes one form of energy into another, it is called **a transducer**. Understanding the basics of microphones will prove helpful for the broadcast performer because choosing the wrong microphone for a given situation can mar the quality of your performance regardless of how good you are at "working" the equipment. Microphones are generally classified by their sound-generating elements (how they change sound into an electrical signal) and by their **pickup patterns** (how they "hear" sound). The two main classifications of microphones by their sound-generating elements are dynamic and condenser. These are not the only types of microphones, but they are the ones most frequently used in broadcasting.

The **dynamic microphone** is also known as a moving coil microphone, as this describes how it changes sound into an electrical signal. The internal structure of the dynamic microphone shown in Figure 2.4 contains a magnetic structure, a wire coil, and a diaphragm. Sound waves entering the microphone strike and vibrate the diaphragm, which is connected to the

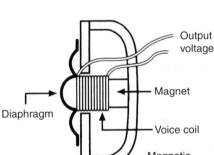

FIGURE 2.4 *Sound generating element of the dynamic microphone. (Image courtesy of Audio-Technica U.S. Inc.)*

coil of wire that is suspended in the magnetic field. Movement of the diaphragm moves the wire coil; and movement of the wire coil in the magnetic field produces an electrical current analogous to the original sound. Dynamic microphones are extremely popular in broadcast circumstances because they are fairly rugged. Often used in field situations, they can withstand a certain amount of the abuse that is almost inevitable when performing outside the studio. Dynamic microphones also provide accurate voice reproduction, good frequency response, and fall within a reasonable budget range for broadcasters. The Shure

FIGURE 2.5 A classic dynamic microphone (Shure SM7B) used in broadcast studios. (Image used with permission. ©2007 Shure Incorporated.)

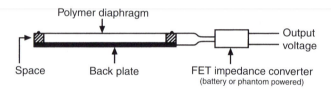

FIGURE 2.6 Sound generating element of the condenser microphone. (Image courtesy of Audio-Technica U. S. Inc.)

FIGURE 2.7 A studio condenser microphone. (Image courtesy of Audio-Technica U. S. Inc.)

SM7B (shown in Figure 2.5), Sennheiser MD421II, and Electro-Voice RE20 are all dynamic microphones frequently found in the radio studio.

The **condenser microphone**, also known as a capacitor microphone, employs an internal structure consisting of a diaphragm-like front plate, a fixed back plate, and an electronic circuit (as shown in Figure 2.6) to change sound into an electrical signal. The microphone's plates are charged, so this type of microphone requires a power supply. When sound waves strike the microphone diaphragm, the distance between it and the fixed back plate is changed. This creates a change in the voltage between the plates which produces an electrical current in the circuit associated with the plates that is analogous to the original sound. Condenser microphones are popular studio microphones because they are of high quality and they produce a signal of exceptional warmth and clarity. The necessary power for the condenser microphone can come from an internal battery or an external **phantom power supply**—a device that sends the low voltage required down the same microphone cable that delivers the sound signal to an audio console or recorder. The Neumann BCM 104, Audio-Technica AT4033CL

(shown in Figure 2.7), and Shure KSM44 are all popular condenser microphones for radio studio use.

Ribbon microphones occasionally show up in broadcast performance situations. This microphone uses a corrugated metallic ribbon suspended in a magnetic structure to convert sound waves into an audio signal in a manner similar to the dynamic microphone. Ribbon microphones were quite popular in the early days of radio because they "colored" the performer's voice with a smooth, warm quality. However, ribbon microphones are extremely sensitive to shock, wind noise, and other abuses that sometimes occur in broadcast settings, and thus lost favor with broadcasters. Other types of microphones, such as the regulated phase microphone, are also rarely found in the radio environment because their characteristics aren't ideal for broadcast applications.

As mentioned above, the other way microphones are classified is by their pickup pattern. A pickup pattern is the area or shape around a microphone in which the microphone best picks up sound. An announcer speaking outside the pickup pattern of a microphone doesn't allow the microphone to pick up his or her voice with optimum quality, so an understanding of microphone pickup patterns is extremely important to the broadcast performer. The most common pickup patterns—**omnidirectional**, **bidirectional**, and **cardioid**—are shown in Figure 2.8. In each case, the name of the microphone pattern describes the actual pickup pattern. An omnidirectional microphone picks up sound equally well in any direction—in other words, it is nondirectional. The bidirectional microphone picks up sound from the front and back of the microphone. The cardioid pattern is considered a unidirectional pattern because it essentially picks up sound from one direction. The name derives from

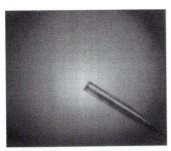

Omnidirectional

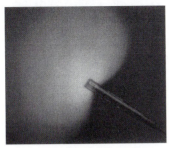

Cardioid

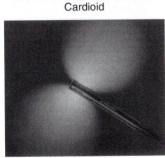

Bidirectional

FIGURE 2.8 Common microphone pickup patterns. (Image courtesy of Sennheiser Electronic Corporation.)

the heart-shaped pattern that allows the microphone to pick up most of the sound from the front, but also somewhat from each side of the microphone.

Pickup patterns that are drawn as a two-dimensional graph—known as a **polar response pattern**—actually represent a three-dimensional space. For example, the omnidirectional microphone picks up sound from the front, back, sides, top, and bottom; think of a large beach ball with the microphone in the center and you get the idea. Most broadcast studio microphones are cardioid—that is, unidirectional—because the announcer is positioned directly in front of the microphone where it best picks up sound. The cardioid pattern also picks up some of the ambient sound of the studio (from the sides), but doesn't pick up much from behind the microphone where the announcer may be manipulating switches, handling paper scripts, or making other unwanted noise.

Microphones are usually mounted to position them properly in relation to the announcer. Video Clip 2.2 shows a typical hand-held microphone being used in a remote situation. A **windscreen** is often used to prevent wind noise or other **plosive** sounds when microphones are used outside the studio. A windscreen is a foam filter (review Figure 2.5) that can be placed over the head or front of the microphone to lessen pops or thumps caused by a sharp puff of air. To free the announcer's hands (perhaps to hold a script), a hand-held microphone is often placed in a floor stand or a desk stand, shown in Video Clip 2.3. The most common microphone mounting for the radio studio is the boom microphone arm, also shown in Video Clip 2.3. Note in each instance that good microphone technique situates the announcer at the proper mic-to-mouth distance and position as explained in the next section.

2.4 WORKING WITH A MICROPHONE

There are two main concepts to remember when working with a microphone: mic-to-mouth distance and mic-to-mouth position. Although you may see many rock singers practically "eating" the microphone, this is not good technique for most broadcast circumstances. A good mic-to-mouth distance is about six inches. Depending on your vocal strength, you may move a bit closer or even a bit further away, but this is always a good starting point and you'll quickly learn what works best for you with a particular microphone. A good approximate measure of the six-inch mic-to-mouth distance is the length of a pen, the length of a dollar bill, or the span between your thumb and little finger, as shown in Video Clip 2.4.

If you work too close to the microphone, it is possible that you may distort the audio signal because your voice is too loud for the microphone to handle. It will also be more likely that the microphone will pick up "pops" (plosive sounds produced when you say letters like p, t, and b), sibilance (excessive s sounds), and even breathing sounds. On the other hand, if you work too far away from the microphone, you'll produce a soft or weak audio signal. Turning up the microphone to compensate for this will just add noise to the audio signal. Proper mic-to-mouth distance is important and good performers pay attention to it.

By good mic-to-mouth position, we usually mean not talking directly into the microphone, but rather, talking slightly off axis to the microphone. The key word here is "slightly"; if you get too far to the side, above, or below the microphone, you can get outside its pickup pattern and actually lower the quality of the audio signal. As Video Clip 2.4 shows, one good technique is to align the microphone with your nose and then tilt the microphone down a bit. That way you end up speaking slightly below the microphone rather than directly into it. This also prevents popping the microphone, and should be considered as important as setting mic-to-mouth distance.

One final word on working with microphones: you'll often be asked to "give a level" when the studio is being set up prior to recording or a broadcast. This just means that you are asked to speak into the microphone so that proper volume levels can be set. Checking the levels may be done by you, if you're working in the studio alone, or by an engineer. The best way to give a level, if you are reading a script, is to read an actual portion of the script aloud, just as you would if you were performing. If you are ad-libbing, voice several full sentences. This gives the engineer enough time to get the mic levels set. If you just mouth a word or two, you'll stop talking before the proper levels are set. Don't ever blow into or tap on the microphone to test levels or see if it's working.

It's possible to damage a good microphone that way. Counting into the microphone ("Testing, 1, 2, 3, 4") is also not always the best way to get good levels, although this is often done. Be aware that people often count with a vocal tone and volume level that is completely different from when they are just speaking. When possible, use a more realistic approximation of the actual performance when setting levels.

2.5 MIC FRIGHT AND WHY BROADCAST PERFORMERS GET IT

On the one hand, mic fright is nothing more than a mild case of anxiety that many announcers experience when called on to perform in front of an audience. On the other hand, it can be nervousness so severe (see Figure 2.9) that the broadcast announcer can't even communicate with his or her audience! It occurs just at that moment when you open the studio microphone or when you are cued that you are on-air, and it doesn't matter if you're actually in front of an audience or if you're all alone in a studio. If you experience a dry mouth, slightly trembling hands, a sweaty brow, or "butterflies" in your stomach, you've got a case of mic fright.

FIGURE 2.9 Mic fright can range from a mild case of "butterflies" to "freezing" to the point where you can't perform at all.

The next chapter looks at the television version of this affliction, known as "camera panic," and you'll see that many of the symptoms, causes, and cures are the same.

Some broadcast performers feel that a small amount of mic fright can actually help your announcing as the adrenaline rush "pumps you up" and this extra energy leads to a better performance. While this may be true for a few people, mic fright, even a mild case, more often has a negative impact on your performance. The nervousness associated with mic fright often raises the pitch of your voice and, as was noted previously, lower-pitched voices are preferred for broadcast performance. You might also find yourself running out of breath, having to gulp for air before reaching the end of a sentence or other appropriate breathing spot. Mic fright often makes the performer lose focus and read too quickly or slowly or speak too softly. Extreme mic fright can cause a performer to "freeze" and not be able to perform at all. A former student of one of the authors, when she was a beginning radio announcer, could not open her mouth and speak when the microphone switch was opened the very first time she was in the studio. She nearly fainted and had to be helped out of the studio. That would be an extreme case of mic fright. Fortunately, she learned what caused the mic fright and ultimately became a fine announcer. An understanding of what causes mic fright will help you discover how to overcome it. Most instances of mic fright are caused by one, or a combination, of these four situations: 1) disliking one's voice, 2) fearing failure, 3) being inexperienced, and 4) being unprepared.

We've all had the experience of hearing our voice played back from a recorder for the first time and immediately stating, "That's not me." It really doesn't sound like you—to you—but that truly is how you sound to everyone else. That's easy enough to explain if you just think for a minute about how you hear your voice and how other people hear it. You hear your voice when your ears pick up the sound waves your voice produces and by sound vibrations that conduct through your skull bone. Other people hear your voice only through the sound waves produced, so what you hear on the recording is what everyone else hears—it's what you sound like to everyone but yourself. That's the key to overcoming this cause of mic fright. You don't sound "funny" to anyone but yourself. Everyone else is already accustomed to hearing you in this manner, and even if you don't like your voice, they've not rejected you because of how you sound. You should also remember that one of the reasons you're reading this text is to improve your voice and how you speak as a broadcast performer. With work and practice, you'll soon like the sound of your voice as it improves with each performance.

A fear of failure will also cause mic fright. No one likes to fail, and a poor broadcast performance, such as stumbling through a script, would constitute a failure. Some beginning announcers try to prevent any failure by just giving a "journeyman" performance. To be sure, they don't make mistakes, but there's also no spark to their effort and it's less than a memorable performance. Good broadcast performers need to push the envelope, and many of the best performances are right on the edge of being disasters. To overcome this fear of failure, begin by thinking about the message of your performance. If you believe in what you are saying, you should be able to communicate this to your audience. It also helps if you think of delivering this message to one other person, not a huge audience. If you concentrate on this one-to-one communication, any fear of failure should melt into the background and not be a factor in your performance.

Sometimes disliking your voice and fearing failure are actually associated with a general lack of confidence. An announcer may adopt an attitude that what he or she has to say just isn't all that important. It's one thing to be unassuming, but quite another to be self-effacing. A dull disc jockey isn't going to capture the attention of the audience. A wearisome news interviewer probably won't grasp the listener's attention. A degree of self-confidence is required to be a successful announcer. It's a self-fulfilling prophecy—if you are confident in your performance and what you are delivering, you will deliver a good performance. One good performance builds your confidence further and leads to additional good performances.

Another major cause of mic fright is inexperience. Unfortunately, all beginning announcers are inexperienced and there really is nothing you can do here except perform and perform and perform. The very first time you read a radio commercial over the air, you'll no doubt experience some nervousness; however, by the time you read the thousandth commercial, your level of mic fright may well be nil. The old adage "practice makes perfect" really is true in this instance. Good broadcast announcers don't necessarily limit their work to actual on-air performances. Many play-by-play sports announcers have sat in the top row of seats at a stadium doing their own play-by-play broadcast into a portable recorder, especially as they were learning their trade. As you become a more experienced announcer, obviously there is less of a chance of mic fright being caused by inexperience.

Being unprepared is the last major cause of mic fright. You've probably experienced trying to "wing it" while taking an exam, and while you may have gotten through it, the results are almost always less than desirable. That's what causes the mic fright: you know you're not ready to go and you know it won't be your best effort. Of course, broadcast circumstances often do require you to ad-lib. For example, most disc jockey work is impromptu in nature, and sometimes a news reporter may be asked to conduct an interview with little or no preparation. (Later in this text, you'll learn about ad-lib announcing and get some practical advice on how to sharpen your skills in this area.) On the other hand, if you're working with a written script, there is no excuse for being unprepared. Pre-reading, copy marking, and practicing with the script will lessen any chance of mic fright.

You should also mentally prepare for a performance. Think about what you are going to say. Are there potential pronunciation problems? What's the appropriate mood of the copy? At what rate should you be speaking? What are the key points? Now, find a moment to relax—both physically and mentally. Many broadcast performance situations won't offer a great deal of time for this, but it may only take a few seconds. At the very least, close your eyes and take a couple of deep breaths. If possible, relax your entire body by letting your muscles loosen up a bit to relieve some of the physical tension. If your shoulders are hunched up, let them droop down a bit. If you're clenching your teeth, let your jaw relax. If you're holding your arms tight to your body, shake them out a bit. The idea is that this preparation, practice, and relaxation will put you into a great performing mode with not a sign of mic fright in your mind or body. If there is one common cure for any of these causes, it's practice—and plenty of it. As you become more comfortable in various broadcast situations, instances of nervousness will become less and less frequent. Remember, you can ease mic fright by 1) preparing your material properly, 2) relaxing just before your performance, 3) believing in what you are saying, 4) having confidence in yourself, and 5) practicing!

2.6 THE BROADCAST CONSOLE OR AUDIO MIXER

Perhaps the key piece of equipment in any audio studio is the **audio console** because the audio signals from all the other equipment in the studio, such as the microphone mentioned earlier, go through the console. Also known as a "board" or mixer, the array of switches, buttons, and knobs shown in Figure 2.10 looks daunting at

FIGURE 2.10 A digital audio console allows the performer to control the audio from all the other equipment in a studio. (Image courtesy of Radio Systems Inc.)

first, but you'll quickly learn that many of the controls are merely repeated. For example, a ten-channel board will have ten volume controls. A channel is a section of the board and its associated switches that allow the operator to control a piece of audio equipment in the studio, such as a CD player or mini-disc recorder. Many digital consoles are actually control surfaces that interface with a companion audio "engine" or router. The studio equipment is wired to the router, and then the control surface is used to manipulate the equipment.

Any audio console or mixer has three major functions: **selecting**, **monitoring**, and **routing** audio signals. The console allows the operator to select whatever piece of equipment he or she needs by manipulating the correct buttons, switches, or slide controls for the channel assigned to that particular piece of equipment. Typical operation requires the console operator to choose the desired source from an input selector switch, turn up the volume using a fader, and choose one or more outputs from an output selector switch.

Since one or more sources are often assigned to a single channel, an **input selector switch** allows the operator to choose the one he or she wants. For example, a CD player and audio recorder may both be assigned to channel 3 on an audio board. Two push-buttons near the top of the channel (often labeled A and B) determine which piece of equipment is active through the channel at any one time, according to which button is depressed. Having more than one piece of equipment assigned to a channel allows the board to have more inputs—a ten-channel board may have twenty or more pieces of equipment going through it. Only one input can be active at a time; however, more than one channel can be used simultaneously. The operator could have a microphone active through channel 1 and a CD player active through channel 4. In fact, that's often done, and that's the way an announcer can talk over the beginning of a song. Since more than one channel can be "on" at any time, an audio console has a secondary, but important, function of **mixing** audio signals. Much of the production work of a board is in mixing several sound sources together.

Volume controls on most modern audio consoles consist of a slider-type control known as a **fader**, like the ones in Figure 2.10. Some boards use a rotary knob, known as a **potentiometer** ("pot") that increases the volume when turned clockwise (review Figure 2.3). Faders are moved upward from the bottom of the board to increase volume. Faders are easier to work with and provide a quick visual reference of what channels are on and how loud the volume is set. To help the operator keep volume controls at an appropriate level, the audio console has **VU** (volume unit) **meters**. These are electromechanical devices that show loudness on one of two scales—a percent scale and a **decibel** scale. The percent scale goes from 0 to 100 and indicates the percentage of audio signal going through the board in relation to the capacity of the board to handle that signal. The scale goes from black to red as you go above 100 percent. It is all right if the VU needle occasionally flicks above 100 percent, but signals that are continuously **in the red** will be distorted. Good **board operators** keep the level between 80 and 100 percent. If you let the signal get too low (usually below 20 percent) you'll get **in the mud** and your audio signal will be weak in relation to the inherent electronic noise that exists within all electronic circuits. Video Clip 2.5 shows the VU meter at various operational levels. Even though you can often monitor the audio signal with speakers and headphones, you'll learn that's not always the best way to control levels and it's better to always keep an eye on the VU meters. Instead of traditional VU meters, some audio boards will utilize **LED** (light-emitting diode) meters—a horizontal row or vertical column of lights indicates the audio signal strength. For example, if there were ten lights, six might light up green, two yellow, and two red. Of course, as with the other style of VU meter, going in the red for very long means a distorted signal.

The *routing* function of the audio console is handled by the **output selector switch**, which allows the operator to control where the audio signal is going as it leaves the audio console. On many boards it consists of three buttons—*program*, *audition*, and *auxiliary* Unlike the input on an audio console, more than one output can be selected at the same time. Program is the normal output mode for an audio console. When this button is depressed, the audio signal from the board is sent to the transmitter if the board's in an on-air studio, or to a recorder if the board's in a production studio. The audition and auxiliary positions are merely additional output routes that the console audio signal can take.

For example, in an on-air studio, program may send the signal to the transmitter to be broadcast, and audition sends the signal to a recorder so the announcer can record portions of his or her programming.

The *monitoring* function of an audio board is accomplished with either speakers or headphones. **Monitor speakers** are high-quality speakers that are fed the output of the audio board. The volume of these speakers is controlled with a separate volume switch that controls only the speakers. In other words, the operator can run these levels as loudly or softly as he or she wants and not affect the volume of the signal going through the board. This is important for the operator to understand, because it's possible to have the board level be too low (in the mud) yet have it sound loud because the monitor speakers are turned way up. This is why you're advised to always watch the VU meters on the board. Keep the board levels in the proper range and you can run the studio monitor speakers at whatever level is comfortable for you.

Most audio consoles also have a plug-in for **headphones**. Headphones are really just tiny speakers encased in an ear muff-type band that rests on your head. They are used for one extremely important reason—when a microphone is "on" in the studio, the monitor speakers will be muted or turned off. This prevents **feedback**—that screeching sound you get from speakers when a sound is produced, picked up by a microphone, sent through an audio console or any type of amplifier, reproduced by the speakers, picked up by a microphone, and so on, over and over until the speakers howl with feedback. Listen to Audio Track 2.1 to hear what feedback sounds like.

Another secondary function of the audio console is **signal processing**. All audio consoles **amplify** the incoming audio signal to some extent with internal amplifiers. Weak input signals (such as from a microphone) will be amplified more than the stronger signal coming from a CD (compact disc) player. Many consoles also contain simple equalizers—various switches and buttons that control the amount of bass or treble applied to the incoming signal. In another way, audio consoles can facilitate signal processing through a "send" and "return" wiring arrangement. For example, reverb could be added to an announcer's voice by sending the voice audio to an out-board signal processor.

2.7 MUSIC PLAYBACK SOURCES

Today, music employed in the radio studio is most often played back from a **CD player** or a **computer-based**

FIGURE 2.11 The CD player is one of the primary music play back sources and this model only takes up one rack space in the audio studio. (Image courtesy of Tascam, a division of TEAC America, Inc.)

FIGURE 2.12 Digital audio storage systems allow the modern radio announcer to play music and other programming elements from a computer. (Image courtesy of Broadcast Electronics.)

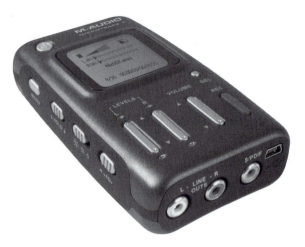

FIGURE 2.13 The Micro Track II from M-Audio has received considerable attention in many radio studio and field recording applications. (Image courtesy of M-Audio.)

so that the announcer can play songs or other material back-to-back.

In making the transition from analog to digital equipment, many stations now play back their music and other programming elements from a digital audio storage system. With mouse clicks and drag-and-drop operations, the announcer can manipulate songs and various programming elements for playback at the proper time. The "log" is displayed on a computer screen (see Figure 2.12) that the announcer can follow and adjust as he or she is broadcasting.

2.8 DIGITAL AUDIO EQUIPMENT

Most of the older analog-based audio equipment, such as traditional cassette or reel-to-reel recorders, have been replaced with their digital counterparts. For example, cassette recorders have been replaced with **compact flash recorders** and reel-to-reels with **desktop audio editors**. Some digital recorders, like the mini-disc, use removable recording media. Configured much like a cassette recorder, it has standard play, record, and stop buttons, but also controls for basic editing functions and has a display window to show timing and other pertinent information about the material on the disc.

Another type of digital recorder (see Figure 2.13) uses a compact flash card, like a digital camera, to record and store audio instead of digital pictures. Operational controls are fairly straightforward and operate much like any traditional recorder unit. Two-channel audio can be recorded in **WAV** or **MP3** files

play back system, replacing the old broadcast turntable that played vinyl records. While the typical broadcast-quality CD player (shown in Figure 2.11) is often quite similar to home stereo units, they are usually more durable. Typical operational controls allow the operator to play, pause, skip forward and backward, and cue the compact disc. Some professional CD players have a "cue wheel" that allows the CD to be rocked back and forth to find an exact starting point; but most cue automatically to the beginning of the music once a specific track on the CD has been selected. An *end monitor* button on some CD players allows the operator to hear the last ten to fifteen seconds of the selected track so that an announcer can determine exactly how a song ends. A **display window** on the CD player shows track numbers and timing information. The most important information for broadcast is the "remaining time," because it's necessary to know how much time you have until the end of the current song and before some other programming element must begin. At least two CD players are usually utilized in a studio

FIGURE 2.14 360 Systems' Short/cut™ Editor can provide fast editing and production of 2-channel audio. (Image courtesy of 360 Systems Professional Digital Audio.)

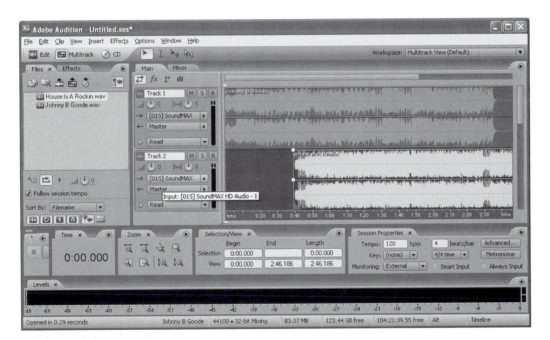

FIGURE 2.15 Most audio production work in the radio station is now being accomplished by computer software programs, such as Adobe Audition®. (Adobe product screen shot reprinted with permission from Adobe Systems Incorporated.)

and then, using drag and drop commands, transferred easily into an audio software program via USB 2.0 for editing or recording onto another medium.

The desktop audio editor shown in Figure 2.14 served as a replacement for the traditional two-track reel-to-reel recorder. In its basic configuration, it could record and store up to two hours of stereo audio. Standard recording controls make it easy to work with; but in addition to recording the audio, you can easily edit what you've recorded. A display window shows the audio waveform, and editing is as easy as setting electronic "in" and "out" marks and electronically cutting or copying portions of audio as desired. A typewriter-style keypad allows easy labeling and setting of "hot keys" for instant playback of selected audio from stored files.

Taking the desktop concept a bit further are editing systems that are used with standard computer systems. Figure 2.15 shows the screen from a software program that, when added to a good computer system with a high-quality digital sound card, produces a full-blown multi-track recorder. This system is capable of easy "point and click" and "drag and drop" editing and even adds the ability to do basic signal processing to the audio. More sophisticated systems, known as **digital audio workstations (DAWs)**, are essentially computer editing systems incorporated into a traditional audio console. It's important to remember that in radio, a performer is also an equipment operator much of the time, and a fairly good operational knowledge of the studio equipment is expected as part of the job.

2.9 CONCLUSIONS

The tips, techniques, and basic concepts for performing in front of the microphone presented in this chapter are important for your development as a broadcast or Internet performer. An understanding of an audio studio environment will make your performance efforts better, as will practice, practice, and more practice. Each time you are in a performance situation, try to apply a few of the concepts presented here. Before long, many of them will start to become second nature and you will be on your way to being a polished performer. As you proceed with this text, you will investigate several specific areas of performance and will continue to learn concepts and procedures that will help make you a professional.

Self-Study

■ QUESTIONS

1. The heart of the audio studio is the _____.
   a) microphone
   b) audio console
   c) CD player
   d) compact flash recorder

2. Which of the following is least likely to occur if you are working too close to a microphone?
   a) popping on *p* sounds
   b) sibilance on *s* sounds
   c) noticeable breathing sounds
   d) weak audio signal

3. Which of the following is least likely to cause an announcer to experience mic fright?
   a) fearing failure
   b) being inexperienced
   c) fearing the wrong type of microphone was used
   d) being unprepared

4. When a beginning announcer gives a journeyman performance—one free of mistakes, but lackluster and less than memorable—he or she is trying to prevent which cause of mic fright?
   a) fear of failure
   b) dislike of his or her voice
   c) lack of experience
   d) lack of preparation

5. As a radio announcer, you've been asked to "give a level" so your engineer can set proper microphone levels. You should _____.
   a) blow gently into the microphone
   b) read or ad-lib several sentences into the microphone
   c) tap sharply on the microphone
   d) speak the standard, "Testing, 1, 2, 3" into the microphone

6. A radio announcer needs to be aware that most audio consoles allow only one channel to be active at a time and plan accordingly.
   a) true
   b) false

7. Which of the following is least likely to be considered a major function of the audio console?
   a) selecting
   b) monitoring
   c) routing
   d) signal processing

8. If the VU meters on an audio console indicate the signal is in the mud, this means the operator has the levels well over 100 percent and the signal will be distorted or muddied.
   a) true
   b) false

9. When a studio microphone is turned on, most audio consoles will automatically mute the studio monitor speakers. This prevents the audio signal from _____.
   a) going in the red
   b) going in the mud
   c) producing feedback
   d) producing plosive sounds

10. Which type of microphone is most likely to be found in a radio studio?
    a) condenser
    b) dynamic
    c) capacitor
    d) ribbon

11. Which microphone pickup pattern can be described as being nondirectional? In other words, there is no one direction in which it picks up sound better than another
    a) omnidirectional
    b) cardioid
    c) bidirectional
    d) hypercardioid

12. In the modern audio studio, which of the following is most likely to be the primary music playback source?
    a) turntable
    b) mini-disc
    c) CD player
    d) digital storage system

13. When a radio announcer is working combo, this means that _____.
    a) the announcer is working with another announcer in the studio
    b) the announcer is working in both the on-air and production studio
    c) the announcer has an engineer to operate the equipment
    d) the announcer is operating the equipment and announcing at the same time

14. What would be a good initial mic-to-mouth distance for a beginning radio announcer?
    a) 2 inches
    b) 6 inches
    c) 10 inches
    d) 18 inches

15. Which piece of digital radio equipment is essentially a computer editing system incorporated into a traditional audio console?
    a) MD
    b) DAT
    c) CD
    d) DAW

■ ANSWERS

If You Answered A:

1a. No. Although the microphone is the first piece of equipment in the audio chain, there is a better response to this question. (Reread 2.3 and 2.6.)

2a. Wrong. This is a characteristic of working a microphone too close. (Reread 2.3 and 2.4.)

3a. No. Fear of failure often causes announcers to experience mic fright. (Reread 2.5.)

4a. Correct. By not pushing their effort, their performance may be mistake free, but it will lack any sparkle. There's often a thin line between failure and a great performance.

5a. Never. Blowing into the microphone could damage a good quality microphone. (Reread 2.4.)

6a. No. You might be getting confused here with the input selector switch which allows only one source to be active through a specific channel. (Reread 2.6.)

7a. No. Audio consoles allow the operator to select various audio sources with an input selector switch. (Reread 2.6.)

8a. No. Just the opposite is happening. In the mud means the levels are low and the weak audio signal is being lost in the inherent electronic noise of the equipment. (Reread 2.6.)

9a. Wrong. In the red refers to having board levels above 100 percent and can occur whether monitor speakers are muted or not. (Reread 2.6.)

10a. No. This is a good second choice as some studios would likely use a condenser microphone; however, there is a better response. (Reread 2.3.)

11a. Of course. The omnidirectional microphone picks up sound equally well from all directions.

12a. No. Turntables are no longer the primary music playback source and are often not even found in the radio studio anymore. (Reread 2.7.)

13a. No. Although two announcers often work together in radio, this isn't the term for it. (Reread 2.2.)

14a. Wrong. Two inches from a microphone would be too close for many announcers and could easily cause popping. (Reread 2.4.)

15a. No. The mini-disc is another form of digital equipment. (Reread 2.9.)

If You Answered B:

1b. Correct. All the other equipment in the studio is manipulated through the audio console making this a key piece of equipment.

2b. Wrong. This is a characteristic of working a microphone too close. (Reread 2.3 and 2.4.)

3b. No. Inexperienced announcers often have mic fright. (Reread 2.5.)

4b. Wrong. A dislike of one's voice could cause an announcer to hold back some, but there is a better response. (Reread 2.5.)

5b. Yes. Reading several sentences of the actual script is an excellent way to allow an engineer to set correct microphone levels.

6b. Yes. This is a false statement because more than one channel of an audio board can be active, but only one source can be active going through a specific channel.

7b. No. Audio consoles allow the operator to monitor various sources through studio monitor speakers or headphones. (Reread 2.6.)

8b. Correct. Levels over 100 percent are in the red and they will be distorted, but in the mud refers to low signal levels, making this a false statement.

9b. Wrong. In the mud refers to having board levels below 20 percent or so and can occur whether monitor speakers are muted or not. (Reread 2.6.)

10b. Yes. Most radio studios use the dynamic microphone.

11b. No. A cardioid microphone picks up sound in a heart-shaped pattern, so it doesn't pick up sound as well from the sides as from the front and hardly picks up sound at all from the rear of the microphone. (Reread 2.3.)

12b. No. While mini-disc players have sometimes replaced cart machines in the radio studio; these are more likely to be used for playing back commercials, promos, and other non-music sources. (Reread 2.7.)

13b. No. Working in two studios at the same time really isn't practical. (Reread 2.2.)

14b. Correct. Six inches from the microphone would be a good mic-to-mouth distance.
15b. No. Digital audio tape is another form of digital equipment. (Reread 2.7.)

If You Answered C:

1c. No. While CD players are one of the major playback sources in the studio, there is a better answer. (Reread 2.6 and 2.7.)
2c. Wrong. This is a characteristic of working a microphone too close. (Reread 2.3 and 2.4.)
3c. Yes. While using the wrong type of microphone may hinder your performance, it usually doesn't lead to mic fright.
4c. Wrong. A lack of experience could cause an announcer to hold back some, but there is a better response. (Reread 2.5.)
5c. Never. Tapping on a microphone could damage a good quality microphone. (Reread 2.4.)
7c. No. Audio consoles allow the operator to route or send the audio signals going through the board with an output selector. (Reread 2.6.)
9c. Right. If the monitor speakers are not muted, the microphone would pick up the audio signal, amplify it, send it through the speakers again, over and over, until a screeching or howling sound was produced.
10c. No. A capacitor microphone is just another name for the condenser microphone. (Reread 2.3.)
11c. No. Bidirectional microphones pick up sound from the front and rear of the microphone, but not from either side. (Reread 2.3.)
12c. No. This is a good choice as many stations do play back music on CD, but there is a better choice for the modern radio studio. (Reread 2.7.)
13c. No. Although an engineer working with an announcer is done in radio, this isn't the appropriate term for it. (Reread 2.2.)
14c. Wrong. Ten inches from a microphone would be too far away for many announcers and would produce a weak microphone signal. (Reread 2.4.)
15c. No. The compact disc is another form of digital equipment. (Reread 2.9.)

If You Answered D:

1d. No. This digital recorder can be used in the studio and for field recording, but it's not a key piece of equipment. (Reread 2.6 and 2.8.)
2d. Correct. Unless the announcer had very weak vocal strength, working close to a microphone probably would not produce too strong an audio signal that is distorted. In general, audible breathing, sibilance, and the popping of letters are the problems you run into from working too close to a mic.
3d. No. Announcers who are unprepared often experience mic fright. (Reread 2.5.)
4d. Wrong. If an announcer gave a mistake-free performance, he or she was probably prepared. (Reread 2.5.)
5d. No. While speaking "Testing … " is often done, it isn't really the best way to give a microphone level. (Reread 2.4.)
7d. Yes. While many consoles have simple equalizers associated with various board channels and also allow audio signals to be looped to outboard signal processing devices, this is not really a major function of the console.
9d. Wrong. Plosive sounds occur when the announcer "pops p's" and can occur whether monitor speakers are muted or not. (Reread 2.6.)
10d. No. Ribbon microphones are rarely used in the modern radio studio. (Reread 2.3.)
11d. No. This is just a type of cardioid microphone with a narrower pickup pattern. (Reread 2.3.)
12d. Yes. This is the best choice because more and more stations are now playing back music and other programming elements from a digital storage device through computer equipment.
13d. Yes. This is what working combo means.
14d. Wrong. Eighteen inches from a microphone would be way too far away for typical microphone technique. (Reread 2.4.)
15d. Yes. This is what a digital audio workstation is.

Projects

■ PROJECT 1

Operate audio equipment.

Purpose
To give you an opportunity to work with audio studio equipment and practice basic radio announcing skills.

Notes
1. Your instructor will probably provide you with a basic orientation to your studio and the equipment it contains; this project assumes you have an understanding of how to operate the equipment in your studio.
2. The most common mistake beginners make is having switches set in the wrong positions. For example, if you open an audio board channel for a recorder that is set up to record, you'll probably get feedback. If you hear the screech or howl of feedback when you turn on a switch, turn it off immediately until you figure out what other switch is turned on but shouldn't be. If you get stuck, ask your instructor or station engineer for help.
3. As a minimum, you'll need some type of blank recording media and a couple of CDs to complete this project.

How to Do the Project
1. Sit or stand in front of the audio console and take a moment to locate and identify the equipment in the studio. Obviously, not all studios are the same, but you should readily find a microphone, CD players, recorders, and, of course, the audio console.
2. You'll need headphones to properly complete the project, so make sure there is a pair available and plug them into the audio console.
3. Set up an audio recorder so you can record your work.
4. Position yourself correctly in front of the microphone. Remember mic-to-mouth distance and position. Start recording, and turn on the microphone channel; increase the volume as you talk into the microphone until you have proper levels. Remember, when you turn on the microphone, the studio monitor speakers will mute, so you can only hear what you are doing through headphones. Watch the VU meters and don't go in the mud or in the red. Record several sentences of ad-libbed material.
5. Turn the microphone and recorder off. Listen to what you have recorded.
6. Put a CD into a CD player; if you have two CD players, put one in each. Set them up to play back through the audio console and practice playing each one. As you're doing so, set the appropriate volume level. Now cue up one song on each CD player.
7. You're going to introduce and back-announce (see step 10) the songs that you've cued up — something the radio disc jockey does all the time.
8. Begin recording again. Turn on the microphone and introduce the first song with some clever ad-lib material that includes the artist name and song title. Rather than start the CD after you've finished your ad-lib, start the CD player while you are talking. The CD volume should be lower than your microphone volume, but we should hear both sources. Most songs have a short instrumental introduction before the artist begins singing; try to end your ad-lib just before the singing starts — this is called "talking up the song introduction." As you stop talking, the CD volume should be turned up to full.
9. Once the song has played long enough to be "established," pause the recorder. Advance the CD to the end of the song. Most CD players have a fast forward button or a cue wheel that allows you to do this. Once you're about 30 seconds or so from the end of the song, pause the CD player.

10. Now begin recording again and start the CD player again. As the song begins to fade out, turn on your microphone and ad-lib some type of material that again gives the artist name and song title. This is a back-announce and lets the listener know what song they've just heard.

11. Start the song on the other CD player and talk up the "intro" and back-announce the outro as you did with the first song. Turn off your microphone and pause the recorder when you are done.

12. Use two new songs from the CDs that you have available and record a couple more song introductions and outros as you did earlier.

13. When you are finished, you should have on your recording the initial ad-lib material you recorded plus four song intros and outros. Make sure this is what you've recorded and that you are happy with the outcome.

14. If you don't like what you recorded, do the project again.

15. If you are satisfied with the project, label the recording with your name and "Song Introductions" and turn it in to your instructor to receive credit for this project.

■ PROJECT 2

Practice microphone technique.

Purpose
To enable you to experiment with various mic-to-mouth distances and mic-to-mouth positions using dynamic and condenser microphones.

Notes
1. This project assumes you have a basic understanding of how to operate the equipment in your audio studio.
2. You could also do the project with just a couple of microphones, appropriate cables, and an audio recorder.
3. If you hear the screech or howl of feedback when you turn on a switch, turn it off immediately until you figure out what other switch is turned on that shouldn't be. If you get stuck, ask your instructor or station engineer for help.
4. You'll need a dynamic and a condenser microphone to complete this project.

How to Do the Project
1. Select a dynamic microphone. Use one with a cardioid pickup pattern.
2. If you're working in a studio, set it up so that you can record from the microphone onto an audio recorder. You could also attach the microphone to a portable recorder with the appropriate cable.
3. Position yourself correctly in front of the microphone. Start recording, and turn on the microphone channel; increase the volume as you talk into the microphone until you have proper levels. Remember, when you turn on the microphone the monitor speakers will mute, so you'll need headphones.
4. While you're recording, change your mic-to-mouth distance from two inches to six inches to ten inches to eighteen inches. Try to keep your volume level the same regardless of your distance, and record into the microphone where you are as you move: for example, "This is a dynamic microphone and my mic-to-mouth distance is now two inches."
5. Now, maintaining a proper mic-to-mouth distance of about six inches, change your mic-to-mouth position, moving completely around the microphone. Again, record where you are as you move: for example, "I am directly in front of the dynamic microphone; now I am ninety degrees to the right of the front of the microphone." If you're in a studio, you probably cannot

get behind the microphone, but you can turn the microphone completely around to get this position.

6. If you have access to another dynamic microphone with a different pickup pattern, such as omnidirectional, repeat the exercise. Make sure you identify exactly what type of microphone and pickup pattern you are recording with.

7. Now repeat the exercise with a condenser microphone. Again, use both a cardioid and an omnidirectional pickup pattern, if possible.

8. Listen to the recording, and write down some observations about the differences you can hear with the different microphones, pickup patterns, mic-to-mouth distances, and mic-to-mouth positions.

9. Devise a chart that summarizes the observations from the previous step.

10. Turn in the chart and audio recording to your instructor to receive credit for this project. Make sure you include your name on both and label the recording and chart, "Working With Microphones."

■ PROJECT 3

Investigate "mic fright".

Purpose
To enable you to survey radio announcers about their experiences with mic fright and query them on performance techniques.

Notes

1. You may want to review Section 2.5 of this chapter to be sure you have an understanding of what causes mic fright and, as a performer, how to eliminate it.

2. You will be contacting several radio announcers, but if some seem reluctant to help you, don't push them. Just select another station and announcer until you've found someone who is happy to help with your project.

3. Make sure you have some ideas about what you want to find out before you begin to contact anyone.

How to Do the Project

1. Select several radio announcers in your market. You could also choose announcers from all across the country, but you'll probably get better response from your local broadcasters.

2. Contact each one by personal visit, telephone, e-mail, or letter. Many station web sites have individual e-mails for their announcers, so you might want to check that method of contact first.

3. Tell them you are doing a project for a broadcast performance course and would like to ask them a few questions about mic fright and broadcast performance techniques. If you are contacting them by telephone or in person, make sure you let them know it will not take long for you to get the information you need.

4. You should have previously decided what information you need to gather, but try to cover the following:

    a. How long have they been a radio announcer?

    b. When they first went on the air, did they experience mic fright? If so, ask why they felt it happened.

    c. How did they overcome their fear?

    d. Assuming they have been an announcer for some time, have there ever been any circumstances recently when they experienced mic fright again?

    e. What do they do to prepare for a performance situation?

    f. Do they have any special techniques for getting timing correct?

    g. Do they have any tricks to ensure correct word pronunciation?

    h. Can they offer you any other tips on performance techniques?

5. When you've gotten the information you were looking for, be sure to thank the announcers for taking the time to help you.

6. Now, using the information you've gathered from several announcers, write a short report about your findings.

7. Make sure you include your name and label the paper, "Mic Fright and Performance Techniques." Turn in your paper to your instructor to receive credit for this project.

CHAPTER THREE

THE TELEVISION PERFORMANCE ENVIRONMENT

3.1 INTRODUCTION

In the previous chapter, you learned how much variation there is in the actual equipment operation you may encounter. While most announcers operate all the equipment in the radio studio when they are on the air, some television performers have the luxury of a crew to operate the equipment behind the scenes. However, in smaller markets, some cable operations, and the Internet, the on-camera talent may wear more than one hat and will often assume equipment operation responsibilities as well. Any performer will benefit from a basic knowledge of the environment in which he or she works and the equipment being used for the performance. This chapter looks at the television broadcast environment—the basic television and cable television studio and the equipment normally found there—and focuses on working with the most fundamental piece of equipment the television performer will deal with—the video camera.

3.2 THE TELEVISION STUDIO

Television and cable facilities can vary widely in layout, depending on the size of the operation and the structural design; however, several elements are common to most of them. The most familiar is the actual **studio**—usually a large room with a high ceiling where the performances and productions take place. This is coordinated by the **control room**, which functions as the nerve center of a video production. A **recording room** is usually nearby, where a variety of machines are housed that will record and play back the various programs and commercials that make up the day's operations. Most of these machines will be digital, although one or two tape-based machines may be preserved for archival work. Even if a production operation does not have a connection to an outlet like a transmitter or satellite uplink, many things are likely to be going on at the same time. Because other equipment supports the studio operation, there may be a separate space know as the **technical center**, or it may be combined with the recording facility. Other areas that may affect talent at different times are the **prop room**, which is really just a very large storage closet, and **editing booths**, where recordings are rearranged and assembled. In addition, there may be **dressing** and **makeup rooms**, **lounges**, and **work areas**. For the television talent, the two most significant areas are the studio and the control room. Video Clip 3.1 shows the key areas of a television facility.

The control room, as shown in Figure 3.1, is equipped with many picture monitors that enable the crew to see what is coming from all the cameras and other video sources in the system. The picture the audience will see is selected through the **switcher**, which also may be called the **SEG** or **special effects generator**. Sound is controlled through the **audio console** or board, which has available controls for microphone volume and other sources of sound such as CDs, minidiscs, and video recordings, plus feeds from networks and satellite trucks. There will also be a device

FIGURE 3.1 The television control room is where various production personnel can manipulate the audio and video for a program. (Photo courtesy of John Carroll University.)

FIGURE 3.2 The television studio houses cameras, microphones, sets, performers and crew. It is where the actual production takes place. (Copyright Kevin G. Reeves, Photographer. Courtesy of Westlake Reed Leskosky.)

FIGURE 3.3 The television lights are mounted and hung from a crisscross grid that is suspended from the studio ceiling. (Photo by Alan Stephenson.)

for creating a wide variety of letters and colors on the screen for titling. This may be known as a **character generator**, by the acronym **CG**, or by a variety of brand names. Lighting and **teleprompter** controls may also be located in the control room.

Television studios are often quite large, not so much to handle big productions, but so that several different sets can be permanently erected and lit, as a means of saving the cost of constantly putting them up, lighting them, and then taking them down. The audience often sees only a small portion of the total studio space. Figure 3.2 shows a portion of the interior of a television studio. Most commonly, studios have three cameras, but some smaller ones may have two, and larger operations may have four or more. Cameras traditionally have had crews to operate them, but many stations have moved to robotic cameras, especially in news studios where the same camera shots are used each day. The first experience with a robotic camera can be a bit surprising for the talent as an unattended camera suddenly moves to another spot in the studio and prepares to take a new picture.

For the talent, one of the most important elements on the camera is the **tally light**, usually a small red light located on the top front of the camera, which illuminates when that particular camera is in use. If the performer is to address the audience directly, he or she will need to speak to the camera that has its light on. A typical studio television camera and tally light are shown in Video Clip 3.2.

In the studio, only the area where the production will actually take place is lit for television. As shown in Figure 3.3, a **grid** suspended from the studio ceiling allows a variety of lights to be hung and positioned for specific television productions. In general, television employs a **three-point lighting** technique using **key**, **back**, and **fill** lights to properly illuminate an area. The lights will seem quite bright at first, particularly because they are viewed against a much dimmer background. You may feel a need to squint until your eyes adjust to the bright lights. It's a good practice to go into the bright area early and get used to the lights, so you can be comfortable when you actually face the cameras during the performance. Some studios now use fluorescent lights, which seem less bright and, as cameras are more sensitive, they need less light. As a result, brightness and heat are less of a fact than they once were. In some cases, you may find the studio quite cool.

Microphones are either worn, held, or suspended over your head. Occasionally you may find that they may be attached to microphone cables, which you will have to consider when moving about during a production. However, most facilities are using **wireless** microphones that eliminate the cable, but may require that you wear a small transmitter. This is usually attached to your belt, in back, at waist level. However, it could also be strapped to a leg under a dress or pants or affixed to your side under a coat. Most **hand-held** microphones have the transmitter built right into them so you don't have to wear a pack. Wireless microphones can be turned on and off, but this is usually done by a production crew member. Be sure the microphone is off during breaks. Every broadcaster knows stories about what can happen when talent is careless about wearing a microphone that has been left "open" after a segment is completed. Jobs have been lost, marriages endangered, and hosts embarrassed by something that was said when a microphone was forgotten or thought to be off. Wireless mics are particularly dangerous because they have no cable to remind you that you are connected. Always turn your mic off or have a technician do it for you before you wander off on a break or begin a conversation you assume will be private. A warning about **clip-on** mics: some people have a habit of bringing their hand up to their chests while speaking. This can result in a loud thump when the hand hits the microphone. This action is almost a reflex for some, and they are not aware that they do it. It is one of the many things you will need to learn and which you must monitor yourself.

Production outside the traditional studio can vary extensively. The advent of small cameras that can operate in minimal light makes almost any site a prospective production location. What you encounter can range from the extensive setup for a major sporting event to a single camera operator working with you. You may even be your own camera operator, as will be described in Chapter 8. News and weather, in particular, will have you in the field, often regardless of the conditions.

3.3 THE TELEVISION PRODUCTION CREW

Unlike radio, in which the talent usually operates the equipment, video production is very much a team effort. The number of people involved will vary according to the facility and the size of the production. At the top of the hierarchy is the **producer** who has the primary responsibility for the content of the production. In larger operations, there may be more than one level of producer. In the studio, the activities will be controlled by the **director**. The director functions somewhat like a quarterback on a football team; he or she decides what the audience will see and hear, in what order, and for how long. In the control room, in addition to the director, you should find an **audio operator**, a **switcher** or **technical director (TD)**, a **CG** operator, one or more **assistant directors (AD)**, and others as needed. Costs have caused crews to shrink and equipment is more versatile, so you could find some doubling up or working without assistants.

In the studio will be found a **floor manager**, who acts as an extension of the director, carrying out the orders received over an **intercom** headphone. Unless you have robotics, there will be an operator for each camera and

any necessary assistants. If a production has many camera moves, each camera may also have a **cable-puller** whose job is to make sure moves are not disrupted by snagged cables. Other assistants may be present to hold cue cards, move props, run teleprompters, and otherwise help as needed. In some situations, particularly when a program is at least partly ad-lib, the producer may move out on to the floor to more closely control program segments and other content decisions. The term most commonly used in this role is **showrunner**.

The audio operator often functions alone, or with one assistant if the production is large. As an on-air person, you'll be asked for **microphone checks**, the process of confirming that your microphone is working properly and adjusting the console so that your voice strength is appropriate. Sometimes the term used will be "Please give a level." Don't fall into the pattern of loudly projecting "1–2–3–4" unless you expect to be speaking that way. Also, don't turn your head and speak directly into the microphone. Count in a modulated, conversational way, or begin to ad-lib or read some script, but do it with your normal tone and volume. Continue your delivery until someone tells you to stop. Few things are as frustrating to an audio operator as the talent who basically says, "1–2–3–4, is that enough?" The key is to do it in your normal voice.

You may notice a very relaxed atmosphere that could be interpreted as a lack of caring about quality. However, the crew is used to working together, and each member knows what to do. The joking will end just as the program starts, and you will find they can get serious very quickly.

3.4 TELEVISION TERMINOLOGY

Although it may not affect you directly as a performer, it is useful to have a sense of the meaning of the terms related to the different types of pictures or "shots" your director might use. Understanding these will guide you in your position and movement. The first basic term would be the **cover** or **wide shot**, which takes in the whole set area. In this kind of shot, you can stand or sit or move within the confines of the set and your audience will still be able to see you. This shot would be particularly useful if you will have a surprise guest walk onto the set during your interview show.

Many shot descriptions are based on the amount of the talent's body that is visible. The **full** shot covers everything including your feet. The **knee** shot cuts off at the knees, and the **hip**, **waist**, and **chest** shots cut off at those places on the body. The waist and chest shots are commonly seen in newscasts. Closer shots may include the **necktie** or **tight chest** shot, the **head** shot, and the **face** shot. The word "tight" is often substituted for "close." As the shots get tighter they become more dramatic. You will see tight close-ups used more in soap operas and in tense interviews. Head and face shots are rarely used for the news anchor or reporter.

Another means of describing shots relates to the number of individuals in the picture. A **four shot** would include all three guests, and the host in an interview. A **three** shot and a **two** shot apply in the same manner, although the director would have to provide more specific information when calling for a three shot if you're working with a panel of five people.

Another type of information that can be useful to the talent is the terms used to describe how the director plans to change from one picture to another. The **take** is an instantaneous change between cameras. It represents a high percentage of changes that will occur in most programs. The **dissolve** is a variable-speed change involving the blending of the pictures from two cameras, and can last more than a second. It creates a different mood and is sometimes used in artistic circumstances or to signify a change of time or location. The **fade** is a change to or from a black screen, and is used at the beginning and end of segments or programs. It too can take more than a second. For the performer, this delay means you will have to hold your position a bit longer as you don't disappear immediately. **Wipes** and **effects** are more novel transitions that can range from something as simple as a moving bar, which changes the picture or something exotic such as a rocket going up or the picture seeming to burn off the screen.

Like so many things in this business, not everyone uses the same terminology, but being familiar with these words will help you understand what is going on and make you feel more comfortable in the environment. You will need to get briefed on critical terms in any new situation.

3.5 CAMERA PANIC

In the previous chapter, camera panic was mentioned as the television counterpart to mic fright. It is a queasiness that occurs just before a performance when the camera tally light comes on or when the talent is cued that he or she is on the air. Like mic fright, camera panic can range from mild to wild. For many performers, it is a stronger feeling than mic fright

because television adds the element of being seen as well as being heard. There is a sense of anonymity in radio that offers some comfort, whereas the camera removes any barrier between the performer and audience.

Further, fear of failure is strong for television performers because nobody wants to make fools of themselves when everybody can see them. On television, you must be concerned with not only your actual performance (for example, reading the script properly) and your general appearance, but also your posture, your movements, your facial expression, your attire, and so on. A "fluff" in any area can play on your anxiety about failure. Of course, being inexperienced and unprepared will cause camera panic, just as it will cause mic fright. Beginning performers can be overwhelmed by television. The lights and cameras in the studio and the crew members necessary for the production process all add to the distraction. However, with practice in this environment it becomes easier and easier. Use every opportunity available to get camera practice. This is the surest way to get over the discomfort. Work on keeping your concentration up and your focus on the task at hand. Adequate preparation is necessary for broadcast talent and will lessen any chance of camera panic or mic fright that comes from not being ready to go.

Because the visual element is so dominant in television, a cause of camera panic can be a dislike of one's appearance. However, if you apply all the things covered in this text, you have no reason to worry. Proper dress, posture, preparation, and delivery will make you look like a pro. Doing those things will likely mean that you are the only one uncomfortable with your appearance.

Occasionally, nearly all broadcasters encounter situations in which they are unsure of, or disturbed by, the circumstances they are covering, and feel off balance. Keeping your poise and letting your professionalism and experience take over will go a long way toward getting you through a difficult time.

3.6 WORKING WITH A CAMERA

Nerves

The television camera is the beginning of the video link that delivers the image of the performer from the studio (or field) to the viewer's TV set or monitor. As a television performer, you should know some basic guidelines for being the person in front of the camera.

For many people, the first few experiences before the camera are unsettling. As noted, camera panic can set in and words that usually flow easily suddenly become stuck in your throat. Hesitations and mistakes come in a deluge. Actually, this anxiety that many experience is quite normal. The primary reason for all the mistakes is the split attention that develops when you go on camera. Suddenly, you are aware of everything you say, how you look, how you're standing or sitting, and just about everything else imaginable. As a result, instead of having 100 percent of your attention focused on what you are saying, you are operating at about 50 percent of your potential because the other half is busy criticizing and worrying about how things are going. This is where practice comes in. The more camera time you get, the easier it all becomes. Work on avoiding the self-criticism and put all your concentration on the presentation. It's another skill that can be learned. Eventually, you'll know the camera is there but you won't care. Any kind of speaking performance can help you adjust. Public speaking is good practice, as is theater work. The goal is to get used to having others looking at and listening to you. Judging by the vast number of people appearing on television, it isn't that hard a skill to master.

Gestures and Speech

Having said that, let's consider some of the things that make you appear to be professional on camera. Those who have had some theater experience know that directors often want gestures exaggerated and speech projected so that those in the back row of the theater will get the message. Just the opposite is true in television, which is a very intimate medium. You operate as if the person you are speaking to is only a few feet away. Gestures and movements are small and underplayed. Speech is conversational. This can be a bit difficult at first because the cameras may be located at some distance from you across the studio. We tend to think that the audience is that distance away, and speak more loudly than necessary. In reality, the audience's ear is the microphone, which you may be wearing or holding close to you. As an experiment, in a practice session, you might ask if the cameras could be brought quite close to you, about four feet away. Ad-lib to the "audience" for a while with the cameras near and then ask to have them gradually moved away. You will feel yourself struggle to hold the style you used when the camera was close, as subconsciously you want to adjust your delivery to the greater distance. With the use of telephoto lenses, the audience can see you in a close-up throughout such a demonstration, regardless of where the cameras actually are located.

Eye Contact and Face

Looking into the camera lens is important because, for the audience, it appears that you are looking directly at them. The lens is your channel to your audience. This does not mean that you should stare as if transfixed. Rather, you should make eye contact as you would with a friend in a conversation. You can glance away to your notes or a script; however, avoid frequent glancing around, because it's very noticeable and annoying to the audience, as is easily seen in Video Clip 3.3. The bottom line is that good, steady eye contact is key to good performance in most television productions, and so it calls for effort on your part to provide it. Communication is most effective when you look someone in the eye.

The look on your face also conveys a message to the audience. It's easy to fall into a blank expression when you are concentrating on a teleprompter or on what you are saying. Except in serious situations, the goal should be to appear pleasant, interested, and involved. Part of your job is to hold the audience, and appearing as an attractive, informed speaker is significant. One easy way to avoid looking amateurish is to remember that the camera might not leave you the instant you finish a segment. You'll look foolish if you heave a big sigh of relief or grimace a split second after you finish what you had to say. Stay "in character," holding a pleasant expression until you are sure the camera shot has changed. In some situations, the floor manager may give you a "clear" signal. On occasion, you may find you have to hold that smile for an agonizingly long period of time. Perhaps the production segment ended sooner than planned or the director isn't quite ready to take a different shot. Whatever the cause, when you must hold an expression to the point where it becomes forced, you'll drift into an **egg-on-face** look, as shown in Video Clip 3.4.

Dress

On television, the way you dress will be important for several reasons. First, extremes of lights and darks do not telecast well because cameras can handle only a limited range. Second, checks, herringbones, and fine stripes also create problems and can appear as a shimmering or moving pattern known as a moire effect. Another reason dress is important is that you may perform in front of a chroma-key background. This effect is frequently used during weathercasts to make it appear that the weather person is standing right in front of a large map. In reality, the talent is standing in front of a large green, or sometimes blue, screen. Since this is an electronic effect, if the talent wears the same color of blue or green as the background, the part of the clothing that is the same color or intensity as the background will become the background map! While that may be amusing, it's the talent's responsibility to choose clothing that is appropriate for the setting. Video Clip 3.5 shows what happens when a performer doesn't dress properly for a chroma-key effect. Other uses for chroma-key backgrounds include music videos, news and sports broadcasts, and commercials. Backgrounds for chroma-keys can be drawn from any visual source, and these days computer-generated pictures are often used. In the movie *Space Jam*, Michael Jordan did his moves alone in front of a green screen and the cartoon characters were added later through the use of computer animation.

Jewelry

Particularly for women, the question of dressing up an outfit with jewelry merits some discussion. Large pins are often shiny and can reflect the lights, causing flashes as you move on the set. They can also cause occasional thumps on the clip-on microphone. Bracelets and bangles can cause the same problems, and can generate stray clicks, particularly if you are using a hand-held mic or working at a table or counter. Earrings follow the same pattern. Large dangling ones, particularly with bright stones in them, can present problems for the cameras and distract your audience. That doesn't mean that you may not have a guest that shows up loaded with jewelry. The director may ask that the jewelry be removed, ask you to break the news to the guest, or, if it's a short segment, try to live with the situation. For the professional, wearing tasteful, simple jewelry that won't cause reflections or create noise is best. It's a good idea to give some consideration to what you have that would fit this category and add some to your collection if you find it is lacking. On-camera checks, in advance, are a good way to avoid problems.

Standing

Now, let's consider standing in front of the camera. The basic rule of thumb here is to stand up straight, lean slightly forward, and stand still. Young performers often have the tendency to put most of their weight on one leg, which can result in one hip sticking out, making the talent look very unprofessional. You also

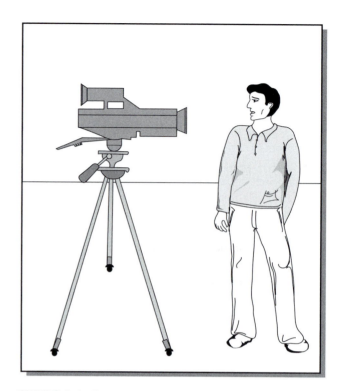

FIGURE 3.4 Poor posture.

cannot rock from side to side, shifting your weight from one foot to the other. You can see a bad example in Figure 3.4. Remember, television tends to exaggerate movement and rocking on camera can cause you to move you in and out of the proper frame and may make the viewers seasick as the camera tries to follow you. If a graphic such as a corner insert is being used, an unaware performer can rock into and go behind the graphic. Video Clip 3.6 shows a television performer "rocking"—notice how distracting the rocking motion is, even when the camera tries to follow the performer. Video Clip 3.7 shows a performer standing on camera—notice how correct posture puts one foot slightly in front of the other; this will help prevent any tendency to rock on camera. What to do with the hands can be a problem. Using one to gesture while letting the other hang quietly beside you is often the best approach. The hand-in-the-pocket stance may be more comfortable for men, but will not be appropriate in many situations.

Sitting

Sitting in front of a camera is similar to standing. Obviously, it's easier to stay still while sitting, but the television performer must still remember the basic rules: sit up straight, lean slightly forward, and keep still, as shown in Video Clip 3.8. When sitting, the same rules as for standing apply: avoid slouching, and sit erect, but relaxed. Leaning too much on one arm-rest can give you a distorted appearance. Watch out, too, for a tendency to slide into a slouch as the program goes on. It can be so gradual that you won't notice until it becomes very obvious to the viewer. Position your body so that it is facing forward or nearly so. Extreme body twists are decidedly unattractive. If you find yourself in a situation where you are directed to a camera that is to the side of you, turn your whole body toward it. Cameras also tend to exaggerate the distance between people, so chairs on the set are often placed quite close together. However, we like to be a certain distance from someone we are conversing with, and being closer makes us uncomfortable. This can cause you to unconsciously lean away from the person seated next to you or across from you, again creating a rather awkward position as seen by the camera. Whether standing or sitting, there is one thing that is certain—the camera will catch whatever goes on in front of it. If you fidget, the audience will see it. So when standing and sitting, be comfortable, but be still.

Objects

Another way to earn a director's respect and to be a polished performer is to become good at handling objects, particularly those to be shown in close-up. The director may designate a spot where all objects are to be held. Be sure to use it. Otherwise, get the object in front of you and hold it steady. It will take several moments for the camera operators to get the shot, so give them plenty of time. You can glance at the studio monitor to see if they have it, but don't try to help position it. The monitor does not show the mirror image to which we are accustomed. It's a "real" image and movements go in the direction opposite from what we expect. Trying to move the object to improve the shot can result in a ridiculous chase where the camera operator is desperately trying to get a shot that you keep changing, as shown in Video Clip 3.9.

If a guest produces something unexpectedly, ask to take it and then hold it steady for the camera. If it's something like an engagement ring, take the guest's hand and admire the ring, while providing that stability the director needs. Be especially careful if a shiny surface is to be shown. Shiny surfaces tend to reflect the studio lights and can result in a glare that makes things impossible to see. The simple tactic of tilting the object slightly forward will cause the glare to be reflected toward the floor, while not harming the view of the object. Book jackets and photographs are one of the most common glare problems and one that you can help with easily. Developing the habit of tilting everything slightly forward will relieve you of remembering to do it each time you handle something for a close-up. Video Clip 3.10 shows a performer incorrectly handling a shiny object.

Movement

You may often find yourself working in an unscripted situation, which requires a greater level of communication between you and the director, who is trying to be sure that the right pictures are ready at the right time and that nothing unprofessional or distracting occurs. Consider a talk show where you are the host interviewing a guest, who is a sculptor. After a period of conversation, you and your guest will get up and cross to an area where there are several pedestals, each displaying one of the guest's creations. Often the time at which you will make the move is only approximate, with you determining the exact moment. But if you stand up suddenly, the director might be in the middle of a close-up of you, which suddenly becomes a shot of your belt buckle, as shown in Video Clip 3.11 or Figure 3.5. Use your conversation to call attention

FIGURE 3.5 *Standing up without warning.*

to an upcoming move, such as, "We have an outstanding display of your work I'd like to take a look at." Don't move immediately, but wait a few moments so the director has time to adjust the shots. You can also telegraph the move by placing your hand on the arms of the chair or otherwise shifting your position to indicate you are about to get up. Video Clip 3.11 also shows how a television talent should get up from a sitting position.

Quite possibly the director will go to a shot of the sculptures while you are on your way there. You will be expected to continue the conversation as you walk. This means walking, talking, and perhaps watching the microphone cords while in the transition. The crew should have made sure you have plenty of cable and that it's not snagged, but a quick check of both your and your guest's cords can save the embarrassment of having a mic pulled off and falling to the floor while you are making the move. If the decision is made to have a camera follow you while the crossing is made, take your time. The camera operator wants to follow you smoothly, so walk at a steady pace, perhaps addressing the audience as well as your guest. Try to avoid turning your back to the audience. Once you have arrived, you will be moving from one pedestal to another, discussing each work. The director will probably have shown you where to stand in each case and which piece to go to next, but again he or she will need a cue as to when you are getting ready to move to the next one. Again, a phrase such as, "I really like this next object" will alert the director to a coming change. It is probable that much of this will be reviewed during the rehearsal, but it's up to you to do your part. Remembering the director's challenges will make you a valued partner. Furthermore, there will be occasions with no rehearsal when you will just have to use your knowledge and experience and make up the actions and words as you go along.

Marks

In a more structured situation, the director may dictate exactly where you are supposed to stand at a given moment. This is sometimes indicated by a small piece of colored tape placed on the floor, with a different color of tape for each performer. If you are on camera while making a move, you will need to use your **peripheral vision** to see your destination. Getting to the correct spot is known as **hitting your mark**. Avoid looking down at the floor and searching for your spot. This takes some practice, but professionals take great pride in never missing a mark. Video Clip 3.12 shows

a performer correctly hitting marks. Frequently, the director will have planned a new shot to take just as you arrive at your mark. The next camera will be pre-positioned. If you miss the mark, you will create a situation where the crew has to make a quick adjustment or use an awkward shot, perhaps showing only one half of your face. Hitting marks is something that can be practiced anywhere. Just set up a mark and walk to it while looking straight ahead or to the side.

3.7 COMMUNICATING IN THE STUDIO: HAND SIGNALS, CUE CARDS, PROMPTERS, AND IFB

One of the first things to be learned in the television studio is that microphones are very sensitive devices that sometimes seem better at picking up things you don't want to be heard than things you do. This means that talking in the studio with a mic open can be dangerous, as previously noted. As a result, other means of communicating have been developed. While the studio crew will be using an intercom headphone system, the talent usually gets operating information in three ways: hand signals, cue cards, and the IFB system. Hand signals were developed in the early days of television and are still commonly used today. However, the signals and their meanings can vary from studio to studio, so it's wise to find out in advance all the hand signs a talent may receive during the course of a production.

Your contact person in the studio is the floor manager. This person is likely to be relaying instructions from the director and will be giving you the various cues or signs at the start of and during your studio presentation. Good floor managers position themselves so that the talent can see the cues without turning their heads. The talent should focus on the lens or other designated point and view the hand signal with peripheral vision. If the cue giver is positioned too far to the side to see easily, during rehearsal, it is not inappropriate to ask him or her to stand closer to the camera. During a production, the floor manager is responsible for getting the cue to the talent and so may be seen crawling behind sets or across the floor to get into the talent's line of vision. However, having received the cue, the talent should never acknowledge it. Nods and similar motions will be very evident to the audience and will be a distraction. Even when you are certain you are off camera, acknowledgments are risky, as it is equally certain that sometime you will be wrong. It is the floor manager's responsibility to watch the talent's eyes to establish that the cue has been seen. Remember, there are no standard cues, but there are some that are used in many television facilities. Video Clip 3.13 shows several key hand signals being given, many from the perspective of the television talent.

Hand Signals

The standby signal, given with the hand overhead with the palm forward, is similar to the starter's words at a track meet—"On your marks, get set …"—just before the gun goes off to start the race. This is usually given about 15 seconds before the show begins and should bring the talent to a full alert position, both mentally and physically. Since the camera will see you at least a moment before you start talking, consider yourself "on" from the moment the standby signal is given. The next cue is you're on or cue talent and is the true start of the segment. The floor manager's hand, held overhead for "standby," suddenly swings down and stops with a finger pointing directly at the person speaking first or at the lens of the camera he or she should be playing to. The "cue talent" signal is almost always given immediately after the "standby" cue, and rarely is either of these cues given alone.

The "look here" cue directs the talent to a particular camera. As noted, studio cameras usually have a tally light to tell you which one is on, but some field cameras do not. In the field, except in major productions, you probably won't have a floor manager. Instead, the camera operator or a producer will give you the cue. In a multiple-camera production, the floor manager will remind you where to look by pointing his or her finger at the camera lens of the camera that is on at the moment. To direct a performer from one camera to another, "a change camera" hand signal is employed. The floor manager will start by pointing at the camera that currently is on, and then sweep that hand downward and bring it up to point at the new camera. The talent can turn smoothly to make a transition or can glance down, as if at notes or a script, and then look up at the new camera. The performer may have to slightly shift his or her body to achieve the best position for the new camera. Avoid looking upward as you go from camera to camera because that is an unmotivated action and may cause the audience to wonder what is going on up in the light grid. Video Clip 3.14 shows talent making a smooth transition from one camera to another.

If you need to change position, the floor manager will seem to be pushing you to the left, right, or back, or pulling you forward with two hands. These signals are very easy to understand. Think of the "stretch-it-out" hand signal as pulling taffy. The fingers are brought together and then pulled apart as if stretching something, like taffy or a big rubber band. It can mean that you are talking too fast or that there appears to be insufficient material for the time remaining, so please stretch it out, perhaps by talking a bit more slowly or by adding ad-libs or planned extra topics or questions. The reverse of the stretch-it-out signal is the "speed-up" cue. It usually consists of the index finger pointed at you and then rotated rapidly at the wrist. It means that you're not getting through the material fast enough, that time is running out, or that what you are saying is boring and you should move on to something else.

Timing

Television segments and programs are usually tightly timed, so it is essential to be alert for time cues and to follow them closely. It is useful to develop a time sense by practicing time estimation with a second-hand until you have some sense of how long 15 and 30 seconds are, in particular. They can be longer than you suspect. It is very disconcerting to your production crew to give you a cue indicating that thirty seconds remain and have you run through your concluding remarks in the next five seconds, most likely leaving them unprepared to close the show and, perhaps, with no way to fill the twenty-five seconds you have left them.

Television timing always deals with the time remaining, so a cue indicates how much time you have left to go. Again, the floor manager should give these cues where you can see them easily and they should not be acknowledged, as it will be very evident. Here, too, there will be variations from studio to studio, but the majority of floor managers will simply hold up two hands with fingers spread for "ten minutes," one hand for "five minutes," and then the appropriate number of fingers for the remaining minutes. At "thirty seconds," a particularly important cue, many studios use crossed, extended arms or index fingers as the cue, while others will form a C with the thumb and index finger as the indication. The "fifteen seconds" mark is another important point, and its signal is often a clenched fist. When the end of a production is reached, a "wrap it up" cue will be given. While this signal may vary, many studios commonly use one hand about six inches above the other and then both rotated in a Ferris-wheel motion. This cue means that you should conclude the segment or the show. Some studios may assist you further by having the floor manager count down the last ten seconds using fingers so that you have a clear picture of the time remaining.

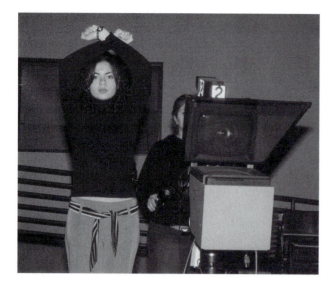

FIGURE 3.6   A common cue indicating that 30 seconds remains. (Photo by Alan Stephenson.)

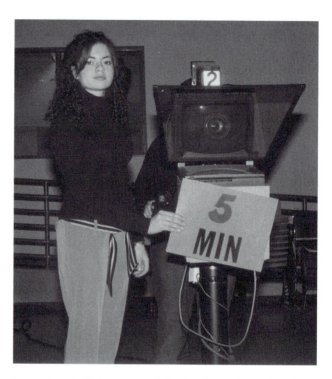

FIGURE 3.7   Using cue cards in the studio. (Photo by Alan Stephenson.)

This should enable you to end professionally, exactly on time. A "cut" signal—slitting the throat with the index finger—is given to show the production is finished. But again, signals vary from location to location. It's up to you to be sure you know the ones being used where you are. Figure 3.6 shows you one example.

Cue Cards

Another way to get information to a television performer is to use cue cards. Cue cards come in three "flavors." In two of them, they are simply substitutes for hand signals, whereas the third group carries script segments. The basic cue card is a heavy poster paper card, perhaps 16" × 18" with significant numbers or words printed on it. Note Figure 3.7. Most studios have a full set of time cards, perhaps starting as high as "30 minutes" and progressing down to "30 seconds" or lower. The word cues on cards could include "wind it up," "slow down," or "speed up," plus any other instruction the studio has found to be helpful. All these are held under the lens of the camera you are addressing or otherwise in your field of view. Video Clip 3.15 shows both correct and incorrect cue card use.

Devices used to provide the script to you during segments or entire shows include cue cards and teleprompters. For example, except for some side chatter, all of a television newscast will be scripted and on the prompter. Script cues are usually hand written on cards that are 20" × 24" or even larger. These are often used when only a short written segment is to be presented. Cards have been used in longer scenes, but

this involves skill in changing the cards without dropping them or getting them out of order. For the talent, moving from the bottom of one card to the top of the next can be a distraction. A well-planned card will finish with an entire sentence or paragraph, so there is a natural pause as you move to the next card.

Teleprompter

Teleprompters have been around virtually since the beginning of television. Originally they consisted of long rolls of paper that were printed on with oversize type. A roll was placed in a box mounted about the lens and the paper was drawn on to a take-up reel by a variable speed electric motor. An operator stood beside the camera and controlled the speed of the paper rolling as the talent read the script. These were useful, but presented problems when script changes occurred. Today, teleprompters are a combination of a small flat-panel computer monitor mounted horizontally below the lens, a special mirror system that is mounted in front of the lens, and a computer that generates the words that will appear. The mirror is a unique variety that enables you to see the words reflected off the screen while allowing the lens to see through the mirror as if nothing was there. The words on the screen are reversed so that they will appear

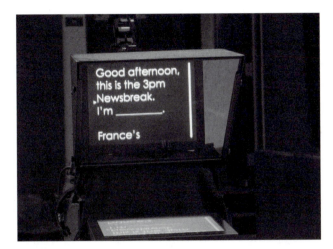

FIGURE 3.8 The teleprompter from the talent's prospective. (Photo by Alan Stephenson.)

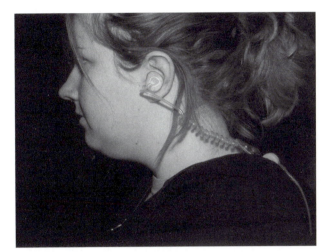

FIGURE 3.9 The IFB communication system earpiece. (Photo by Alan Stephenson.)

normal when viewed in the mirror. The speed at which the new words appear is adjustable. Usually they flow up from the bottom of the screen. Figure 3.8 shows you the talent's perspective.

Whether reading prompters or cue cards, professionals make it look easy; in reality, they are often reading copy they have never seen before. There is a story of old-time performer Arthur Godfrey breaking up at his own jokes on his television show. The reason was he was so good at reading the prompter that he never rehearsed and often had not heard the jokes before. The goal, of course, is to read the copy and make it sound conversational, delivering it as you would in an unrehearsed statement you are creating as you speak. This takes concentration and practice. Video Clip 3.16 shows a performer utilizing a teleprompter. We will devote more attention to working with teleprompters in Chapter 8.

IFB

In recent years, the IFB, or interruptible foldback, has become a common means of communicating with the talent. This is an earpiece, usually made out of transparent plastic, which is worn by the talent during the production. A wire or tube extends behind your head and often to a small intercom pack you'll be asked to wear. A little observation should enable you to spot them on most news and talk program performers. See Figure 3.9. These provide a means for someone in the control room to speak directly to the talent who is on the air. In some cases, interview guests wear them as well. The first experience using one will be distracting, since it means that while you may be trying to

speak intelligently or read a teleprompter, someone is giving you instructions in your ear. A good communicator will try to keep these directions very short and sandwich them in between your statements. Hundreds of people do it successfully every day, and you can, too. Several practice sessions should prepare you. Try to keep what you are saying in the foreground of your mind and hear the instructions in the background. Video Clip 3.17 shows the use of the IFB system. The IFB systems have become so common that you are almost certain to be expected to use them, so getting experience whenever possible is essential.

3.8 MAKEUP

Makeup is part of the business for most performers. It is added to enhance your appearance and hide flaws. The advent of HD, high-definition television, has changed the field of makeup considerably. For several reasons, standard television was very forgiving. Thick makeup could be used. Primarily, the definition of the television picture was not particularly good, and excesses and variations were not revealed. The ability to see fine detail in HD, about ten times sharper than analog, means that any error such as unevenness, missed spots and poor shading will jump out at the viewer. For some, the greatest concern is that the new system reveals age lines and blemishes vividly.

Makeup for HD should cover all exposed skin, the face, neck, hands, and arms. If a professional makeup artist is available, they will probably use an airbrush system which applies the makeup in tiny dots that are gently sprayed on to the skin. This quickly dries into an even, non-shiny finish and is so light that most talent forget they are wearing it. One of its great advantages is that it will hide just about anything, including tattoos. This approach is used on many network shows.

There are powders that are particularly effective in HD. These can be applied personally using a thick bristled brush and rubbed into the skin. Some powders have tiny reflective particles in them which can cause problem reflections. Any powder makeup should be viewed under bright light before use, to be sure this is not a factor. Everyone should use a foundation and a blush to add contours and definition. Women and some men will need eye makeup and lip color as well. Performers should be careful of applying too much makeup. Follow the guideline "less is more" for high-definition situations. Professional application of makeup takes time and practice. Elaborate or dramatic makeup is best left to the professional makeup artist, but anyone interested in television performance should have a basic understanding of the process. Many local stations will expect you to apply the makeup yourself. Once completed, makeup should always be checked on camera. It is important to avoid lines, streaks or shiny spots and to be sure the makeup is thoroughly blended.

3.9 CONCLUSIONS

This chapter has offered many useful tips and techniques for performing in front of the camera. These basic concepts are important for your development as a video performer in the mass media industries. An understanding of the studio environment will make your performance efforts better, as will practice. Each time you are in a performance situation, try to apply a few of the concepts presented here. Before long, many of them will start to become second nature and you will be on your way to being a polished video performer.

Self-Study

■ QUESTIONS

1. Television performers don't need any knowledge of the broadcast studio because a production crew will always be there to handle the equipment operation.
   a) true
   b) false

2. For television talent, the two most significant areas are the _____.
   a) studio and tape room
   b) studio and control room
   c) studio and prop room
   d) studio and editing booths

3. Which of the following is the best and quickest means for the talent to know which camera is on-air?
   a) tally light
   b) IFB
   c) cue cards
   d) hand signals

4. In the studio, the person responsible for giving the talent directions is the _____.
   a) director
   b) technical director
   c) floor manager
   d) producer

5. Which of the following is least likely to cause camera panic?
   a) dislike of one's appearance
   b) fear of failure
   c) distractions by the crew
   d) experience and preparation

6. Which of the following is not effective in working with a camera?
   a) large, exaggerated gestures
   b) eye contact with the camera as if it were a friend
   c) pleasant facial expression
   d) plain, simple clothes without small patterns

7. All of the following are important for the talent to do when holding objects to the camera except _____.
   a) tilting shiny surfaces so the light does not reflect and result in glare
   b) holding the object steady until the director and camera operator can get the shot
   c) moving the object to help the director and camera operator get a good shot
   d) using the monitor to help in placing the object, remembering that the direction of movement is opposite of what you would expect

8. During an unscripted program, it is the talent's responsibility to communicate movement to the director, perhaps by his or her conversation with the guest.
   a) true
   b) false

9. Which signal is almost always given immediately after the "standby" cue?
   a) Look here
   b) Cue talent
   c) Change position
   d) Wrap it up

10. Which hand signal would be given to alert the talent he or she is talking too fast?
    a) a clenched fist
    b) a motion imitating cutting the throat
    c) an index finger pointed at the talent and rotated rapidly at the wrist
    d) a motion imitating stretching a rubber band

11. Since the television production is very much a team effort, which production crew position functions somewhat like a quarterback, deciding what the audience will see and hear?
    a) technical director
    b) floor manager
    c) director
    d) camera operator

12. Television, much like theater, requires the talent to utilize exaggerated gestures and projected speech to get the best performance.
    a) true
    b) false

13. Which means of communicating with talent during a video production is most direct?
    a) cue cards
    b) IFB
    c) hand signals
    d) CG

14. If a performer has to hold a pleasant expression (often at the end of a production) to the point where it becomes forced, it will probably drift into a moire effect.
    a) true
    b) false

15. A dislike of one's appearance is one cause of camera panic. Which of the following is not a way television can distort a performer's appearance?
    a) performers often look heavier than they are
    b) a performer's movements can be exaggerated
    c) camera angles can reveal new elements of a performer's appearance
    d) TV lighting can make a performer appear washed out or sickly

■ ANSWERS

If You Answered A:

1a. No. Most radio performance situations require the performer to operate the equipment and even television talent should have a basic knowledge of the studio equipment. (Reread 3.1.)

2a. No. While the talent will be in the studio during the program, the technical center is where the program is recorded and the production crew will take care of this function. (Reread 3.2.)

3a. Correct. The red light on top of the camera indicates which camera is "hot."

4a. No. The director controls the entire production from the control room. To relay messages from the director to the studio talent is the job of the floor manager. (Reread 3.2 and 3.3.)

5a. Incorrect. The television camera can distort images and show you as you have not seen yourself. This can cause panic and nervousness, but remember, you are probably the only one who is uncomfortable with your appearance. (Reread 3.5.)

6a. Correct. For theater performances, large, exaggerated gestures are necessary. On television, these gestures appear unnatural. The television lens can get close-ups when necessary; therefore, it is distracting to the audience to use large gestures.

7a. Incorrect. Objects often need to be tilted slightly toward the camera so that glare or distortions are avoided. (Reread 3.6.)

8a. Correct. The talent must help the director get the shots as camera movement and adjustment can take some time, so this is a true statement. Talent should telegraph movement by indicating what will happen next, perhaps when talking with a guest.

9a. No. "Look Here" is the hand signal used to direct talent to a particular camera. (Reread 3.7.)

10a. Wrong. A clenched fist is often used to indicate 15 seconds remaining in the production. (Reread 3.7.)

11a. No. While the technical director will push buttons to put specific camera shots on-air, he or she isn't making decisions about those shots. (Reread 3.3.)

12a. Wrong. Just the opposite is true in television. Gestures are underplayed and speech is conversational. (Reread 3.6.)

13a. No. The floor manager would have to be told first by the director which cue card to show to the talent. (Reread 3.7.)

14a. No. The forced expression is known as egg-on-the-face. Talent clothing with small checks or fine stripes can create a shimmering pattern on camera that is known as a morie effect. (Reread 3.6.)

15a. Wrong. TV performers will often "electronically" gain a few pounds and appear heavier than they really are. (Reread 3.5.)

If You Answered B:

1b. Correct. Broadcast talent should have a basic knowledge of the studio environment in which they perform and the equipment utilized to complete a performance, so this is a false statement.

2b. Correct. The studio is the performance area. The control room is where the program is coordinated and from where talent will receive directions.

3b. No. The IFB is not the best way for talent to know which camera is on-air even though it is an earpiece into which the director or someone in the control room can talk to the talent during a program. (Reread 3.7.)

4b. No. The technical director sits in the control room and presses the buttons on the switcher to choose which picture will be broadcast. (Reread 3.2 and 3.3.)

5b. No. Fear of failure can cause you to loose confidence in your ability, which will show on your face and in your voice and result in a very poor performance. (Reread 3.5.)

6b. Incorrect. The conversational quality that television performance requires means eye contact should be direct toward the camera lens, but not result in staring into the camera. Think of communicating with the audience as you would a friend, occasionally glancing away from direct eye contact that can feel too intense. (Reread 3.6.)

7b. Incorrect. Holding the object steady is the most important thing the talent can do. (Reread 3.6.)

8b. Incorrect. In unscripted situations, the director relies on the talent to help maintain a professional look to the show. This means that the talent must indicate movement, often with comments such as "I think it's about time to go to the demonstration," so that camera shots can be framed and taken in an appropriate way. (Reread 3.6.)

9b. Yes. At the beginning of a production, the "standby" hand signal is usually followed by the "cue talent" hand signal, which is also known as the "you're on" cue.

10b. Wrong. A hand signal cutting the throat, known as a cut signal, is given to indicate a production is finished. (Reread 3.7.)

11b. No. The floor manager will just carry out orders he or she receives and often relay information, via hand signals, to the talent. (Reread 3.3.)

12b. Correct. This is a false statement because just the opposite is true in television. Gestures are underplayed and speech is conversational.

13b. Yes. An IFB (interruptible fold back.) is an ear piece device that would allow the talent to hear someone directly from the control room.

14b. Yes. This is a false statement because this forced expression is known as an egg-on-the-face look.

15b. Wrong. Movements are exaggerated on television so an awkward movement can be blown out of proportion. (Reread 3.5.)

If You Answered C:

2c. No. The prop room is an area talent should be aware of, but generally talent will have little contact with the prop room's organization, functions, or purchasing. (Reread 3.2.)

3c. No. Cue cards are not really the best way for the talent to know which camera is on-air. They are used to help the talent read copy. (Reread 3.7.)

4c. Correct. The "extension" of the director in the studio is the floor manager.

5c. Incorrect. The television studio is a busy, sometimes noisy place. During a program, people continue to move around the studio. If you let these distractions affect you, your performance will suffer. (Reread 3.5.)

6c. Incorrect. Facial expressions are very important on television and should be pleasant, but not exaggerated or forced. (Reread 3.6.)

7c. Correct. The talent can help the director by holding objects steady instead of moving them around, which can result in missing a close-up shot altogether.

9c. No. The "change" position hand signal is used to move the talent from one location to another. (Reread 3.7.)

10c. Wrong. This hand signal would do just the opposite, because it is used to tell the talent to speed up. (Reread 3.7.)

11c. Yes. The director of a TV production decides what the audience will see and hear, in what order, and for how long. He or she is the quarterback of the production crew.

13c. No. The floor manager would have to be told by the director which hand signal to give to the talent. (Reread 3.7.)

15c. Wrong. Various camera angles and screen sizes show very stark images often revealing elements of your appearance that are new to you. (Reread 3.5.)

If You Answered D:

2d. No. Although you may be interested in editing a segment for your program, the editing booths are used by editors whose job it is to combine recorded segments. In small markets you may be involved in some editing. (Reread 3.2.)

3d. No. Hand signals may help the talent to switch cameras during a production, but they are not the quickest means of communicating to the talent. The signal must come from the director to the floor manager to the talent, which causes a slight delay, so this is not the best way for talent to know which camera is on-air. (Reread 3.7.)

4d. No. The producer is responsible for hiring and obtaining a budget. During the production itself, the producer may not even be there. (Reread 3.2 and 3.3.)

5d. Correct. Confidence comes from practice and being prepared. The more experience you gain, the more you know you can handle any situation in the television studio.

6d. Incorrect. Plain, simple clothes without high-contrast colors (black/white.) are important on television. If you wear clothes with small patterns like herringbone or checks, they will look like they are moving on camera: a moire effect. (Reread 3.6.)

7d. Incorrect. The talent should not try to help the director by using the monitors. Movement appears opposite to what you may expect and therefore takes some practice. Position the object and hold it steady until the director and camera operator have time to complete the shot. (Reread 3.6.)

9d. No. This hand signal is given to indicate that the end of the production has been reached and the talent should "wrap it up." (Reread 3.7.)

10d. Correct. This stretching hand signal is used to alert the talent to slow down or stretch out the material.

11d. No. While the camera operator will frame various camera shots, he or she isn't making the decisions about those shots. (Reread 3.3.)

13d. No. A CG (character generator) is not a device used to communicate with talent in a TV production. (Reread 3.7.)

15d. Correct. A properly lit studio, using standard three-point lighting techniques, will show a performer as natural and lifelike.

Projects

■ PROJECT 1

Practice camera performance.

Purpose
To give you an opportunity to work in the television studio environment and practice basic camera and announcing skills.

Notes
1. Your instructor will probably provide you with a basic orientation to your television studio and the proper use of a script, cue cards, hand signals, and teleprompter. This project assumes you have a basic understanding of the television studio environment and knowledge of hand signals.
2. Remember to dress properly. Avoid patterns, high-contrast colors (black/white), shiny material, and jewelry that may reflect too much light.
3. Remember to use direct eye contact with the camera. This requires you to know the script fairly well.
4. Remember to glance down occasionally to break eye contact so that you don't seem to be staring at the audience. Look down as if you are referring to a script, even if you are using cue cards or a teleprompter.
5. As a minimum, you'll need about two minutes of copy to complete this assignment, cue cards on twenty- by twenty-four-inch cards (usually white poster board and black ink), and a blank recording medium. Your instructor may supply the script and cue cards.

How to Do the Project
1. You will need to have a crew for this assignment and your instructor will probably provide the necessary people. In the studio with you, you probably will have a minimum of two people—a camera operator and a floor director. In the control area will probably be a director, audio operator, and a recordist.
2. Sit or stand in front of the television camera. Standing may give you more energy, but there is always the problem of what to do with your hands. You can use the script as a prop or your instructor may give you other directions. If you are standing, hold the script at about waist level and to the right or left side. If you are sitting, be sure to sit up and keep the script in front of you. When using a teleprompter or cue cards, keep the script in the same place(s) but be sure to "use" it by glancing down as if you were reading.
3. Glancing down may cause you to lose your place. Before coming into the studio, practice where in the script you want to glance down. Mark the copy with a color pen to remind you of your place in the script or where you will glance down.
4. Go over the hand signals with the floor director before you begin. Be sure you understand the signals and can see them without moving your head or eyes. The floor person should stand in your line of sight so that you can see the signals in your peripheral vision. For this assignment, you probably will use only a few signals: stand by, cue talent, speed up, slow down, wrap it up, thirty seconds to go.
5. Record the copy using the script, then using cue cards, and finally using a teleprompter (if available).
6. Review the recording. Evaluate your eye contact, head movement, body movement, and the manner in which you took the cues.
7. If there are any takes that you do not like, record those parts over again.
8. If you are satisfied, turn the recording in to your instructor to receive credit for this project.

■ PROJECT 2

Practice taking hand signals in the television studio.

Purpose
To give you a chance to demonstrate your knowledge of studio hand signals and your ability to respond to them while speaking.

Notes
1. Review Section 3.7 to refresh your memory of the various hand signals that are used in the television studio.
2. For this project, you will need to prepare an ad lib segment. It can be something quite familiar, such as your autobiography, an experience you've had, or your opinion of some topic. There should be enough material for you to talk easily for at least three minutes.
3. You should practice the delivery several times before going to the studio so that the presentation comes smoothly.

How to Do the Project
1. You will need a studio crew to operate the cameras and a floor manager to give the signals. A field camera can be used to record a total view of the project. If possible, your microphone should be fed to the field camera so your delivery can be more clearly analyzed.
2. Begin as a seated talent, waiting for a cue to begin.
3. The floor manager gives you "stand by" and "you're on" cues. You commence your monologue, addressing the camera indicated.
4. The floor manager then gives you a continuing series of cues designed to have you change cameras, get up, move around the set, talk faster and slower, concluding with "one minute," "thirty seconds," and "windup" time cues. You should finish on time. One possible sequence is listed below. If you do not have a cue for one of the commands, you and your floor manager can develop it.
5. Your goal will be to respond to all cues promptly and correctly, while continuing to give your presentation without stumbling or showing any evidence that you have been taking cues.
6. As this simulates a live production, you will get only one take to do the project.
7. Label the recording "Hand Cues," add your name, and turn it in to the instructor to receive credit for this project.

■ PROJECT 3

Record a movie review utilizing a teleprompter script.

Purpose
To give you an opportunity to get the feel of the challenge of proper teleprompter delivery.

Notes
1. Review Section 3.7 of this chapter to refresh your memory on teleprompter use.
2. For this project, assume you are a feature reporter on a news program giving a weekly movie review. It's your station's idea to promote interest in old films because they often broadcast them on weekends.

3. Become familiar with the script (shown below) before attempting the project.
4. You can also practice reading the script from a teleprompter by using the appropriate track on the DVD that came with this text.
5. Your instructor may decide to do this exercise as a class project.

How to Do the Project

1. Enter a copy of the script into the teleprompter system.
2. If you do not have a teleprompter, you could do this project with cue cards. In this case, write the script on several large cue cards.
3. You'll need a minimum TV crew to operate the equipment, hold cue cards if necessary, and assist you in recording your movie review.
4. You should practice a few times before beginning the taping.
5. If you have to use cue cards, be sure they are held directly under the camera lens. The camera should be as far back as you can comfortably read the copy. Make sure your card holder knows the last line of each card and can smoothly and quietly change from one card to the next at the right time.
6. Record your presentation. You should have a copy of the script on your desk or counter, in case the teleprompter fails. You only get one take on this recording, as your segment would most likely be part of a live newscast. You can assume you have been introduced by the anchor.
7. Label your recording "Movie Review," your name, and turn it in to your instructor to receive credit for the project.

Script for Teleprompter

If you haven't seen a good Western in a while, rent Fred Zimmerman's award-winning *High Noon*. For taut action and fine writing, there aren't many much better. Driven forward by Tex Ritter's delivery of the title song (he was John Ritter's dad), the music tells the story of the older sheriff who marries a younger woman and is about to leave town when he learns that a villain he had sent to be hung has been released. He's on the way back to get revenge and will arrive on the noon train. Three of the killer's old gang are already in town to join in the shoot-out. One interesting aspect is that the film time is almost real time, as the action starts after ten a.m.. and climaxes shortly after twelve. The film is eighty-five minutes long. The sheriff, long-time star Gary Cooper, struggles to line up deputies to help, but the town deserts him. You're constantly reminded of the time factor by an array of ticking clocks that seem to be everywhere, and by Dmitri Tiomkin's fine orchestrations that frequently repeats notes that sound like a clock. It all concludes with a traditional gunfight, with a mildly surprising ending. A young Grace Kelly, Lloyd Bridges, and Katy Jurado are also featured. High Noon, our outstanding classic movie of the week. I'm [say your name] with your weekly movie review.

CHAPTER FOUR

VOCAL DEVELOPMENT*

4.1 INTRODUCTION

Most of us have had the experience of being at a social function and noticing someone who looks attractive. After some maneuvering, you get to meet them or at least get closer. Suddenly that person starts talking and all the attractiveness disappears. The way you talk can have an immense effect on your social life and your career in and out of mass media. Your voice is the most important physical quality for effective broadcast performance. As a radio announcer, your voice is the only way the audience will be able to understand the message. As a television performer, you will be seen as well as heard, but to understand the importance of the vocal portion of television, just turn down the volume the next time you watch TV. While you may be able to follow what is on the screen, you will quickly lose the actual content. Even if you do not find a job in an announcing situation, your voice will continue to be one of your most important assets. The sound of your voice and your ability to communicate ideas are essential in any career.

The development of vocal quality requires understanding, training, and practice. Most of us never give much thought to this because we speak every day. But if you plan a performance career in broadcasting or any other field, you need to understand how your body produces and can improve your voice and the aspects of the delivery that are used to enhance a message. This chapter begins with a basic description of the physical parts of the body that are necessary for full vocal development, continues with a discussion of those characteristics of your voice that you can develop, and ends with a look at some voice problems that can hinder broadcast performance.

4.2 HOW SOUND IS PRODUCED

While different performance situations require different skills and techniques, the process of producing vocal sound is always the same. It is not necessary to know the complete anatomy of the upper body involved in breathing and sound reproduction, but a basic understanding of the key parts of the body which contribute to the process will help you improve your voice and develop your vocal performance. Figure 4.1 shows a simplified diagram of the parts of the body involved with the physiology of vocal production.

Most of us think that we breathe with our lungs, but actually our lungs do not do most of the work. Because the lungs do not have muscles, other muscles must keep the air flowing in and out when you inhale and exhale. The most important of these is the **diaphragm**. The diaphragm is a flat muscle which separates the **thoracic cavity** (location of the lungs and heart) from the **abdominal cavity** (location of the stomach and intestines), which is below the diaphragm. The diaphragm extends from under the rib cage in front, across to the back bone, and forms a complete base under the thoracic cavity. Our lungs are suspended above and rest on the diaphragm. When the diaphragm contracts, it moves downward and draws air into the lungs. When it relaxes, the stomach muscles contract to force the air upward through the **trachea**, a tube, to the **larynx**, which is a slightly larger cylinder made of cartilage. We also call it the "voice box" or the "Adam's Apple." This is the location of the two vocal cords, which are actually more like membranes (see Figure 4.2). When you are silent, the membranes are relaxed and the passage is open. When you are speaking, these membranes

---

*This chapter includes material adapted from the *Broadcast Voice Handbook: How to Polish Your On-Air Delivery*, by Ann S. Utterbach, Ph.D. Chicago, Bonus Books, third edition, © 2000.

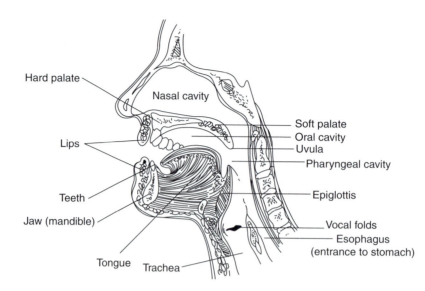

FIGURE 4.1 The upper portion of the vocal mechanism extends from the vocal folds to the opening of the mouth and nose and includes the pharynx, tongue, cheeks, jaw, lips, palate, and nasal cavity.

FIGURE 4.2 The vocal cords or folds (shown here as if you were looking down the throat) are separated during breathing, but during speech production, they come together and vibrate as air flow from the lungs passes between them. Variations in pressure and membrane tension produce varied sounds.

4.3 DIAPHRAGMATIC BREATHING TECHNIQUE

The best vocal quality begins with proper breathing technique (see Video Clip 4.1), which requires an understanding and practice of diaphragmatic breathing. The diaphragm muscle is what allows us to breathe naturally. As mentioned, when we inhale, the diaphragm muscle contracts, causing it to move downward, drawing air into the lungs. As the diaphragm moves downward, it pushes on the abdominal cavity and forces the abdominal area outward. This movement of the abdomen makes it easy to feel if you are breathing deeply. You should feel expansion of the stomach area and all around the back. The lower chest area should also expand. Then, as the breath is exhaled, when the diaphragm relaxes, the muscles of the stomach contract to push the air out. The gradual relaxing of the diaphragm controls the airflow so that air is released slowly rather than all at once. Good announcers have excellent control over breathing because it affects their delivery.

If you are unsure how to feel the abdomen, here are two easy ways to practice. First, lie down flat on the floor. Place a book on the lower part of your rib cage. Breathe in and out until you can make the book move up and down. An easier way may be to sit forward in a chair with your elbows on your knees. Breathe normally and focus on your abdomen until you feel the movement of your muscles. The trick is to be able to feel these muscles when you are performing. Just being

tighten and come together. Air is forced between these two touching edges, causing them to vibrate rapidly, generating a sound that is not particularly pleasant— more like the sound generated by blowing through a trumpet mouthpiece without the trumpet attached.

The air continues upward through the trachea into the head and mouth. The bones and sinuses of the head serve as **resonators**, to improve the sound, the way the pipes of a trumpet or trombone do. More on this in 4.10. In the mouth, the teeth, tongue, jaws, and palate act as **articulators** which shape the sounds into words. Proper use of these tools will have a significant impact on your speech, tone and breathing. Review Figure 4.1 to be sure you can follow the path air takes from the lungs/diaphragm area until it leaves your mouth as sound.

aware of how it should feel will help you to use your muscles properly for breathing. The control of breath adds to better voice projection and a more relaxed sound. Learning to breathe by doing exercises for diaphragmatic breathing will help to develop the muscle and control breath. Improper breathing causes a thin sounding voice or tenseness in the voice. Diaphragmatic breathing will relax the larynx and vocal cords, which will result in a slightly lower pitch and therefore a more pleasant sound to your voice. Breathing will also be less noisy, so is not likely to be picked up on the microphone. When your larynx is relaxed and you are using proper breathing techniques, you can speak for longer periods of time without hoarseness.

4.4 PROPER BREATHING POSTURE

The proper breathing posture, while standing, is feet apart with weight slightly on the balls of your feet. Knees should be slightly flexed and your hips should be straight rather than shifted to one side or the other. The back is also straight and, as you breath in, your abdomen should push out, but your chest and shoulders should not rise. Breath control takes regular practice. If you are seated, it is best to sit toward the edge of the chair with your feet flat on the floor and your back straight. This allows for the maximum expansion of the diaphragm. Since you really can speak better when standing, many radio studios are designed for a "stand-up" operation. The counters and racks that house the equipment are built at an appropriate height for the average announcer to be standing while speaking and operating the equipment. Of course, many broadcast situations, especially in television, require the performer to be seated.

Good performance technique dictates that you keep your posture appropriate for good diaphragmatic breathing, regardless of the circumstances. You should review Video Clips 4.1 and 4.2, which show proper posture for television, and note how they relate to good breathing posture.

4.5 AVOIDING THORACIC BREATHING

Diaphragmatic breathing is the natural way our bodies take in air; unfortunately, many of us have been taught to give up this style of breathing for another, less efficient way called **thoracic breathing**. Someone along the way may have told you to pull your stomach in and push your chest out, even though this is just the opposite of the way our bodies were built to breathe. Look in a

FIGURE 4.3 Thoracic breathing.

mirror and take a breath. Watch yourself. Did you raise your shoulders as you inhaled? If you did, you are using thoracic breathing. It is what many of us do most of the time, instead of using the greater lung capacity that is available through the proper use of the diaphragm and abdomen. You can get an idea of what it looks like in Figure 4.3. When you breathe improperly, air is drawn into only the upper part of the lungs. For broadcast announcers, this is not helpful because you are using a very small portion of your total lung capacity. The result is often a thin, unenergetic sound that causes you to need a breath every few words. This makes performing difficult and makes reading a broadcast script sound choppy. Diaphragmatic breathing is used by singers, actors, trained announcers, and even athletes and musicians who need plenty of air and strong breath control.

4.6 KEY ELEMENTS OF VOCAL DEVELOPMENT

We'll begin by noting that just about everyone in performance actually has two voices, or more accurately, speaking styles. The first we'll call the **personal voice**. This one you use with friends, and it can be loaded with slang, bad pronunciation, and poor delivery. That you can keep in your personal arena. We want to develop your **performance voice**. This is the sound you bring when going into a broadcast or any other performance situation that requires good speech.

Each broadcast performer is unique; we all sound different and there are some very specific reasons this is so. Announcer voices that are deemed excellent are usually well developed in three areas. First, they speak in a lower range with a pleasing, resonant voice. Second, they speak at a pace that promotes easy comprehension by the listener. And third, they speak with exceptional clarity. A few performers come by this naturally, but just about everyone can improve the speaking voice they have. As you're developing your own performance voice, you will be able to manipulate several variables that will help characterize your style of speaking. The elements that you have some degree of control over include volume, pitch, rate, and tone. You will also have to develop and improve your articulation and pronunciation in performance situations. We'll explore more techniques in Chapter 5.

4.7 VOLUME

Volume is the loudness or softness of your voice—in other words, your vocal amplitude. It contributes to the perception of energy and enthusiasm that you, as a performer, communicate to the audience. Volume is controlled by the muscles that affect proper breathing. Practice speaking and reading copy in a variety of volumes to get the feel of it. In broadcast performance situations, you can also control the volume of your speech by using the microphone and audio console. But be careful here. Sometimes new announcers think that the volume control on the audio board can be used to increase the volume of the voice, rather than putting adequate energy into the delivery. That's not true. While a soft voice can be boosted electronically, it will still have a weak and lifeless quality to it. The volume controls on the audio board should never be used to enhance what is lacking in your natural voice. Another way to think of this is to consider **projection**—the process of pushing the sound out of your mouth. When we speak to someone at a distance, we give the sound more of a push with our stomach muscles. Experienced announcers have developed the ability to project their voices, whereas beginning

announcers often hold back on projection. This is another situation in which proper breathing and use of the stomach muscles are important.

Variations in loudness and softness add to the interpretation of the copy. If what is read to the audience is always loud or always soft, it sounds boring and the announcer sounds uninterested. When using the louder range of your voice, be cautious of talking "at" the listener, rather than talking "to" the audience. You should work on developing a range of speech from loud to soft and remember that broadcast speech is most often conversational and should convey a one-to-one quality. Audio Track 4.1 contrasts an announcer talking "at" the listener and an announcer talking "to" the listener using a variety of loudness and softness in a conversational tone.

4.8 PITCH

Pitch is the highness or lowness of your voice—in other words, the frequency of your vocal sound. In the early days of radio, the announcer was expected to have a deep, bass voice with formal, crisp articulation. It was a style of speaking that was heard nowhere else but on the radio. Today, a deep voice and formal articulation are no longer required for broadcast announcing. What is desirable is for you to use your full pitch range, with emphasis on the naturally lower portion of your speaking voice. However, don't make the beginning announcer's mistake of taking on an affected "announcer's voice," which is pitched too low, like the television character Ted Baxter from the *Mary Tyler Moore Show*. To speak as low as you possibly can for any length of time puts a strain on your voice. For most performers, the best pitch would be about one-quarter up from the lowest pitch at which you could speak. In general, lower-pitched voices are more pleasant to listen to than high-pitched voices. Males have an advantage here, as their longer vocal folds put the typical male voice about an octave lower than their female counterparts. For this reason, women may need to be more conscious of favoring the lower range of their vocal pitch. Young women may find it necessary to actually think, "Start lower" when about to read a piece of copy.

4.9 RATE

Rate is the number of words you deliver during a given period of time as you speak or read a script.

FIGURE 4.4 Fast talker.

While there is no correct rate, typical "out loud" delivery usually falls in a range from 160 to 180 words per minute (wpm), with about 160 wpm being an accepted broadcast pace. This is probably not as fast as your normal conversational rate, but will help with articulation and make it easier for the audience to understand. The higher your speaking rate, the more likely it is that you will make mistakes and be harder to understand. Figure 4.4 gives you an idea of what it sounds like to the listener. In commercial performance situations, your speaking rate will often be determined by the copy you have to read and the number of words you must read within a fixed amount of time. For example, you may be given a 60-second script that contains 120 words on one occasion, and one that contains 175 words the next time. Your task will be to read both scripts within the 60-second time frame.

We are usually fairly poor judges of how fast we actually do talk. As you practice, it's a good idea to record yourself so that you can play it back and hear your rate as other people do. Work for that good basic rate of 160 wpm, but be aware that many announcing situations are also going to require you to adjust your rate. Figure 4.5 is a reading rate exercise to help you establish what your typical rate is. Audio Track 4.3

lets you hear an announcer speaking at 160 words per minute. A class of undergraduates was timed reading this passage without any instructions about rate. They averaged 230 words per minute, a long way from the appropriate rate.

4.10 TONE

Tone is the quality of sound that is made, also known as the voice's **timbre**. It is affected by what surrounds the vibrators. The vibrators could be strings on a guitar or violin, the reed on a clarinet, or your vocal cords. Musical instruments are a good example of how the surroundings of the vibrators affect the quality of the sound. If an acoustic guitar and a piano play the same song at the same time, you can easily tell when the piano played or when the guitar played. This is because, although both are playing the same notes, the material that surrounds them vibrates or **resonates** the sound in different ways. These differences are called **tone quality**. The human voice is similar to musical instruments. The body surrounding the vocal cords is different for each person and therefore will resonate the sound in a different way. We know this because we can recognize the voices of many different people even if they are saying exactly the same thing.

Learning to use resonance is one of the keys to developing a good broadcast voice. As noted, to produce sound, a flow of air from the lungs passes between the vocal cords, which causes vibrations. The sound is then directed to the resonant cavities of the chest, throat (larynx and pharynx), and head (mouth, sinus cavities, nose). The task for the performer is to relax enough to allow the sound to be channeled to the various resonant chambers that enhance the quality of sound. Often you do not realize the importance of the resonating chambers until you have a cold and some of those chambers are blocked, leaving you with a "stuffy" sound. You can feel your body resonate or vibrate by doing a few simple exercises. First, just hum. The tune isn't important. You will feel a vibration in the bridge of your nose. Now, place your fingers on either side of your nose and under your eyes, and hum again. You should feel the slight tingle in your hands. Now open your mouth and say, "Ah." The vibration should stop. Keep the sound going and move your tongue to block the flow of air so that it can only go out your nose. You should feel the tingle again. Placing the sound in your chest, throat, or nasal cavities to enhance resonance takes practice. Using the naturally lower pitch of your voice will help

TIMED COPY PRACTICE

1 Alfred had been away in the military for four years. Because of distance and his own
2 lack of cash, he had been home twice in that entire time and had been out of the country
3 for the past two years. He arrived in New York after a cross-country flight, and took a
4 bus for the last 70 miles out into the country of the rural Catskill Mountains where
5 he had grown up. After all the travel and being away so long, he was anxious, excited
6 and apprehensive all at the same time. Finally he began to see a few familiar sights that
7 told him he was arriving in his old territory. He wondered what it would be like to see his
8 family again. He knew that both his kid brothers would be bigger now, as both had
9 become teenagers while he was away. He hoped most things would be the same, but
10 realized that there were many things that he had not seen in the four years he'd been
11 gone. You can't do everything when you're home on leave for just a couple weeks.
12 Finally the bus started up the long street that led to the terminal. Alfred went a little
13 numb as he had in tough circumstances in the service. "Just deal with the situation," he
14 reminded himself. The bus wheeled into the station and pulled to a stop. Alfred
15 gathered his bags and started up the aisle. As he hit the steps going out the door,
16 he heard a voice shout, "There he is!" It was his mother, with his father and brothers
17 close behind. In a circle of hugs and kisses, four years seemed to evaporate.
18 Within a few days it would begin to feel like he had never been away. It was over
19 and he was home.

(The following is the word count. For example, if you read to the word "flight" on line 3, you read 50 words. You can determine your rate by reading for 30 seconds and doubling the result, or just read for one minute. Mark the last word spoken within the time.)

25—twice in—line 2	125—He knew—line 8	225—the station—line 14
50—flight—line 3	150—would be—line 9	250—he heard—line 16
75—After all—line 5	175—everything—line 11	275—four years—line 17
100—a few—line 6	200—went—line 12	300—was home—line 19

FIGURE 4.5 Speaking rate test.

4.11 ARTICULATION OF SOUNDS

Sounds must be shaped into recognizable words, and the **articulators** are the physical parts of our body that do this work. These parts include the lips, teeth, tongue, jaw, and hard and soft palates (see Figure 4.6). Good articulation means producing sounds that are clear without being overly precise. As a broadcaster, it's very important for you to articulate words clearly because your voice will be carried over a long distance and through many electrical devices. What might be heard perfectly well in a face-to-face

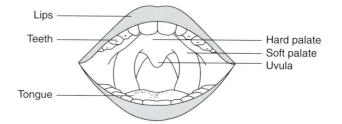

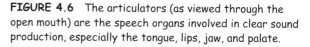

FIGURE 4.6 The articulators (as viewed through the open mouth) are the speech organs involved in clear sound production, especially the tongue, lips, jaw, and palate.

conversation could be distorted by the time it reaches the audience.

The most common cause for inarticulation is a "lazy mouth." If the articulators do not move or move sluggishly, it is difficult to form words clearly. Say this simple sentence and notice the movements your tongue has to make: "Let's take the local bus to that market." Say the sentence slowly and feel how your tongue moves from your front teeth to the soft palate. Tongue positions are only one part of the combinations of movements required by the articulators for speech. If the tongue is to move freely, the jaw must be relaxed. Clenched teeth can affect resonance and limits the movement of all the other articulators. Good announcing requires a relaxed, open mouth. The soft palate located in the back of your mouth must be flexible to move up and down. If the soft palate is left closed, or up, this can result in a very nasal sound with little or no resonance. Essentially, you are cutting off the flow of air into your nasal passages and the sound that is produced is similar to when you have a cold or sinus trouble.

Lazy speech habits can be overcome by opening the mouth, moving the lower jaw, and using the lips, tongue, and teeth in an exaggerated manner, forcing yourself to be precise. Some beginners manage to speak while barely opening their mouths or using little lip movement. Spend some time observing yourself in the mirror and observing professional speakers for comparison. Initially, you may find this to be very uncomfortable and have a feeling that you are overdoing it. But like using the diaphragm to breathe correctly, exercising the articulators can result in an improvement in clarity and a better on-air voice. It isn't something that can be cured in a moment. You need to be conscious of the mistakes you are making and to focus on getting the words out correctly and clearly. The articulators also depend on lubrication—saliva—to work properly. Dehydration causes a reduction of saliva, which makes articulation more difficult. Tension may affect the production of saliva, sometimes causing too much and sometimes not enough. Taking a few sips of water helps to lubricate the mouth and relax the throat. Excess tension may also be lessened with proper breathing technique.

4.12 PRONUNCIATION

In broadcast performance situations, it is essential to pronounce words correctly. This involves two things: determining what the accepted form is and then making sure you get it right on the air. Pronunciation is the way in which words are spoken by uttering the proper sound and stressing the proper syllable(s). Pronunciation has to do with accent, whereas enunciation has to do with clarity of sound. As noted earlier, most broadcast stations prefer Standard American English, which is grammatically correct and relatively unaccented. However, some successful announcers, such as Howard Stern or Larry King, have made a name for themselves using their regional accents.

Mispronounced words will alienate listeners and cause both the announcer and station to lose credibility. Broadcasters are therefore expected to pronounce words correctly. The causes of mispronunciation are many, from simple unfamiliarity with the correct pronunciation to serious speech impediments. Pronunciation guides are usually provided in broadcast wire copy, and most stations have dictionaries and other reference sources for correct pronunciation. The rule of thumb is that an announcer always looks up words with which he or she is unfamiliar, and it's good practice to double-check some words that you think you know, but about which you may be uncertain. Equally as important is practicing the word several times, rapidly, out loud, to get your mouth used to shaping the word. Repeat it until you can pronounce the word effortlessly. It will save later embarrassment. Also be careful with the articles "a" and "the," which might be pronounced "ay" and "thee" when reading aloud. For mass media, the preferred pronunciation is "uh" and "thuh." This pronunciation sounds less formal and matches the conversational style.

Foreign pronunciations are also something you may encounter. Many news stories use foreign names and words, and increasingly the United States is importing foods and other products from around the world, so copy includes more foreign words than ever.

In the case of foreign names and places, it may take a little effort to get it right, but if you're doing the news, it's essential. Contacting the network, native speakers, or even the consulates and embassies may provide you with the correct sound. In the case of more common foreign words, the general rule is to pronounce the word as an American would, not necessarily as the native speaker would. For example, many languages roll the "r"; American English does not. So if there is a word such as "burro" in the copy, it would be pronounced like "burrow," not with the rolled Spanish "r" sound. "Paris" is another word where the American pronunciation differs from the French. Correct pronunciation in the United States would be "Pare-iss" rather than "Parr-ee." However, a fairly popular French cheese is Camembert, which is pronounced "Kam-em-bear," not "Kam-em-bert." You also should be aware of local pronunciations of place names. For example, Cairo, when talking about the Egyptian city, is "Ky-ro," with a long "i" sound, but Cairo, the city in Illinois, is pronounced "Kay-ro." The

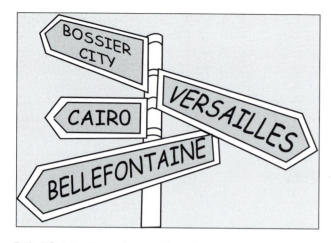

FIGURE 4.7 *Know where you're going.*

town of Bellefontaine in located in central Ohio. In some parts of the country, or if you've studied French, you would assume it was "Bell-a-fon-tain." However, in that community, it's "Bell-foun-ten." Other examples, illustrated in Figure 4.7, would include Bossier City in Louisiana, pronounced "Boh-zer," and Versailles, Kentucky, pronounced "Ver-sales." One more tricky example can be found in western New York, where Nunda is pronounced "Nun-DAY," not "Nun-dah."

One other group of words for which the new announcer must be prepared are communities, lakes, and streams whose names are derived from other languages. In the United States, particularly in the east, many names are drawn from the Native Americans who once lived there. These are often long and strange-looking, and invite mispronunciations. A sampling of these include Skaneateles and Schaghticoke, communities in New York, and the nearby Kayaderosseras Creek, a significant stream, but the locals abbreviate it to KAY-der-ross. In Maine, you find the Passamquoddy tribe of Native Americans, and the name also applies to a bay of the ocean. New Hampshire contains the famous Lake Winnipesaukee. In Louisiana, you'll encounter the Atchafalaya River and find it also applies to a large swamp. The point of all this is to alert you to the likelihood that you will encounter names that look baffling and some which will lead you to assume you can pronounce them, but locally it's different. Good broadcast announcers, when they move to a new geographic location, make an effort to learn important local pronunciations— names of local streets, nearby towns, and city officials, for example.

Correct pronunciation of names is important because most people aren't happy when their names

are mispronounced. Even those who claim not to care, often do. The rule here is to pronounce names as the individual desires, not how you imagine the name might be pronounced. For example, NFL quarterback, Brent Favre, pronounces his name "Far-vah," even though, when looking at the spelling, an announcer might assume that it would be "Fav-er" or "Fav-reh."

Regional accents are found in various parts of the United States and Canada. Many cities along the East Coast of the United States have very distinctive accents. For example, the Boston accent tends to drop the "r" sound so that "car" sounds like "cah" and "park" sounds like "pock." Although regional accents may be acceptable for smaller market radio stations, once again the general rule of thumb in broadcast performance is to speak using Standard American English.

The other part of correct pronunciation is avoiding slips on the air, under the pressure of time. A common aid used by announcers to help with pronunciation is phonetic spelling: The announcer writes out the word as it sounds, not as it is spelled, dividing the word by its syllables and adding helpful reminders such as accent marks to guide pronunciation. For example, you may be reading a commercial for an ice cream store that is promoting a special strawberry parfait. You may want to remind yourself of the pronunciation of "parfait" so you write it phonetically above the word as "par-'fay." Notice that in this example, the second syllable "fay" is written as it should sound, no concern about spelling.

There are many systems that can be learned to help you write out words exactly as they sound. Wire service copy and the International Phonetic Alphabet are two such systems. The problem with some systems is that they use symbols that are not found on the teleprompter word processor. One of the easiest to use is from the Associated Press, which does not use any special symbols.

Looking at how words might be written phonetically, we encounter the problem that some of our vowels, particularly "a," are pronounced in several different ways. Assuming you know the correct pronunciation of a word, and it has "a" sound like that of "father," it would be written "ah." (facetious—fah-SEE-shus). If it sounded more like the "a" in "raw." it would be spelled "aw" (taught—tawt). If the sound was a "long a," such as in the word "ate," use "ay" (training—tray-ning). For the short "a," just use the letter "a" as in "ap-li-kay-shun." For the short "e" as in Fred, just use an "e," but if the "e" sound is long as in "treat," use a double "ee."

An "i" with a short sound can be written with just the letter, but a long "i" can be "eye" or "y". The letter "o"

(These are samples from the Associated Press Pronunciation Guide. One group is for news figures and the other is for sports-related individuals.)

Words from World Affairs

Shinzo Abe -- shin-zoh ah-bay
Mahmoud Ahmadinejad -- ah-muh-DEE'-neh-zhahd
Banda Aceh -- BAHN'-duh AH'-cheh
CNOOC -- SEE'-nook
John Demjanjuk -- dem-YAHN'-yuk
Moammar Gadhafi -- MOO'-ah-mahr gah-DAH'-fee
Carlos Ghosn -- GOHN
Guangzhou -- gwahng-joh
Yaser Esam Hamdi -- YAH'-ser EE'-sahm HAHM'-dee
Hamid Karzai -- HAH'-mihd KAHR'-zeye
Kazimierz Marcinkiewicz -- KAH'-zhee-myehrsh mahr-cheen-KAY'-vihch
Jean-Marie Messier -- zhan mah-REE' MEH'-see-ay

Names from Sports

Hideki Matsui -- hih-DEK'-ee mat-SOO'-ee
Dirk Nowitzki -- noh-VIHT'-skee
Miguel Ojeda -- oh-HAY'-duh
Hakeem Olajuwon -- ah-KEEM' ah-LAH'-zhoo-wahn
Jose Maria Olazabal -- oh-lah-THAH'-bul
A.J. Pierzynski -- peer-ZIN'-skee
Stacy Prammanasuh -- prah-mah-nah-SOOD'
Albert Pujols -- POO'-hohls
Branko Radivojevic -- rad-uh-VOY'-ih-vihch
Miroslav Satan -- MEER'-oh-slahv shah-TAN'
Mark Teixeira -- teh-SHEHR'-uh
Iroda Tulyaganova -- EE'-roh-dah too-lee-GAHN'-uh-vuh

FIGURE 4.8 Samples from the Associated Press Pronunciation Guide.

has multiple possibilities also, and can be spelled "oh," "oo," "ow," or "oy," according to the pronunciation. With a "u," most situations can be covered by using with "uh," or "yoo." With the consonants, most are written in their normal form. However, in many cases, a "k" is used for a hard "c" and an "s" for a soft "c." The combinations like "ch," "sh," and "th," are written in the normal way. To assist your pronunciation, you can print the dominant syllable in capital letters, to remind you where the emphasis goes, as in "air-ah BEE-ka," the name of a coffee shop.

4.13 SUBSTANDARD PRONUNCIATION

Another type of pronunciation problem that is often one of the beginner's biggest weaknesses is bad pronunciation reached another way. In conversations with friends, we use all sorts of shortcuts and slang. This includes incorrectly pronouncing words or delivering them in an unclear way. While this may work in personal situations, it makes you sound very unprofessional in the broadcast world. The two primary problems are laziness and force of habit. These errors fall into several categories you should be familiar with so you can be careful to avoid them.

The first and perhaps most common error is that of **omissions**—leaving out part of the word. Within this category, dropping the "g" off words, for example, is very common. How often do you hear or say "runnin'," "walkin'," or "talkin'"? The same applies to the host of other verbs in our language that end in "ing."

A different example would be "mirror," which often can be heard as "mire." It takes conscious effort to avoid dropping endings.

Sometimes omissions occur within words: "winter" becomes "winner," and "hundred" comes out "hunnerd." Some other words to be alert for include "don't" which can become "dohn"; "little," which can sound like "lil"; "recognize," which can be heard as "rec-a-nize," "lenth" instead of "length" and "assesory" instead of "accessory." There are many more. Sometimes speakers will add a sound instead of leaving one out. The late President John Kennedy was noted, as are many New Englanders, for adding a sound, so that "law" became "lawr," idea was "idear," and "Alabama" became "Alabamar." Some other examples of **additions** include pronouncing the silent "l" in "salmon," saying "re-member-ance" instead of "re-mem-brance," and adding an "r" to our nation's capital so that it becomes "Warsh-ing-ton." A variation on additions can be the **substitution** of other sounds for the correct ones. Some examples would include "budder" for "butter," "mudder" for "mother," and "the-ate-er" for "theater." **Distortions** are also quite common. Some examples include "jist" for "just," and a group which is particularly common: "git," "fergit," and "forgit."

A few other examples of common pronunciation errors include "chil-dern" instead of "chil-dren," "hunderd" instead of "hun-dred," "per-fessor" instead of "professor," and "per-scription" instead of "prescription." Another common problem you can encounter is the slurring of words, running them together: "Did you eat?" becomes "Jeet?" "What are you doing?" becomes "Whatcha doin'?" There is also "going to" which becomes "gunna" and "wanna" instead of "want to."

The first step in becoming conscious of your pronunciation is to record yourself and analyze your work. It's a good, though sometimes painful experience to critique yourself after every recording, and it will do more to help you improve than virtually any single exercise. Select a newspaper article of modest length, record it, and critique the results. In your critique, consider the following points:

1. Am I dropping endings of words?
2. Are some consonants indistinct or omitted within words?
3. Do I hear words being slurred together?

Here are some sentences to record and evaluate. Below them are things to check for after the recording. Pause between each sentence.

1. The police officer came running up behind the bank robber.
2. Just as the car turned the corner, it hit a pedestrian walking across the street.
3. The druggist asked the young man where he got the prescription.
4. William Johnson was arrested and charged with being an accessory to the robbery.
5. Terry Brown took the kickoff and ran the length of the field.
6. As John started his college years, he decided to say "goodbye" to his childish behavior.
7. The runaway car crashed through the plate glass window and destroyed the mirror on the back wall.
8. John's first class was European History, one he would just as happily forget.
9. The lawyer said that Mr. Smith was a gentleman who should not be charged with assault and battery.
10. The police officer said he had gone through a different door into the library and so was able to recognize the robber as he fled.

Words to Watch

1. running (runnin')
2. walking, street (walkin', stree')
3. prescription (perscription)
4. accessory (assessory)
5. length, field (len'th, fiel')
6. goodbye (guh'bye)
7. mirror (mire)
8. history, just, forget (his'try, jist, fergit)
9. gentleman, battery (gennelman, bat-tree)
10. different, library, recognize (diff'rent, li-bree, rec-a-nize)

Correct pronunciation will take some concentration for a while, as some habits can be very deep seated, but it's essential. In your efforts to improve, however, don't become so precise with each word that the effort becomes obvious. Strive to make your words clear and correct, but make the delivery unobtrusive.

4.14 COMMON VOCAL PROBLEMS

A vocal problem that has become a plague for many is the extensive use of **fillers** when speaking. Fillers are used to fill the gaps in your conversation, while you take a moment to think, or they are just a bad habit. Common fillers are "Uh," "Um," "Ya know," and "OK."

FIGURE 4.9 Ferocious fillers.

These crutches have become so common that it is questionable whether some people would be able to speak if they didn't have them. While everyone uses a filler occasionally, constant use is distracting and degrading. The authors have encountered situations where a speaker couldn't get through one sentence without three "Ya knows." The fillers "OK" or "Right" also are sometimes used as often as every two or three sentences. Becoming conscious of this habit is the first step toward eliminating it. You can get the idea from our speaker in Figure 4.9.

A variation of the filler that has crept into our language is the use of the word "like" in all kinds of inappropriate situations. Again, you will find speakers who can't get through a sentence without using it at least once. One television producer, desiring to use a particular artist as the host of an art series, determined to drive the fillers out of the individual's speech. During rehearsals, he sat in the studio with an empty glass and a knife. Whenever a filler was uttered by the talent, the producer struck the glass with the knife and the talent had to start over. The talent admitted that though he wanted to kill the producer, the approach worked.

The reality is that it is difficult to get rid of these bad habits. Ad-lib situations are particularly tough, for without the script to lean on, the old patterns begin to appear as soon as you start focusing on what you want to say. Students, starting a presentation, have been determined not to fall into the trap, and then used a filler within the first few words. Hearing yourself doing it is the first step, but it won't be easy. However, it can be done with time and effort. It is well worth it, for few things make an announcer sound more amateurish than the regular use of one or more of these words or sounds. You might as well wear a sign around your neck that says "Beginner!"

Announcing can be more difficult than expected; what is heard by the audience may sound completely different from what you hear in your head. For example, some common problems related to variations in pitch are monotone, sing-song, and whiny vocal styles. The **monotone** announcer doesn't vary pace or pitch, leading to a lack of inflection and a boring sameness in his or her delivery, as you can clearly hear by listening to Audio Tracks 4.1 and 5.1 again. Everything sounds the same and the announcer sounds uninterested in the copy or the audience. The **sing-song** announcer stresses words or phrases in a pattern of inflection that is repeated throughout the copy, such as putting emphasis on every fourth word. Another example of a singsong pattern that was popular a few years ago was the sound of the Valley Girl. Audio Track 4.2 provides an example of one type of sing-song announcer. The announcer with a **whiny** vocal style speaks with a too high, nasal pitch that tends to elongate the vowel sounds. *Saturday Night Live*, at one time, had a whole skit built around characters called "The Whiners" who spoke in this way. Audio Clip 4.4 provides the sound of a whiny announcer. As you should surmise, in all these cases, the listener's attention will shift from the content of what the announcer is saying to the announcer's delivery style. This makes it difficult for the announcer to actually communicate a message. It's also impossible to add any variety to a delivery style if a single way of speaking has already been established.

Other common vocal problems are related to lack of resonance or improper breathing. These include **nasality**, **thin voice**, **breathy voice**, or **husky voice**. Nasality is caused when the air is blocked from the resonators by the tongue or soft palate. A sample of the result is heard in Audio Track 4.5. Often this is just a bad habit or is caused by tension. Relaxing the jaw and mouth and lowering your tongue can help rid you of this problem. As previously noted, if your sinuses become blocked due to a cold or allergy, you will also have a nasal sound to your voice. A thin voice is a voice that lacks resonance, has no power, sounds weak or colorless, and lacks any authoritative sound. It is caused by weak or shallow breathing, pitching the voice too high, or inadequately moving your resonators. A good example of a thin voice was Truman Capote, the author. Follow the suggestions for diaphragmatic breathing to improve a thin voice. A breathy voice, as the name suggests, sounds breathy or airy, as demonstrated in Audio Track 4.6. Although some may think this is a sexy sound, like actress Marilyn Monroe's voice, it usually indicates a problem with breathing. Proper breathing includes both the inhalation and the exhalation of air. You may be taking in a deep breath in the proper way, but letting the air out too rapidly. This causes a sudden release of breath and results in an airy sound. Controlling the muscles during exhalation will help correct this problem. Keep muscles tight around the abdomen, pull in the stomach muscles slowly, and don't use more air than necessary. You'll find this requires concentration and practice, but it will pay off.

A "gravelly" or husky voice sounds harsh and unpleasant. Often it seems as if the announcer needs to clear his or her throat. There may be a physical cause to this vocal problem. For example, many heavy smokers or someone suffering from laryngitis will sound excessively hoarse. It's also a problem caused by misuse of your voice. After shouting for a period of time or trying to artificially pitch your voice too low, your voice can take on a raspy, harsh quality. Singer Kim Carnes has a husky voice, as did trumpet player/singer Louis Armstrong. Again, the use of proper breathing technique and a higher pitch, if you're speaking too low, can correct this difficulty. Often, resting your voice for a period of time will help temporary hoarseness, such as laryngitis.

Other problems often encountered by broadcast performers are excessive **sibilance** and **popping**. Sibilance is the overemphasis of the "s" sound and can be heard in words that include s, sh, and sometimes z. Popping is caused by a "pop" of air in words with p, b, t, d, k, or g. Both of these problems tend to be exaggerated by microphone usage, as heard in Audio Tracks 4.7 and 4.8. As noted in Chapter 2, a windscreen or a pop filter may help to eliminate this sound. The announcer can also try different placement of the mic and speak slightly off to the side of the mic to reduce or eliminate this problem.

4.15   MAINTAINING A HEALTHY VOICE

As a mass media performer, you must take care of your voice because it's a valuable asset and without it you could lose your livelihood. Unfortunately, being a professional requires regular use and sometimes misuse of your voice. You can abuse your voice by excessive shouting or screaming. While some of that may be necessary on the job, try to avoid it wherever possible. Excessive strain on your vocal cords can lead to nodules or polyps, which are fleshy growths on the vocal cords, also known as phonal trauma. An injured voice can take a long time to heal, so it's better to prevent problems than to treat them. Baseball pitchers would never enter a game without a proper warm-up. They know that their control would likely be off, they could damage their arms, and even shorten their careers. The same idea applies in other performance areas as well. Stage actors warm up their voices before the show, and singers do scales or other exercises. Humming, reciting some verse, and even rolling your head around will loosen the muscles and cords so you can go on the air without straining your voice.

Another key to care of your voice is adequate moisture. Dry mouth can make it very hard to speak easily. Keeping your mouth and throat hydrated makes it possible to speak easily over a long period of time and will reduce strain on your voice. Keep a glass of water handy and take a sip during music or other breaks. If you hear someone clearing his or her throat before speaking, you're hearing the worst thing one can do for the voice, as this merely strains the throat. The best way to keep your throat moist is to drink plenty of water each day. Water is best and you should definitely avoid coffee, dairy products, alcohol, and caffeinated soda, as they dry out or thicken mucus in your throat.

Another thing to remember is that you are using a microphone that has an amplification system. This means you don't need to generate as much volume as you might in non-amplified situations. Learn to vary your volume without shouting. You can generate excitement and even shock without straining your voice. Try to keep your throat and chest muscles relaxed, as this too will reduce strain and keep you from tiring. Keeping relaxed will help your sound as well.

Finally, if you've used your voice excessively, you need to plan some withdrawal time in which you don't speak. Don't talk for a couple of hours before or after heavy voice use. That's not always practical, but if you can work it into your schedule, it's to your advantage. To a broadcast announcer, the voice is much like a tool kit to an auto mechanic. Neither would get very far without the tools of the trade.

4.16 CONCLUSIONS

Development of the voice is a process that announcers continue to work on during their entire career. A pleasant, energetic voice is the broadcast standard that you should work toward. This begins with the use of diaphragmatic breathing and an understanding of the physical development of the muscles that support the breathing process. Volume, pitch, rate, tone, articulation, and pronunciation are all aspects of the voice that can be enhanced with practice. Professional announcers make their job seem easy, but behind that seemingly casual style is a well-developed voice. As we begin to look at the various broadcast performance areas, you will see that the techniques related to vocal development are well used.

Self-Study

■ QUESTIONS

1. The most important muscle/s for proper breathing is/are the _____.
   a) lungs
   b) diaphragm
   c) resonators
   d) vocal cords

2. Proper diaphragmatic breathing includes all of the following except _____.
   a) the back should be straight
   b) the abdomen should push out
   c) the chest should rise
   d) the knees should be flexed

3. The tone quality of your voice is primarily affected by the use of _____.
   a) resonators
   b) articulators
   c) pitch
   d) volume

4. The proper use of the lips, teeth, tongue, and jaw, referred to as the _____, helps produce clear vocal sounds.
   a) resonators
   b) projectors
   c) pronouncers
   d) articulators

5. The broadcast standard for speaking is Standard American English at about 160 words per minute (wpm).
   a) true
   b) false

6. If your voice is soft, the best way to increase its strength is to use the volume controls on the audio board.
   a) true
   b) false

7. A common vocal problem that is related to resonance is a _____.
   a) sing-song pattern
   b) monotone
   c) breathy sound
   d) nasal sound

8. A career in broadcast announcing should not be considered unless you have a voice with a deep, low pitch.
   a) true
   b) false

9. The use of a high-quality condenser mic may help to enhance _____.
   a) resonance
   b) articulation
   c) pronunciation
   d) volume

10. Which of the following is the proper performance guideline to follow for pronunciation?
    a) pronounce foreign words as a native speaker
    b) maintain individuality by using regional accents
    c) always pronounce "the" as "thee"
    d) be familiar with copy to avoid pronunciation mistakes

11. Which of the following is least likely to define an excellent broadcast announcer voice?
    a) speaking with a low, pleasing, resonant voice
    b) speaking at a pace that promotes easy comprehension
    c) speaking at a loud volume level
    d) speaking with precise articulation

12. Which of the following illustrates the articulation problem of omission?
    a) saying "wabbit" instead of "rabbit"
    b) saying "warsh" instead of "wash"
    c) saying "chick" instead of "chic"
    d) saying "winner" instead of "winter"

13. Which of the following variables of your speaking voice do you have the least ability to manipulate?
    a) volume
    b) pitch
    c) rate
    d) tone

14. Television performers do not have to be concerned about vocal delivery; it is much more important for them to be concerned about their appearance.
    a) true
    b) false

15. Which part of your vocal apparatus directs air over the vocal cords?
    a) vocal folds
    b) pharynx
    c) larynx
    d) trachea

■ ANSWERS

If You Answered A:

1a. No. The lungs are not muscles, they are like sponges to hold the air. (Reread 4.2 through 4.5.)

2a. No. Keeping the back straight is part of proper breathing technique. (Reread 4.3 and 4.4.)

3a. Yes. The vibration of sound in the head produces tone quality.

4a. No. Resonators are used to produce a full, rich sound. (Reread 4.2 and 4.11.)

5a. Correct. The generally accepted speech standard is a relatively unaccented speech properly spoken at this rate, so this is a true statement.

6a. No. The volume controls should not be used to make up what is lacking in your voice. (Reread 4.7.)

7a. Incorrect. A sing-song pattern is caused by the announcer repeating emphasis or stressing words in the same pattern. (Reread 4.14.)

8a. No. Although true in the past, a deep, low-pitched voice is not the vocal standard today. (Reread 4.8.)

9a. Correct. A high-quality microphone may be used to help the tone quality of your voice.

10a. No. Correct foreign pronunciation is often modified in broadcast circumstances. (Reread 4.12 and 4.13.)

11a. No. Most broadcast announcers speak in a lower range with a pleasant, resonant voice. (Reread 4.6.)

12a. Wrong. This illustrates an articulation problem when one speech sound is substituted for another. (Reread 4.13.)

13a. No. Most people have a fairly good range between the softest volume at which they can speak and the loudest. (Reread 4.7 through 4.10.)

14a. No. Proper use of the voice is important for all performers. (Reread 4.1.)

15a. No. Vocal folds is just another, more accurate, name for your vocal cords. (Reread 4.2.)

If You Answered B:

1b. Yes. The diaphragm is the most important muscle for proper breathing.

2b. No. When the diaphragm pushes down, the abdomen should push out. (Reread 4.3 and 4.4.)

3b. Incorrect. Articulators are used to make the speech sounds clear. (Reread 4.10 and 4.11.)

4b. No. Projection is a result of proper breathing and energy. (Reread 4.2 and 4.11.)

5b. No. The broadcast standard is a relatively unaccented speech properly spoken at about 160 words per minute. (Reread 4.9.)

6b. Yes. This is a false statement because strength of voice is best controlled by proper breathing technique rather than the audio board's volume controls.

7b. No. A monotone problem is caused by lack of pitch changes. (Reread 4.14.)

8b. Correct. This is a false statement because, today, the broadcast announcer needs to have a pleasant voice and not just a deep, low-pitched voice.

9b. No. Articulation depends on the performer properly using lips, tongue, teeth, jaw, and soft palate to clearly speak words. (Reread 4.10 and 4.11.)

10b. Incorrect. Although a few individuals may be successful in maintaining a regional sound, this limits your ability to move to other markets. (Reread 4.12 and 4.13.)

11b. No. Most broadcast announcers speak at a pace that promotes easy comprehension. (Reread 4.6.)

12b. Wrong. This illustrates an articulation problem when a speech sound is added to a word. (Reread 4.13.)

13b. No. Most people have a fairly good range between the highest pitch at which they can speak and the lowest. (Reread 4.7 through 4.10.)

14b. Correct. This is a false statement because television performers communicate with both appearance and voice.

15b. No. The pharynx is the area between the mouth and nasal passages. It is above the vocal cords and is a resonator. (Reread 4.2.)

If You Answered C:

1c. Wrong. Resonators vibrate the air for a full, rich sound. (Reread 4.2 through 4.5.)

2c. Correct. This is not part of proper breathing, but shows that breathing is shallow and coming from the chest area rather than the diaphragm.

3c. No. Pitch is the highness or lowness of the voice. (Reread 4.8 and 4.10.)

4c. Incorrect. Pronunciation is the way words are accented. (Reread 4.2 and 4.11.)

7c. No. A breathy voice is caused by a problem with breath support. (Reread 4.14.)

9c. Incorrect. Pronunciation is the responsibility of the announcer and depends on the correct use of accent and inflection. (Reread 4.10.)

10c. No. This pronunciation is too formal. Broadcast announcing uses a more informal style of pronunciation so "the" becomes "thuh." (Reread 4.12 and 4.13.)

11c. Yes. Most broadcast announcers speak with an intimate, conversational voice. It is usually not necessary to speak at a loud volume level and doing so can make it seem like the announcer is speaking "at" the listener.

12c. Wrong. This illustrates a pronunciation problem. Chic is pronounced as "sheek" and not "chick." (Reread 4.12.)

13c. No. Most people have a fairly good range between the slowest rate at which they can speak and the fastest. (Reread 4.7 through 4.10.)

15c. No. The larynx is the voice box and it is where the vocal cords are located. (Reread 4.2.)

If You Answered D:

1d. No. Vocal cords or folds vibrate to produce sound, but they are not muscles. (Reread 4.2 through 4.5.)

2d. No. The knees should be flexed because this is part of proper posture to allow for a relaxed use of your muscles. (Reread 4.3 and 4.4.)

3d. No. Volume is the loudness or softness of the voice. (Reread 4.10.)

4d. Yes. Articulators are used to make speech sounds clear.

7d. Yes. By blocking the resonant chambers with your tongue or soft palate, the voice sounds nasal, as if you have a bad cold.

9d. Incorrect. Volume is really dependent on the announcer's proper use of breath support and projection. (Reread 4.7 and 4.10.)

10d. Correct. The audience expects an announcer to use proper pronunciation.

11d. No. Most broadcast announcers speak with precise articulation that provides exceptional clarity of content. (Reread 4.6.)

12d. Correct. This illustrates the articulation problem of omission, in which necessary speech sounds are omitted from words.

13d. Yes. While you can develop your voice tone quality somewhat, a lot of how you sound depends on the "body" that surrounds the vocal cords.

15d. Yes. The trachea or wind pipe directs air over the vocal cords.

Projects

■ PROJECT 1

Practice articulation.

Purpose
To develop speech clarity by proper movement of the articulators: teeth, lips, tongue, jaw, and soft palate.

Notes
1. Practicing tongue twisters can be helpful in enabling you to easily handle everyday phrases. Although you may never read copy as complicated as this, these exercises will help you become aware of the importance of moving the articulators to avoid lazy mouth.
2. At first, it will feel as though you are moving your mouth too much. However, this is necessary to clearly articulate the words.
3. If you need assistance in recording, in the studio or with a portable recorder, ask your instructor or station engineer for help.

How to Do the Project
1. Practice reading the copy below for this project out loud.
2. When you are comfortable with your ability to read each phrase slowly, but with clear diction and proper articulation, record the practice copy.
3. Play back the recording and listen to yourself critically.
4. Do not erase your first recording, but rerecord the copy and try to improve on your articulation as well as repeat each phrase faster.
5. Label the recording with your name and "Articulation Exercise." Turn it in to your teacher to receive credit for this project.

Articulation Copy
A. If I assist a sister-assistant, will the sister's sister-assistant assist me around the angled amber a-toll?
B. Betty bought a bit of butter, but she found the butter bitter, so Betty bought a bit of better butter to make the bitter butter better.
C. Kris Kringle carefully crunched on candy canes while a cupcake cook in a cupcake cook's cap cooked cupcakes with crisp crusts that crackled crunchily.
D. Do drop in at the Dewdrop Inn and see a dozen double damask dinner napkins.
E. Erin hears an excited executioner exercising his excising powers excessively unless her ears err here.
F. Friendly Frank flips fine flapjacks while four furious friends fought for the phone as fat frogs were flying past fast.
G. Gertie's great-grandma grew aghast at Gertie's grammar as cows grazed in groves on grass which grows in grooves in groves.
H. How has Harry hastened so hurriedly from the huge hog hunt?
I. Ike ships ice chips and inchworms itching in inch-long ice chip ships.
J. James just jostled Jean gently, but jolted Joan.
K. Karen's cutlery cuts keenly and cleanly, but Ken's cutlery can't carve.
L. Larry sent the latter a lovely lemon liniment and a letter later.
M. A minx mixed a medicinal mixture, while a moose noshed much mush.
N. Nine nice night nurses nursing nicely napped near-by.

O. Old oily Ollie oils old oily autos.

P. A pleasant place to place a palace is a place where a palace is pleased to be placed.

Q. Karen gave a quick kiss to Ken. Ken gave a quicker kiss to Kim. Kim gave the quickest kiss to Kerry.

R. Regal Ruby Rugby recalled round the rugged rocks the ragged rascal ran.

S. Sister Susie sat on the sea shore sewing shirts and short-silk sashes for sailors and six short slow shepherds as the sunshine shown.

T. Ten tame tadpoles tucked tightly in a thin tall tin as the two-twenty-two train tore through the tunnel.

U. An undertaker undertook to undertake an understanding. The undertaking that the undertaker undertook was the hardest undertaking the undertaker ever undertook to undertake.

V. Virginia vowed vengeance very vehemently.

W. William, will you ask which witch wished to switch a witch wristwatch for a Swiss wristwatch?

X. Rex's hex: X-mas wrecks perplex and vex.

Y. Yes, local yokels were yodeling and yanking yellow yo-yos yesterday.

Z. Zizzi's zippy zipper zips.

■ PROJECT 2

Practice proper pronunciation and avoidance of substandard enunciation.

Purpose
To develop an awareness of poor pronunciation and promote a clear speaking style.

Notes
1. Becoming more aware of common poorly pronounced words will be helpful in developing a good speaking style for radio, television and cable performances.
2. Before beginning the exercise, you should review sections 4.11, 4.12, and 4.13 of this chapter.
3. You can practice as much as you want to, but can record the project only once, in a continuous take.
4. Your instructor may have you complete this project several times during the term.

How to Do the Project
1. Practice reading out loud the paragraph below. You should be able to easily read the text in 60 seconds.
2. When you are comfortable that you can read the entire text in a clear speaking style, record the copy onto an audio tape or other recording medium. If you need assistance in recording in the studio or with a portable recorder, ask your instructor or station engineer for help.
3. You can practice as much as you want, but you can record the project only once, without stopping. You may not exceed sixty seconds in length, although shorter is acceptable.
4. Play the recording and listen to it critically. After listening, write a one-page evaluation noting any problems you had with the reading.
5. Label the recording and evaluation with your name and "Clear Speaking Style." Turn in both to your instructor to receive credit for this project.
   (Note: As this is not a news broadcast you do not need to make any reference to the quote marks in the copy.)

Jim had a bad cold and sounded so different his friends almost didn't recognize him on the phone. Walking to the library he met his statistics professor and explained to him that he had had a temperature of ninety-nine point one. The professor laughed and said he must have partied too much and ought to get more rest. "Let me tell you one thing," he said, "you are going to face a hundred temptations. Don't let a few little trips into the city cost you a good grade. I recall you have a history of starting well in class and subtly sliding. Let me warn you not to forget you have twenty days until the end of the semester." Jim said "Good bye" and continued walking and kept thinking "I don't want to fail that course. I'm just going to have to sit down and put in an extra thirty minutes of study every day, even though that is going to be very tedious."

■ PROJECT 3

Practice pronunciation.

Purpose
To help you increase your working vocabulary and make sure that you are correctly pronouncing words that are often mispronounced.

Notes
1. Even though many people think they know how to pronounce commonly used words, they are frequently incorrect. Broadcast announcers are expected to pronounce words correctly.
2. You will be recording words on CDs, MP3s, or audio cassettes, so make sure you're familiar with the operation of the necessary equipment or ask your instructor or station engineer for assistance.

How to Do the Project
1. For each of the words in the following list, research the correct pronunciation.
2. Provide a phonetic pronunciation guide for each word (as is often done with wire service copy). For example: Word Phonetic Guide Almond AH'-MUND
3. Now record each word onto a CD, MP3, or cassette tape. Be sure to leave a blank space of about two seconds between each word.
4. Put your name and "Word Pronunciation" for the heading of your paper. Label your cassette tape in a similar fashion.
5. Turn in the finished paper and the tape cassette to your instructor to receive credit for completing this project.

Word List

accessory	hospitable	realtor
athlete	illustrate	sandwich
barbiturate	jewelry	theater
caramel	liaison	unguent
consortium	mischievous	vase
deluge	negotiate	worsted
envelope	ophthalmologist	yeoman
facade	palm	zoology
genuine		

CHAPTER FIVE

PERFORMANCE DEVELOPMENT

5.1 INTRODUCTION

In the previous chapter, we began to focus on how to develop your voice. Having a pleasant speaking voice is the first step in being a professional performer. In this chapter, the plan is to take that good speaking voice and learn how to use it to develop a delivery style that is appropriate for broadcast performance situations. The most sought-after general delivery style in mass media is a conversational tone—the ability to speak to hundreds, thousands, maybe even millions of listeners or viewers, yet make it sound as if you are talking one-to-one. Most broadcast situations make this fairly difficult to accomplish for two reasons: first, you lack direct feedback that gives you a reaction to what you are saying; and second, you are often reading a script written by someone else, rather than saying your own words. Figure 5.1 shows this contrast between normal conversation and broadcast

FIGURE 5.1 Normal conversation contrasted with broadcast "conversation."

conversation. The best broadcast performers overcome this environmental handicap and seem to be relaxed and conversational to the listener and viewer, even though they receive no audience feedback. The modern broadcast announcer also has to be more than a reader of words and is expected to be able to interpret and communicate the message of any script. This chapter begins to show you how to develop a natural performance style.

5.2 DEVELOPING A BROADCAST DELIVERY STYLE

You won't develop a broadcast delivery style overnight; it takes time and is the combination of developing a good voice, learning how to use the techniques and becoming a good reader of copy, particularly material you haven't written. A few beginners assume they can "sight read" cold copy. This is unlikely. It's hard enough mastering material that you've practiced. The best thing to do is record yourself regularly and be critical of the results. Having someone else review the recording with you will be a good check. This is a practice even veteran pros do regularly. Some comedians even record their entire performance and analyze it, trying to determine why one joke worked and another failed. You can also record a sentence or two, listen to it, and record it again, trying to make improvements. Work on the same short passage until it sounds the way you want it and then go to another and repeat the process. You really can't overdo it.

Another thing to remember is that reading copy silently is worth about 10 percent of reading it aloud. Just running the words through your mind will not show you the problems, the delivery style and the correct pronunciation that reading aloud will. Don't do it in a half voice either. Get where you can project a little. Do it regularly and be critical. You will make progress.

Textbooks and coaches often speak of developing a **conversational style**. But how does that sound, and how do you do it? One thing for the new announcer to keep in mind is what we'll call **audience distance**. That is the apparent distance to your listener, and it may seem quite large. In a television situation, many beginners feel the audience is where the cameras are, and project their voice to that distance, particularly when the camera is some distance away. This can be compared to the theater performer whose director reminds actors to project to reach the back row of the auditorium or the professor who strives to keep the back row of the classroom alert. Such an effort will lead to over-projection in many cases and largely eliminate the intimate sound you want in many situations. Your audience's ear is located where the microphone is, and that is probably only six or so inches from your lips.

Getting the feel of projecting over different distances can be accomplished with a small experiment, but one you will want to do it with a good friend. Start reading a piece of copy from six or seven feet from your friend, remembering that you are speaking to that individual. Get the feel of that delivery. Then take a stride closer to them so that you are about four feet away. It should feel a little different, and you may want to adjust the projection. Then take another stride, so that you are about eighteen inches away. (This is why we recommended it be a friend.) You are very likely to feel uncomfortable in your delivery. Stay at that location for a minute or so, still speaking, and get the feel of the delivery for that distance. Now start moving back, but maintain the style you used when up close. This is the intimate sound that you want to be able to use in many situations. It is likely to feel strange at first, but if you practice it and learn how to call upon it when it is appropriate, it will be very useful. An alternative, if it's available, is to start ad-libbing to a television camera located only about two feet from your face. Note the feel of the situation. Now have the camera suddenly moved about six feet away. You'll likely find that you have to struggle to sustain the intimate style you used when the camera was close, yet that is a style you want to develop. As an alternative, you can get some of the same feeling just talking to a wall. Get close and visualize the person, start speaking and feel how you adjust as you step away. Strange, but effective.

Another factor to think about from the beginning is **audience number**. We use a different style when speaking to a large group than we do when speaking to two or three. In broadcasting, hopefully, you will have a large audience. However, that needs to be put aside and everyone addressed as if they were just immediate family. Some performers have spoken about taping pictures of a few friends around the camera lens or just beyond the microphone in radio, to remind them to whom they were speaking. Developing the habit of listening to how people speak in different situations may not add to your popularity, but can give you some insight into how we address groups in different situations. The more you become conscious of this the more progress you will make. One last strange suggestion: Extend your arm and curve the fingers back toward you. In general, this represents your audience, about four people located about two feet away, so talk to your fingers. Now, with this material as background, let's begin looking at technique.

5.3 PERFORMANCE ELEMENTS

In most careers, the professional practitioners have a "kit" of tools that make them stand out from the non-professional and help them do their jobs well. Such is the case in mass media performance. In a very real sense, your voice is the foundation of your success, but how you use that voice is a bigger factor in how successful you will be. The techniques of skillful voice use can be called the **performance elements**—the changes you make during a delivery to make copy more interesting and understandable. Learning to use these "tools" well, and knowing when to employ them, are the trademarks of a "pro."

The performance elements are so intertwined that it is difficult to explore them individually, because more than one element is often involved at any moment. If we were to identify one element as the most important, it probably would be **inflection**. This element is critical in giving life to copy and in making it readily understandable. Inflection deals with pitch—the range of high, middle, and low notes that are most evident when we listen to a singer. Everyone uses pitch variations in their conversations, but when presented with some copy to read, the variability often disappears and what we hear can approach a monotone. Another word for pitch is "tone," and, of course, monotone means "one tone"—about as dull a sound as you can get.

The first step in using inflection is to get a sense of how it feels. You can do this by some singing or the simple exercise of saying "low, high" in the lowest and highest pitch you can muster. Get the feeling of what it is like to consciously cause your pitch to rise and fall. Use the sentences in the practice material at the end of this chapter. Practice reading them in the style in which they are written. Next, read a piece of copy, listening to the amount of inflection you are using. Then read it again, exaggerating the inflection on many of the words. This is one exercise where you can't really overdo it. Once you have given it several reads, try reading the copy again, but adjust the inflections to the level you feel is appropriate. Recording your speech is a good way to evaluate how you are progressing. Since inflection is such a critical tool, it is worth spending some time on it. It's worth remembering that there are very few sentences that should be delivered without inflection. Virtually everyone needs some. Many students feel they are inflecting adequately, but after listening to their recording, discover they need more. For many it will feel like you are overdoing it so that you're uncomfortable. In many cases, you will still be a little short of enough. Compare Audio Track 5.1 in which the announcer uses little inflection with Audio Track 5.2 where proper techniques are used.

Besides making the sound more interesting, which is very important for a broadcast, inflection helps us make certain words stand out in the message. It is one of the ways we give a word or phrase **emphasis** in a message. Particularly by inflecting upward, we can cause the audience to be more aware of the important words in our message. Another way to generate emphasis is with loudness. By pushing more energy into a certain word, it stands out in the copy. Emphasis, however, is a little like hot pepper sauce in that it can be overused. We've all heard commercials where the announcer seems to think every word in a commercial message is critical. Of course, if that's the way the sponsor wants it, the speaker is just doing the job as the client wishes. Most sentences of average length will only have two or three key words that deserve to be emphasized. It's important to identify which words those are, so that you don't waste emphasis on words that really aren't as important.

Volume or loudness is another tool you have available. Here again, the key is to vary it. Some passages can be delivered in a slightly softer voice, while others should stand out by turning up the volume a little. Variety is so much the key to good delivery that you want to use every avenue you have. Dropping the volume now and then should not make you unintelligible, but it can make you more interesting.

Another versatile tool is the **pause**. You can create emphasis by pausing before or after an important word. Pauses have other applications as well. They break up copy and help create interest, as well as give the audience a moment to absorb what you have said. You don't want to fall into the habit of pausing in a predictable pattern, because that creates a **choppy** sound that quickly becomes uninteresting and unprofessional. In addition to making a specific word stand out, a pause can create interest by where you place it. Sometimes these locations are not at obvious points, but can be within a sentence to add understanding as well as appeal. Using the simple sentence, "Alfred had been away in the military for four years," we could add brief pauses after the word "Alfred" and after "military." That name also has a natural up and down inflection in it, as you can go up on the "A" and down on "fred." The pause after "military" can be smoothed by drawing out the "y" just a little before you say "for." The next sentence in that copy is, "Because of distances and his own lack of cash, he had been home only twice in that entire time and had been out of the country for the past two years." Try reading it with a short pause after "distances," and after "cash," "twice," and "time." Placing some emphasis on "distance," "lack of cash," "twice," and "two years" will make the significance of his return stand out. Try inflecting upward on "twice." Don't let your pitch drop when you pause, as the choppy sound will appear. Avoid the temptation to rush through the copy. As you become more skilled at using the performance tools, you will be able to speed up a bit without losing their impact.

Pauses have another important role in reading copy. They provide a chance for you to get a little **breath**. You don't want to go on so long that you fade as you run out of air, and the audience hears a big gasp when you finally reach a point where you can stop. The space between sentences is an obvious place to breathe, as are the pauses at some commas. If the sentence is long, find a place where you can add a pause, without affecting the meaning, to get some air. When you reach that breath point, try to wait until the end of your pause to take the breath, as the new phrase will distract the audience from the sound of you inhaling. Planning to breathe more often will reduce the likelihood that your breathing will be evident. You may find it helpful to mark important breath points in the script. Using these pauses leads us to another available tool, that of **rate variation**. We don't deliver copy in a steady flow of words like water from a faucet. Rather, to add interest and clarity, we vary the rate, reading some phrases faster than others. Slowing pace can add emphasis, while speeding up tends to make a phrase more secondary. This takes some conscious planning at first, but with practice it will seem natural. Listen to Audio Clip 5.3 for an example of pauses and rate variation. By adding inflection, emphasis, and pauses in addition to the rate variation, the interest in what you have to say will be heightened. Careful selection of the locations for inflection and emphasis will make the material easier to understand as well.

Joining these tools is **phrasing**, which is the process of grouping words that form an idea, and then delivering that group smoothly together. Using the first line of the Alfred sentence, "away in the military" is one idea

and should be delivered as such. Likewise, consider "for four years," "because of distances," "lack of cash," "he had been home," "in that entire time," and "had been out of the country," "for the past two years." All form word groups that should be read as a unit. To vary the sound, don't use the same length of pause between each phrase. Let some be very brief, and extend others by a fraction of a second. Watch for any tendency to repeat a pattern, as that will tend to carry you toward a "sing-song" sound. Stretching the last sound at the end of a phrase will help you pause without becoming choppy. And, don't let your pitch drop after any of them.

Flow initially seems to contradict some of the other ideas that have been presented, but that's not actually the case. Even though it's important that each word be properly enunciated, phrases constructed, and pauses included, carrying these too far can result in an overly precise, stilted delivery that sounds very unnatural. Some beginners strive to complete every word so thoroughly that there is a tiny pause after each. Others will say two or three words and then pause, and then repeat the pattern, so that a very choppy sound emerges. Listening to delivery, either while you're reading or via a recording, can help you become aware of your habits. Use the inflectional technique of holding the tone to signal that more is coming. In a choppy delivery, the tendency is to drop the pitch a little at each pause point, which signals an ending when you didn't intend it.

One of the challenges that many students find is reading smoothly without stumbles and restarts. This is primarily the result of insufficient concentration and essentially guessing what the next word will be without looking at it. Being thoroughly familiar with the copy, and controlling reading rate will help. However, it can take a fair amount of effort to get your concentration and focus to the level where you are reading the words that are actually there. Most re-starts seem to come at the beginning of a sentence, so be alert to that. Some students have more trouble with this than others, so evaluate yourself honestly on it, and get plenty of practice. **Mood** is another vocal tool that is often overlooked. In some stories, the mood is quite evident, while in others it may not be so obvious. Mood is a factor in commercials as well as news stories, and because of the problem/solution pattern of a commercial, the mood may change within the space of the message. You may start in a serious or concerned tone, and switch to an upbeat mood as the wonders of the product are described. Mood possibilities are obvious, but to consider some examples, we

Here's a little exercise to help you learn about mood and inflection. Take the simple word "Hello". Say it aloud as you would if you were happy to encounter a friend. Now, say it as if you had run into someone you really didn't care for, but didn't think you should ignore. Next try it as you would when meeting someone you thought was attractive and you were flirting a little. Finally, explore how you would say it when meeting someone in the corridor at school. Someone you really didn't know, but good manners dictated that you acknowledge them as you pass.

FIGURE 5.2 *An inflection and mood exercise.*

could encounter *a serious* mood in reporting on a disaster or concern for a missing child, *happiness* when reporting a pleasant weather forecast, *elation* when reading a commercial about a great sale, and *humor* when telling of some harmless mistake or incident. Obviously, there are many gradations and variations in between, such as *pensive, cordial,* and *angry.* Any copy needs to be examined for mood prior to delivery, remembering that mood shifts may be buried in the text. You need to identify and highlight any changes before you deliver the reading.

Start by giving some thought as to how you will use your voice to express the appropriate mood. How would you show that mood to a friend? Even in radio, your facial expressions can help to produce the right sound. If reporting a funny story, it's fine to put a chuckle in your voice and a smile on your face. A grim look can help convey the mood of a serious story. The mood must match the message. A bad choice can make you sound foolish or uncaring. Don't be like a young reporter who greeted the audience with a "Hi," when about to report the story of a fire that killed two students.

Energy has been mentioned in several places in this text because it is so important. Without it you will never develop the professional sound it takes to be successful. Like inflection, it is one of the more valuable tools you have available. Some beginners find it difficult to put enough push in their delivery to sound alive. For these folks, the first step is to become aware that you are holding back, by critiquing recordings of your delivery. Next, alone or with a partner, get somewhere you are comfortable and just overdo it. There are short passages at the end of this chapter. Read them with as much steam as you can generate. Be as loud as you can. If you have a partner, try to top each other. After doing this exercise a few times, it may be easier to project more energy, and therefore, more life, into the copy.

Every announcer needs to consider the appropriate amount of energy to use in each circumstance. Some will always be needed, but consider the message, the audience, and the circumstances. A commercial for a big carpet sale may call for nearly shouting, while a news story on an accident will take much less vocal energy. If you are the host of a classical music show, you'll need even less, but you still need to sound alive, interested, and appreciative of the music you are playing and the audience that is listening. Listen to working pros in a variety of formats and gauge how much energy they are using in each situation. Using too much energy and overdoing it can be as unprofessional as sounding flat.

One of the benefits of doing radio is that you can use your body to help get you to the right level. Work standing up, gesture, make faces, punch the air if it helps you sound alive. On television, you don't have quite as much flexibility, but facial expressions, gestures, and nods of the head will make you look and sound more alive and effective.

Emphasis, inflection, pauses, flow, and the other performance techniques are all tools of the professional announcer, and most of them are used in every delivery. Properly applied, they make the message more understandable and more interesting. If the copy demands a high word rate, the pauses will be briefer, but shouldn't be lost altogether. Inflection needs to be used regardless of speed, as it is a key to understanding. Some students, when listening to recordings of themselves do not even hear the lack of inflection and the other performance elements. Giving yourself an honest critique is also a skill to be developed. The **air check** is a regular tool of the pros who want to maintain and improve their work. It's the basis of their livelihood. Frequent practice and self-evaluation will help you build skill in using these performance elements.

PERFORMANCE TIP 5.1

Reading a "string"

A **string** is the name we can give to a listing of items within a news story. As an example, the following might be the characteristics of a high-priced Hollywood home that had been put up for sale. "IT HAS SIX BEDROOMS, EIGHT BATHS, A GYM, FORMAL DINING AREA, AN ATRIUM IN THE LIVING ROOM, A SKYLIGHT THAT OPENS AUTOMATICALLY AND A MOAT." The question is, how to read it in an interesting and meaningful way. It would be very easy to rattle through the list in a dull and uninspired manner. Read each item with a difference in performance elements. Give each a different inflection and use a variation in rate and even a pause or two in strategic places to give you and your audience a brief break. Many strings are three items long, as our culture seems to be attracted to that number. The first item could be read in a regular pattern, the second could be inflected upward followed by a slight pause and the third with a slight downward inflection to show that it is the end of the list. Returning to the list above, if we just used the first three, it could go "six bedrooms," and the inflection upward on "eight" and stay up in pitch on "baths," then, drawing out an "and" (which we'll add to make it more readable) then come down in pitch "a moat." It will take some practice to do this inflecting automatically. Identifying strings in copy before you start will make your reads more understandable and easier for the listener.

5.4 COPY MARKING

The first step, when working with a script, is to read it out loud, as practice. Focus on finding the words that carry the meaning of the message so that you will emphasize those **key words** during the performance of the script. The key words alone usually carry a concise summary of the message of the script. For example, in the sentence, "The huge end-of-the-month sale begins this Saturday morning at Anderson's," it's not crucial to know the sale is "huge" or that it's an "end-of-the-month sale," or that it begins in the "morning," even if that's nice to know. What is key is that there is a "sale Saturday at Anderson's." Read the copy aloud several times, trying the emphasis on different words to see which are the most effective. The key words should highlight the important elements of the story or commercial.

Normal punctuation will help you read any written material, but to help you interpret broadcast copy, you should plan on marking the script further. **Copy marking** means using a system of graphic symbols to indicate how you feel the script should be read. Basically, it's adding supplementary punctuation to the script. For example, you might underline a key word to remind you to give that word extra emphasis when you deliver it. The idea is that the marks should assist you in reading the copy and should not become a distraction that might cause errors in your reading. At first, copy marking will seem a tedious task that takes too much time, but you will eventually find that it becomes second nature and it will help you to become a better broadcast performer.

Of course, there will be times when you will not have the chance to actually mark up the script, but you'll find after a period of time that you can do it mentally, if not physically. Some professionals avoid copy marks altogether as they fear that they might be a distraction. Since there is no standard method or technique for marking a broadcast script, you can develop your own system, however, here are some commonly used marks you can adapt. It's important to keep copy marks simple and to be consistent in how you use them, so there is no delay in determining what they mean. You can underline a word or phrase to give it extra emphasis. For example, "Anderson's Big 25th Anniversary Sale starts this Saturday!" How you actually give emphasis to "this Saturday" is also open to interpretation, as noted in the previous section. You might slightly raise the volume of your voice, but you could also change the tone or pitch of your voice, and you might slow the pace of your reading to call attention to the phrase. If you want to indicate even more emphasis, use a double underline, for example, "Anderson's Big 25th Anniversary Sale starts this Saturday!"

A forward slash is used to indicate a pause, much as a comma would; however, it usually means a slightly longer pause. For example, "Anderson's Big 25th Anniversary Sale starts / this Saturday!" You can indicate an even longer pause by using two slashes, as in ". . sale starts // this Saturday!" Each slash indicates an approximate beat or "one-thousand-one" count.

A two-headed arrow drawn under a word or phrase indicates that you need to vocally "stretch out" the word or expression. For example, "Anderson's Big 25th

Anniversary Sale" would remind you to read "Big" more like "Bbbiiiggg."

To indicate that a word or phrase should be spoken more quickly than the rest of the script, you'd draw a squiggly line under the word or phrase, like this: "Don't miss Anderson's Big 25th Anniversary Sale! All sales are final. Sale ends at midnight this Friday." On the other hand, to indicate that a word or phrase should be spoken more slowly than the rest of the script, you would put dots under the word or phrase, like this: "Don't miss Anderson's Big 25th Anniversary Sale! All sales are final."

Brackets are often used to group words into phrases so you know you want to read those words as one complete thought. For example, ["Anderson's Big 25th Anniversary Sale] starts this Saturday!"

Smart broadcast announcers will "flag" certain words in their scripts, especially those words that might cause trouble with pronunciation. To do this, simply draw a box around the entire word, and write the correct pronunciation just above the flagged word like this:

noo'klee-uhr

"Bigger than a nuclear explosion . . it's Anderson's Big 25th Anniversary Sale!"

If you have a personal problem pronouncing some word, it's a good idea to highlight it in some way to remind you to be careful. Even if you have a tendency to say "git" instead of "get" a mark in your copy will help you avoid that error.

Voice inflection is often noted with an arrow above the word or phrase. If you want to remember to raise the pitch of your voice as you read it, draw the arrow so the shaft bends upward as you go from left to right over the word or phrase. If you want to pitch the voice lower as you read a phrase, draw the arrow above the phrase so the shaft bends downward as you go from left to right. The point of the arrow is always at the end of the word or phrase. For example, "Anderson's Big Anniversary Sale ends this Friday at midnight."

There is one other use for the arrow. Some sentences have several points in them that could be the end. Returning to our Alfred copy, in the second sentence , "Because of distance and his own lack of cash, he had been home twice in that entire time and had been out of the country for the past two years." If, by chance, the word "time" happened to be at the end of a line, it would be very easy to read it with a downward inflection signaling the end of a sentence, and creating a problem

for you when you discovered there was more. A straight arrow is often put over a word that happens to be located at the end of a line on the script, but is not the end of the sentence, to remind the announcer not to take a pause there. In other words, the phrase or thought continues on the next line. The straight arrow also can be used at the end of a sentence to alert the reader not to drop the pitch when there is more information in the next sentence. Dropping pitch at the end of a sentence signifies that the idea is complete. This can result in a very choppy sound if you drop too much at the end of each sentence. It can also be confusing to the listener who assumes you just finished the idea, and then you continue. The amount you drop the pitch depends on whether you have just completed an idea or the whole piece of copy. Save the biggest drops for the true end of the piece.

Anyone who has done much copy reading has encountered the problem of reading a line and then, just as you are finishing it, realizing that it is a question and you've been presenting it as a statement. A forced, sudden raising of the voice sounds very unprofessional. The Spanish language has a device that can be useful here. They use an upside down question mark or exclamation mark at the beginning of a question or exclamation. To alert an announcer that a sentence he or she is about to read is either a question or an exclamation, upside down punctuation can be put at the beginning of the sentence. For example, "¿Do you want to save $1000?" Since these sentences call for a different tone or inflection than sentences ending with a period, these marks make sure you aren't caught unaware by giving you an alert as you *start* the line, not when you are just finishing. You might like to enlarge the question mark or exclamation point at both ends of the sentence just to be sure.

Regular punctuation also gives the announcer an indication of how the writer wants the script read. For the period, comma, question mark, and exclamation point, the traditional meaning of these punctuation marks is the same when applied in broadcast copy. The colon and semicolon are usually not used in broadcast copy. While not an exhaustive list, some of the other punctuation marks as used in broadcast copy are noted in the following paragraphs.

You know that in normal syntax, an **ellipsis** (…) indicates words missing from a sentence or quotation. However, in broadcast copy, the triple periods are often used to indicate a pause. Likewise, a dash (–) or even three hyphens (—) can be used to indicate a pause. These pauses are usually thought of as longer than a comma pause, but shorter than a concluding period pause; however, there is no standard convention and it is up to the announcer to interpret this in his or her own style.

The **hyphen** (-) can be used to indicate that several words are linked into one common idea. Such terms as *book-of-the-month* or *jack-of-all-trades* are easier to read if you can readily see that the group of words represents one idea. The hyphen is a handy device to help smooth out broadcast copy. For example, "The Johnson Company end-of-the-year sale starts next Wednesday!" Use hyphens wherever it will help your reading. Another example would be in this sentence, "The star's real name was *James Robert Jones Senior.*" You could easily drop your voice on "Jones," and find that the "Senior" was awkward. Hyphens between each name will help you remember. However, when a hyphen is put between single capital letters, you should read each letter separately, such as "F-B-I"; no hyphens mean that you should pronounce the letters together as an **acronym**, such as "NASA."

Quotation marks are used occasionally in broadcast copy. First, they may indicate an actual quote. Since the marks aren't seen by the listener, the announcer must make the quote stand out through the copy. If the copy read as follows: The mayor said, "No new taxes this year," the announcer could indicate this quote with a change of vocal inflection on "no new taxes …" or by inserting a phrase like "and I quote" in the copy: The mayor said, and I quote, "No new taxes this year." In either case, don't close out a quotation with the awkward word "unquote"; simply continue with the next line of copy. Either the announcer will convey that the quote is finished with his or her delivery style, or the script will make it clear that the quote is completed. However, if it is a controversial statement, something like "unquote" may be justified.

Parentheses ( ) are normally used for **de-emphasis** of a word or phrase, but in broadcast copy they are most often used to indicate directions to the announcer, and whatever is included inside the parentheses is never spoken. For example, you might see a script like this:

> Announcer: (READ WITH URGENCY) "Don't miss the one-day clearance sale at the Flairtique Gift Shop."

The last marks to consider could be used in a situation where copy editing is being done while you are in the process of recording the spot—for example, if the ad agency suddenly decides there is a better word to use than the one in the script. Draw a single line through the word and write the new word in pencil immediately above it. If it's decided to go back to the original expression, you'd just have to erase the replacement word. If the copy is too long and a word or phrase is cut, thoroughly cross out the deleted words so there is no chance of reading the wrong copy. Remember, **marking copy** and punctuation marks will help guide you, but your job as the broadcast performer is to interpret the script in your own unique style. Chances are you have been hired to do so exactly because you have a special style.

5.5 WORD USAGE

You can build your vocabulary by employing a feature found in *Reader's Digest* called "Word Power." A list of words, both fairly common and more unusual, is given along with three possible meanings for each word from which you select the proper definition. Correct answers are provided as well as an example of the correct usage of the word. An online version of this feature can be found at wordpower.com. If you're an aspiring broadcast announcer, it truly would pay to take this monthly quiz or develop a similar plan to increase your vocabulary because broadcast announcers make their living using words. They are expected to properly manipulate the words they are using. It's more difficult to do if you're not sure of the meaning of certain words. An additional source to strengthen your knowledge of words is the website, www.wordsmith.org, that will send you a daily email with a new word and its meaning and applications. There's no cost to subscribe and it could help you get some new words for your vocabulary.

Correct pronunciation and usage of words are absolutely necessary for the broadcast performer, but there are several other categories of words to which performers should be especially sensitive. Jargon and slang are similar types of words in that both encompass a "private" vocabulary that has made its way into common usage. **Jargon** usually refers to specialized language or words used by a specific profession, while **slang** can be thought of as informal street language or words used by a specific social group. However, it's often difficult to differentiate between the two. Jargon and slang may not be as grammatically correct as regular conversational speech, but they often provide colorful and very expressive ways of communicating. It seems strange to think that expressions like PC (personal computer), byte (binary digits processed by a computer), and spam (junk e-mail) were once only used within the computer industry. As computers became common household objects, much of the jargon was absorbed into mainstream speech.

The important point for performers to remember is that sometimes jargon or slang may only be understood by a small segment of the audience. It is up to the performer to make sure to clarify the meaning of words or expressions that may be unfamiliar to the general listener or viewer. In a similar manner, slang terms often have meaning to certain demographic or ethnic groups, but may not always be understood by the general population. Many groups have "in words" which are known primarily by members of the group. That's part of the fun of being in the group. Dr. Connie Eble of the University of North Carolina gathers college slang words and has a book, *Slang and Sociability: In-Group Language Among College Students*. In it, she lists contemporary terms that students have provided her. She reports such terms as *Geck*: (from Gecko) an annoying person; *Manky*: unappetizing or disgusting; and *Snorgle*: to cuddle. Many campuses may use some of the terms in the book and perhaps have some others as well.

Even the broadcast industry has many slang expressions—for example, the term *ear candy* refers to easy-listening music and the expression *flash and trash* is often used to describe local television news stories that feature sex, violence, and other sensational topics to boost **ratings**. Again, the broadcast performer needs to be aware that not all slang or jargon words or expressions will be understood by the entire audience. This doesn't mean you shouldn't use these expressions, but you may need to clarify their meaning for your audience.

Some expressions that started out as slang terms have been used so much and for so long that they've become clichés. A cliché is defined as an overused or worn out expression. It's likely you know many cliches, because they are so overused. For example, complete the following phrases:

dry as a _____
neat as a _____
quick as a _____
preaching to the _____
sharp as a _____

You should have been able to complete these easily with *bone*, *pin*, *wink*, *choir*, and *tack*. A broadcast announcer or performer doesn't need to completely avoid cliches because, on the positive side, they do convey a common idea with a minimum of words, but remember that they became cliches because they were used too often. Broadcasters should strive for

new ways to convey ideas and certainly avoid a steady use of cliched expressions.

A **redundant expression** is one that uses more words than necessary to convey an idea. In other words, redundancies are needlessly repetitive. This is one group of expressions that broadcast performers should try to avoid. Since time and clarity are important in broadcasting situations, performers should be economical with their words. The first step in avoiding redundant expressions is to listen for and recognize them in your speech. A *true fact* is a redundant expression because a fact is anything that is true. *Abundant wealth* is redundant because wealth means affluence, opulence, and abundance. *Visible to the eye* is redundant because visible refers to something that can be seen. Other redundant expressions you might have heard include *free gift*, *armed gunman*, *green in color*, *unexpected surprise*, and *filled to capacity*. This should give you an idea of redundancies so you can readily recognize others that you hear or may use in your speech. Consider the example in Figure 5.3.

The French phrase *mal a propos* means "badly to a purpose" or something inappropriate or inopportune. The Americanized *malapropism* refers to the misuse

FIGURE 5.3 A very redundant department.

of a word or expression by giving it a garbled or mixed up meaning, usually by using an incorrect word that sounds like the intended word. It's named for Mrs. Malaprop, a humorous character in the 1775 Restoration comedy, *The Rivals*, who frequently garbled her speech. In speaking of another character, Mrs. Malaprop said, "He is the very *pineapple* of politeness" when she obviously meant pinnacle. While they usually bring a chuckle to the listener, malapropisms should be avoided in broadcast delivery because they are speech blunders. Other examples include "UFO's are optical *conclusions* (illusions)" and "Her brother was a civil *serpent* (servant)." Baseball great Yogi Berra is one of the greatest malapropists of all time. His famous quips include, "A nickel ain't worth a dime anymore," "Always go to other people's funerals, otherwise they won't go to yours," and "Ninety percent of the game is half mental." Check Figure 5.4 for another example.

FIGURE 5.4 *A very colorful imagination, indeed.*

Another speech blunder is a **solecism**. This is a word or phrase that is not grammatically acceptable. The best example is the use of the word *ain't* as in "I ain't going to school today." Other solecisms include "between you and I" instead of "between you and me," and "they was" instead of "they were." Solecisms like these are unacceptable in 99 percent of broadcast performance situations. Announcers are expected to use grammatically correct speech.

A final speech mistake that plagues broadcast performers from time to time is the spoonerism. **Spoonerisms** occur when certain syllables of spoken words are transposed, resulting in other words that can produce a humorous result. The term "Spoonerism" comes from the name of Rev. William Spooner who lived in England in the second half of the nineteenth century. He switched syllables constantly, particularly when he was upset. He is supposed to have reprimanded a student by saying "You have tasted two worms," when he meant "You have wasted two terms." Spooner became so well known for this type of error that it was named for him. It usually happens unconsciously, and happens to many in broadcasting. Announcer Harry Van Zell once introduced U.S. President Herbert Hoover as Hoobert Heever and Lowell Thomas addressed British minister, Sir Stafford Cripps as Sir Stifford Crapps. Broadcasters often call these "bloopers." Broadcast archivist Kermit Schafer has published a series of blooper books that include a few spoonerisms among other broadcast gaffes. From his *Best of Bloopers*, Schafer notes that *Tonight Show* host Johnny Carson once introduced puppeteer Shari Lewis as a "girl who is one of the bust pepiteers in the business!" Schafer also captured a PGA announcer stating, "And now Johnny Tee is on the pot ... of course I mean John Pott is on the tee!" A befuddled newscaster once announced, "This is your eleven o'clock newscaster bringing you an on-the-pot report ... I mean on-the-spot retort . . . I mean on-the-tot resort ... oh well, let's just skip it!" Figure 5.5 offers another example.

5.6 LANGUAGE CHANGES

Broadcast performers need to be aware that the language they use changes on a regular basis. New words are added to various dictionaries each year, and that certainly marks the official acceptance of a word into everyday usage. *The Physics Factbook* reports that there are about 500,000 words in our language and another 500,000 scientific and technical terms beyond that.

FIGURE 5.5 Thank you, Rev. Spooner.

Further, some words are in usage for a while before they become "official," and sometimes older words take on new or additional meanings, but each era seems to bring a batch of new words and expressions into our common usage. For example, in the 1960s we acquired *area code, velcro, cassette, Jacuzzi,* and *microwave oven.* The 70s, brought us *hatchback, palimony, streaker, disk drive,* and *bar code. Karaoke, airhead, rust belt, yuppie, cineplex,* and *people meter* came from the 1980s. In the 1990s, we added *roller blade, snail mail, DVD, spam, phone tag,* and *Generation X.* Since the turn of the century, we've added *tree hugger, hottie, road rage, metrosexual, blogosphere, nanobot* and *subprime,* with more certain to come.

One of the main cultural forces that have changed our language over the past few years has been the concept of PC or **political correctness.** Announcers, more than ever, need to be sensitive to using language that may offend or exclude individuals or segments of the population. The male orientation of the English language certainly falls into this category. In the past, the word *mankind* was often used to indicate the entire human race, and *he* or *his* was employed even when referring to both sexes. Many nouns and verbs also had a male slant, such as *businessman,* although the work was just as often being done by a female.

Common sense tells us that such gender-specific references can frequently be eliminated with alternative expressions that are usually more accurate and more colorful. Instead of *mankind,* use *humanity,* and replace *businessman* with *executive.* If it's somewhat awkward to use "his or her," try to reconstruct the phrase, such as changing "Each listener should send in his or her request as soon as possible" to "Each listener's request should be sent in as soon as possible."

Revising your language to eliminate potentially offensive references is good performance practice, but don't carry it to an absurd level. "*Manhole* cover" probably doesn't need to become "*person hole* cover," and just because we have a *Jack O'Lantern* doesn't mean we must have a *Jill O'Lantern.* Again, common sense often dictates proper language usage.

Another area in which the announcer must be fairly sensitive is in how to refer to people. This includes ethnic terms and age references. The first rule for the broadcast performer is to be aware that in many instances someone's age or heritage is not relevant at all. Unless noting it will help the audience to understand the topic or story, it shouldn't even be included. There are no standard age classifications and in most instances, if mentioning age is important, you're better off giving an exact age and not using a category. However, there will be some circumstances when it might make sense to use a general age reference. Child or *boy* or *girl* is usually appropriate for those under twelve years of age, while *teenager, youth, adolescent,* or *juvenile* are terms for people during their teen years. Adult is reserved for someone over eighteen years of age, as is *man* or *woman,* and *young adult* for those between eighteen and twenty-one. The term middle-aged is used for those between forty and sixty-five and those over seventy are called *elderly* or *seniors.* Those over seventy-five years of age may be referred to as *old,* but many people of that age do not like the expression. While other terms like *kid* (under twelve) or *senior citizen* (above seventy) are also frequently used, they are just as frequently disliked by those being described. A good broadcast performer is sensitive to this and will use an age reference only if it is significant to the circumstance.

Someone's heritage is perhaps the most sensitive reference that an announcer may mention. Like age, ethnic background should be used only when it helps the understanding of a story. Indian has not been an appropriate term for the original citizens of North America for some time. Today, terms like *Native American* and *American Indian* are used, although the latter term isn't always acceptable. *Negro* or *colored person* has given way to *black* or *African-American*. Although there is a National Hockey League team called the Vancouver Canucks, to call an inhabitant of Canada a *Canuck* would be an insult. The term is a derogatory label for French Canadians; the more appropriate term is simply Canadian, even though some Canadians might not find Canuck to be offensive. In a similar fashion, *Polack* is not appropriate, but *Pole* or *Polish-American* can be used to describe someone of Polish heritage.

A broadcast performer should also be aware that some members of ethnic groups in the United States do not like being identified as "hyphenated Americans." In fact, many of the terms that we use to categorize people do not meet with universal approval. *Latin American, Hispanic, Latino,* or *Chicano* have all been used to describe people with Mexican, or Central or South American ancestry, but not all members of these ethnic groups agree with these designations. In addition to being sensitive to how socially acceptable a term might be, a performer is also expected to utilize the correct term. For example, someone from Scotland is not scotch, but rather a *Scot*—the former referring to a drink, not a person. *Oriental* is fine when referring to a rug, but is not appropriate when referring to a person. *Asian,* or a term based on the country of origin such as *Chinese* or *Japanese,* is preferred. Phrases like *Indian giver, Mexican standoff,* and *Chinese fire drill* are considered to be ill-mannered and offensive and should be avoided.

5.7 AVOIDING AMATEURISH ANNOUNCING AND INEPT DELIVERY

This and the previous chapter have sought to provide some insight into what it takes to become a professional announcer, but a quick review of what characterizes a poor delivery style should prove helpful before moving on.

Beginning announcers often hesitate slightly before reading or saying a difficult word. This merely calls attention to the fact that they are uncomfortable with the pronunciation of that word. The polished announcer is able to keep his or her word flow constant, whether a phrase contains difficult words or not. As discussed in Chapter 4, beginning announcers also often add needless vocalizations, such as "uh," "ya know," or "um" to their speech. These "verbal tics" detract from the message the announcer is trying to present and should be avoided in order to move beyond the amateurish level

of performance. Another earmark of the beginning announcer is a performance that includes mispronunciations or grammatical errors. The audience expects announcers to speak perfectly and they cannot mispronounce words.

A common error for beginners, and one that makes their inexperience really stand out, is letting their voice trail off on the last word or two of a sentence. The pattern, called a **throw away**, makes those words sound unimportant and sometimes unintelligible. Some students do it several times in each paragraph. Unfortunately, in both commercials and news, the last words may be very essential to the story, or may be vital to the punch line of the kicker. Sometimes the error sounds more like clipping the last syllable off the final word. The problem seems to arise from the focus on the next sentence and the premature loss of energy on the one currently being spoken, although it even happens with the last sentence to be read. Students find that this is not an easy habit to conquer, even though it seems simple. It occurs commonly enough that avoiding it should be a constant concern of the performer, even to the point of putting emphasis marks under the last words in the script to be certain they are not lost. Otherwise, your status as a beginner will be very evident.

A few beginning announcers have an inept delivery style because they have a poor reading ability. Sometimes poor eyesight is the problem and that's easily corrected, but often the problem is simply an inability to correctly read a script without stumbling, hesitating, or just misreading lines. Practice will help, and being aware that this is a problem will prompt the announcer to take extra care when reading a script. **Concentration** is a big factor. Professionals give reports in the midst of all sorts of distractions. At first you are conscious of everything around you, to the point that your attention to the script may wane. Work on mentally blocking out your environment and focusing totally on the copy. This, too, takes practice, but it's well worth the effort.

Beginning announcers often read or speak with indistinct speech—that is, they mumble or slur words and phrases. This is a problem of weak enunciation. Whether you ever go into broadcasting or not, this is a habit to which you should give serious attention. Anyone who attempts to lead, or give directions while mumbling, is destined to have problems and it could jeopardize any career. Slowing delivery and concentrating on completing every word is a way to start. It will yield an overly precise speech, but getting used to saying each word completely will get you on the right track. If the listener can't understand you, you have no chance.

Other illustrative problems of beginning announcers include an improper rate of speech (either too slow or excessively fast), misplaced emphasis (either pausing when they shouldn't or stressing words that shouldn't be stressed), and a "dead" delivery (one that lacks vitality or enthusiasm). If your announcing approach includes any of these characteristics, you must work to eliminate them now.

5.8 AUDIENCE RAPPORT

The reality of today's society is that a rising percentage of the population lives alone. As a result, the radio is often on to provide a form of companionship. That being the case, why does one broadcaster do so much better with the audience when the news being reported or the music being played is virtually identical to that which is heard on other stations? Why do listeners admire and even talk about some announcers in reverent tones? Why does the audience become very involved in any mishaps or successes in certain broadcasters' lives? It's called **rapport**, and although it's a very nonspecific concept, there are some clues about what is involved in this important connection with an audience.

In part it has to do with knowing your audience. What is attractive to one group may not be to another. One characteristic an announcer must have that applies in virtually every situation is to be **knowledgeable**. Whether it's country music or world affairs, your audience expects you to be up-to-date and know what you're talking about. Regardless of the subject, trying to fake it won't succeed very long, as someone out there will know more about the subject than you do, and will call in, write, or pass the word that you don't know what you're talking about. To build a connection with your audience, work at being current on your information, and admit it if you don't know something.

If your audience is younger, you will probably need to be seen as cool, hip, and aware of the latest trends. This will make you appealing and someone with whom they want to be associated. If your audience is older, they will generally expect you to be more sophisticated and interesting, and present a more mature image. Being community spirited will also add to your appeal. Supporting charity events, finding new homes for pets, and advocating for causes will make you more attractive. Being approachable—within

reason—signing autographs, and chatting with people in public will also add to your standing. The reality is that it only takes a few instances in which you make sarcastic remarks, brush people off, or are otherwise obnoxious to destroy how the public feels about you, so be particularly careful when you're tired or are having a bad day. To summarize, you need to come across as an interesting person that your audience would like to know better.

When discussing what it takes to be a successful broadcaster and to build audience rapport, there is no word more important than integrity. It means that you are trusted and what you say is believed. Even though, as a human, you occasionally make a mistake, everyone believes it really was a mistake because "Jim or Jane would never do that on purpose." When your integrity is well established, it serves as a shield to protect you when there are lapses. This protection can carry you through some bad times, as long as you don't call on it too often. However, integrity is a base, not the whole element in connecting with an audience. The audience also needs to see you as a friend. That comes through in the way you talk, the way you greet people, and the way you conduct yourself in public. Just as we talk about the announcer needing a pleasing voice, that same performer also needs a pleasing personality. You need to be interesting. These are internal characteristics that can't really be taught, but you should be aware that before an audience will build an emotional bond with a performer, they must find that performer personally appealing. If they don't, it will be hard for the performer to establish any rapport with the viewer or listener.

5.9 CONCLUSIONS

A broadcast performer needs to use the English language correctly, use words and expressions freshly and creatively, and be sensitive to potentially offensive phrases. An intimate, conversational style is preferred in most performance situations, and marking broadcast copy can help the announcer stress key words and concepts in the script. Very few of us are naturally polished performers, but almost all of us can improve our announcing style. None of this comes without some effort by the performer, and practice will be one of the keys to becoming a successful broadcast talent. The next few chapters take a look at specific performance situations and the techniques and procedures necessary to become a professional announcer in each area.

Self-Study

■ QUESTIONS

1. According to the copy marking system presented in this chapter, a squiggly line under a phrase would mean _____.
   a) to vocally stretch out the expression
   b) to raise the pitch of your voice as you read the expression
   c) to read the phrase faster than the rest of the copy
   d) to read the phrase slower than the rest of the copy

2. The expression "dry as a bone" is an example of a _____.
   a) slang expression
   b) redundant expression
   c) malapropism
   d) cliché

3. According to the copy marking system presented in this chapter, a two-headed arrow under a word means to _____.
   a) vocally stretch out the word
   b) raise the pitch of your voice as you say the word
   c) read the word more quickly than the rest of the copy
   d) read the word more slowly than the rest of the copy

4. The phrases "completely encircle" and "true fact" are examples of _____.
   a) spoonerisms
   b) redundant expressions
   c) cliches
   d) jargon expressions

5. To rip and read a script is good technique because it saves time, and time is an important element of most broadcast performances.
   a) true
   b) false

6. Which technique is a broadcast announcer least likely to employ when stressing a key phrase in commercial copy?
   a) slightly pause before and after the phrase
   b) increase voice volume when speaking the phrase
   c) lower voice volume when speaking the phrase
   d) speed up when reading the phrase

7. In normal punctuation, an ellipsis (…) is used to indicate that words are missing from a sentence or quote; however, in broadcast copy, the triple periods are often used to indicate _____.
   a) several words that are linked into one thought
   b) vocal directions to the announcer
   c) the end of a sentence so the announcer will lower inflection
   d) a pause, usually longer than the pause indicated by a comma

8. Which general age reference is not normally used to describe those under twelve years of age?
   a) juvenile
   b) child
   c) kid
   d) boy or girl

9. Which heritage reference could be used if it helped the understanding of a news story or script?
   a) Canuck—an inhabitant of Canada
   b) Polack—an inhabitant of Poland
   c) Chicano—someone of Mexican descent
   d) Scotch—an inhabitant of Scotland

10. The most sought-after delivery style in broadcasting is a sing-song tone because it is rhythmic and pleasing to listen to.
    a) true
    b) false

11. Which vocal element is described by the process of grouping words together to form an idea and then speaking that group smoothly when delivering broadcast copy?
    a) inflection
    b) phrasing
    c) energy
    d) loudness

12. As a broadcast performer, which characteristic would be least helpful in building audience rapport?
    a) being up-to-date/knowing what you're talking about
    b) building trust with your audience
    c) chatting with the public and signing autographs
    d) the ability to correctly read a script

13. For most broadcast performers, the ability to speak to thousands of listeners or viewers yet make it appear that you are talking one-to-one is fairly easy to accomplish.
    a) true
    b) false

14. Which of the following is not really a characteristic of an amateurish announcer?
    a) pausing before difficult words
    b) adding verbal tics to one's speech
    c) making a spoonerism
    d) slurring words or phrases

15. Bounce, whack, and bling-bling are all _____ expressions that an announcer may need to clarify for his or her audience.
    a) slang
    b) cliches
    c) redundancies
    d) jargon

■ ANSWERS

If You Answered A:

1a. No. The copy mark for stretching out a word or phrase is a two-headed arrow under the phrase. (Reread 5.4.)

2a. Wrong. Slang expressions are street expressions; usually the language of a specific social group. (Reread 5.5.)

3a. Yes. The copy mark for stretching out a word or phrase is a two-headed arrow under the phrase.

4a. Wrong. Spoonerisms occur when certain letters of spoken words are transposed, causing a humorous effect—in other words, your "tangue becomes tongled." (Reread 5.5.)

5a. No. To rip and read means to read the script on-air with no practice, copy marking, or prereading. It's a practice that should be avoided. (Reread 5.2.)

6a. No. Using pauses would be a good way to stress key words. (Reread 5.3.)

7a. Wrong. The hyphen (-) is used to link words into one thought, such as "end-of-month sale." (Reread 5.4.)

8a. Yes. Juvenile is usually used for someone in their teen years.

9a. Wrong. Canuck is an insulting term for many Canadians. (Reread 5.6.)

10a. No. A conversational tone is the most sought-after broadcast announcing style. A singsong style should be avoided. (Reread 5.1 and 5.2.)

11a. Wrong. Inflection refers to using pitch variations when delivering copy. (Reread 5.3.)

12a. No. Being up-to-date and knowing what you are talking about will help build a connection with your audience. (Reread 5.8.)

13a. Wrong. Because you lack direct feedback to what you're saying and because you're often reading someone else's script, being conversational in broadcast performance situations is not easy to accomplish. (Reread 5.1.)

14a. No. Beginning announcers often hesitate slightly before difficult words. (Reread 5.7.)

15a. Correct. These are all slang expressions commonly heard on college campuses.

If You Answered B:

1b. No. An upward rising arrow over the phrase would be the copy mark for an upward inflection. (Reread 5.4.)

2b. Wrong. A redundant expression uses more words than necessary to convey an idea. (Reread 5.5.)

3b. No. The copy mark for indicating that the announcer should raise the pitch of his or her voice while speaking a word is an upward rising arrow over the word. (Reread 5.4.)

4b. Correct. Redundant expressions are needlessly repetitive. For example, a fact is a true statement so you need to say only "fact."

5b. Yes. This is a false statement. While timing is usually critical in broadcast performance, rip and read should be avoided because it means reading a script without practice, copy marking, or prereading.

6b. No. Using volume is one of the most common ways to emphasize key words. (Reread 5.3.)

7b. Wrong. Parentheses ( ) are used to give the announcer vocal cues, such as (Read With Urgency.). (Reread 5.4.)

8b. No. Child is a correct term for someone under twelve years of age. (Reread 5.6.)

9b. Wrong. Polack is an insulting term for someone of Polish heritage. (Reread 5.6.)

10b. Yes. This statement is false because the most sought-after delivery style in broadcasting is a conversational tone and sing-song patterns should be avoided.

11b. Correct. The vocal element "phrasing" is accurately described.

12b. No. Being trusted will help build a connection with your audience. (Reread 5.8.)

13b. Correct. This is a false statement because being conversational in broadcast performance is not easy because you lack direct feedback to what you're saying, and you're reading a script written by someone else.

14b. No. Beginning announcers often add needless vocalizations, such as "ah" to their speech. (Reread 5.7.)

15b. No. A cliché is an overused or worn out expression. (Reread 5.5.)

If You Answered C:

1c. Yes. Use a squiggling line under a phrase that should be read faster than the rest of the script.

2c. Wrong. A malapropism is an expression with a mixed-up or garbled meaning. (Reread 5.5.)

3c. No. The copy mark for reading a word more quickly than the rest of the copy is a squiggling line under the word. (Reread 5.4.)

4c. Wrong. Cliches are worn out expressions, like "quick as a wink." (Reread 5.5.)

6c. Yes. Normally, you would raise your voice to stress key words.

7c. Wrong. The period (.) is used to indicate the end of a sentence and you would normally lower your vocal inflection to indicate this. (Reread 5.4.)

8c. No. Kid is a correct term for someone under twelve years of age, but often disliked by those being addressed with it. (Reread 5.6.)

9c. Correct. While there isn't universal agreement, Chicano has been used to describe people with Mexican ancestry.

11c. Wrong. Energy refers to using enthusiasm and vitality when delivering copy. (Reread 5.3.)

12c. No. Chatting with people in public and signing autographs will help build a connection with your audience. (Reread 5.8.)

14c. Yes. Spoonerisms occur when certain letters of spoken words are transposed causing a humorous effect. The broadcast bloopers can unconsciously happen to the most seasoned broadcast performer.

15c. No. A redundant expression is one that uses more words than necessary to convey an idea. (Reread 5.5.)

If You Answered D:

1d. No. A series of dots under the phrase would indicate that you should read the phrase more slowly than the rest of the copy. (Reread 5.4.)

2d. Correct. A cliché is an overused or worn out expression.

3d. No. A series of dots under the word would be the copy mark for reading the word more slowly than the rest of the copy. (Reread 5.4.)

4d. Wrong. Jargon refers to the private language of a profession, such as "byte" or "netiquette" coming from the computer industry. (Reread 5.5.)

6d. No. Using rate is a good way to stress key words. (Reread 5.3.)

7d. Correct. In broadcast copy, the ellipsis is often used to indicate a pause.

8d. No. Boy or girl is a correct term for someone under 12 years of age. (Reread 5.6.)

9d. Wrong. This is not even a correct term for an inhabitant of Scotland; it's a liquor. The correct term is "Scot." (Reread 5.6.)

11d. Wrong. Loudness refers to using volume changes when delivering copy. (Reread 5.3.)

12d. Yes. The ability to correctly read a script is important, but it is expected of all professional performers and won't necessarily build audience rapport.

14d. No. Beginning announcers often mumble or slur over words and phrases. (Reread 5.7.)

15d. No. You're close here, but jargon usually refers to a specialized language or words used by a specific profession. There is a better answer. (Reread 5.5.)

Projects

■ PROJECT 1

Copy mark and record a script.

Purpose
To give you an opportunity to mark a broadcast script to indicate how it should be read when recorded.

Notes
1. Use the copy marking system introduced in this chapter to complete this project.
2. You will be recording the script after it has been marked, so make sure you're familiar with the operation of the necessary equipment.

How to Do the Project
1. Look over the radio commercial script in Figure 5.6.
2. Photocopy or type the script onto a sheet of paper. Double-space if you type the script.
3. Determine how you would read this script and how you would mark the copy to indicate this.
4. Mark the copy in pencil, so you can readily make changes.
5. Read the script aloud a few times to be sure this is the way you want the copy read.
6. Re-mark the copy in ink. Make sure you put your name on the script.
7. Record the script, either in the studio or using a portable recorder.
8. Make sure you interpret the script as you've marked it.
9. Play back the tape. If you're not satisfied with the results, rerecord the spot until you get it exactly as you want it.
10. Turn in your marked script and the recording labeled "Copy Marking" to your instructor to receive credit for this project.

Like it or not, winter is on its way. Are you ready? Do you need broken windows replaced, insulation installed, or leaks and holes repaired? Then call the Robert Bolton Company. We're experts in the repairs you need. We're licensed, bonded, and insured, and we'll do the job right, and at prices you can afford. We'll even work evenings to fit your busy schedule. Let the Robert Bolton Company improve your home. Call the Robert Bolton Company at 683-221-4400. That's the Robert Bolton Company, 683-221-4400. You'll be glad you did. (91 words)

FIGURE 5.6 Radio commercial script.

■ PROJECT 2

Compile jargon, cliche, and redundant word lists.

Purpose
To build a base of words and expressions that should be avoided or used sparingly in broadcast performance situations.

Notes
1. You may not use any words or expressions used as examples in this chapter.
2. Your jargon list may include slang words or expressions.
3. It may prove helpful to speak with someone much older than yourself, such as a grandparent, to come up with cliché expressions.
4. The reference section of your school or local library can be a great resource, as can the Internet.

How to Do the Project
1. Review Section 5.5 of this chapter on Word Usage, especially the parts on jargon, cliches, and redundant words. For an upward inflection, raise the pitch of your voice. (Think "up HIGH.") For downward inflection, drop your pitch, as in "down LOW." For an upward and downward inflection, start at a low pitch and go to a higher one for the second word.
2. Using whatever resources you can, collect a list of jargon, cliches, and redundant words or expressions.
3. You must include a minimum of ten of each; however, additional credit will be given for longer lists.
4. For jargon and cliche words or expressions, include a brief description that explains what the word or expressions means.
5. For redundant expressions, provide a brief explanation of why the word or expression is redundant.
6. Type your lists in neat columns. Make sure you put your name on the project and add a heading labeled "Word Usage."
7. Turn in your paper to your instructor to receive credit for this project.

■ PROJECT 3

Practice pronunciation.

Purpose
To help you increase your working vocabulary and make sure that you are correctly pronouncing words that are often mispronounced.

Notes
1. Even though many people think they know how to pronounce commonly used words, they are frequently incorrect. Broadcast announcers are expected to not mispronounce words.
2. You will be recording words, so make sure you're familiar with the operation of the necessary equipment or check with your instructor or station engineer for assistance.
3. This project is a continuation of Project 3 at the end of Chapter 4, but utilizes a new word list.

How to Do the Project

1. For each of the words in the following list, research the correct pronunciation.
2. Provide a phonetic pronunciation guide for each word (as is often done with wire service copy), such as the following:

Word	Phonetic Guide
Almond	AH'-MUND

3. Now record each word, making sure to pronounce them correctly. Be sure to leave a pause lasting about two seconds between each word.
4. Put your name and "Word Pronunciation" as the heading of your paper. Label your recording in a similar fashion.
5. Turn in the finished paper and the cassette recording to your instructor to receive credit for completing this project.

Word List

accompanist	clique	err
bouquet	dais	forte
bulimia	disparate	gala
harass	mores	species
heinous	nuclear	statistic
irrevocable	often	status
juror	penalize	toward
library	preferable	vegetable
memorabilia	reprise	

■ PROJECT 4

Practice inflection (pitch variation).

Purpose
To develop an ability to interpret broadcast copy by using variations in pitch.

Notes

1. Pitch variation can be difficult to hear, and often it feels as if you are doing too much. However, practice should include exaggerated inflection as if you are reading a children's story. This will help tune your ear to pitch variations.
2. You will be recording these exercises on audio cassettes. If you are unsure about operating your portable recorder or studio equipment, check with your instructor or studio engineer.
3. The noted inflection should be given on the underlined word.

How to Do the Project

1. Practice reading the copy for this exercise out loud.
2. When you are comfortable with your ability to read the copy with the appropriate inflection, record the material.
3. Play the tape and listen to yourself critically.
4. Now rerecord the exercises and try to improve your vocal inflection, starting after your previous recording.
5. Label the recording with your name and "Inflection Exercise." Turn it in to your teacher to receive credit for this project.

Inflection Copy
(Upward inflection)

1. Will you finish now?
2. Do you think I care?
3. Should I send you an e-mail?
4. Would you finish this today?
5. Did you ever visit Paris?

(Downward inflection)

1. What will Professor Harris say?
2. Why is she so upset?
3. Why are you complaining?
4. Where would you send the students?
5. Who knows what he did?

(Upward and downward inflection)

1. Stop worrying.
2. Don't go.
3. Please come back.
4. Give me a call soon.
5. Stop trying to trick me.

Practice Material

■ ONE-LINERS (DELIVER WITH LOTS OF ENERGY)

1. This is Golden Oldies WVOL.
2. Solid Gold WVOL.
3. Stay tuned, we'll be right back after these messages.
4. It's 10 o'clock and time for Dandy Don Douglas.
5. At Manny's Carpet, we sell for less.
6. Now here's Fred with an interesting guest.
7. The weather-watch forecast, exclusively on the news station, WEAI.
8. Remember, if you see news happening, call 241-9959, the WEAI News Tip Line.
9. Wall Street's opening prices, every day on news radio WVOL.
10. At the top of your dial, golden WVOL.

■ MORE QUICKIES

1. You're watching *Around the World in Eighty Days.*
2. For the finest in fresh fruit and vegetables, come to the Franklin Market, 3130 West Madison Street.
3. The Amethyst Bank guarantees you the highest rates on your CD in the Greater Stillwater area.
4. For a really fine meal, come to the Wishing Well Restaurant, on Route 9, three miles north of town.
5. When you need tires, the Middleton Auto Center is the place to go.
6. Partly cloudy today with a high in the middle 70's and some rain clouds moving in about sunset.
7. Are you forgetting someone's birthday? Call the Flower Basket for speedy delivery of a lovely bouquet that will keep you out of trouble.
8. The hometown heroes did it all today, as the Blue Falcons topped Union University 41 to 17.
9. Slugger Barry Woods drove in five runs with two homers and a single as the Hawks downed the Bruins 6 to 3.
10. The annual Art in the Park festival will take place June 12th through 14th in its usual spot, Roswell Park, off West Mill Run.

CHAPTER SIX

COMMERCIAL ANNOUNCING

6.1 INTRODUCTION

The underlying purpose of radio, television, and cable programming is to draw an audience. Access to listeners and viewers is then sold to advertisers in the form of commercials. Broadcast and, to a degree, cable stations rely on the sale of commercials to generate enough revenue for the operation of the facility. Many different announcing situations will put the performer in the position of reading and recording commercials. A good performer in those commercials is likely to find a steady source of income, whether the announcer is a member of a station staff or a freelancer who picks up jobs as an individual. This chapter explores the various forms of commercials, ways of properly analyzing commercial copy, and delivering script lines in a professional manner. It's also your first opportunity to apply the skills you've gained in earlier chapters, such as controlling the rate of your words or marking copy, in a very practical situation. The ability to "sell" on the air is extremely important in your development as a broadcast performer.

6.2 SOURCES OF BROADCAST COMMERCIALS

The origin of a commercial will vary with market size and the advertiser. In larger markets, and particularly with large advertisers, the commercials are likely to be developed by advertising agencies that then deliver the finished copy or a completed recording to the station. In smaller markets, which are where most new announcers will get their start, the situation may not be so highly structured. In addition to the output from local agencies, your copy may be written by the salesperson who sold the account. Some salespeople become very adept at preparing potential commercials and use these drafts as a part of the sales pitch, particularly with clients who have done little advertising previously. Hearing an interesting approach can do much to convince a potential advertiser. In other situations, a station staff member, such as a continuity writer, may write copy. The station may have one or more "creatives" whose job it is to come up with a steady stream of new ideas and commercial copy. At the other extreme, some commercials are done live from fact sheets from which the on-air talent chooses the words that will be used on-the-spot. These commercials give the appearance of being testimonials and are preferred by some advertisers, particularly where the talent is very popular and respected.

6.3 COMMERCIAL FORMS: RADIO

Anyone who listens to the radio is aware of the wide range of forms that commercials can take, from a simple message read by an announcer to expensive, carefully produced mini-dramas that pack an amazing amount of material and action into a few seconds. Actual commercial content can extend from a simple statement of the qualities of a product or service to very subtle presentations in which the product is associated with implied benefits or fads. A good performer will be familiar with the most common formats a radio commercial can take and be aware that various formats are often mixed together.

Regardless of the source, the most basic commercial consists of copy presented with no music or other effects. Known as a **straight read commercial**, this type of **spot** relies on the skills of the announcer to bring the copy to life, as you can hear in Audio Clip 6.1. Since it's a basic production with no music or sound effects to enhance it, the straight sell spot is one of the most difficult to pull off successfully. **Performance elements** such as emphasis, pausing, inflection, and rate become critical in the straight read commercial. In addition, the announcer is often chosen for this type of spot based largely on the tone of his or her voice and the enthusiasm it conveys.

A variation of the straight read commercial is the **fact sheet commercial**. In this instance, the announcer has a listing of the basic information and product characteristics that should be included in the spot, but it includes little or no direction on how to create the commercial. Because there is no script or commercial copy, the announcer must ad-lib the spot, which is much more difficult than you might think. However, good ad-libbers make it seem so natural, it suggests that anyone can do it. Actually, selecting the appropriate words as you are talking and making them seem sincere takes practice and preparation. Of all the commercial forms, the straight read and fact sheet can be the most challenging because the announcer has only his or her voice to make the commercial come alive. We will cover more on ad-libbing in Section 6.10.

A **music bed** is a common element in many radio commercials and can be added to "punch up" a straight read commercial. In this case, music plays while the copy is presented, as you can hear in Audio Track 6.2. The music needs to be appropriate for the style or mood of the spot and should not be distracting or too loud. In small radio stations, the announcer is probably also adding the music bed, either in a recording session or live, so a critical element is the balance between voice and music. Experience suggests that, when in doubt, it is wise to hold the music a bit below what seems acceptable—most advertisers want to hear every word for which they are paying. A variation of the music bed is a sound effects bed that adds atmosphere to a commercial, such as pounding surf and seagulls to suggest a place on the ocean's shore.

The **donut commercial** is a combination of a recorded message, usually provided by an advertising agency, plus local live copy. The recorded message is often a jingle with singing at the beginning, music only or even silence in the middle, and more singing again at the end of the spot. In the middle of the spot, when the singing stops, the local announcer reads the appropriate information, perhaps the local source of the product, over the background music. This idea of local copy read over a "hole" in the jingle, with recorded material around it, gives it the name "donut." The performer must have a good feel for timing with this type of spot because the local information must fit exactly in the middle section.

The **live tag** is a variation of the donut in that all the recorded copy comes first, and then the announcer adds a bit of information that connects the message, usually to a local advertiser. Again the tag is most often the name and location of a local merchant selling the product mentioned. As before, the critical element is time—the announcer must effectively read the copy in the time provided. Timing is particularly important with the donut, since the last of the announcer's words must not overlap the start of the second segment, nor should there be silence from too rapid a reading.

The **spokesperson** commercial often employs some well-known sports or music figure, although anyone widely known may be used. For the radio announcer, opportunities to become spokespersons do exist and can provide pleasant additional income. Often the spokesperson is the owner or manager of the business doing the advertising. Some of these appearances are quite effective and others are not. For the announcer, the role may be an on-air introduction of the sponsor or providing help to record the spot without having the sponsor seem foolish. A cute variation of the spokesperson spot was a series of commercials done by using the five-year-old son of a local car dealer. This young man was quite a talker and, by extensive recording and editing, the station was able to create a humorous conversation between him and the station announcer. The salesperson who developed the idea found it quite effective and ultimately syndicated a series of "Tommy" commercials that were heard across the country.

Commercials that include multiple voices, music, sound effects, or even singers are known as **high production value** commercials. Perhaps the best example is the dramatization commercial, one of which you can hear on Audio Track 6.3. In these spots, announcers present the commercial message in a dialogue form while acting as characters in a "slice-of-life" situation. Music and sound effects usually embellish this type of commercial. An announcer may have a limited role in adding a tag or product information that can't easily be presented in dialogue. These mini dramas are some of the most elaborate spots on radio and play to the medium's ability to be a theater of the mind. (Listen to a variety of commercial styles from Lisa Brooks on Audio Clip 6.4).

6.4 COMMERCIAL FORMS: TELEVISION AND CABLE

Many of the commercial forms utilized for radio are also used for television, often with minor variations and, once again, the astute performer will be cognizant of the basic television commercial formats. One of the key developments for the television commercial announcer has been the rapid rise of cable advertising. Lower cable rates have enabled small advertisers to get into the television medium on a regular basis. Many of the ads are relatively simple, such as interviews with the owner or customers of a business, views of the establishment, and occasionally some halfhearted attempts at comedy.

For the television announcer, the **voice-over** has the greatest potential for additional income. In a voice-over commercial, the sales message is given by an off-screen announcer while video of the product is seen on the screen. Video Clip 6.1 is an example of a typical television voice-over. The challenge here is to fit the copy into the space that has been provided and to adapt the presentation to the mood of the spot. Voice-over work is a big part of commercial performance and will be discussed further, later in this chapter.

In television, as in radio, the spokesperson format is very popular. A readily recognized person is paid to speak about a particular product. At the local level, these can be very simple, but they can also be extensively produced at the national level. Some years ago, Lee Iacocca, who was then head of Chrysler Corporation, became quite famous when he stepped in as the company spokesman in a series of commercials in which he pledged that his cars would be outstanding. The company sold many automobiles and at least part of the credit goes to the spokesperson spots aired during that period.

A variation on the spokesperson spot is the **testimonial commercial**. In a testimonial, the person speaking on behalf of the product is actually endorsing the product based on his or her use of the product, such as when LeBron James of the Cleveland Cavaliers appears in Nike commercials. These commercials often use local sports figures or others who are hired to endorse the product. The general concept is that if this product is good enough for this famous person, then it must be good enough for the average person.

In many cases, these individuals have little on-camera experience, so an announcer may be added to the commercial to introduce or stabilize the situation.

This is by no means a complete list of all commercial styles, and many television commercials will contain elements of several approaches. Regardless of the actual commercial format, let's consider how the announcer approaches commercial copy and prepares for a professional delivery.

6.5 CONSIDERING THE BASIC STRUCTURE OF THE COMMERCIAL

If you divide a broadcast commercial into beginning, middle, and end segments, you'll see that, in general, it follows a basic motivational structure that includes four stages: getting attention, creating a need, satisfying that need, and urging action. Consider a simple radio commercial like the one in Figure 6.1. The beginning of the spot is designed to capture attention or hook the listener. One of the most common attention-getting devices is to ask a question, as this spot does ("Does your lawn look like a dandelion patch?"). You could also make an unusual statement ("The typical lawn is home to over 738 dandelions!") or perhaps use a sound effect (Boing! Boing! "Ahh, more dandelions popping up in your front lawn.") to accomplish the same task. In the middle of most commercials, you create a need ("a lush, green, weed-free lawn") and then satisfy the need ("Sunny-Grow").

Many commercials follow this problem-solution format. Notice how the product is conveniently the perfect solution for the problem. The middle of the commercial is also where you find out more about the product. In our example, this is information like "a special seed

---

CLIENT: Sunny Grow

LENGTH: 30 seconds

(GETTING ATTENTION) Does your lawn look like a dandelion patch? (CREATING NEED) Almost everyone wants a lush, green, weed-free lawn, but no one likes the work it takes to have one. (SATISFYING NEED) That's why you need Sunny-Grow—the lawn mixture that does two jobs at once. Sunny-Grow feeds your lawn with a special seed and fertilizer blend at the same time its killing those pesky dandelions. You simply spray Sunny-Grow on your lawn using your garden hose and the Sunny-Grow self-dispensing bottle. There's no hard work at all . . . and you'll soon have a beautiful lawn! (DEMANDING ACTION) Get easy-to-use Sunny-Grow today at your favorite home supply store.

FIGURE 6.1 *Basic commercial structure.*

and fertilizer blend" or "simply spray Sunny-Grow on your lawn." Finally, the spot ends with a call for action or what is known as the stinger ("Get easy-to-use Sunny-Grow today."). The end of a commercial often includes the sponsor's name and location or the advertiser's slogan. Not every commercial will so conveniently break down into these elements, but a good initial step in analyzing a commercial is to see if you can recognize the motivational elements it does contain.

6.6 OTHER FACTORS TO CONSIDER WHEN ANALYZING A COMMERCIAL

When analyzing a commercial, start by determining just what the commercial is seeking to accomplish; in other words, decide what the **goal** of the spot is. Selling a product is not the only possibility. Obviously, many companies are selling a product or service, but sometimes the advertiser is interested in image. Banks, insurance agencies, and health maintenance organizations often will have the goal of creating a positive image of the organization and its employees in the mind of the consumer. Such commercials often speak of the strength of the companies, the speedy service when you are in need, and the knowledgeable, caring people that make up their staffs. The announcer needs to take the time to get a clear idea of what the people who created the copy were trying to accomplish. Once you have ascertained the goal of the spot, you're ready to proceed.

Next, determine the **mood** of the spot. Get your preparation underway with two or three silent readings of the script just to get the feel of the message. Is it serious, humorous, friendly, or informal? It's your job to be sure that the audience understands "where you are coming from." You must decide what tone of voice is appropriate. If it's a serious matter, your vocal tone should reflect that mood. You will need to articulate clearly and perhaps be just a shade understated. Too much energy can come across as a parody. Notice if the mood changes at any point in the spot. Often commercials have a somewhat serious tone at the beginning, when the problem is presented, and change to a lighter tone when the solution is offered.

Sincerity becomes critical in this situation. It may be necessary to have a fairly high word rate if that's what the writers have given you, but you must not lose sight of the mood of the piece. Energy is important in commercials because you are seeking to attract and hold attention, but tone and energy also are key factors in setting the mood. Take time to think about how the spot should sound.

If the mood of the spot is humorous, take extra caution in developing your delivery style. Too often beginners feel that the way to do a commercial is to include humor. However, comedic commercials can be dangerous, as it's easy to overdo the humor. What you think is funny may not seem so to the audience or the sponsor. Humor can be great if you have the talent to truly make a commercial funny. A few on-air people over the years have even gotten away with making fun of a product, but there haven't been many and they were well established before they tried it. Remember, you're kidding about the company or product that is actually paying your salary, and a line that's over the top could put you on the street. Usually when there is potential for humor, there is also potential for disaster and any commercial, even something that is funny the first time, will become boring after it has been heard over and over, as most commercials usually are.

Next, consider what the **message** is or what the advertiser is trying to get across. What action is the advertiser seeking? What is the specific idea? What actions are the listeners being encouraged to take? Many commercials seek to drive home the "act now" aspect. Listeners are more likely to buy if they are urged to do it now. This is the reason for lines like "sale ends Friday," which often show up in the stinger of the spot, so you need to deliver it with the correct style. If there is a telephone number to call, it should get careful attention and not get lost in other aspects of the copy.

Consider, too, for whom the message is intended. The style of the delivery will be influenced by the **intended audience**. The tone, rate, and inflection would be different for a commercial aimed at teenagers than for one aimed at people considering a retirement home. When you are outside the station, it's valuable to listen to conversations whenever you are in a public place. The intent here is not to eavesdrop, but to get a better sense of how people speak to each other. The better you understand that, the better you will be at speaking to them in a commercial. In addition, it could help you in dramatized commercials where the appropriate delivery could land you an extra job.

After initially becoming familiar with the copy, it's time to consider how to deliver it. Start by identifying the key words. Most audiences do not sit and concentrate on the radio message because they are doing other things while listening. Therefore, the key words are the ones you want them to hear. Review the section in the previous chapter on using inflection, duration, volume, and especially pauses to stress key words. Singer Frank Sinatra was famous for his phrasing. He used the need

"*If I don't feel it, if it's not real, then it's not going to sound real when it comes out of my mouth. Even if you're selling soap—so and so's soap is the best—you have to believe that is the best soap that you're selling or it's not going to come across.*"

FIGURE 6.2 Lisa Brooks, on-air host, newscaster, and commercial talent, KOMO, Seattle, WA.

to get an occasional breath to his advantage by effectively pausing at key points in the song to let the message sink in. He's said to have learned this technique from watching horn players in the band sneak a breath in the middle of an instrumental passage. A good commercial announcer can use this type of technique, too.

Emphasis, or stressing key words, is one of the most important aspects of your commercial delivery, for it has considerable impact and can greatly influence the meaning of the message. Consider the short, simple sentence, "Jack bought a new car." If we emphasize the first word, "JACK bought a new car," we suggest that we're stunned it was Jack. Perhaps we expected his sister Jill would be the one to go for the new car because Jack is a person who doesn't like to spend money. Putting the emphasis on the next word, "Jack BOUGHT a new car," we could be expressing surprise because Jack repeatedly said he would only lease one. Moving the emphasis further, "Jack bought a NEW car," we're apparently astonished because he always preferred used vehicles. Finally, putting the emphasis on the last word, "Jack bought a new CAR," implies that we had been expecting Jack to buy another type of transportation, maybe a motorcycle or minivan. When reading commercial copy, be sure to select the emphasis point carefully to ensure that the proper message is delivered to your audience.

PERFORMANCE TIP 6.1

Breathing, from Lisa Brooks

Like singing, good commercial delivery starts first with the breath. It is important to connect with your breathing when you read aloud. Shallow breaths from primarily the throat and head do not flesh out your sound as much as breathing from your diaphragm. A good vocal coach from the choir might be a good way to go for specific tips. Breathing in deep, regular steady breaths helps to relax you. It is very tough to approach a microphone when you are nervous.

6.7 IMPORTANCE OF TIMING

An announcer's ability to consistently read advertising copy within the allotted time is obviously one of the keys to success. Regularly being long or short is an invitation to look for another job. Further, good timing can make you stand out at an audition, as it suggests you are a professional performer. Good timing is a skill that can be developed. A professional will have several delivery rates that can be called on in different

situations. A stopwatch and a collection of scripts from old commercials can help you start developing a sense of timing. Most commercial copy will include time indications. If it's a straight read commercial, the time will probably be 30 seconds or occasionally 60 seconds. Get familiar with the copy, decide where pauses and emphasis go, and then start the watch and give it a reading. Examine the results and consider how you can adjust. Are there some pauses that could be extended a fraction of a second? Can you increase the overall tempo slightly to save time? A point to keep in mind is that we tend to read faster when reading silently, so do your timing while reading the copy aloud.

Don't just read words, but consider your sound. Listen to the tempo of the words. An experienced driver can tell if the car is doing 35, 55, or 65 mph, just by its sound. How many words did you read in 30 seconds? Stay with this piece of copy until you can consistently hit the allotted time. Then switch to a different radio script and repeat the process. When you have that one down, go back to the first copy and see if the rhythm is still there. Now look for another piece of copy that is quite different in style, mood, or intended audience and get that one in shape. Keep at it until you can consistently get very close to the time no matter what copy you use. With that skill, it will be easy to adjust a little for each new piece of copy you are asked to read. Don't select scripts that all have roughly the same number of words. Effectively reading copy with a lesser word load is a challenge, too. It isn't just a matter of slowing down. Your use of performance elements becomes particularly important to give the message vitality.

Realistically, some commercials have many words jammed in, and it will be your job to fit them into the time available in a clear and interesting way. Some commercial scripts may indicate the number of words in them. Become familiar with the number of words you read easily in 30 seconds so that you will have a reference point. With that base in mind, you will know whether to speed up your delivery and the approximate amount. Preparing for this situation, it's wise to look for word-heavy copy or set out to do one of your standard pieces in 25 rather than 30 seconds. Don't just speed up—set a time/word goal and work toward it. Vary the copy in terms of mood and intended audience. It isn't likely that you will have many commercials where you will have to stretch the copy, but some practice delivering lines more slowly will help your versatility.

Practice is the primary way of getting rate of delivery under control. In addition, the elements of clarity, emphasis, and pauses are also important because they help listener understanding. First, really get to know the copy. It's hard to read an unfamiliar script well, even if it's not very fast. Asking your brain to process unfamiliar copy, and get the words out rapidly and effectively, is approaching overload. Read at a comfortable rate for as many times as it takes to know the phrase or word that's coming next. Then, work on

"I'm lucky, I've pretty much got a 30-second and a 60-second clock ingrained in my head at this point, so if you give me a piece of copy I can tell you, this is 42 seconds and you want me to do it in 30 seconds. You just have to adjust. Sometimes you can't adjust and you have to edit words. That becomes a relationship between the producer and the performer"

FIGURE 6.3 *Another comment from Lisa Brooks, Komo, Seattle, WA.*

speeding up. Here's the challenge: As you go faster, clarity and inflection must be maintained. With a heavy word-load, it will be easy to slide toward a monotone. After you've made some progress, try timing yourself. It may be a little discouraging, but keep at it. Work at maintaining the performance elements, and don't let your concentration sag as you read the words for the 15th time.

As mentioned, reading copy with a lesser word load is not just a matter of slowing down. Now your inflection, phrasing, and pausing become even more important. Pauses can be a bit longer and additional ones can be slipped in after key words. Inflection can be increased a little to emphasize the significance of the subject. Try drawing out the last syllable of some words. But, you can't just deliver a series of words with a pause after each one. The flow and the meaning must still be maintained, even though the pace is reduced. Again, practice with a watch, and concentrate on communicating and sounding interested. Even if you never do a commercial in your life, the skill of timed delivery, with proper mood, emphasis, and inflection, will be a benefit in many fields.

Probably the only exception to these guidelines is the "disclaimer" statement. These can be heard at the end of an ad that carried some enticing offers. The disclaimer is there to keep the spot legal by noting that there are certain restrictions and limitations. In rare cases, you'll be asked to read this extremely fast and forget about the vocal techniques. A monotone is fine, because, to be realistic about it, the intent is to get the audience to "turn off" and not hear the more restrictive rules. More likely, you'll be asked to read at a normal rate without many vocal techniques, and then your voice will be electronically processed to speed up the delivery without changing the pitch.

PERFORMANCE TIP 6.2

Preparation, from Lisa Brooks

I would recommend taking a script, reading it, and underlining the words you need to emphasize. Words such as the client's name. Adjectives that describe the product are frequently emphasized. Pausing is frequently a personal inter-pretation. Look for commas, colons, semi-colons—things the client has put into the copy to give you a clue. If there's an ellipse: ... , I give that a hesitation rather than a short pause.

6.8 ENERGY: HARD SELL VERSUS SOFT SELL

Very few commercials are made in which the talent sounds about half awake. Even with what is known as a soft sell approach, a certain degree of energy is required. One of the accepted elements in selling is that you need to catch and hold the attention of the potential buyer. This means that you will need to sound alive and enthused. It doesn't mean that you should constantly sound like the stereotypical used car salesman, but extra effort is usually expected. It's interesting to note that for some beginning announcers, a little extra energy can feel like a great deal. In many situations, you may be used to underplaying just a little, perhaps to seem cool, so the soft sell style may come naturally to you. For others, you may be too loud or expressive and have to learn to rein yourself in. It's best to get a second opinion, so ask a friend to evaluate your delivery.

Hard sell and soft sell delivery styles are opposites. The hard sell commercial has a feeling of tension and excitement. The announcer seems to be almost shout-ing, but isn't actually. However, hard sell announcers do speak at a higher volume and at a faster rate than soft sell announcers. The soft sell commercial con-veys a feeling of relaxation and the announcer seems to speak in much more conversational tones. Which approach you use may be the choice of the advertiser and certainly will be influenced by the mood of the commercial and the word count. Audio Track 6.5 con-trasts the soft sell and hard sell delivery styles.

So how do you lift up your energy level? Waving your arms or running in place can get you warmed up, at least for a few minutes. While actually reading the commercial, work standing up, if at all possible. Don't be afraid to gesture and get yourself into it. Here again, judgment is called for. If you're working with a producer, he or she can help you find the right energy level. A professional announcer will have a variety of levels that can be tapped at the push of a mental button.

When you try a level, listen to the producer's com-ments. If it was too much or too little, file away how that delivery felt for use at another time, when more or less is needed. Once your delivery receives the produc-er's approval, one of your goals should be to be able to go back to that approved level again without additional coaching. You should be able to recapture that level not only in the next take, but the next day if necessary.

6.9 GESTURES AND FACIAL EXPRESSIONS

Two of the most important aspects of selling products during television commercials are how you show prod-ucts and how you react to those products. Your gestures will be subtle movements to stress a copy point, denote the product, or actually handle the product. The most important point is to never "mask" the product label with your fingers or hands. This will take practice, especially if you have to do more than hold the prod-uct, such as pouring a drink or opening a package. The product label must also always be pointed toward the camera lens. This can be a problem if you must pick up the product and then set it back down again, especially if you are somewhat behind the product and can't see the label. A trick some performers use is to mark the product directly opposite the center of the label so they can easily orient the product whether from the front or back. We've previously mentioned that most items should be tilted slightly forward to prevent glare from the studio lights into the camera lens. When holding a product, keep your arms close to your body and keep the product itself close to you. This will accomplish two important goals: first, it will help keep the prod-uct steady so that close-up shots won't find the product shaking, and second, it will convey a positive feeling toward the product in the viewer's mind. In other words, if you didn't like the product, you might put some distance between yourself and it. Video Clip 6.2 shows a performer handling, correctly and incorrectly,

FIGURE 6.4 Don't hide the sponsor's name!

a generic product package. Also note Figure 6.4 for another reminder.

Three key gestures are commonly used to call attention to a product: the **caress**, the **cradle**, and the **hug**. To caress a product is to simply glide the fingertips of one hand gently along the side of the product, as shown in Video Clip 6.3. This is usually done just as the line of copy mentions the product name. Holding a product in the palm of your hand, as in Video Clip 6.4, is known as the cradle. A larger product may actually require you to cradle it with your arms, but the concept is that you are holding the product with the same affection that you would have for a tiny kitten. To hug a product is not like a face-to-face hug, but rather an arm-around-the-shoulder gesture, as shown in Video Clip 6.5. Large cards with product information or even mannequins displaying a product can be handled in this manner. Remember, the key is to be natural and lifelike, not artificial and stiff.

As a television commercial announcer, your eyes are extremely important. The viewer will follow your eyes and look where you look. That's good when you want them to look at the product, because you merely have to

do so and they will, too. However, it can be bad because viewers will notice a performer who seems disinterested in a product or who must stare at a TelePrompTer to remember the script. You'll often use a whole range of facial expressions, such as a smile, a wink, or an arched eyebrow, when dealing with a product. If it's a product that you taste (a soup, a soda, or something similar), you'll use your skills to anticipate and then actualize the product. Good performers can admire the product as they anticipate how good it is going to be and then, after actually tasting it, express, nonverbally, that it was better than even they thought it would be. Video Clip 6.6 shows an example of this admiration of a product. It helps to sell a product and it's what good commercial performers get handsomely rewarded to do. This anticipate-actualize technique may be used for other products, but it always works well with food products.

6.10 AD-LIB COMMERCIALS

Many sponsors like to have the talent do ad-lib spots. This is a situation where you are handed a fact sheet and expected to come up with an interesting, attractive presentation. As an on-air performer, you will probably find it easier to do if you use the product or service before you talk about it. At the very least, an announcer should get as familiar as possible with the subject of the commercial. You'll have that fact sheet, but your own reactions may seem more genuine and this is what everyone is after.

Ad-lib does not mean unprepared. In many cases, the first thing you will want to do is plan a scenario or thread. You might also call it a skeleton. It is the structure on which you will hang your presentation. If your commercial was for some sort of easy-to-prepare meal, the scenario might be built around the fact that as a college student living in an apartment, you don't have much time or experience preparing meals. If it was a coffee or some breakfast drink, you might talk about the problems of getting up and getting to work or class and how this product speeds you on your way. Making it personal makes it seem more genuine.

In the process of developing your thread, refer to your fact sheet and decide what sequence of points works best with the story you're telling and how you're going to get started. Then decide how you'll get to the second point and the third. It probably won't be possible to cover all the elements provided on the fact sheet. If you use too many, it won't sound genuine. Also, don't let yourself fall into the pattern of just reading the statements off the fact sheet. It's best to look back to the microphone after seeing what comes next. You may want to rewrite the points in your own words and in the sequence you want to use. Remember, you're talking to your audience, not reading copy. Plan what you would add if there is time and what you would cut if you're running long. The last thing to plan is your exit. How are you going to get out of this bit gracefully? It should have a conclusion, perhaps a punch line, but almost certainly should return to the product or service you're promoting, probably with the name of the source or sponsor.

Another approach would be to consider what qualities of the product are meaningful to you. How would you describe them? What few key words will get the idea across in an interesting way? The announcer must create a word picture, emphasizing the significant qualities or benefits. Try to relate your comments to your reactions, or those you expect the audience to have. Remember that ad-libbing commercials is not an exercise in exaggeration. You are supposed to be sincere and believable. A good practice drill for an ad-lib commercial is to pick up a product and talk about it for 30 seconds. Don't always select something that you are very familiar with. Could you persuade yourself to buy it?

6.11 ACTING

Announcers who do commercials are called upon to actually be actors and actresses as well. There is a clear degree of acting involved in being excited over a product, but often the demands can go well beyond that. Particularly in the smaller markets, the announcer may be called upon to be a variety of serious and comical characters, sometimes of various ages. For these different roles, the ability to do voices is both a talent and a developed skill. The rise in computer animation makes it likely that there will be an increase in its use in commercials as well. Animation technology is getting cheaper and simpler to operate, so that its use in smaller television markets is probable. All these animated characters are going to need human voices to make them come alive, and the professional announcer can fill that need.

If you are doing radio or voice-overs, your age or what you look like has little bearing on your work. However, for television commercials you have to give who you are some consideration. A 20-year-old is not likely to be cast as an old man unless the commercial is a spoof of some sort. However, many commercials do not want to use individuals with movie star looks; they want the actors to appear as real as possible. That

means that the tall, short, and overweight have a good chance of being chosen, as there are more people who look like that than there are those who look like Leonardo DiCaprio or Anne Hathaway.

While an entire course in acting can't be covered in a few paragraphs in a book, there are a number of ideas that can help you get started. Even the rawest beginners have more resources than they realize. We all have known many people, all with their own peculiarities and experiences. In the commercial, time is very tight, and therefore the qualities of each character must become clear very quickly. We tend to have stereotypes about what various people look like and how they act. We feel we know what a truck driver, a police officer, a doctor, and a professor probably look like. This is often unfair and inaccurate but, nonetheless, it plays a big part in who gets cast for a part in a commercial.

Study the characters to learn about them. Each word in the copy has been chosen to help the audience understand who the characters are and what to expect of them. Have you known someone who sounds a bit like this character? How did that person talk, move, or react to situations? Your job will be to help the audience quickly understand who you are. If you will be playing a character who doesn't seem to have any special qualities, one technique is to make up a personal history for him or her. Where did she grow up and go to school? Is he married, with kids? What does she like and dislike? These bits of information will help you get a bearing on how to present the character.

Clearly, the sound of your voice will be one of the key elements of your portrayal. How would this person sound? Does she speak rapidly or slowly? Does he speak clearly and precisely or does he slur his words a little? What gestures would be typical? Acting is behaving naturally in a make-believe situation. Therefore, the more you observe how others conduct themselves, the more you will have to draw on when playing a character. You will need to appear involved in whatever scene you are in. Look at and listen to your acting partner. Try to pace your responses so the characters sound the way they would in a conversation. Let your body movement be a part of the response. If you are serious about doing commercials, spend time watching actors on television. As usual, they make it look easy, but it isn't. There are skills you can learn. Consider getting involved in theater work for more experience. Be alert for notices of audition opportunities. Although you may not be selected, auditioning is another way to get experience and learn from what others are doing.

PERFORMANCE TIP 6.3

Talent Selection

Talent selection really starts with understanding what I am looking for, and that's usually based on the script that I'm working with or the show I'm trying to produce. I need to find a talent that fits that design, the role that has been created by the writer. For a TV game show for kids around eighth grade, we needed someone who could communicate with those kids. We wanted a personality that was quick, humorous and could grab attention, yet mature enough and savvy enough to handle the situation. Someone able to speak on their terms and make them feel comfortable. Someone probably between 20 and 30, with a young appearance. We first had a general briefing for everyone and then, for auditions, set up two tables with our interns playing the eighth graders. We gave the candidates the opening lines, and then they had to ad-lib the contest for about five minutes. The choice happened to be the first guy we auditioned. He really understood what we wanted.

For a young person, my advice would be first, know yourself. If you're inexperienced, start looking for roles that fit who you are. Don't try to go outside the boundaries of yourself. Working in theater is an excellent way to grow. There are plenty of community theater opportunities.

Dennis Knowles holds a bachelor's degree in journalism and advertising and a master's degree in film production from Ohio University. He worked eight years in advertising before going back for his second degree. He is a producer at WVIZ-TV and is involved in independent film production. He has won numerous awards including three Emmys.

6.12 COMMERCIAL VOICE-OVERS

For many performers, voice-over work is a specialization that is very attractive. The opportunities are primarily in television, film, and Internet, they mean that your voice does the work, but you never appear on camera. This eliminates the common concern that, by becoming too associated with a particular product or service, you eliminate any opportunity for other jobs over a long period of time. Dell Computer did a lengthy series of "Steven" commercials, which many

Lisa Brooks is a successful commercial and voiceover artist. She shares the following information:

Frequently you are asked to do auditions for commercials, either through your agent, if you have one, or as an independent contractor. You will be expected to submit mp.3 files. Often the client will email you the copy, so you must be proficient in recording your own voice-over auditions on your home computer or in a studio, and must know how to convert them to mp.3 and email them to the client. Often you have less than a day to get it done.

At the beginning of the audition, it is important to "slate." You say your name and your agent, if you have one. It might be "Hi, I'm Lisa Brooks with The Actors' Group. Then begin your audition. When you finish, just say "Thank you." It is important to give your best read in that audition. No false starts or laughing, just do the job like you had already been hired.

More and more voice-over actors are setting up studios in their home rather than go to a commercial studio to record. Even those at the very top level are doing it.

"Wild tracks" is a term used by producers who don't necessarily have a script or are not sure where the commercial will go. They say "Give me a few wilds of the line ...Taste's Great." You give them four or five different versions and let them choose. Some commercials are built completely from "wild lines" where a producer or director picks and chooses from many options from many actors to build a single commercial.

Sometimes an actor is asked to improvise. The producer might tell you, "You are at a party and meet someone for the first time. You have two words, What do you say to them?" What would you say, "Hi there", "What's up". "Nice party", "Great tie"?

FIGURE 6.5 Thoughts from a pro.

felt limited the young actor's opportunities in other situations. Voice-overs are found in television commercials, news, public service announcements, and documentaries. In addition, there are lip-sync jobs, substituting your voice for an actor who looks right for the role, but just doesn't sound right. The project can range from a few seconds within a commercial or PSA to an assignment in a two-hour documentary.

Many voice-over specialists work at developing a variety of sounds to broaden their appeal. Creating a range of voices can be helpful to you too. Essentially, a television commercial voice-over is done like a radio commercial, with the same range of energy and the same sort of time demands. However, you might have only a sentence or two, as you may be providing information on the product or noting that limitations apply to the offer. Mark your copy carefully and don't be afraid to ask for more information on some point or on how the producer wants the copy delivered. Pay particular attention to your energy levels and style, as you will be expected to retain these through what could be multiple takes. Listen to Audio Clip 6.6 to hear a portion of

a performer's audition CD. You'll find a more detailed look at voice-over work in Chapter 11.

6.13 PUBLIC SERVICE AND PROMOTIONAL ANNOUNCEMENTS

A **public service announcement** (PSA) is a spot run by a broadcast or cable station that promotes nonprofit organizations or government agencies. For example, you've probably heard or seen spots for the United Way, the Red Cross, or the U.S. Department of Transportation. Audio Track 6.7 lets you hear a radio public service announcement. These spots usually try to raise funds for the organization's cause, or promote safety and other social benefits if the audience follows the message of the announcement. Broadcasters cannot charge for PSAs, but they air them to help fulfill their license obligation of "serving the public interest" and to promote goodwill within their specific markets. Since they take up time when commercial announcements could air, you're more likely to hear PSAs during times for which the station hasn't sold a lot of commercials. National PSA campaigns, using most of the same formats as commercials, are often produced by major advertising agencies and feature celebrity announcers who donate their efforts to the nonprofit organization. The delivery style for an announcer, whether national or local, is usually fairly straightforward and leans toward a soft sell approach.

A **promotional announcement**, or **promo**, is a spot run by an individual station or network to promote itself. Promos usually highlight upcoming shows, special programming, or key personalities of a station, but also are used to convey the general image of a broadcast station. Listen to Audio Track 6.8 to hear an example of one type of station promo. The basic style of a promo is much the same as a commercial. Promos range from the basic straight voice announcer, such as a television voiceover promoting the next program that is run over the credits of a show that's ending, to a high-production-value spot. Broadcast announcers capable of handling radio and television commercials will find that they are called upon to be the talent for public service and promotional spots, as well.

6.14 CONCLUSIONS

The perceptive announcer recognizes that commercials support the American system of broadcasting. As a broadcast performer, the ability to deliver a commercial message is a skill that will serve you well. There are many types of commercial formats for radio, television, and cable, and they all require talent to effectively deliver their message. While most broadcast commercials are structured to follow a basic motivational sequence, it is the announcer's skill in analyzing the copy and then interpreting the script that truly makes the commercial sell to the audience. Commercial announcers utilize all the basic performance skills, but especially the ability to understand and convey the mood of a commercial, the ability to read the script in the allotted time, and the ability to become an actor for the length of the commercial spot.

Self-Study

■ QUESTIONS

1. The spokesperson commercial is the same as a testimonial commercial.
   a) true
   b) false
2. Which commercial format is more closely associated with television than with radio?
   a) straight read
   b) voice-over
   c) donut
   d) dramatization
3. Which commercial format is more closely associated with radio than with television?
   a) testimonial
   b) dramatization
   c) voice-over
   d) ad-lib
4. Which of the following is not a common method to capture audience attention at the beginning of a commercial?
   a) ask a question
   b) make an unusual statement
   c) give sponsor name and location
   d) use a sound effect
5. Selling a product is the goal of all radio, television, and cable commercials.
   a) true
   b) false
6. When comparing the hard sell and soft sell delivery style, the hard sell commercial is characterized by all of the following except _____.
   a) lower pitch
   b) faster rate
   c) higher volume
   d) feeling of excitement
7. Broadcast advertising copy is least likely to be written by _____.
   a) a salesperson
   b) an ad agency
   c) the announcer
   d) a continuity writer
8. One of the most difficult types of commercials to perform is straight reading.
   a) true
   b) false
9. Music that is played in the background while copy is read is called a _____.
   a) donut
   b) bed
   c) theme
   d) tag
10. The biggest challenge for the announcer when doing voice-over work is to _____.
    a) fit the copy into the time that has been provided
    b) develop a character
    c) make the copy sound natural
    d) select the correct words on the spot

11. All of the following are factors to consider when you analyze a commercial except
_____.
   a) mood
   b) goal
   c) action
   d) salary

12. Timing is a skill that can be learned.
   a) true
   b) false

13. Which of the following is generally true about television commercial performance?
   a) how you look has no bearing on being hired
   b) stereotypes are often used to determine character traits
   c) you probably should have movie star looks to succeed
   d) your age has no bearing on being hired

14. A type of announcement that is run by an individual station to promote itself is called
a _____.
   a) PSA
   b) spot
   c) voice-over
   d) promo

15. A gesture that is used in commercial work in which you hold a product in the palm of
your hand is called a _____.
   a) caress
   b) cradle
   c) hug
   d) mask

■ ANSWERS

If You Answered A:

1a. No. While these are quite similar commercials, this is not true because the spokesperson merely speaks on behalf of a product while the testimonial announcer endorses a product he or she has used. (Reread 6.3 and 6.4.)

2a. Wrong. If anything, straight read commercials are more common to radio than television. (Reread 6.3 and 6.4.)

3a. No. The testimonial commercial format is common to both radio and television. (Reread 6.3 and 6.4.)

4a. Wrong. Asking a question is one way to hook a listener or viewer. (Reread 6.5.)

5a. No. This is not a true statement because, while many commercials strive to do so, it's not the only possibility. For example, some commercials strive to create a positive image of a company. (Reread 6.6.)

6a. Correct. Lower pitch would be a characteristic of the soft sell commercial.

7a. No. At smaller stations, a salesperson often writes commercial copy. (Reread 6.2.)

8a. Correct. This statement is true since there is no production, so this commercial format relies heavily on the skills of the announcer to bring the copy to life.

9a. No. While there is part of the typical donut commercial when copy is read over music, this is not the best answer. A donut is a type of commercial format. (Reread 6.3.)

10a. Yes. Fitting the copy into the appropriate time and with the visual portion of the spot is the biggest challenge for the voice-over announcer.

11a. No. Mood is an important area of analysis for an effective performance. (Reread 6.6.)

12a. Correct. This is a true statement and using a stopwatch and practice will help to develop this skill.

13a. False. Television is a visual medium and looks are an important factor. (Reread 6.9.)

14a. Incorrect. PSA is a public service announcement. (Reread 6.13.)

15a. No. A caress is gliding your fingers along the side of the product. (Reread 6.9.)

If You Answered B:

1b. Yes. This statement is false because, while similar in concept, there is a distinct difference between the spokesperson and testimonial commercial.

2b. Correct. The voice-over is a basic television commercial technique.

3b. No. The dramatization commercial is common to both radio and television. (Reread 6.3 and 6.4.)

4b. Wrong. Making an unusual statement is one way to hook a listener or viewer. (Reread 6.5.)

5b. Yes. Many commercials are selling products, but others promote the image of a company, making this a false statement.

6b. Wrong. Faster rate is a characteristic of the hard sell commercial. (Reread 6.8.)

7b. No. Ad agencies often write commercial copy. (Reread 6.2.)

8b. Incorrect. A straight read commercial relies heavily on the skills of the announcer. (Reread 6.3 and 6.4.)

9b. Correct. Music played underneath the announcer's voice is known as a music bed.

10b. No. Although important, developing a character is more a concern for an acted scene. (Reread 6.9 and 6.11.)

11b. No. Determining the goal of a spot is the first and most important aspect of analysis. (Reread 6.6.)

12b. Incorrect. Timing is not innate, but can be practiced and learned. (Reread 6.7.)

13b. True. Character development is very limited by time and stereotypes can be helpful to develop character traits.

14b. No. This is another name for a commercial. (Reread 6.3 and 6.13.)

15b. Correct. The cradle is one of the commonly used gestures in handling products in television commercials.

If You Answered C:

2c. Wrong. Donut commercials are more common on radio than television. (Reread 6.3 and 6.4.)

3c. No. The voice-over is a basic television commercial format. (Reread 6.3 and 6.4.)

4c. Correct. Sponsor name and location can certainly be found in a commercial, but it's more likely to be given at the end of a spot.

6c. Wrong. Higher volume is a characteristic of the hard sell commercial. (Reread 6.8.)

7c. Correct. The announcer's primary job is to perform, not to write, broadcast copy. However, this doesn't mean an announcer will never write broadcast copy.

9c. No. A theme is usually the signature music of a program or performer played at the beginning and ending of a program. (Reread 6.3.)

10c. No. Sounding natural is always important, but perhaps most important when doing a testimonial or spokesperson type of commercial. (Reread 6.4 and 6.11.)

11c. No. The better your understanding of what the advertiser wants from the audience the better you will deliver the copy. (Reread 6.6.)

13c. False. Many advertisers want talent who look like real people, not movie stars. (Reread 6.9.)

14c. No. A voice-over refers to an announcement that is heard over visuals. (Reread 6.4 and 6.13.)

15c. No. A hug is a gesture that is like an arm around the shoulder. (Reread 6.9.)

If You Answered D:

2d. Wrong. The dramatization commercial is commonly found on both radio and television. (Reread 6.3 and 6.4.)

3d. Yes. Ad-lib or fact sheet commercials are more likely to be found on radio.

4d. Wrong. Using a sound effect is one way to hook a listener or viewer. (Reread 6.5.)

6d. Wrong. A feeling of excitement is a characteristic of the hard sell commercial. (Reread 6.8.)

7d. No. Continuity writers are creative people who write commercial copy. (Reread 6.2.)

9d. No. A tag refers to an announcer adding a statement at the end of a commercial; perhaps giving the sponsor's location or hours for a special sale. (Reread 6.3.)

10d. No. Selecting the correct words on the spot is the challenge for ad-libbed commercials. (Reread 6.4 and 6.11.)

11d. Correct. The amount you get paid will not help in your analysis of the copy.

13d. False. Age is an important factor in your overall look. (Reread 6.9.)

14d. Correct. A promo promotes the station and its programming.

15d. No. Masking means that you are covering up the product name. (Reread 6.9.)

Projects

■ PROJECT 1

Analyze and record a radio commercial.

Purpose
To develop your announcing skills for a straight read commercial.

Notes
1. Review the discussion of the straight read commercial in this chapter.
2. For a straight read commercial, concentrate on variations in pitch and pace, pauses, word emphasis, vocal quality, timing, and *energy*!

How to Do the Project
1. Use the radio script in Figure 6.6 for this project.
2. Analyze the copy by first considering the structure of the commercial. Divide the copy into beginning, middle, and end segments. Is there a hook? Does the commercial follow a problem-solution format?
3. Use copy marks to remind yourself where to pause, change pace, and otherwise interpret the copy. You must turn in your copy with your performance marks to receive credit.
4. Write a detailed description of the audience for whom this message is intended, including demographic and psychographic characteristics. In other words, create a picture of the person to whom you are communicating.
5. Write a description of what you, as a performer, want to communicate. One or two short sentences are all that is necessary. What are the goals of the commercial? What is the mood of this spot? Then, list two or three key words that will help you understand the meaning of the copy.
6. Record the commercial on a CD or audio cassette.
7. After listening to your finished spot, do a brief written self-analysis, concentrating on your energy, your use of changes in pace, your use of pauses in the timing and naturalness of sound.
8. Turn in the recording, the written material, and the copy to your instructor to receive credit for this project.

CLIENT: Mrs. Mulligan's Muffin Shop
LENGTH: 30 seconds

ANNOUNCER: Who doesn't like fresh, homemade blueberry muffins? But these days, how many busy people have the time to bake? Mrs. Mulligan does . . . and that's why Mrs. Mulligan's Muffin Shop is so popular. Mrs. Mulligan's bakers prepare delicious, homemade muffins—fresh every day. Blueberry Royal, Cinnamon Apple Crisp, Banana Nut Nugget, and more than two dozen other varieties, all baked to perfection. Take a tasty treat home tonight from your nearest Mrs. Mulligan's Muffin Shop.

FIGURE 6.6 Radio commercial script.

■ PROJECT 2

Record a television commercial.

Purpose
To enable you to practice the use of facial expressions and gestures as a television announcer.

Notes
1. Review the use of gestures and facial expression in this chapter.
2. Props will be provided by the instructor, but you can practice by using any small object.
3. Watch some television commercials to determine how gestures are used.
4. You will need to have a television crew work with you to record this project, so your instructor may schedule this as a class assignment.

How to Do the Project
1. Using the script provided in Figure 6.7, record a television commercial.
2. Direct your performance toward the camera lens. Concentrate on variations in pitch and pace, word emphasis, vocal quality, timing, and *energy*!
3. Dress appropriately for television performance and the product of the commercial.
4. Use movement (a caress and one other type) and facial expressions to sell the product. Read the copy carefully to determine the appropriate use of gestures.
5. Since you cannot read the copy on-camera, memorize the script or use a TelePrompTer or cue cards.

CLIENT: Cola Pop Soda
LENGTH: 30 seconds

VIDEO	AUDIO
FADE FROM BLACK TO MCU	There's a place . . . (POINT TO TALENT THROAT) deep in your throat that lets you know you're thirsty. Call that spot the "thirst trigger" and call this the "thirst quencher."
ZOOM IN TO CU	(HOLD UP PRODUCT) Cola Pop Soda
CUT TO HEAD SHOT OF TALENT	Thirst trigger . . . (POINT TO THROAT)
CUT TO CU OF PRODUCT	Thirst quencher (CARESSES PRODUCT)
ZOOM OUT TO MS OF TALENT	Cola Pop Soda is America's number-one drink . . . and you'll love the refreshing and satisfying taste. Cola Pop Soda comes in convenient family-sized 2-liter bottles or 12-pack.
ZOOM IN TO MCU cans	. . . Calm your thirst trigger with the thirst quencher . . . a frosty Cola Pop Soda.
FADE TO BLACK	

FIGURE 6.7 TV commercial script.

6. Turn in your copy with performance marks.
7. Write a description of the audience. Visualize one person with whom you are communicating.
8. Write a description of the motivation and mood for delivering the commercial. In other words, what are you trying to communicate—sincerity, surprise, anger? One or two short sentences are all that is necessary.
9. List the product advantages emphasized in the copy.
10. Turn in the recording and the written requirements to the instructor to receive credit for this project.

■ PROJECT 3

Ad-lib a radio commercial from a fact sheet.

Purpose
To develop your ability to plan and present an interesting ad-lib commercial.

Notes
1. Review Section 6.10 on ad-lib commercials before trying this project.
2. Study the fact sheet and plan a scenario or thread for your presentation.
3. Avoid just reading statements off the sheet.

How to Do the Project
1. Use the radio fact sheet in Figure 6.8 for this project.
2. Plan a scenario for your presentation. Can you develop a way to make it personal?
3. Decide what sequence of points will work best. Which point will you start with? Which one will come next? How will you move from one point to another? How will you gracefully exit the spot?
4. Since it is an ad-lib spot, you only have one opportunity to record it.

Commercial Ad-Lib Fact Sheet

SPONSOR: Bramwell, Inc.
PRODUCT: Bramwell's Herbal Tea
LENGTH: 0:30

Points:--

    No caffeine
    Can be enjoyed as brewed or sweetened with honey or sugar
    Special blend of ginseng and other selected herbs
    Clearly balanced for superior, rounded flavor
    Naturally relaxing
    Pleasant interlude in a busy day
    Contains hibiscus flowers
    Distinctive taste and aroma
    People all over the world enjoy the natural benefits of drinking tea
    Package—24 bags to a box

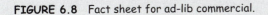

FIGURE 6.8 Fact sheet for ad-lib commercial.

5. Arrange for an audio booth or other recording facility. Your instructor may permit use of your computer.

6. Use a clock or watch with a sweep second hand and start "at the top" of any minute. Your goal is to ad-lib a 30-second spot.

7. Stop after 30 seconds are up.

8. After a short break, make a second recording, with the goal of recording a 60-second spot using the same material.

9. After listening to your finished spots, do a written self-analysis concentrating on your sincerity and believability. Would you be persuaded to buy this product? Did you use energy, inflection, pacing, and other vocal elements to communicate the points? How was the timing?

10. Turn in your recordings and your written analysis to the instructor to receive credit for this project.

Practice Material

■ FACT SHEETS: AD-LIB COMMERCIALS

SPONSOR: Rico's, Inc.
PRODUCT: Rico's Rice
ITEM: Boil-in-the-Bag Rice
LENGTH: 0:60

Points:
  Simply immerse in boiling water
  "Gripper tabs" for easy removal
  Ready in 10 minutes
  No measuring or fuss
  2 cups of rice per bag—meal for two, or
    one hungry person
  Microwaveable
  Tastes better than any other boil-in-the-
    bag brand
  100% natural ingredients
  Trusted for over 60 years
  Low fat
  Cholesterol free
  High in fiber, thiamin, niacin, and iron
  Four 2-cup packages per bag
  A healthy, low-cost meal
  Add green peas and mushrooms for an
    extra treat
  "The foundation for good health"

SPONSOR: Rosewell Coffee Co.
PRODUCT: Rosewell Instant Coffee
SIZE: 8-ounce jar, a large economy size
LENGTH: 0:30

Points:
  Quick and easy to make, no waiting
  Easy to store in your desk
  Motto: "The flavor really lasts"
  A rich and full-flavored American classic
  Consistent flavor
  100% pure coffee, no fillers
  Can be made in the microwave
  Specially selected beans
  Packaged in glass to preserve flavor
  Carefully blended and roasted

SPONSOR: Hopewell Bakeries
PRODUCT: Hopewell's Multigrain
Cereal Bars
LENGTH: 0:30

  8 bars to a box
  Low fat
  Made with real fruit:
    Strawberry, blueberry, apple
    cinnamon, raspberry, chocolate chip,
    oatmeal, and apple raisin
  7 vitamins and minerals
  No preservatives
  Individually wrapped
  Energy and great flavor
  Motto is: "Hopewell for Happiness and
    Health"

SPONSOR: D'Amico Quality Foods
PRODUCT: D'Amico Soups, Particularly
  Beef Barley
LENGTH: 0:60

  19-ounce can
  Ready to serve
  No need to add water
  Heavy soup made of savory beef
  A variety of garden vegetables
  Great seasonings
  Plenty of hearty barley
  Low fat
  3 vitamins and iron
  Only 130 calories per serving
  Great taste

■ COMMERCIAL COPY

Short Commercials

0:15

Are you a do-it-yourselfer? If you change your car's oil, adjust the spark plugs, or replace the alternator, then Freddie's Auto Superstore is the place for you. We've got tires, brakes, headlights, and filters. Everything to make your car purr. That's Freddie's Auto Superstore at the corner of Church Street and Broadway. (52 words)

0:15

Valentine's Day is just around the corner. Plan a romantic evening for that special someone at the Garden Restaurant. We have wine, soft music and candlelight, as well as the finest food in town. Plan a special evening at the Garden Restaurant, 1750 Richmond Road. (45 words)

0:30

Fitness is good for everyone. It trims your waist, increases energy, and just makes you feel good. The Workout Center is ready to help you get fit. We have all the machines, free weights, and a wonderful pool that's Olympic size and heated. At the Workout Center, we also have experts who will help you plan and carry out a successful fitness program. Bring out the Real You. Come to the Workout Center in the Lakeland Shopping Center, just off I-90 at the 306 exit. (85 words)

0:30

Where do you go when your eye doctor gives you a new prescription? If you live in the Hudson Valley, you should check out All Eyes on You, in Albany and Poughkeepsie. As dispensing opticians for 15 years, All Eyes on You has brought style to the necessity of wearing eyeglasses, and we have all the latest fashions. You should look good if you wear glasses, and we'll see to it that you do. All Eyes on You—you'll love the way you look. (84 words)

0:30

I'm here at Madeira Foods, checking up on the specials you'll find here this weekend. There are excellent buys on fresh fruits and vegetables. Like extra fancy Indian River ruby red grapefruit, three for a dollar ninety-nine. Or iceberg lettuce, two heads for ninety-nine cents. And, don't overlook the relishes—green onions or radishes, two bunches for sixty-nine cents. Here's where you'll really come to appreciate Madeira Foods. Their low, low prices add up to a total bill that winds down the cost of living. So pay a visit to Madeira foods this weekend. (93 words)

■ DIALOGUE COPY

Fresh Brew new coffee maker Radio Copy (Dialogue spot)

SFX:	Alarm goes off.
WIFE:	Oh, no! Honey, I overslept!
HUSBAND:	Well… I didn't. Good night.
WIFE:	You've got to get up and turn the coffee maker on.
HUSBAND:	Didn't I tell you…
WIFE:	Didn't I tell you "what"?
HUSBAND:	To buy Fresh Brew's new Super Coffee Maker.
WIFE:	Yes, but I told you our coffee maker still works.
HUSBAND:	But does it have an automatic, state of the art, timer like the Fresh Brew's new Super Coffee Maker?
WIFE:	No, but it still works…
HUSBAND:	And does our old coffee maker make the best coffee?
WIFE:	The coffee is okay.
HUSBAND:	Just okay?
WIFE:	Yes, it's okay and I'm okay with that.
HUSBAND:	The Fresh Brew new Super Coffee Maker is guaranteed not to make just okay coffee, it's guaranteed to make great coffee.
WIFE:	And how do you know that?
HUSBAND:	Go to their website freshbrew.com and read the results of an independent taste test. Fresh Brew's new Super Coffee Maker finished Number One as the tastiest coffee
WIFE:	Well, you convinced me. Where do I get the Fresh Brew new Super Coffee Maker?
HUSBAND:	You can buy it anywhere or even buy it on-line and they'll throw in a free coffee cup.
WIFE:	Alright, I'm sold. After work tonight we'll go buy one, okay?
HUSBAND:	Sure, now let me sleep a little longer.
WIFE:	Sure you don't want a cup of coffee?
ANNOUNCER:	If your coffee is just okay, then you might sleep better knowing you'll awaken to a cup of Fresh Brew's Super Coffee Maker coffee. Mm-mm-mm. Smell the bean!

(Prepared by Robert Noll and Pamela V. Merkys)

CHAPTER SEVEN

INTERVIEWING

7.1 INTRODUCTION

The broadcast interview is the basic instrument for gathering information for radio, television, and cable. For example, radio announcers often conduct celebrity interviews on the air. A quick glance at a television schedule shows that many hours during the day are filled with talk shows. Radio and television newscasts usually include short sound segments taken from longer interviews with persons in the news, although all or most of some programs may be devoted to one important newsmaker. Some cable networks carry interview shows for the entire broadcast day.

Interviews can be very interesting and fun. They look easy, but actually require a lot of preparation. Frequently, beginning announcers are uneasy when conducting interviews and can be intimidated by a well-known guest or are unprepared with information about the topic or person. The best broadcast interviews are conducted like well-planned conversations and can range from a very short sound bite to 60-minute or longer talk shows. Good interviewing is a combination of practice and preparation. With preparation, practice, and awareness of the skills covered in this chapter, you can develop into an accomplished, professional interviewer.

7.2 TYPES OF INTERVIEWS

There are many kinds of interviews, but the two basic types are news and feature interviews. News interviews are specifically designed to gather information about a news event, a person in the news, or a current issue. They tend to be shorter than feature interviews, but not always. For example, interviews on television programs like *Meet the Press* may last up to a half hour. Feature interviews are designed to entertain or to provide in-depth information about an interesting person or issue. Feature interviews often focus on certain people because of who they are (celebrities), what they do (an interesting or unusual occupation), or what they have accomplished (a 90-year-old man parachutes out of a plane to celebrate his birthday). Both news and feature interviews can be done in the studio or on location. Today, many interviews are highly edited, and often the audience only hears one or two responses from a much longer interview. A negative result of these sound bite interviews is an unwillingness of people to be interviewed for fear their remarks will be taken out of context and used inappropriately. This style of interviewing also creates a false impression for the beginning interviewer that interviewing is unplanned and requires little skill. However, nothing could be further from the truth, as even short interviews have to be well planned, organized, and prepared to accomplish your goals in a limited amount of time.

7.3 BASIC STRUCTURE OF THE BROADCAST INTERVIEW

Broadcast interviews tend to fall into two categories: those that will be longer and broadcast more or less complete, and those from which brief segments—called **sound bites**—will be edited. For the longer or "whole program" interview, the opening is particularly important. However, in a sound bite, an introduction is not necessary as the news anchor or reporter will present the segment with a lead-in to give the audience some orientation to what they will hear or see. Frequently the interview segment is just one part of a longer report.

Although it will vary a little, depending on the nature of the produced opening, you will want to follow a general five-step pattern for your interview: 1) the opening, 2) an introduction, 3) the questions and discussion, 4) a reintroduction, and 5) a close. The introduction is the time when you establish yourself and the reason for the interview. Although you will need to adjust to what is said as part of a recorded opening, the interview normally begins with a brief statement that includes the name of the show, the name of the host, the name of the guest, and the interview topic. Even if much of this is covered in the produced opening, you can still greet your audience and re-identify yourself, perhaps slipping in the name of the program as well: "Good evening, I'm John Smith. Welcome to The Conversation Corner."

If the interview is topic-oriented, you will want to make a brief statement about the subject to be discussed so that the audience understands what you will be covering and why. It could relate to news events, discoveries, local problems and issues, or even some pertinent fact such as that people over 100 are one of the fastest growing age groups in the country, if that fits the situation. This establishes why the interview is taking place and leads to the introduction of your guest. You want to avoid getting into what might be called biographical questions (for example, Where were you born?; Where did you go to college?; What's your favorite ice cream?). There should be a focal point for your conversation: a book written or at least enjoyed, an unusual experience, an accomplishment. If you have a good answer for the question, Why this interview? you are well on your way toward a good one. Knowing your topic will take you a long way toward your opening remarks, which are intended to catch the audience's interest and get you off to a good start. Try to avoid just starting, "My guest today is …" Here's a simple example: *"Jumping out of an airplane, with only a few pounds of fabric to keep you alive, is not something that appeals to me. However, my guest today loves the experience and has just completed his one hundredth jump … and he's 75 years old. I'd like you to meet. …"* That short statement attracts some attention, establishes what you are going to talk about, and should intrigue much of your audience into staying with you for a while. Not all openings can be that brief and be that interesting, but it's a place to start.

Next, introduce your guest, being sure to get the name and title/job correct. The introduction should be used to establish the guest's credentials, sometimes called the **qualification**—in other words, tell the audience why the guest is qualified to speak on the topic. If the person is the subject, a bit about his or her background, experiences, or unique aspects can be used to explain why the audience should find the person interesting. If the guest is someone who will be making statements about a situation and is something of an expert, your introduction should include some of those qualifications. Why should anyone pay any attention to what they have to say? Here's an example of a qualifying

introduction. *"The Declaration of Independence is over 225 years old. The Bible and the Koran are much older than that. We know that documents written hundreds of years ago still exist. Did you ever wonder how that happens? Our guest today is Dr. Albert Jones of State University, who is an authority on old documents and quite a collector of them as well. We're going to explore how you find old documents, how you preserve them and what kind of costs are involved."* The topic may not be as exciting as jumping out of a plane, but shows how a guest might be "qualified."

Next, welcome your guest. This helps to establish a friendly atmosphere and to develop rapport, but avoid trite remarks like, "Thanks for finding time in your busy schedule …" The basic guideline is to address the guest as the average listener or viewer would. Politicians and professionals usually get a more formal address, such as Senator Jones, Doctor Smith, or Miss Brown. Most sports stars and Hollywood celebrities can be addressed by their first names such as Tiger (Woods), Peyton (Manning), or Britney (Spears). If the interview is to be short, parts of the greeting may have to be omitted, but still try to project a cordial image.

The third step is the interview itself. At the beginning of your career, you probably will be asked to interview many local people on many topics. Often the best part of the interview occurs after the person has talked for a while, has developed a level of trust with the interviewer, and has relaxed. This is when an effective interviewer can use his or her knowledge and skills to create a successful interview. (Developing and asking questions will be covered in later sections of this chapter.)

In any communication setting, trust is important for a relaxed and interesting conversation, and the same is true for interviewing. Trust is developed through the relationship between the interviewer and interviewee. Since many of the people you interview you have not met before and will likely not see again, trust can be best established by treating guests with dignity and respect. Trust begins with the first encounter. Tone of voice, facial expression, and body language all contribute to its development. Trust is not developed by letting the guests control the interview or letting them have prior approval of questions. A knowledgeable host who uses effective listening techniques goes a long way toward establishing trust. No one wants to place faith in someone who doesn't seem to know what he or she is talking about or isn't interested in what the interviewee has to say. Most political and public figures are used to giving interviews and many have had bad experiences, so building trust may be difficult with them. However, if you plan to have a long career in the field, you must develop the ability to establish trust—and remember that once trust is lost, it is not easily regained.

The fourth part of an effective interview is reestablishing the credentials of the guest. Unless the interview is shorter than five minutes, you should reintroduce the guest and topic near the midpoint of the interview. On television, a graphic can be used that keys the name or the topic on the screen without disrupting the flow of the interview. On radio, you need to pause between questions and give the reintroduction. You might go to "We are talking with …" In either situation, a good time to reintroduce guests is after a commercial break because it provides a natural interruption in the program.

The final part of an interview is the close. In most cases, a brief thank-you to the guest and a mention of the guest's name and topic one more time are sufficient. Try to avoid clichéd endings such as, "I see our time is up" or "We hope you enjoyed the show." These, too, have become trite, overworked expressions. A better way to end is to summarize what the guest has said, especially if the topic was complicated. A way to set the tone for the close is to ask guests if there is anything else they would like to add. If they have felt that you ignored a point that is important, this provides an opportunity for them to respond and helps to maintain rapport with them for the future. However, you don't want to offer that opportunity when you have only a few seconds left, as they might have several minutes' worth of material they want to cover. Often, the close is a good opportunity to promote the next interview, if you know who the guest will be, and if the program is aired on a regular schedule. As with the introduction of the interview, it's good practice to write down the closing comments so you can finish smoothly. You'll need to write them so they can be easily adjusted to fit the time requirements at the end of the program. You don't want to read either the open or the close, but writing them out will help you remember them. Watch Video Clip 7.1 to see how the five basic elements mentioned above are developed into a television interview. Video Clip 7.2 shows a student's interview broken down into the five elements. Also see Figure 7.1 to see notes from another student's first interview.

An additional step may be needed for television interviews. If your interview was done outside of the studio and the final product will be edited later, then you need to include **cut-in shots**. These are close-ups (CU) of you and the guest responding to each other, both verbally and non-verbally, as shown in Video Clip 7.3. You may even re-ask questions to an empty chair after the interview, just to have them on tape and to give the editors additional material to use. Sometimes the videographer may ask for a CU of you writing in a notebook or doing some other activity. The key here is to make the actions natural and seem as if they are happening within the interview. Cut-ins need to match in terms of lighting, clothing, hair style, and makeup. That's why they are best done immediately after an interview. Cut-ins are also used in studio settings, especially if the interview is taped and will later be edited. The purpose here might be to show you reacting to a guest response, so you may be asked to laugh or smile or look pensive. Be sure to focus your eyes where the guest would be in making the shot. You also should avoid responding with "uh-huh" or "okay" because they often overlap with the speaker and are difficult to edit out.

In this day of satellites and long-distance fiber optics, it is quite possible that you will be called upon to conduct an interview with someone who is not in the studio, but may be hundreds, even thousands, of miles away. Further, you might have two or more guests simultaneously who are located in other different parts of the world. You would probably see them on a split-screen studio monitor, perhaps a large flat panel that is part of the set. You could have four or more different guests on the screen at the same time.

The technological reality is that on these long satellite hookups, the connection may be made through two or more "birds" with the signal returning to the ground station, as it works its way around the world. Although the electronic signal moves very fast, the time it takes for these jumps of 22,500 miles each way, plus the black box processing on the ground, can add up, so that the signal may take as long as two or three seconds to reach its destination. This means there will be a delay between when you ask your question and when your guest hears it. The longer the delay, the more disruptive this pause becomes. The lag can vary with different locations. As satellite time is leased just for the period you plan to use it, different satellite combinations may be used and the delays may be greater on some days than others. If the delay is relatively short, just ignore it, but if it's long, it is often better to acknowledge it with a brief comment like, "The delay is long today." While it can break the rhythm of the conversation, treat it as if the guest is just taking a moment to think.

A student's first interview can be nerve racking. Here is how one student handled it. (It was preceded by an announcer's introduction.)

"Thank you and welcome to Conversation Corner. I'm Mary Smith. I'm sure that in the audience we have one or two aspiring authors. Unfortunately, not everyone is going to get the chance to be published. My guest today is published author and professor at State University, Jane Jones. Thank you for being with us today, Jane."

She then clarifies the topic of the interview and goes into her first question.

"What we're going to go over today is the writing process. How you get your ideas for your novels and how long it takes you to get them down on paper and published. You have four novels, how did you get the inspiration for the first one?"

The author responds, talking about her main character and Mary uses a follow-up question.

"And, how much of her story was, in fact, your story?"

Midway in the interview, Mary had to do a break for a message. Here is how she handled it. Then you see how she handled the return.

"Thank you very much. As soon as we return, I'll get on with the questions, but right now we're going to go to a commercial."

"Thank you very much and welcome back to Conversation Corner. I'm Mary Smiths and I'm here with published author and professor at State University, Jane Jones.

Before the break we were talking about how you established a "place" with your character, Terry, for your first novel. Did any aspects of her carry over into your other novels?"

Finally, let's take a look at the closing.

OK, it seems that we're almost out of time, so I want to thank you (directed to the guest), and hope that this has been beneficial to the writer/hopefuls of the audience. Once again, our guest has been Jane Jones and I'm Mary Smith with Conversation Corner.

Certainly there are ways this might have been done better, but it is one student's effort. How would you have handled it?

FIGURE 7.1   Notes from a student's first interview.

On a further note, satellite links are usually scheduled for very close to the exact time and length of the planned interview. This could mean that your guest might be cut off, even in mid-sentence, and it will be up to you to cover the incident gracefully and perhaps fill any time remaining. "We seem to have lost the satellite connection" will cover most situations and a summary of what the guest said should fill the time. A dilemma can occur when you know the guest was to make a statement that wasn't heard. The temptation will be for you to make it. If it seems appropriate to do so, you might say "I believe our guest was going to say ..." and summarize the comment.

When working with multiple remote guests, remember that although you can see them, they probably can't see you or the other guests. They are connected to the two-way audio via an earpiece. You need to direct traffic by regularly naming the person to whom you are asking a question or from whom you are seeking a comment. Guests could start responding to each other excessively, so you might have to step in if the discussion gets off subject or is running long.

7.4 THE INTERVIEW SETTING

In a radio studio, the guest and host will probably face each other while sitting at a table or counter, as shown in Video Clip 7.4. You will speak into separate microphones that are usually on a mic stand or boom in front of each person. To make sure the guest is comfortable in a situation where microphones or other equipment are between you and the guest, take a few moments to talk casually before beginning the interview. Asking about the weather, the guest's trip to the studio, or some other insignificant topic can settle the person down if he or she is nervous. An audio engineer or the host (announcer), who may be operating the equipment, will ask for sound levels. Each person who talks on the program will have to speak so that the volume can be adjusted for correct technical sound. Encourage your guests to speak in their normal voice.

If headphones are to be used, make sure that the guest has tried them out before the interview. Since there are live mics in the studio, the monitor speakers must be muted or electronic feedback will occur. Therefore, headphones are usually worn to hear the interview and any other sources of audio, such as telephone calls, that may be mixed in. For many people, this setup will be unfamiliar and even uncomfortable, so one of your jobs as a host will be to put the guest at ease. Briefly explain the operation of the studio, especially if this is your guest's first visit to a radio or television studio. Equipment can be intimidating, so explain what you will be doing and what will happen. This helps to relax the guest, and you will end up with a better interview. One way to help guests relax is to maintain eye contact with them while they are answering your questions. Try not to read or keep your head down, but look the guest right in the eyes.

The usual television studio interview set consists of chairs, or a desk with chairs on either side. Occasionally they will be set up in a more face-to-face manner. Video Clip 7.5 shows a typical TV interview setup. This may be part of an elaborate living room set or merely positioned in front of a curtain. In television, the right side of the screen is considered dominant, and if the host is put there, he or she becomes as important as the guest. Both Oprah Winfrey and David Letterman use this configuration because the comments they interject during the interview are as important to the program as whatever the guest says. Likewise, if the guest is on the right side of the screen, he or she becomes dominant. Larry King uses this approach because the emphasis of his program is more on the guest and topic. Both guest and host in a television interview usually wear small, inconspicuous microphones that the floor director or other crew member will help attach properly. Depending on the actual interview set, a boom or desk mic may also be used.

Television studios are very busy places and can be distracting to your guests. Be sure to orient them to the studio setting, explain the role of the floor manager and other crew, but ask them to look at you and not at all the activity around the studio. As in the radio studio, the host can help the guest by maintaining direct eye contact. In the television studio, working with the floor manager and director can be key to your success. Make sure you've reviewed the hand signals with the floor manager and be sure the director understands your organization and any special shots you might need, such as a close-up on an item the guest has brought in.

Camera shots are important in the television studio. The host often looks directly at the camera for the opening, the close, and any breaks, but during the interview a variety of shots may be used. One common perspective is the **over-the-shoulder shot**, shown in Video Clip 7.6, in which the guest appears in a full front view and the host "frames" the side of the shot with his or her back to the camera. With this angle, the camera seems to participate in the conversation.

Another approach is the **profile shot,** shown in Video Clip 7.7, in which the guest and the host look at each other and the camera seems to be listening in on the conversation. The host should be aware of various camera positions and also rely on directions from the studio crew or the director speaking through an IFB to communicate camera changes. As noted in Chapter 3, an IFB is the earpiece that television performers wear so the director can communicate directly to them during a performance. Another way in which the host keeps track of the camera positions is the tally light. One other thing to keep in mind is that camera angles can accent poor posture. If you slouch or lean sharply to one side, this can be very noticeable. As Figure 7.2 suggests, "Sit up straight."

Some interviewing skills can be practiced but others can't, because it really comes down to how well you put it all together during a live or prerecorded

FIGURE 7.2 Sit up straight!

interview. Many interviews are recorded, but ultimately aired as if they were live, with little or no editing. Successful interviews begin with research and
preparation, knowing the purpose of the interview,
knowing how it will be used (for example, sound bites,
information), and understanding the intended audience and the goal (entertainment, information, per-
suasion) for the interview.

7.5 RESEARCH AND PREPARATION

Although interviews often seem spontaneous and
unrehearsed, they require time and effort in preparation. Prior experience and knowledge in an area
certainly help, but thorough research about your topic
is essential for an effective interview. It helps develop
the focus of your story and defines what you want the
audience to understand or know. This means reading
local newspapers, national papers like *The New York
Times* and *USA Today*, and news magazines such as
Newsweek and *Time*. Books and conversations with
friends may also lead to interesting ideas.

Finding interesting guests and topics can be a challenge. Not everyone makes a good interview subject.
Choose an interview topic or person that you and your
audience would find interesting. In order to do this,
you will need to know something about your audience. Your radio or television station can provide you
with such demographic and lifestyle information for
its audience, to help you choose a topic. For example,
if your audience consists primarily of young families

with both parents working, an interview on child care
might interest them.

Things to consider when choosing a guest include
celebrity, personality, importance, accomplishments,
entertainment value, knowledge, or sense of humor.
Some guests you will have to invite while others will
be knocking at your door. Often celebrities or authors
make tours to promote their latest work and can be
booked easily for a program.

Begin by researching the topic and person. Start
with what you find interesting and investigate what
you don't understand. Chances are that if you don't
understand something, your audience won't either.
Basic library skills and a familiarity with the Internet
and electronic databases are critical for the interviewer. You can access stories and newspapers from
around the world using the Internet. Newspaper
archives and computer databases such as Lexis/Nexis
are valuable tools. Become familiar with sources like
Who's Who in America, and the *Reader's Guide to
Periodical Literature*. Other references include biographies and local newspaper coverage of an individual's
accomplishments. If such materials are available, try
to read any recent books or articles written by a guest
to get a sense of that person. This knowledge can help
you ask better questions and guide the discussion.
A useful technique is to write down interesting statements or quotes from what you've read. These may
not be used verbatim during the interview, but may
remind you or the interviewee of some interesting
aspect of his or her life. Ask for a copy of the person's

resume if he or she is a professional. Another source of background information involves talking to colleagues or associates of the guest. This type of information gathering also requires interviewing skills. Questions during the on-air interview can often arise spontaneously from this type of preparation. Be curious and be current. The audience wants to listen to new ideas and stories or issues to which they can relate.

The most important thing to remember is that good preparation equips you to determine a focus for the interview. Time is usually too short to develop more than two or three main ideas. What ones do you choose? Know your audience and decide what would be most interesting to them. Preparation also helps keep you focused during the interview. Your energy and attention must be directed at the person being interviewed. If you are worried that you don't understand the material or might get lost, the interview will lack focus.

Another area to consider when planning an interview is time. For the beginner, the judgment of time is difficult. For interviews that are longer than a sound bite and are going well, time will fly by, but for some, time can seem to drag. You need to plan to have more than enough material to fill the entire time period. This is particularly valuable when you find yourself with a guest who is prone to giving short answers. Your list of questions could be used up rapidly. Experience will be your biggest aid, but some over-preparation will help you survive until that sense of time develops. Even then, it's usually easier to shorten a discussion that it is to expand one when you don't have enough material.

7.6 PREPARING INTERESTING GUESTS AND TOPICS

It often helps to do a pre-interview with a guest, although some experienced interviewers prefer not to, as they feel it may kill spontaneity. However, you don't want your interview to become an undirected "chat." As you finish your research and plan your questions, ask yourself, "What is my goal in this interview?" The answer should be more than "To fill x minutes." You need a direction, information you want to reveal, or a side of the guest that is significant that you want to show. Some guests feel nervous about an interview and want to have some control over the situation. You may get requests for the actual questions in advance. However, this is not a good idea as it will take away from the spontaneity of the interview and produce a feeling, as you can get rehearsed responses. The guests should have a general idea of the areas you will

discuss so they can be prepared, and if you've done a pre-interview they probably can guess several questions you will ask. In some instances, showing the questions ahead of time may be the only way you will get an interview with an important guest, but you will have to decide if it is worth it.

For the beginning interviewer, the pre-interview is a valuable tool. It can be done in person, over the phone, or via e-mail. The pre-interview allows you to introduce yourself and build rapport with your guest, and it can help you avoid asking inane questions that will show your ignorance. This is a good time to check name pronunciation and any other difficult words (jargon) that might come up during the interview. If you've done your research, you might just say, "I'd like to talk about_____." You can inquire about the guest's points of view or experiences with the subject. Often in discussing experiences you will stumble across things that would be interesting to include. But don't get wrapped up in a lot of details such as where the guest grew up, went to school, or his or her favorite hobbies, unless these are pertinent to your goal with the interview. Keep considering how each idea relates to that goal. It's appropriate to ask if your guest has some experience or story that would be interesting to your audience. You may not use it, but these stories can serve as padding and may also help your guest open up to you. Be careful not to conduct an interview instead of a pre-interview. Once you get a basic sense of something you'll be discussing, move on to the next area. Save some of your curiosity for the show.

Remember that in the interview there will be occasions when you are asking questions to which you already know the answers. You are the audience's representative. Audience members will not know as much about the guest as you do. So ask questions or clarify statements that will help them understand and enjoy the interview.

Be sure to tell the guest up front how long the pre-interview and the interview process will take. This is especially important for television—since you are working with many people and pieces of equipment, the chances of things needing to be redone or taking longer to set up are greater than in radio. Communicate a realistic time frame to your guest. People—especially busy people—need a reasonable estimate of the time involved so they can plan their day.

Field Interviews

Another form of the interview that can be quite different from the longer studio situation is the news interview in the field. These are almost always shorter and are aimed at getting one or more statements that can be included in a news reports on some incident or event. Here the interviewer is not as interested in the overall discussion as in a clear statement of what the interviewee saw, heard, or experienced. These segments, often only 20 seconds long, are to add validation, a personal perspective, or an eyewitness experience. As a result, there is less preliminary discussion so that the whole interview may last less than five minutes and the desired segments will be lifted out. Much of what you ask will be devoted to getting the information for your report while encouraging the subject to make the focus statement or "sound bite." Sometimes the individual will say several good remarks so that more than one can be used at some point in your report, perhaps even providing a summary statement.

In this situation, you will need to get the person talking and guide them with questions, even if you have to butt in occasionally. It may take questions like: "How did you know the person?" "When did you notice the fire?" "Describe what you heard (or saw)." You might even use "How did you feel about that attack on the elderly person?" You are seeking reactions, observations, and even opinions, which is a bit different than a studio interview in which you may choose to challenge something your guest has said. Remember that in the field your interviewee is qualified only by what they have seen or heard. They aren't the same as an expert you might have in the studio.

As the interview proceeds, you are listening for that statement that you can use in your report and may elect to bring the encounter to a conclusion quite promptly if you get what you want, or decide that this subject isn't likely to provide what you need. Still, be sure to thank them for their time and contribution, but don't commit yourself to use any of it, as the person could have all their friends watching and could be disappointed and angry if you find something else that you feel is better. Remember that your full story may not be more than 90 seconds long.

7.7 DEVELOPING INTERVIEWING SKILLS

Like most things in life, good interviewing takes practice. There are some individual skills you can practice even when you're not in an interview setting. Listening, asking questions, and planning the interview, especially the open and close, are key skills a good interviewer will need to develop.

Listening

Listening is an active process and requires energy and commitment. It is not passive, even though it is often thought of that way. We live in a society that uses communication devices that require little energy or effort, like listening to music or watching television. Active listening in an interview is both mental and physical, and involves paraphrasing, asking questions, and expressing understanding of the speaker's ideas or feelings. Listening requires concentration, but it can be learned. Because we do it so much, we assume we know how to listen and many good interviewers make it look easy. However, a quick, critical look at interviews on television or listening to radio interviews tells us that interviewing often is not done well. Sometimes the interviewer asks complex questions, talks too much, or loses control of the interview. Effective listening is the key to overcoming these problems.

What do you listen for? First, listen for words the audience may not understand. This could include abstract or vague ideas, as in "The mayor faces a number of problems." What problems? Second, listen for words that may be unique to the field or subject being discussed and ask for an explanation of terms. Use of **jargon** may appear to give a sense of credibility, but if the audience does not understand what is said, the purpose of the interview goes unfulfilled. For example, if your guest blurts out, "That wig picker Kristine Martin summed it up nicely when she said ..." it would be helpful if the audience knew that a wig picker is a psychologist and not a hairdresser.

Third, listen for cues. The guest may make a statement that could lead to interesting new areas of questioning. In particular, look for opportunities for **follow-up** questions, questions that continue a line of thought from the previous question, or a shift to a new aspect of the topic. For example, a student was conducting an interview with a laboratory technician who mentioned that his job included destroying chemicals. Although ecologically this could be a hot issue, the student missed the opportunity to ask what methods were used to destroy the chemicals safely.

Reacting to answers shows that you are listening. However, avoid responding with comments like "yes," "no," "uh-huh," or "okay." There are a number of reasons to avoid these verbal tics. First, it sounds unprofessional and is poor performance practice, as we've already noted. Second, it may give the impression to the audience that you agree with the person when perhaps you do not. Third, if the interview is to be edited, it can make the job more difficult since you are often not on camera and a voice that apparently comes from nowhere can be distracting. The best type of listening reaction is nonverbal. This includes smiling, head nodding, and direct eye contact. The interviewee still needs to feel he or she is being heard, even if you are not verbally responding. However, do not fake attention. Appearing to listen is not the same as listening.

For the beginner, it's very easy to get so involved in what you are going to ask that you focus on your notes and not the guest. Not only is this rude, but you may easily miss a key comment that could be very significant to your interview. You could also look very amateurish by asking a question the guest has just answered.

If your preparation has been thorough, you may hear contradictory statements or a new view being expressed. Ask for clarification. This is where your research pays off and distinguishes the exceptional interview from the mediocre. Paraphrasing—restating what the person has just said—is a very good way to show your guest you are listening and also helps to clarify ideas for the audience. Paraphrasing might take one of the following forms: "Do I have it right that you feel ….?" "As I understand it, your position is that …" The interviewee will then agree or disagree with your restatement of his or her words, and will frequently elaborate further. This is a relatively easy way to open people up and get them to talk about what they love. Summarizing what has been said is also a good way to let your guest know you were listening.

During the actual interview, do not refer to something the guest said before you were on-air. This is impolite to the audience and they will feel left out. If you need to prompt the guest about a topic from the pre-interview, use something like "Before the show you told me …" If you refer to a newspaper or magazine article, be sure to give enough background so the audience understands the context of the questions. Remember, the idea is to let the other person shine, not you. Interest and focus should be directed toward the guest. Giving your personal point of view is usually inappropriate. If you remain invisible and let the person come through, you have been successful.

Planning

It is a good idea to plan questions even if you don't use them. In fact, you probably won't use them all and often will change the order of questions depending on what happens during the actual interview. During the interview, base questions on what the guest says. Think of your interview as a conversation, not just a list of questions that will be asked one after the other. Part of a good interview is the spontaneity that occurs between the guest and host as the interview develops. Having a list of questions is a source of security, especially if you are new to the task of interviewing or are unfamiliar with the guest or topic. A list of questions on a clipboard or small note cards is acceptable even on television, as shown in Figure 7.4. Also, have a pen or pencil with you and take notes during the interview. If the person says something you want to follow up on, a few key words jotted down will remind you, but keep the note taking brief.

Asking Questions

In general, there are two basic types of questions, open-ended and closed ended. Try to avoid **closed-ended** questions, which are questions that can be answered with a simple yes or no or other one-word answer, such as, "Where did you go to school?" or "Do you like your job?" This type of question can result in a very stilted interview, but it can help initially to get the person talking, so a few closed-ended questions may be asked early in an interview. Experienced interviewees, like politicians, often know that it is best to elaborate, but if you are working with someone who is new to being interviewed, especially on television, he or she will not elaborate and so it is best to avoid this type of questions.

Open-ended questions provide the guest with the opportunity to elaborate in the answer and let the audience get to know the person. For example, "What types of things did you find interesting about Ireland?" will elicit more appealing answers than "You were just in Ireland, weren't you?" Another type of open-ended question that may elicit detailed or interesting answers is the hypothetical question, such as "What would you do if …" or "Where do you see yourself in five years?"

Make sure you ask only one question at a time. Asking two questions at the same time, known as a *double-barreled* or complex question, is a too frequent occurrence on television and radio shows and causes confusion for the audience and the interviewee. If an interviewer asks something like, "Mayor Casey, what will this increase in our sales tax mean? Will the money go to education or social services or another city program and just how much money does the city anticipate collecting?" the response is liable to be, "Could you repeat the question?" Often multiple questions occur when the interviewer asks a closed-ended question and then immediately follows up with

Megan Mosack, interviewer and talk show host, WIBW, Topeka, Kansas.

"It is so important when we are interviewing someone to listen to the person we are asking questions of. Often times we ask the question and we're so concerned about what's coming up next, we miss what they said, and sometimes what they said is key to the next question you ask." (Listen to more of Megan Mosack's thoughts on interviewing on Audio Clip 7.1.)

FIGURE 7.3 Listening when interviewing.

FIGURE 7.4 The TV interviewer can use a clipboard or note cards to list key questions or take notes, but they should be handled as unobtrusively as possible. (Photo by Alan Stephenson.)

an open-ended question. It may happen because the interviewer feels the need to fill air time. However, an interview is easier to follow and more clearly focused if you ask only one question at a time.

Asking questions that are easy and friendly is important at the beginning of the interview. By reading material about the person, you can get a sense about what is important to your guest. Begin with that. Save difficult or controversial questions until the middle or end of the interview. Sometimes you have to make an on-the-spot decision about when to ask a question; an opportunity to ask a particular question that you are interested in may not occur when you think it should. That is another reason why listening and preparation are so critical to a good interview. Know your subject so you can intertwine and relate ideas and topics on the spot.

Be careful about asking questions that show bias or seems to seek a specific answer. This is a **leading question**. For example, beginning a response with "You don't think that ..." implies that the person is wrong in thinking a particular way. In 1999, talk show host Rosie O'Donnell caused quite a stir when she got into a debate with actor Tom Selleck over the gun control issue. Selleck, who has spoken on behalf of the National Rifle Association, was on the show to promote a movie and was taken by surprise when the interview shifted into this unplanned area. A very tense discussion followed that upset many people.

Other examples of leading questions could include "Most people think that, don't you?" or "You would vote against capital punishment, wouldn't you?" Remember to ask questions that will highlight the knowledge of the guest. Try to avoid asking questions that show off your own knowledge. Sometimes playing dumb is a great way to get people to open up and explain their topic. Remember that the purpose is to get your guest talking.

Avoid inane questions with obvious answers like "Were you glad you survived the crash?" See Figure 7.5 for another example. Also try not to answer the questions you ask: "You voted against the bill. What were you thinking? Your statements at the time indicated you felt we were giving up more than we were gaining."

FIGURE 7.5 Were you disappointed when you lost, Mr. Jones?

This may cause your guest to feel unimportant and also may not elicit very interesting information. If the person changed his or her mind, you are now in the awkward situation of having trapped them into explaining their contradictions. This may cause a negative tone and alter the effectiveness of the interview.

Probes are follow-up questions to get more depth and detail from the interviewee. Sometimes they are used to create conflict or controversy. If your guest does not answer a question, rephrase the question and ask it again. Often people are insecure about doing an interview and need to be asked questions more than once. Politicians may purposely avoid answering your questions and public relations representatives may want to give you only their standard responses. If you run into a guest who seems evasive or does not answer the questions, don't just drop the subject. Try a few times to ask the question in a different way. Your judgment comes into play here, because if you try too much you may alienate your guest and the rest of the interview could be difficult. However, probing provides the possibility of an exciting interview. Probe by paraphrasing—restating what you think you heard—and asking follow-up questions.

Don't feel compelled to jump in with a question if the guest stops talking or does not answer immediately. Although **dead air** is not generally acceptable in broadcasting, some different guidelines apply during an interview. If you jump in too fast, you may interrupt the guest's thought or not get a very good answer. Remember, sometimes people are nervous and need time to warm up, or they may simply need a few seconds to formulate a response. In some cases, they may not like the question and are just stalling in the hope that you'll come up with a different one. Don't be afraid to wait them out.

Developing questions for an interview is a skill that improves with practice. One tip is to "know what you want to know." Preparing possible questions is important process for the beginner. Since there are so many situations and subjects for which you could be developing inquiries, it's difficult to offer specific suggestions, but below are fifteen "question starts." Think about how you could complete the question in an appropriate way for your guest or situation. The "starts" can be used in many ways and even reshaped to use more than once in the same situation. Consider how you could expand the list.

Question Starters
1. Why did you …?
2. How did you react to …?
3. Describe your experience with ….
4. How long does __ take?
5. How does this work?
6. How do you feel about …?
7. Why undertake this?
8. How can you justify …?
9. Tell me about ….
10. Could you explain how this works?
11. Why didn't you …?
12. What is it that …?
13. Why is the cost so high?
14. Could you describe what you saw?
15. What have you learned about …?

Transitions, or moving from one subject area to another, can be awkward. Commercial breaks may help to establish a natural sequence, but they do not always happen when you want them to. Transitions, as with all good interviews, require knowledge of the subject and active listening by the interviewer. They can often be general, such as "In the introduction I mentioned your interest in …" or "As you said earlier …" More specific transitions can relate to the interview

CHAPTER SEVEN

itself. Summarizing what was just discussed and relating it to the next area often works well and provides the opportunity for listeners who just tuned in to follow the conversation. For example, "We've been discussing the reasons why busing of school children for integration did not work. Now let's look at some of the reasons why busing has been considered successful."

Humor can be used to keep and maintain interest in an interview. However, humor is difficult to do well. It is a skill, but also requires an analysis of the audience and situation. Beginners sometimes try to use humor when it isn't appropriate and can seem to be degrading the guest. Often when humor is attempted, what one group of people may find funny, another may not. Using humor at an inappropriate time can make you look very foolish. Be especially careful of trying sarcastic humor as it may hurt you or your guest. Laughing at yourself, whether you made a mistake or are making fun of something you did earlier, is probably the only type of humor that one could say is safe in all situations.

7.8 DRESSING FOR AN INTERVIEW

A general rule of thumb to follow for dress is to be conservative. However, there is a lot of leeway in this guideline. For example, in radio, since you are not seen by the audience, dress may be more informal. Your style of dress may be related to whom you will interview or where the interview will take place. For example, politicians or business executives may find it easier to relax if you dress more formally. Television interviews with athletes or those done over a holiday weekend may work better if dress is informal. Of course, follow the general guidelines for television dress as discussed in other chapters of this book.

7.9 KEEPING CONTROL

One of the most difficult aspects of an interview for beginners is retaining control of the interview. This does not mean talking or interrupting when the guest gives answers you don't like or don't expect. It does mean you have to draw out people who are not too talkative and restrict people who talk too much. Interruption is a key skill to learn for the latter situation. Paraphrasing and asking open-ended questions are the keys to the former. Interrupting a guest is often the only way to maintain control of the interview. This is especially important if you have a guest who

rambles or is trying to focus the interview on his or her interest and not the interest of the audience, which you have determined. In one case, a guest turned away from the host and toward the on-air camera, and proceeded to launch a several minute tirade. The host, a little inexperienced and trying to be respectful of the guest, let him get away with it for far too long.

There are a few ways to approach this. Listen carefully to the guest's response and jump in when the person is taking a breath. This way the interruption will occur during a natural break in speaking and will appear to be less rude than just interrupting the person's speech. Sometimes a nonverbal pat on the arm or leaning forward in your chair alerts a guest that you want to say something. Occasionally, you may have to jump in and firmly re-ask a question or remind the guest of the focus of the interview—for example, "I understand your interest in this topic, but our audience wants to know …" In extreme cases, you may have to talk right over the answer and become more aggressive, but always remain polite: "Forgive me, but …" One other reminder is to avoid letting the guest physically take the microphone. If you hold the mic, you can always interrupt the interviewee by moving the mic away from him or her and toward you. Of course this doesn't work if the guests each have their own microphone.

In another situation, you could have a guest who takes your first question and turns it into a monologue that will last the whole show if you permit it. Again, you may have to do some interrupting to get control. The monologue may be interesting, but the guest is then controlling the whole interview, not you. In the case of a guest who rambles, you may have to use closed-ended questions to force him or her to focus on the subject. A series of one-word answers can help to get the guest back on track and can help you regain control of the interview. However, this is generally not an effective technique and should be used only when absolutely necessary.

7.10 KEEPING A NEUTRAL VIEW

One issue that is important to consider is your expression of opinion. Of course, an audience may guess your viewpoint, and no one is totally objective. By the very nature of the people you choose to interview or the topics you cover, you are indicating preferences. However, during the course of the interview it usually is not appropriate to express your opinion of what the guest has said. For example, suppose you have asked your guest, "How do you react to the war in Afghanistan and Iraq?" and the guest responds that he is totally in favor of such action. You may have an opinion that disagrees with this, but your job is to draw out the guest and find the reasons for that opinion, not to disagree and create a conflict on the air. Realistically, this may not be the case for some talk shows where controversy and disagreement are important features of the program.

7.11 TALK RADIO

Talk radio evolved in the two decades, some say to allow the conservative audience to have a voice in a liberal media environment. The general format of talk radio shows is a call-in to a host or host with a guest, about various topics, as heard in Audio Track 7.2. Phone screeners are used to help select callers who seem likely to be interesting, and tape delay systems provide a safeguard to delete unwanted language or possible libelous statements. A performer in this format generally works a three- or four-hour shift, five or six days a week.

Talk radio programs have centered on news and politics, sports and fishing, sex and relationships, cooking, cars, and a multitude of other topics. The skills needed include the ability to conduct a good interview with a guest and the ability to converse with callers. The demands for this type of interview include being well read in the news of the day. If you wanted to host a specialized talk show, such as a fishing show, you would need to be a recognized expert or extremely knowledgeable in that field. Another skill demanded of radio talkers is the ability to switch gears frequently. Sometimes callers do not follow the same topic one after the other.

While radio interview shows often do not have high ratings, both local and national call-in talk shows are quite popular. They generally have a loyal following and are cheap to produce. Talk radio hosts such as Rush Limbaugh or Howard Stern may be considered by many to be too forceful, but their personal appearances usually draw large crowds, attesting to their popularity. Listen to Megan Mosack's interview with Rabbi Daniel Lapin about *The Passion of the Christ.* Note how she develops questions to move the interview along, how she reintroduces him twice, and summarizes at the end. Then hear her pose questions to the audience to encourage call-ins. (Audio Clip 7.3.)

7.12 TALK TELEVISION

In recent years, talk television shows have grown in number. These shows usually have a well-known host whose job it is to manage a conversation between the guest(s) and the audience members. Audience participation is an important aspect of these programs. The show might begin with the host briefly interviewing the guest on the topic. These shows may include a panel of guests, and the host's job is to involve the whole panel in presenting the issue without having one or two people dominate the conversation.

There are some other unique talk formats on cable television. For example, CSPAN offers a television call-in program with different hosts and news or political representatives every morning. WABC carried *Imus in the Morning*, which is also broadcast nationally on WRFD, a cable and satellite television service. It is actually a talk radio program in New York that includes many interviews. A broadcast performer interested in talk television may find more opportunity in the cable field than in the broadcast television area.

7.13 SPECIAL INTERVIEW SITUATIONS: POLITICIANS AND ATHLETES

Interviews with politicians are an important part of the democratic process. During national and local elections, you may be called on to interview many political candidates. Even during a non-election year, politicians frequently want to appear on-air to promote their agendas. Your job is to present objective, impartial interviews with all political candidates and to provide the audience with balanced and fair information about the record of each person. This can be especially difficult in today's environment. Polls indicate that the public does not trust journalists and that part of the problem is a perceived liberal bias. Although the fairness doctrine, which guaranteed fair coverage, is long gone, it is still a broadcaster's ethical responsibility to provide a wide range of views for the public.

Politicians always present a challenge to the interviewer because most of them are well rehearsed and smart about the interview process. To provide information to the audience, you may need to be a bit more aggressive with a politician than you would be with other interviewees. It is probable that the politician has an agenda and will not cooperate with you until he or she is given the chance to say what is important to him or her. Therefore, it is usually best to let politicians say what they came to say so you can get on with the topics that you have determined are most important for your audience. Remember that if you are interviewing a politician regarding a controversy, it is your obligation

```
┌─────────────────────────────────────────────────────────────────────────────┐
│                    INTERVIEWING DO'S AND DON'TS CHECKLIST                      │
│                                                                               │
│  DO                                    DON'T                                   │
│                                                                               │
│  Come prepared                         Ad-lib your way through an interview    │
│  Research guest and topic              Monopolize the conversation             │
│  Make a tentative list of questions    Stick only to prepared questions        │
│  Know your audience                    Ask more than one question at a time     │
│  Use verbal and nonverbal feedback     Jump in to avoid silence                │
│  Use humor carefully and only where    Give your opinion                       │
│    appropriate                         Give guest questions before the          │
│  Write out open, close, and first        interview                             │
│    question                            Comment with "uh huh," "I see," or       │
│  Listen actively                         "okay"                                │
│  Use open-ended questions              Ask leading questions                    │
│  Interrupt when appropriate            Ask closed ended questions               │
│  Maintain control                      Be untruthful about your identity to     │
│  Be objective                            obtain an interview                    │
│  Know legal guidelines                 Answer a question at the same time        │
│  Be familiar with ethical standards      you're asking it                      │
│  Enjoy the person and topic            Ask obvious questions                     │
│  Ask for explanation of jargon or      End an interview with "I see our time    │
│    ambiguous terms                       is up"                                │
└─────────────────────────────────────────────────────────────────────────────┘
```

FIGURE 7.6 *Interviewing checklist.*

to have credible sources to back up your own ideas. Rumors and gossip are never sufficient.

Although all interviews require general preparation, a political interview requires that the interviewer be familiar with the record of the politician. This record can be obtained through public documents, articles in the press, or voting records.

Although the political interview provides the interviewer with many challenges, the sports interview can be a lot of fun, but also frustrating. Often athletes are preoccupied before a game and are tired afterward. Many are inexperienced public speakers. Noise and confusion in dugouts, locker rooms, and at sports arenas may make hearing a problem, since these interviews are usually conducted on-the-scene. Generally, sports interviews are edited for later use and the final version often includes only the responses to your questions. In contrast to political interviewing, you should assume that your audience is familiar with the sport and record of the athlete you are interviewing, so you don't need to provide a lot of background information.

7.14 CONCLUSIONS

Interviewing is an important aspect of being a broadcast performer. Although countless interviews occur in the media today, many are ineffective and merely consist of simple sound bites. Effective interviewing requires preparation and development of specific skills. Preparation includes research about the person and the topic. Skills include listening, asking questions, paraphrasing, and developing trust with the interviewee.

The advent of talk radio and television, while not a traditional format since the interviewer/host is responsible for providing a forum for audience participation, has added to the mix of interview opportunities today. Due to the relatively low cost of producing interview programs as well as the proliferation of channels, talk shows will be an important aspect of the media for many years to come. Review the Interviewing Checklist in Figure 7.6 to summarize some of the key points made in this chapter.

Self-Study

■ QUESTIONS

1. Which question is most appropriately worded for an interview?
   a) Why did you leave your position with the government?
   b) Because of the problems with children's access to pornography, don't you think that there should be censorship on the Internet?
   c) Do you approve of television ratings?
   d) Mr. McCain, are you disappointed that you lost the election?

2. Which question is not appropriately worded for an interview?
   a) Why do you think people join cults?
   b) Tell us why you left your position with the government. It was because you disclosed some financial difficulties to the press, wasn't it?
   c) What are your plans for the future?
   d) Is there anything you would like to say that I did not ask you during the interview?

3. Active listening _____.
   a) needs to be practiced because it can be learned
   b) includes responding to the interviewee with "yes," "no," or "okay"
   c) is nothing special since we listen all the time and anyone can do it
   d) is not necessary for effective interviews since the time is usually so short

4. Interrupting is an important skill for an interviewer to learn.
   a) true
   b) false

5. All of the following are important steps to prepare for an interview except _____.
   a) speak to colleagues and associates for background information about a guest
   b) plan a list of questions, even if they are not all used during the interview
   c) share the planned questions with your guest before the interview
   d) read material that the guest has written, if available

6. Which of the following is not something to listen for during an interview?
   a) vague words or phrases, such as "a number of problems"
   b) jargon words that may be unfamiliar to the audience
   c) cues that can refocus the interview
   d) opinions that you agree with, so you can discuss the topic from your point of view

7. It usually is not important to establish trust during an interview since most of the time you will not interview the same person again.
   a) true
   b) false

8. The general structure of an interview includes three parts—an open, a close, and the interview itself.
   a) true
   b) false

9. To move from one subject area to the next, a good interviewer uses _____.
   a) probes
   b) transitions
   c) cues
   d) humor

10. Since it's show business, a television interviewer should dress the part with clothing in stark colors and designs and glittering jewelry.
    a) true
    b) false

11. Which of the following is least likely to be a feature interview?
    a) an interview with a major league pitcher about his no-hit game
    b) an interview with a woman about her professional shopper business

    c) an interview with a politician about a pending sales tax increase

    d) an interview with a 90-year-old man about his skydiving experience

12. Which of the following could most likely be left out of an interview?

    a) introduction

    b) welcome

    c) questions

    d) close

13. Which television talk show host has an interview set that puts his or her guests on the dominant side of the TV screen?

    a) Jay Leno

    b) Oprah Winfrey

    c) Larry King

    d) David Letterman

14. Some television talk shows have been referred to as "food fights" because they cover a "smorgasbord" of topics each week.

    a) true

    b) false

15. Interviewing athletes can be especially challenging for all of these reasons except _____.

    a) some athletes have poor communication skills

    b) often interviews with athletes are conducted in noisy, busy environments

    c) many athletes are preoccupied with game details

    d) many interviews with athletes require extensive background information about the sport

■ ANSWERS

If You Answered A:

1a. Correct. This question is open-ended and allows the guest to respond as he or she feels is appropriate. The interviewer can easily probe with follow-up questions to elicit additional information if necessary.

2a. No. This question is open-ended and allows for a lot of discussion. (Reread 7.7.)

3a. Yes. Active listening is a skill, and with practice over time an interviewer can readily develop in this area.

4a. Correct. This is a true statement because interrupting, when appropriately used, is a necessary skill to control the interview.

5a. No. Obtaining background information, by speaking to colleagues and associates of a guest, is a very important aspect to preparing an interview. (Reread 7.5 and 7.6.)

6a. Incorrect. Asking for an explanation of something that is unclear is a necessary aspect of interviewing. (Reread 7.7.)

7a. No. Without a level of trust between the interviewer and interviewee, a good interview will not be possible. (Reread 7.3.)

8a. Incorrect. There are five basic parts to most interviews. (Reread 7.3.)

9a. Wrong. Probes are used for follow-up questions. (Reread 7.7.)

10a. No. Conservative dress is the rule. TV cameras may have problems with bright colors or plaids and the lights will cause those baubles to be distracting. (Reread 7.8.)

11a. No. Feature interviews often focus on celebrities. (Reread 7.2.)

12a. Wrong. The introduction sets up the entire interview and gives the audience vital information about the program, guest, and topic. (Reread 7.3.)

13a. No. Leno's humorous comments are as important as the guest's responses, and emphasis is put on the host if he appears on the right side of the TV screen. (Reread 7.4.)

14a. No. While a variety of topics may be covered, the term "food fights" refers to the name calling and physical violence that guests often become involved with on these shows. (Reread 7.12.)

15a. Wrong. Some athletes are poor speakers, making the interview process challenging. (Reread 7.13.)

If You Answered B:

1b. Incorrect. The question is leading. Rephrase the question to allow the person to express his or her opinion. (Reread 7.7.)

2b. Yes. This question is leading and may box the interviewee into a specific answer or may cause the interviewer embarrassment if incorrect.

3b. No. This type of response is annoying and interferes with later editing. If you are off camera it may be unclear to the audience from where these verbal tics are coming. (Reread 7.7.)

4b. Incorrect. Interrupting is important to use to control the interview, especially with guests who talk too much. (Reread 7.9.)

5b. No. Prepared questions provide you a smooth start and add to a sense of security, so this is an important step in the planning process. (Reread 7.5 through 7.7.)

6b. Incorrect. Listening for unusual words and asking the guest to explain them will help the audience to understand the guest. (Reread 7.7.)

7b. Yes. Trust is an essential ingredient to a good interview, so this statement is false.

8b. Correct, this is a false statement. There are usually five parts to an interview: an introduction, a close, the interview, a welcome, and a reintroduction.

9b. Correct. Transitions are used to change topics.

10b. Yes. This is a false statement. Unless the interviewer is trying to cultivate a specific persona, conservative dress (including jewelry) is best on television.

11b. No. Feature interviews often focus on people who have unusual occupations. (Reread 7.2.)

12b. Correct. While a welcome creates a friendly atmosphere and helps establish rapport with the guest and audience, some feel it has become a cliched time waster.

13b. No. Winfrey's interaction with the guest is important to the style of the show, and emphasis is put on the host if she appears on the right side of the TV screen. (Reread 7.4.)

14b. Yes. This is a false statement because the term "food fights" refers to the name-calling and physical violence that guests often become involved with on these shows.

15b. Wrong. Often interviews with athletes are conducted on-the-scene, in noisy locker rooms, for example, which makes them challenging. (Reread 7.13.)

If You Answered C:

1c. Incorrect. This is a yes/no question. Rephrase to allow for some detail. (Reread 7.7.)

2c. No. This question gives the guest an opportunity to explain his or her projects and may be a good way to end the interview. (Reread 7.7.)

3c. No. Active listening requires energy and the knowledgeable use of a set of specific skills. (Reread 7.7.)

5c. Yes. It is usually unwise to share questions with a guest as it takes away from the spontaneity of the interview responses.

6c. Incorrect. Cues are important to hear so you can pick up on ideas and explore them during the interview. (Reread 7.7.)

9c. Wrong. Cues are used to develop an idea or refocus the interview. (Reread 7.7.)

11c. Yes. A political interview would most likely be a news interview.

12c. Wrong. Of course not; an interview must have questions. (Reread 7.3.)

13c. Yes. King's guests are on the right side of the TV screen, which puts emphasis on the guest and topic rather than the host.

15c. Wrong. Many athletes are preoccupied with game details even though they are expected to give an interview, making the process more challenging. (Reread 7.13.)

If You Answered D:

1d. Incorrect. He obviously would be upset over losing an election. Rephrase to have him express his feelings or thoughts. (Reread 7.7.)

2d. No. Although yes/no questions are usually ineffective, this is a good question to end an interview to give the person a chance to say what he or she was not given the opportunity to say during the interview. (Reread 7.7.)

3d. No. No matter the length of time you may have with a person, active listening will enable you to get the best interview possible. (Reread 7.7.)

5d. No. Knowing as much as you can about the person being interviewed will increase the likelihood that the interview will be successful. Reading his or her writings is a good way to understand your guest's perspective. (Reread 7.5 and 7.6.)

6d. Correct. Expressing your own opinion is usually not appropriate since the focus of the interview should be the guest.

9d. Wrong. Humor can be used to maintain interest, but is difficult to use. (Reread 7.7.)

11d. No. Feature interviews often focus on people's accomplishments. (Reread 7.2.)

12d. Wrong. While the close is the end of an interview, it's important to summarize the interview, thank the guest, and promote the next program. (Reread 7.3.)

13d. No. Letterman's humorous comments are as important as the guest's responses, and emphasis is put on the host if he appears on the right side of the TV screen. (Reread 7.4.)

15d. Correct. The interviewer, when interviewing athletes, assumes that his or her audience has a great deal of knowledge about the sport and the individual athlete, so very little background information is necessary.

Projects

■ PROJECT 1

Record a radio interview.

Purpose
To give you the opportunity to research, plan, and conduct an interview in a radio setting.

Notes
1. Be sure that you are familiar with the audio equipment you will use. If you are concerned that you will be unable to operate equipment and interview the subject, arrange for someone to help you.
2. The interview may be recorded in a radio studio or using portable audio equipment, but be sure that all the equipment is operating properly before starting.
3. The topic of the interview should be appealing to and appropriate for a college-aged audience.
4. This should be an unedited interview, conducted without interruption.
5. Follow the basic interview model discussed in this chapter.

How to Do the Project
1. Your instructor may assign another student in your class for you to interview. Plan to meet with this student outside of class time to discuss possible topics and to gain personal information for your introduction. Topics could include hobbies, activities, or a special topic about which he or she is knowledgeable, such as an environmental issue. The instructor may also require that the interviewee be someone from outside the class.
2. Do some basic library research on the topic. From that research, develop a list of 10 questions. Be sure to include a bibliography.
3. Write out an introduction and close for the interview.
4. Record a five-minute interview with no breaks onto a CD, MP3, or other approved medium.
5. Play the interview and critique yourself based on the interviewing checklist in Figure 7.6.
6. Turn in the recording, the list of questions and bibliography, the introduction and close, and your critique to your instructor to receive credit for completing this project.

■ PROJECT 2

Record a TV interview.

Purpose
To give you the opportunity to research, plan, and conduct an interview in a television setting.

Notes
1. Television requires a number of people to make a performance happen. Be sure to explain your project idea to the entire crew.
2. The topic of your interview should be appealing to and appropriate for a college-aged audience.

3. Be sure to explain the equipment or studio setup to your guest to make him or her feel comfortable.
4. If the interview is conducted in a television studio, your instructor will arrange for a crew as part of the class. If done on location, be sure you have arranged for someone to operate the camera for the segment who knows how to operate the equipment properly.
5. The program will be 10 minutes long and not be edited.
6. There will be a 30-second break halfway through the interview. Plan your reintroduction for after the break.
7. Follow the basic five-part structure of an interview, as outlined in this chapter.

How to Do the Project

1. Arrange to interview a faculty member, staff member, or administrator at your university. Be sure to clear the date, time, and place with the person you will be interviewing.
2. Arrange for a pre-interview time and request a resume, if available.
3. At the pre-interview, discuss possible topics and set the time for the actual interview. Based on the interview topic, develop a list of 10 possible interview questions and a short introduction.
4. Conduct library research on the background of the topic and develop five additional questions and a bibliography.
5. Write out your open, the close, the reintroduction, and your possible questions on index cards or paper that can be put onto a clipboard.
6. Record the program.
7. Play the interview and critique yourself based on the interviewing checklist in Figure 7.6.
8. Turn in your interview recording, written materials (including your bibliography), and your critique to your instructor to receive credit for this project.

■ PROJECT 3

Plan an interview.

Purpose

To acquaint you with the resources available to an interviewer when planning to interview a well-known person.

Notes

1. Choose a well-known person in entertainment, politics, or sports.
2. Be sure to use library resources such as biographical information from *Current Biography* magazine. There should be a lot of information available, especially on the Internet; however, be aware that some sources will be more credible than others.
3. Choose an angle or focus for the interview. Try to plan an interview on one aspect of the person's life or contributions. An interview that tries to cover too much will not be as interesting to the audience.
4. The interview topic should appeal to and be appropriate for a general audience, as might watch the most popular television station in town.

How to Do the Project

1. Get the approval of your instructor for your choice of a well-known personality.
2. Research the person's background and try to obtain copies of things he or she has written, if appropriate and available. Develop a bibliography.
3. Develop a list of possible questions that could be used for an extended, half-hour interview.
4. Describe the audience in terms of demographic and psychographic characteristics. Explain how the planned interview questions relate to the audience or why you think the audience would enjoy this interview.
5. Turn in the list of questions, bibliography, and audience explanation to your instructor to receive credit for this project.

CHAPTER EIGHT

NEWS ANNOUNCING

8.1 INTRODUCTION

Broadcast journalism can be an exciting and challenging aspect of a performance career. It's an area of performance that has changed a great deal in the last decade. On the radio dial, **National Public Radio (NPR)** continues to provide a flow of indepth, often award-winning, newscasts. However, there is some concern over the limited amount of radio news that is generally available. Although some of us turn to radio as a source of news at some point during the day, television still tends to be the primary news source for most people. News magazine programs from the television networks that once aired weekly are now on the air two or three times a week. The six and eleven o'clock newscasts continue to be the most important time slot for local TV stations.

A new area for news performance is developing because newspapers are supplementing their coverage with news videos on their websites. Most are seeking to make the Internet a major source of revenue.

In 1980, when the **Cable News Network (CNN)** signed on with a 24-hour news service, the opportunities to work in television news expanded. The success of CNN has led to other news and information services, such as MSNBC and Fox News, which also reach an international audience. The increased opportunities for anchors and reporters are especially important for women and minorities. A variety of on-camera (talk show host, financial reporter, weathercaster) and behind-the-scenes positions (editor, producer) were also created for these around-the-clock news services. In addition, performance skills such as news writing and ad-libbing have gained extra emphasis as cable news operations frequently go live with breaking stories and devote longer periods of time to covering a story than do traditional radio and TV operations. More recently the Internet has become a major source of news for many. In addition to written stories and blogs, streaming video, iPod downloads and postings to such sites as YouTube provide a wide variety of audio and video opportunities to know what's going on in the world.

Broadcast journalism entails the accurate dissemination of facts about stories, events, and ideas to the public using electronic media signals. It includes the selection, preparation, and presentation of information. The term **newscaster** has been used to describe a performer specifically employed to deliver the news. It often carries a slightly derogatory connotation that suggests the individual is merely an efficient reader of a script. The preferred, and perhaps more accurate, term is **broadcast journalist**, as this describes an individual who gathers, writes, edits, and arranges the news as well as reads it on-air. The focus of this chapter is on the presentation of news by the anchor and reporter. However, a brief look at the selection and preparation of news is important in understanding the complete role of the news broadcaster.

8.2 DETERMINING NEWS VALUE

What is news anyway? News is an acronym for north, east, west, and south, and this implies that news is what happens all around us. It can be local, national, or international events that affect the public. Most dictionaries will define news as information about recent happenings, usually delivered through newspapers, radio, or television. Today we must add the Internet, ipods and cell phones. In a mid-1960s interview with *TV Guide*, broadcast journalist David Brinkley said, "News is what I say it is. It's something worth knowing by my standards." However, most practitioners would agree that the reporter alone does not determine what news is. News value standards, as noted in the following paragraph, are used by journalists to ascertain what is news.

To determine whether an event is newsworthy, journalists use a variety of criteria, including proximity, timeliness, human interest, significance, conflict, and prominence.

For local programming, news is what happens close to us geographically, the *proximity* of the event. For example, a bank holdup in Iowa won't be of much interest to someone in Florida, but a shopping mall fire in Springfield, Illinois, will have a lot of news value to the Springfield area audience. *Timeliness* is another important criterion for news value—news is what is happening now. Broadcast journalism is unique among news forms because of its *immediacy*, or ability to report news as it is happening. When a news event has reached the point of "it happened yesterday," it has lost a great deal of news value for the media. *Human interest* relates to the emotional impact a story may have. What people are interested in, whether it is monumental or trivial, is often newsworthy. Even though it may occur on the other side of the country, the birth of sextuplets would have fairly high news value across the nation because of its emotional interest.

How an event may affect the audience determines its *significance* and news value, as does the number of people directly affected. For example, an increase in the Ohio state income tax rates would be important for nearly everyone in the state, but an increase in the liquor license fee for that state would have less news value as it has impact on a much smaller group and thus less significance for the whole audience. An event often becomes news because it is unusual or out of the ordinary; for example, *conflict* has a high news value. Two adjacent nations living peacefully side-by-side isn't news, but those two nations threatening to declare war against each other is. We've already mentioned that the general significance of an event is its news value criterion, and so is the prominence of the newsmaker. A neighbor down the street getting tipsy at a strip bar isn't newsworthy, but a congressman in the same situation would raise the news value of the event considerably.

Finally, how *visual* a story is can determine its news value for television, and this criterion must be considered. This has become a controversial area in determining news value because sometimes stories are included more for their visual element than for any news value. For example, a story about a decrease in an important economic indicator might be given less news value because the visual element includes only a spokesperson delivering the announcement, perhaps with a chart or graph showing the decrease. A department store fire with visuals that include leaping flames, billowing smoke, and firefighters scurrying around could be judged to have more news value because it looks good on television. In reality, the economic story could have a far greater impact on

the audience than the fire and probably should have the greater news value. There is no doubt that visual impact must be given some consideration for television; however, it should supplement and not replace the other news value criteria.

One additional note about news: most news stories are categorized as either hard news or soft news. **Hard news** is what most people think of when you say news—a bank robbery, a plane crash, or an increased trade deficit. It's usually a breaking or ongoing event that is important because it has impact for the listeners and is information they should know. It has the element of immediacy. **Soft news** is sometimes called feature news and is information that might be interesting or even enjoyable to know about, but has far less impact on the listener. Soft news is usually not dated. Although there are exceptions to this, the story could run today or next week and be just as viable for the audience—for example, a story about a local senior citizen who has collected Mickey Mouse figures for the past 50 years, or tips on how to prevent frostbite could make good soft news stories. Every news story has importance to a particular audience, and the specific target audience is critical to broadcast stations. Generally, each program service knows its target audience and expects reporters to write and choose stories for that particular audience.

8.3 NEWSCASTER CRITERIA

The criteria that make a good newscaster include both physical and personal qualities. In addition to all the attributes we've noted earlier in the text as important for any media performer, the newscaster should pay special attention to factors that build a credible and authoritative style. *Credibility* is the degree to which the audience perceives you as reliable and trustworthy, and it's absolutely essential for a journalist. Credibility is established by the way you report stories, your history for accuracy and how you present yourself. In radio, this authoritative presence is communicated to the listener to a large degree by the announcer's voice. Your news voice needs to convey a serious tone, to be clear and free from accents, and always to utilize correct pronunciation.

While a music announcer may try to develop a peculiar style with a distinct mannerism, a news announcer should have a style that is unobtrusive. Any mannerism can be distracting and get in the way of the message, which is the news. Tone of voice should be sincere and show interest in the story. The wrong inflection can make it seem as if the newsperson is making fun of the community or a person in that community, and no one likes that no matter how novel the subject matter. Clearly articulating words and correctly pronouncing local names are musts. Listeners expect that the pronunciations they hear in a newscast will be accurate. Mispronunciations or slurred or mumbled words will greatly damage your credibility and the news effort at your station. Listen to Audio Track 8.1 to hear an example of the typical radio newscaster.

For the television and cable newscaster, appearance will be another important criterion. The telegenic appeal of newscasters is determined by their manner of dress, hairstyle, and other physical characteristics. Male newscasters almost always wear a suit and tie or sport coat and tie ensemble, although TV news anchor Dan Rather, on occasion, broke this mold by wearing a sweater while delivering his network newscast. Female newscasters have more flexibility in their clothing choices, but should stick to fairly basic outfits that present a professional image. While there is no need for a female newscaster to wear man tailored clothing, frilly blouses do not often work well on television and can be distracting to the TV viewer. The best rule of thumb is to be well dressed but conservative. Remember that flashy colors or complex patterns can cause camera problems, and some colors will be inappropriate if chroma-key technology is being used. Flashy jewelry can also cause camera glare and could be magnified on camera, so basic, conservative jewelry is best.

Hairstyles are also important and the newscaster should again avoid extremes of taste. This element will be less critical for men, but a good stylist can help strengthen your appearance by covering up or toning down other facial characteristics. Women will be more closely watched regarding hairstyle, and some female newscasters have been assailed for a drastic change in hairstyle or color. Some employment contracts actually forbid extreme changes of hairstyle without management permission. If you merely watch several of the local newscasters in your market, you'll quickly see what hairstyles are considered appropriate for television. You'll also notice that most newscasters, male or female, have perfect teeth and complexion and few wear glasses. Obviously, some physical imperfections in these areas can be corrected by professionals. Dermatologists can clear most skin problems and dentists can repair crooked teeth. If you're serious about being a newscaster, you may want to consider correcting these problems now.

While eyeglasses are certainly not prohibited on television, contact lenses are preferred. Glasses often cause glare and also present an obstacle between the newscaster's eyes and the TV viewer. Of course, good eyesight is a must since much of the TV newscaster's job is reading copy from a teleprompter. The use of this device is standard in the studio and, with portable prompting devices now readily available, is becoming more common on-location as well. There was a time when some television reporters seemed to have been hired solely because they looked good on camera, but this is no longer the case. While a pleasing appearance is important, you must also have good journalistic and performance skills to be successful.

A solid, broad-based education is also very important for a newscaster and helps build credibility. News stories cover a wide range of issues, and familiarity with topics from local government, to education, to the arts will be helpful because these are all areas you may cover. A lack of knowledge in these subjects ultimately will be detected by the listener and will undermine your credibility. A good sense of local, national, and world geography will help you place where the news is happening and avoid inaccuracies. Knowledge of history and political science will help you convey an understanding of the roots of today's news stories. A news announcer must also stay up-to-date with current affairs. Reading newspapers and news magazines, and watching and listening to network-level radio, television, and cable news will keep you abreast of events and allow you to deliver the news authoritatively. Other skills that you learn in college, such as utilizing research techniques, formulating the right questions to ask, and knowing what you don't know, help add to your credibility as a journalist.

8.4 NEWS SOURCES

The newsperson depends on a variety of sources of information to write the news. One critical source of information is the news agency **wire service**, such as the Associated Press (**AP**) or Reuters. Some networks, such as ABC, also provide a news wire. These news services have reporters around the world and distribute a variety of reports to all stations that are members. The news is delivered to the radio station via satellite or phone line on a closed-circuit feed, which is a direct link from the news source to the local station. The information is then fed to computer terminals set up with the appropriate software to capture the news data. Information can include ready-to-read world and national newscasts, feature stories, sports, stock market information, entertainment news, and other broadcast-ready copy. Most wire services also offer state and regional news. Use of wire service material lends credibility to local stations because, without having to pay for individual reporters, the station has access to current news events, whether they are regional or international.

While news wire copy is broadcast-ready, it is often rewritten by the local newscaster to either better fit the station's style, correct mistakes (which do creep into news wire copy), incorporate some local angle to the story or adjust the length of the segment. Figure 8.1 shows a news summary as sent by the AP news wire. If a station is associated with a network such as NBC, CNN, or AP, it has access to information through its **affiliation** with that network. The network provides audio and video feeds, which include complete newscasts and clips that can be incorporated into a local newscast. Some wire services also provide a separate audio/video service that operates in a similar manner. Networks usually provide a complete newscast at the top and bottom of the hour, and sports, business news, and other feature information at specific times during the hour. Like the wire service, the network feed is usually delivered via satellite, microwave or fiber optics.

The broadcast newscaster also depends on the local newspapers. Since the newspaper probably will have many more reporters than the station gathering news, a broadcast newscaster can utilize the paper for both story ideas and actual stories. While some radio news operations have been known to read stories from the newspaper verbatim, proper news technique would dictate rewriting the newspaper story and giving credit to the newspaper. Often the reporter will merely get ideas for a story from the paper and then develop the story with his or her own contacts and resources. The broadcast newsroom also monitors police, fire, and other local emergency radios with scanners to keep alert to breaking news stories. While much of what is

---

AP-8th NewsMinute

Gunman attacks meeting. . . Sugar plant explodes. . . Shuttle's in space

KIRKWOOD, Mo. (AP) _ A man who'd lost a lawsuit against his city outside St. Louis, Missouri, is blamed for opening fire at a council meeting, killing two police officers and three city officials. The mayor is critically hurt. The gunman was killed by police. He'd been a contentious presence at previous meetings, but the mayor decided against banning him from proceedings.

PORT WENTWORTH, Ga. (AP) _ Firefighters in Georgia are still battling flames at a sugar refinery that exploded last night. Six people are missing. No official word on what sparked the blast at the plant in a Savannah suburb that left dozens injured. Officials suspect volatile sugar dust.

FINDLAY, Ohio (AP) _ Ohio's governor tours flood-ravaged Findlay today, along with other affected areas in two counties. The water along Findlay's Blanchard River finally began to recede yesterday. But forecasters say Grand Rapids' historic downtown area could be threatened today by the Maumee (mah-mee) River.

HOUSTON (AP) _ The crew of the space shuttle Atlantis is getting ready to check their space-craft for damage that may have been inflicted from yesterday's launch. At least three pieces of foam came off the fuel tank two minutes into liftoff. Atlantis is set to reach the space station tomorrow, where a 2 billion dollar lab will be delivered and installed.

VIENNA, Austria (AP) _ Oil prices are rising today as investors see a more stable stock market. Dow Jones Industrials climbed higher yesterday after recent sell-offs. Energy investors often interpret the stock market as a barometer of economic health.

(Copyright 2007 by The Associated Press. All Rights Reserved.)

FIGURE 8.1   An Associated Press NewsMinute. (Reproduced with permission of the Associated Press.)

picked up is minor fender bender type material, learning of a major freeway accident or downtown fire at the same time the emergency service does, allows the broadcast journalists to both report the event and get on-the-scene reporters dispatched immediately.

Other sources of information that local stations rely on are press releases, the **video news release (VNR)**, and news tips. The basic press release provides background material on an event and is often produced by public relations firms for specific clients ranging from entertainers to the federal government. There is considerable ethical concern about the increased use of press releases as a source of news as stations have cut back on the hiring of local personnel. Local stations often do not identify the origin of a press release and the audience mistakenly assumes it is a legitimate news story rather than a story provided by an agency interested in promotion of its client. The broadcast newsroom also receives tips about possible news stories from its listeners and viewers. Some stations heavily promote this by giving special numbers to call ("If you see breaking news, call WDMA, at …") and offering a reward for the best news tip of the week.

Finally, broadcast journalists utilize their own reporting skills. These skills include researching, interviewing, and developing sources. Compiling a list of people to contact can help you understand a complicated story or provide background information. These people may provide you with leads or other information about a new story. Most media reporters maintain a list of contacts (both individuals and organizations) they call each day, which can provide them with news on a regular basis. Some newscasters are assigned a **beat** or specialty area, such as education, government, or health and medicine. The reporter would need to acquire specialized knowledge in that area and would be expected to

regularly contact sources to develop news stories. Such a list can be a big asset in times of breaking news. It's also a good idea to keep a **future file**, which can be as simple as a group of file folders labeled for each day of the month or some similar arrangement. In the folders, under the appropriate date, the journalist keeps possible future news story ideas. It could be a press release for an event taking place later in the month, or a note about an important meeting happening next week, or anything else that might be developed into a news story. Another wise move for a beginner is to get out and meet your contacts. When you arrive on a new job, go and connect with them. Find out what phone numbers they prefer you use, and other people to contact if they are not available. Develop an email list as well. It will speed your work and bring you respect. Don't forget to thank them also, as they will provide the information that will ease your day.

8.5 WRITING BROADCAST NEWS

Writing in an appropriate, conversational broadcast style is critical. A simple rule to follow is to write the way you talk, also referred to as "writing for the ear rather than the eye." You'll have to be slightly more formal and precise than you would be in everyday conversation. For example, the use of slang or incorrect grammar is not acceptable, but remember that the words you write are to be heard by the audience, not read. Learning to write in this style takes practice and lots of it, but here are some basic copywriting guidelines to follow that should make your performance much easier to deliver and get you started effectively writing for the ear. Seasoned pro Megan Mosack stresses the importance of writing in Performance Tip 8.1.

PERFORMANCE TIP 8.1

Broadcast Writing

Megan Mosack, of WIBW in Topeka, Kansas

"There are several things I wish I would have know before I got into the broadcasting industry, and the most important one is the importance of writing. That is clearly the most important thing you can learn and master in the broadcast industry. In fact, the ability to write well will open many, many doors for you that you never expected would be opened for you-just because you have an understanding and strong grasp of the English language and how to use words."

(Hear more of Megan Mosack's comments on writing on Audio Track 8.2.)

In general, it is best to keep your words simple and clear and your sentences short and precise. Do not include too many facts because it is difficult to understand so much information at once. Numbers should be rounded off; for example, $2586 should be written as "more than twenty-five hundred dollars." Avoid abbreviations and acronyms unless they are well known, such as Dr., Mrs., or FBI. Broadcast news writing should be concise, and you should learn to edit out unnecessary words. Use of **contractions** makes the copy sound conversational and also keeps it short. Accuracy is critical, and you should never write anything you don't understand. Be sure that you attribute ideas and quotes to the correct sources. **Attribution** means referencing the source of a news story or statement within a story, such as "Mayor McShea told reporters there would be no tax increase this year." You don't want to be the source of the story. Keep attribution words simple, such as "says," "told," or "reported" for indirect quotes, and "in his [or her] words" for direct quotes. Another potential error to keep in mind is the danger of convicting someone before the courts have done so. Always use the words **alleged** or **accused** in any crime report until you are sure there has been a conviction.

The use of "quote, unquote" is awkward and is only used if there is concern over the exact source of the quote because of its critical nature. Often you can use the "quote," but omit the unquote, using a slight pause and a change of voice instead. On sensitive material, you may want to use the "unquote" as well.

One of the first points to remember is that you know much more about the story than your audience does. Further, they will only get to hear it once. They cannot ask, "Would you please explain that?" Remembering the acronym COIK may help. It stands for "Clear Only If Known." It suggests that something is understandable only if the listener already knows considerable about it. You don't want to do a report that only a few can follow.

In broadcast news stories, ages and titles are usually given before the name so that the audience is prepared to hear a name (for example, 10-year old James Smith). Because of broadcasting's immediacy, the following guidelines are used: 1) write in the present tense, 2) use active rather than passive voice, and 3) keep time references close to the verb. "Today, the president is announcing his view on the new tax law" is easier to read aloud than, "A new view on the tax law was announced today by the president." Writing for broadcast news also includes the use of special script formats. You will probably be writing using a computer, and will likely be using specialized scripting software. However, if you're writing on paper, use one

---

CHEMICAL EXPLOSION
0:45 3/27, 9 AM
S. Miller

One person is still missing this morning after a massive explosion at the Dow Chemical plant in Elgin, Illinois. The force of the blast blew half the roof off the West 95th Street plant. A worker who was standing only 10 feet away when the tank blew up is missing and feared dead. Plant investigator Jeff Denver believes the explosion occurred as workers began mixing chemicals for paint thinner.

INSERT #102 Investigator Denver
RUNS: 0:10
OUTCUE: ". . . look at our controls"

Five other workers were also hurt and two firefighters received minor injuries. The explosion reportedly shook homes seven miles from the plant. Investigation into the accident continues.

###

FIGURE 8.2   Radio news script.

side of standard 8-1/2 × 11-inch paper and double-space your work. Radio news copy begins with a slug line that indicates the reporter's last name, the date, the newscast time, a story identification, and the story length. The script is written using the full length of the page and a standard end mark is inserted after the last line. End marks in broadcast scripts are either "###" or "-30-." Figure 8.2 shows a sample radio news script format. When **actualities** (the recorded sounds of the news event) are used, the script includes the length of the actuality and an **out cue**. The out cue is the last few words on the recording, so the newscaster is prepared to begin reading again when the actuality ends. Review Figure 8.2 for an example of a radio script.

Television news follows the same basic broadcast style as radio, but also includes the use of a special script format, as shown in Figure 8.3. The television news script begins with a slug in the upper-left corner that includes the writer's name, date and time of the newscast, and a subject description or title. The upper-right corner often includes a timing of the complete story. The television news script page is divided in half, because it's really two scripts combined. On the

left-hand side are the visual aspects of the newscast—these are the technical instructions for the director. Key commands are usually written in ALL CAPS. On the right-hand side are the words the newscaster will read. Usually, initials are inserted at the beginning of each news story, indicating which anchor is to read that particular story. The script style will vary slightly depending on the complexity of the story, which can range from the anchor simply reading a story on-camera to reading a lead-in for a field-reporter story or live remote. Realistically, some stations may have somewhat different systems.

Broadcast news copy is organized in a "pyramid" style, meaning the most important points of the story are given in a concise lead sentence and then the remaining details of the story are given in descending order of importance. The news story is told by giving the basic "who, what, when, where, why, and how" information in very short, simple sentences that are easy to read out loud. The **lead** sentence tells the listener what the story is about and usually contains only a few of the above facts. Try reading this newspaper report out loud: "A huge snowstorm blew across the

---

CHEMICAL EXPLOSION	0:45
3/27, 10 AM	
S. Miller	
JM (Anchor on CAM)	One person is still missing this morning after a massive explosion at the Dow Chemical plant in Elgin, Illinois.
	-Anchor VO-
Anchor VO	The force of the blast blew half the roof off the West 95th Street plant. A worker who was standing only 10 feet away when the tank blew up is missing and feared dead. Plant investigator Jeff Denver believes the explosion occurred as workers began mixing chemicals for paint thinner.
SOT: 0:12	-SOT-
SUPER: JEFF DENVER	OUTCUE: ". . . and take a look at our controls"
JM (Anchor on CAM)	Five other workers were also hurt and two firefighters received minor injuries. The explosion shook homes seven miles from the plant. Investigation into the accident continues.
	###

FIGURE 8.3 Television news script.

Midwest yesterday with whiteout conditions and drifts up to 8 feet high, canceling flights, forcing motorists off roads, and keeping mail carriers from their appointed rounds." Were you able to read the sentence without taking a breath? In contrast to broadcast newscasters, newspaper reporters include as many facts (who, what, when, where, why, how) as possible in the first sentence (lead). Additional details are included in follow-up sentences, in order of decreasing importance. The editor can trim the copy from the bottom up, to fit the space available, without losing important information. This style of writing, known as the inverted pyramid, will not work in broadcasting because it is awkward to read, no one really talks that way, and the listener or viewer would get confused with all that information coming in a single sentence. When writing broadcast news, just remember the KISS principle: keep it simple, Sam (or Susan)! The who, what, when, where, why, and how are included in the story, but not all in the first sentence.

Broadcast news is always written to time. The reporter times the story by reading *out loud* with a stopwatch. If you don't read the news aloud, it will not time out properly, as most people read faster silently than they read out loud. Another way to time a news story is to count lines or words. Four lines of radio copy (about 40 words) usually last around 15 seconds. In the computerized newsroom, script-writing software can be put to use to time the news script. News copy may also be read directly off the computer screen, scrolled at the appropriate read rate for the newscaster. To ensure a newscast will time out properly, news broadcasters often prepare extra copy called **pad** or **fill**. This consists of a some additional material that can be read to fill extra time or discarded if it is not necessary.

8.6 THE RADIO NEWSCAST

The individual stories that a media journalist develops during the day become part of a newscast. For radio, this is often a two- to five-minute report that might be broadcast every hour. Stories to be covered are usually selected by a news director and then given to a field reporter to be developed. At radio stations, all the news jobs may be accomplished by one person. The final stories for the newscast are selected by the news director based on news value and the target audience.

Once the stories are selected, their order is determined. This is usually referred to as "stacking." Stations often have a set pattern for the organization of stories. If all the news is being produced locally, local news will usually come first, unless there is a national or international story of major significance. Some stations may first air a network newscast that covers the national and international news, and then follow that with a complete local report. Each station determines the overall structure its newscasts will follow. Usually, traffic and weather are important aspects of the newscast, especially during **drive time**. Sports, stock market reports, and health stories have also become important factors in news content, but inclusion depends on the station's target audience and time available.

The length of individual news stories varies from about 10 seconds to 2 minutes. The shorter stories are usually straight reading and are preferred for radio. In broadcast journalism, time is important. If stories are 30 seconds each, the number of stories that could be covered in a 5-minute radio newscast is only 10. If commercials, weather, and traffic are included, the number of actual news stories declines. Therefore, reports are often less than 30 seconds long.

Since radio is an auditory medium, radio news should employ as many actualities as possible. An **actuality** is the sound of the news event or the voice of an actual newsmaker. For example, during a radio news story about the U.S. Congress, an actuality might consist of comments by the local congressional representative. Television uses actualities called **sound bites**, which include the voice and face of the newsmaker. A television news report is usually made with several sound bites, which are joined with additional copy into a completed story, called a **package**. A television news story as well as a radio report may also use natural sound (**nat sound**). For example, as the president addresses the press corps in the Rose Garden of the White House, applause, laughter, or a police siren may be heard in the background. This **ambient noise** adds interest and immediacy to the story.

During editing, sound may be worked into the program in several forms: a sound bite alone, a sound bite with nat sound, or even a sound bite and nat sound at reduced volume with the reporter's voice at full level. This technique is often used as a reporter leads into a sound bite segment. When the recording does not include natural sound, the newsperson usually reads a script over the video in what is known as a **voice-over**. Another way to get sound, other than the anchor's voice, into a newscast is to have a radio reporter call in to the station and record a **voicer**. This is an oral news report from the scene of the event. A voicer and an actuality can be combined into one complete story.

At the end of the actuality, the newsperson needs to let the people back at the station know the story is finished. This is usually done by giving a tag line that closes the story and a standard closing line, usually something like, "For WDMA, this is Robin Smith reporting live at the county courthouse." The news anchor must be aware that when "For WDMA…" is heard, it's the cue to get ready to announce again.

Since much of what we hear in the news is serious, even depressing information, a radio or television newscast frequently tries to end with a **kicker** story. A kicker story is a humorous or human-interest report that may put a smile on the listener's face. The wire services usually include a kicker at the end of their hourly news summaries and have features sometimes called news quirks, such as those shown in Figure 8.4, that can be rewritten as kicker stories.

8.7 THE RADIO NEWS ANCHOR

The radio news anchor is the on-air performer who delivers the news to the listener and is also usually the news director for the station. Modern radio news is largely done by one individual, except at large-market stations or networks and all-news stations where larger staffs are common. At most radio stations, a single person writes, edits, and announces one or more newscasts per hour during his or her shift.

The primary job of the radio news anchor is to oversee and put together the entire newscast (producing). This includes selecting and writing stories in addition to performing. Other duties include introducing stories produced by field reporters or from other news sources, such as a wire service or network. Since stations do not want to repeat the same stories every hour, the radio anchor must spend time updating and rewriting the stories between newscasts.

The radio news anchor at a local station probably does field reporting, too; however, if the staff is small, he or she may be totally confined to the studio. This means that the anchor must obtain all information for the newscast while working from the studio. In this case, the anchor relies heavily on wire services, network feeds, and the telephone. The anchor may be responsible for following up a local story, but at a small station this would primarily mean making phone calls to his or her sources.

At a larger station, the anchor would be part of a news team. In addition to studio work, he or she may also be responsible for covering local events, such as a city council meeting. This could mean a demanding schedule, as meetings are often at night and the job on the air is usually during the morning drive time. However, the anchor position is usually the highest paid news position, and most radio newscasters who begin as field reporters are working toward obtaining an anchor slot. Listen to Megan Mosack's comments on the importance of knowing your community in Audio Clip 8.3.

Another of the realities of modern radio is that, with the ownership of large numbers of stations by a single company, many news reports may originate from the same studio, with the anchor tailoring each report to a specific station or community by making references to local people, landmarks and events.

8.8 THE RADIO NEWS REPORTER

The job of the radio reporter is to write and report stories from the scene of a news event. Often these stories are recorded, brought back to the studio, and then edited for the best possible sound reproduction and length. However, filing a story live from the field adds a certain element of credibility, even if the audio quality is slightly inferior to studio quality. There are a number of ways to file an audio story from the field, including phone lines, cell phones, two-way radios, and broadcast lines. The field reporter also relies heavily on the basic audio recorder and microphone. The rapid proliferation of cell phones now makes it virtually impossible for a radio field reporter to be out of contact with the station. The job of the reporter is to use the phone to send recordings, or live reports, back to the station. Many devices can be used and, because a radio reporter is usually alone, a working knowledge of this equipment is essential.

A better way to send a signal is through a broadcast line. The cost of a line can be high, so usually they are not cost-effective for short periods. A press room, perhaps in a city hall, could be an ideal place for a broadcast line to be installed. Reporters should familiarize themselves with the location of broadcast lines and the equipment necessary to use them. Some news operations have a news van equipped with a two-way radio system. The reporter can drive the van to the scene, cover the news event, write the story, and report back to the station via two-way radio.

For many years, the cassette recorder was the basic tool for the radio reporter to gather sound at the scene of a news event. However, several digital recorders that

MORNING PREP - MORNING PREP - MORNING PREP - MORNING PREP
KICKERS

MEN IN PINK

BUFFALO, N.Y. (AP) _ It takes a real man to wear pink -- six of them. The Blue Devils will be wearing pink today when they take to the ice. The guys on New York's Fredonia State college team will trade their usual jerseys for pink ones, along with matching socks in their game with rival Courtland State. It's part of an effort to raise money and awareness for breast cancer research. Assistant coach Greg Heffernan came up with the idea. His mother Jane is a breast cancer survivor. Fans can think pink as well. Pink T-shirts and breast cancer awareness ribbons will be sold at the game. Some of the pink jerseys will also be sold in a silent auction, to benefit the American Cancer Society.

UNINVITED VISITOR

NEWARK, Del. (AP) _ Sara Kelly Sheats-McDonald might seem like a nice enough houseguest. According to authorities in New Castle County, Delaware, she phoned the homeowner at work, let the dog out and helped herself to a snack. But police charge this guest wasn't invited. According to officers, the homeowner received a call from Sheats-McDonald at her office. The woman noticed on the caller ID the call was coming from her own home phone number. Police say when they got to the home, they found that Sheats-McDonald had lit candles and helped herself to cake and soda. She now faces burglary and other charges.

FAKE BUG MAN

RUSTON, La. (AP) _ Something about the exterminator bugged police. Now, Richard Taylor is charged with posing as the bug man or a maintenance man to rip-off dorm rooms and apartments in the Louisiana Tech area. Authorities charge he used the ruse to steal laptops and other valuables. The crimes were first reported last month. This week, police in Ruston, say a suspicious tenant called a property manager about the so-called maintenance man. The property manager chased the suspect to the campus stadium, where police busted Taylor.

COOLER MAILBOX

OGDEN, Utah (AP) _ How does a cooler sound for some cold mail? Record snow in the West is giving rise to drifts and creativity, too. The snow is burying homeowners' mailboxes. So, Christopher Lizotte uses a blue 5-gallon Igloo cooler to get his mail. He notes it's waterproof and meets all the government requirements by simply carrying a label with the words "US Mail" and his address. Postal officials in the Ogden, Utah, area report other residents are putting out buckets, bags or even just a board stuck in the snow for their mail.

KOMODO DRAGONS

WICHITA, Kan. (AP) _ Zoo keepers in Wichita are reporting an apparent virgin birth -- of Komodo dragons. Officials at the Sedgwick County, Kansas, Zoo say their two Komodo dragons are female. As far as they know, these particular endangered reptiles have never been exposed to a male. The two baby dragons were hatched less than two weeks ago. The experts say there are two other known cases of Komodo dragons being hatched without male fertilization. But the zoo keepers say they'll do DNA testing on the mama and baby Komodos to make sure there was no daddy dragon involved.

by Jamie Friar

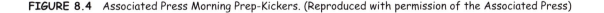

FIGURE 8.4 Associated Press Morning Prep-Kickers. (Reproduced with permission of the Associated Press)

record directly onto a hard drive, are now being used by many reporters in place of cassette recorders. Listen to a news interview with Senator John Kerry, conducted by Lisa Brooks and Eric Slocum, on Audio Clip 8.4.

8.9 THE TELEVISION NEWS TEAM AND NEWSCAST

Unlike radio, where one or two people may be responsible for putting together and airing the entire newscast, television requires a team effort. While the viewer sees the on-air performers, there are many other people behind the scenes who make it possible for the newscast to come together. The news team is made up of the on-air talent and a production crew. Gathering the news requires an assignment editor, producers, editors and videographers (sometimes called "photogs") in addition to field reporters. In general, a TV news staff outnumbers a radio news staff by about ten to one. This means that your ability to work with others is critical to your success in television news.

The news director is the top broadcast journalism job. This individual is in charge of the overall news operation. In television, he or she is usually not an on-air talent and will deal more with personnel and policy decisions around the newsroom. The second-in-charge for most news teams is the news producer, who is responsible for the on-air style of a newscast. While an executive producer is responsible for the overall look of the newscast, on a daily basis, line producers, associate producers, and field producers are responsible for various segments of the news program. The producer balances story content, determines how many stories to include, sets the story lineup, and watches the timing of the newscast. The stories used for the newscast are selected by the producer based on news value and target audience, but ratings are always an important consideration, especially for the local television channels. Much of their revenue is generated during the commercials that air during the local newscast. An assignment editor (AE) has the main responsibility of deciding which reporter (and crew) will cover a particular story. The AE coordinates everything that goes on to cover the day's news. In addition to assigning stories, this includes lining up interviews, handling news phones, monitoring scanners, checking the news wire, and viewing the competition. Other key television news team jobs include videographer (shoots news video), video editor (edits raw footage into news story), writer (writes news scripts), and ENG technician (coordinates remote equipment for live, on-the-scene broadcasts).

Add the regular television crew people to all these, and you quickly see how much of a team effort a television newscast can be! As a beginner, you should realize that your first job may not be on-air, but rather as an associate producer or desk assistant. Neophyte journalists often help reporters with packages and may be assigned to write additional copy.

As mentioned earlier, the stories a broadcast journalist develops during the day later become part of the station or network's newscasts. For television, this often includes a 30- or 60-minute newscast at noon, one in the evening (5:00 or 6:00 pm), and one at night (10:00 or 11:00 pm). More recently, some stations have started 4:00 PM newscasts. Many stations also offer early morning newscasts as part of their total news effort. Once the stories are selected, the news producer determines the order in which they will be broadcast. This may be international, national, then local stories, or there may be a focus on local news with a few international or national stories mixed in. Sports and weather are other important aspects of the television newscast. Specialty information, such as traffic, entertainment, or stock market and health reports, is often included in a news broadcast, depending on the target audience.

A local television newscast often follows a pattern close to this one:

News	(15 minutes)
Sports	(4 minutes)
Weather	(2 minutes)
Commercials	(6 minutes)
Open/Close/Transitions	(1 minute)

Obviously, you can proportion the elements differently, but if you decide to give an extra minute to weather, you need to ask yourself, from where does that minute come? In broadcast journalism, time is crucial. The length of stories varies from 30 seconds or less, to more than 2 minutes. On television, the shorter stories are usually straight, on-camera reading by the anchors, probably with an *over-the-shoulder graphic* included. As seen in Video Clip 8.1, an over-the-shoulder graphic is a picture, chart, or other visual element appearing over the left shoulder (usually) of the anchor as the news copy is read. Longer stories can include additional visual elements, such as a recorded segment or a story from a general assignment reporter. Stories without some visual component often are not included in the television news lineup.

8.10 THE TELEVISION NEWS ANCHOR

One of the most visible roles in television news is that of the news anchor, whose job it is to present the newscast to the audience. This includes reading news stories and introducing reporters in the field. Sometimes the news anchor acts as the producer and therefore is responsible for the overall look and content of the news. Some anchors write the news copy and then deliver it, but are not responsible for the style or contents of the program. Many local news anchors would fall into this category. Some news anchors are excellent at announcing the news, but do not write or produce the news. Their job is to present the news in the best possible way. Anchors generally receive the most recognition, and are usually the highest paid people in the field of broadcast news. See Amy Basista's tip on getting the right mood for a story in Performance Tip 8.2

The typical local television news effort usually includes two anchors—a male and female, as shown in Video Clip 8.2. They alternate reading news stories throughout the newscast, giving the viewer some variety. The qualities most associated with successful news anchors include good appearance, news savvy, credibility, and ability to communicate well. If the anchor has a personality that also displays some charm and wit, he or she will have less trouble finding a position in broadcast news.

PERFORMANCE TIP 8.2

A News Anchor's View of Delivery

Amy Basista, news anchor at WCMH-TV/News Channel 4, NBC in Columbus, Ohio, says, *"I'm not reading a story, I'm telling a story. I always try to put myself into the story. If it was a fire story where someone was killed, I ask myself how the family would want me to sound."*

Teleprompter

If you have any role in news presentation, particularly in the studio, you are going to be involved with the teleprompter. Smooth delivery using this device will be essential to your success. While it will be challenging at first, many hundreds of people do it successfully every day, and you can learn it, too. Of course, the primary goal is to look and sound like you are conversing rather than reading. The first step to get you there is practice, but there are numerous techniques to apply as well.

At the anchor desk, some newscasters sit, while others stand. In either case, you need to exhibit good posture, but with a relaxed appearance. This means sitting or standing erect, without leaning forward on the counter. In most situations, you'll want the news copy in front of you—preferably one story to a page, in case you get instructions to delete or add a story via the IFB. Both for appearance and emergencies, you will need to check your copy after each story. This brief pause helps the viewer to understand that you're changing stories. The pause shouldn't be long, but will help keep the right story in front of you, in case the teleprompter suddenly fails. Many stations find the viewers prefer to have you appear to use the copy, even though your delivery is coming 100% from the prompter. In most cases, you'll want to keep the copy flat or with the edge toward the camera raised only slightly. Holding it at 45 degrees will cause the lights to be reflected back on your face, changing the lighting. It also can become a wall that you don't want between you and your viewers.

How do you appear to be just talking when, in fact, you're reading from a script? First, all the vocal skills that have been previously covered come into play—inflection, pauses, emphasis, and pace are all essential. In a television newscast, a monotone reading is going to sound terrible. In addition, being as familiar with the copy as possible will help your performance tremendously. Certainly practice the difficult words, but become well acquainted with the flow of each story, so that you aren't surprised by something you run into, such as when a sentence goes off in a direction you didn't expect. Beginners often do not become as familiar with their stories as they should.

FIGURE 8.5   The anchor's view of the teleprompter. (Photo by Alan Stephenson.)

Next, in reading the prompter, you should set the pace. Your operator's job is to adjust to your delivery, not the other way around. Don't feel you have to rush. Remember, you're likely to feel the need to hurry. You may want to find a comfortable rate during practice and have that speed held during your report. The prompter will show you four or five lines, but since the type will be large, each line will have perhaps only three words in it. Look at the center of the middle line and try to hold your attention there. Avoid having your eyes tracking across each line. While holding your eyes steady, you can use your peripheral vision to see the oncoming words. Having some of the words in your mind, you can then split your attention between the delivery of the current phrase and what's coming next on the teleprompter—difficult sounding, but doable.

The final step is getting away from the "death stare," where you are so locked in on the prompter that your body becomes motionless and your face, a grim deadpan. Your face and hands are critical tools in successful teleprompter delivery. When we talk normally, we use head nods and a variety of facial expressions for emphasis. The more animated your face becomes, the more real you seem. We communicate a great deal with our eyebrows, and these should be a regular part of your tool kit for broadcast delivery. Small smiles, frowns, nods, and eyebrow moves contribute to making you seem involved and interested, and can help with the viewer's understanding of the story as well. Small gestures with the hand not holding the copy can also be added. Being expressive and animated without overdoing it makes you a much more interesting newscaster to watch, and gives you a

professional appearance. See Video Clip 8.3 for a comparison of styles.

If you stumble over your words, correct yourself and go on. The operator should slow the speed of the teleprompter for a moment until you recover. If it's a big mistake or a bit funny, a shake of the head will let the audience know you're human and will make them more likely to support you. Of course, a steady string of errors is not good, so concentration, preparation, and practice are your friends. (See Video Clips 8.4 and 8.5 for prompter practice. Scripts are at the end of the Practice Material in this chapter.)

8.11   THE TELEVISION NEWS REPORTER

The job of the television reporter is to go out of the studio and report the news on-the-scene. As previously noted, some reporters may have specific beats like city hall or local entertainment, but most television news reporters work as **general assignment reporters**. They work on stories or cover breaking news assigned to them by a producer or assignment editor and are also expected to come up with story ideas of their own. Usually they work during a specific time of day called a shift. When they receive an assignment, the reporter researches the story, makes phone calls, sets up interviews, and goes on location to cover the story, usually with a videographer. Once on the scene, the reporter is responsible for interviewing people there and putting together a story. The videographer and reporter work together to be sure that visuals are taken that best tell the story. Video shot on-the-scene is called *raw footage*. The reporter might remain in the field longer to cover any late-breaking developments during the newscast. Some TV stations build their whole news philosophy around an action-news concept in which extra emphasis is put on stories that are reported live from the scene of an event.

Field Reporting
Field news reporting takes two forms, the **package** and the **live shot**, and, if you do them well, you greatly increase your potential of being hired. The portion of either that focuses on the reporter, is referred to as the **standup**. The package is a comprehensive report that may have been developed over most of a day, or even longer. It is prerecorded and edited, and may include interviews, voice-overs, *b-roll footage*, and reporter stand-ups, either at the start or finish or both. (B-roll footage is a recording made of a scene in which no one

is speaking, although there may be ambient sounds.) In some cases, the reporter may do a live open; introduce a longer segment that was recorded, edited, and narrated earlier; and then conclude with another live segment. In other cases, everything is prerecorded. When mixing live and prerecorded segments, try to use a consistent tone and pace so that the change from live to recorded isn't obvious. You may want to read the section on voice-over work in Chapter 11 to guide you.

In the recorded standup, most stations will expect you to do three things as a part of the recording: first, you will need to "slate" the piece, stating what the story is about, which "take" you are about to make, and perhaps the date. This is followed by a "countdown," usually 3-2-1 followed by a pause. In other situations, it may be 5-4-3 followed by the "2" and "1" said silently to yourself. This creates a blank space for the editor. In either case, it's important to keep the same rhythm during the entire count, for editing purposes. The slate and countdown also serve to get your mouth and voice working so that your first word isn't something that will go on the air. The third element is to take several steps (3 or 4) toward the camera as you begin your story. Movement toward the camera is the strongest direction in television and gives the viewers the feeling that you are coming to tell them something important. Take a step before you start talking. Remember, though, that each station may have a slightly different procedure for packages. A variation that is becoming more popular is the result of the lightweight cameras now in use. In this case, the operator walks backward while the reporter walks forward, always remaining the same distance from the camera. The walk can last the duration of all of the report in some cases. In this situation, the reporter must be aware of the route, although in most cases, it is along a sidewalk or through a building. Reporter Bill McGinty says that news directors love to see reporters walking and talking.

Once the field work is complete, the reporter returns to the studio where the package will be put together. At small television stations, the reporter may do the video editing, and write the story that goes with the video footage. At larger facilities, the reporter will be expected to log the footage, locating the sound bites, video segments and nat sound, listing the in and out cues for each. The reporter then writes the story using those cues. If properly done, the video editor should be able to assemble the piece using those instructions. A special skill here is to write to the video lengths so the timing is precise. Frequently time is short and the work has to be accomplished rapidly.

FIGURE 8.6 Reporter Carol Sullivan, of WKYC-TV, Cleveland, performs a standup.

Live Standup

The true challenge comes in the live standup because in the recorded package you can do several "takes" until you are satisfied. The live standup is one take, with everyone watching. There are several things to do before you step in front of the camera. For the beginner, the first step is to really know the story—understand it, including any implications it has or changes it may cause. Consider what is the most important aspect of the story. Then think about what the audience needs to know at the beginning to comprehend the rest of the story. You may need to provide some background—what happened before, and things you've been told may happen in the future. Realize that you may feel you know the story, but when the tally light comes on, some of that knowledge could vanish and you could be forced to rely on your notes. Although notes are common, and we'll return to them in a moment, the tendency can be to rely on them too heavily. Practice your report, off camera, without using notes, or limit yourself to one glance at them. This will help you measure if you have control of the story and what points you need to study further. In many cases, you will only have a minute or so for the report, so it is essential to determine and understand the key points. Repeating, many beginner problems result from not truly knowing the story. You should be able to tell it without notes, off camera. Read Pro Bill McGinty's advice in Performance Tip 8.3.

PERFORMANCE TIP 8.3

Tips from a Pro on Storytelling

Telling Stories

Reporters tell stories, so tell a story and don't forget that stories have beginnings, middles, and ends. When you are telling a story, try to think "Big Picture" and don't get caught up in too many details. Focus your story on 2 or 3 thoughts that you think are important and then find the people to interview who will best help you tell that story. If your story is about a property tax increase, don't just talk to the Property Appraiser at the Government building. Go to a neighborhood and interview the people who will have to pay the increase. *Stories are about people.* You don't need to interview 10 people, find one person and tell his story, or talk to 3 people on the same block and tell the story of the "Elm Street" neighbors and their new tax increase.

Get your story done quickly; learn to be a fast accurate writer, and a quick editor. If you master that, you will save yourself a massive panic attack at the end of the day. Don't miss your slot in the newscast because of "wasting time." Circumstances beyond your control, weather, traffic, equipment problems, are one thing, but missing slot because you didn't budget your time well is a one way ticket to the news director's office.

When covering big stories, realize you may have to turn several reports for your station and other stations all in the same day. *Time management* is everything. Get out the door early, and if people don't call you back, go to their office. People don't typically understand the deadlines of a reporter, so it's important to impress upon them that "sooner is better and tomorrow won't work." Most importantly, don't sit at your desk and make calls/research on your computer. And old friend (and a boss) once told me "News doesn't happen in the newsroom" ... so get out the door and make your calls from your cell, even if you have to make those calls from the bagel shop around the corner. You are more likely to find a story there than you will in the newsroom.

Tips from a pro. Bill McGinty is a reporter and anchor with KHQ-TV in Spokane, Washington and has more than 15 years of experience. See his biography in Chapter 13.

Notes are appropriate, but keep the quantity limited. You may want to write out your opening line, but after that use just one- or two-word reminders. Of course, you can also write down complex numbers or quotes that you wouldn't be expected to carry in your head. Plan a logical sequence for your points, and determine how you're going to close. More beginners stumble getting out of a story than getting into it. Consider, too, what you would skip if you are signaled that you are running long, and what you would add if you were running short. Establishing these things before you get on camera will make you far more comfortable than trying to figure out how to stretch or get out on time while you are talking to your audience. Students have a tendency to expect to rely on their notes too much. They write out too many words, sometimes several sentences, and then stumble trying to read them. While every story is a little different, if you have more than 20 words on your pad, you are probably over the limit.

The physical form of the notes is another factor to consider. If you choose to use a few sheets of paper, you can be sure the wind will come up and double them over, just when you need them. A small hard-backed pad is best, so you can control it with one hand. Write large enough, dark enough, and legibly enough so that you can read your notes quickly and easily. Hold the pad in your left hand at about waist height. Don't fall into the pattern of raising it every time you want to refer to your notes. Try to make their use unobtrusive. Just don't overuse them, as your audience will spend more time looking at the top of your head than at your eyes. The cartoon in Figure 8.7 is supposed to be funny, but it won't be if it happens to you.

How you start your report depends partly on how you are introduced, what's going on, and where you are. You may have an earpiece so you can hear how the anchor leads into your report. If so, tailor your open to fit with it. The anchor will probably introduce you in the **toss**, so you may want to return the greeting and then define where you are in relation to what you're covering. "I'm standing in front of ..." may be a reasonable beginning. See Video Clip 8.6. Be sure to remember the factor of mood in your opening and through the entire story—the mood and the story must fit.

Here are a few other tips to remember. A good rule of thumb regarding your appearance is to dress to fit the scene. While normal business attire is fine

FIGURE 8.7 *Cartoon: Bad notes.*

FIGURE 8.8 *Cartoon: Windy day.*

for most reporting circumstances, a more casual out-fit may be more appropriate if reporting from a flood scene or interviewing a farmer in the middle of a plowed field. Have a bag under your desk with seasonal wear, jeans, a polo shirt, warm sock, shaving kit with bathroom essentials, etc. Be prepared to adjust to your story and even go out of town for a report.

On camera, stand straight and look into the lens. Strive to be conversational, using good vocal techniques to communicate. Watch for any tendency to rock or fidget. Unfortunately, this situation is one where it is very easy to fall into "fillers"—the "uhs" and "ums" and even "ya knows" that sound amateurish. Hold the microphone in your right hand, at mid-chest level, about six inches from your mouth. If you're using a clip-on, don't hide it under a lapel, as it will muffle the pickup. If you have long hair, you may want to plan some means of controlling it. Having hair falling in your face or flying around can distract both you and your audience. Figure 8.8 illustrates what can happen. Avoid what, for some people, is almost a nervous habit—repeatedly pushing your hair back behind your ears. Ignore other distractions unless they relate to the story. Sooner or later you will have people waving in the background or otherwise being distracting. As a reporter, you may have to do standups in the middle of a crowd. Focus on what you are saying.

At first you may have trouble deciding what to do with your hands. Try to ignore them or use them for a few small gestures, but avoid putting them in your pocket. If you're using a hand microphone, it will be hard to point to something. It may be easier just to refer to it and perhaps comment on some visible element near the point to which you are drawing the audience's attention. Using a relatively small pad may make it possible to hold it with two fingers of your left hand and move the microphone to that hand when you need to use the right hand to point at something. If you must turn to point something out, only turn as far as necessary and then quickly turn back to your audience. Turning your back to the audience, except in very rare cases, is considered bad form. This is a lot to keep in mind, but these are things you can practice. For your delivery, just record the audio of a story and critique yourself. Do that often enough and the skills will develop.

Field reports aren't always short. Occasionally, you could find yourself covering an ongoing situation where you will be ad-libbing for a longer period of time, perhaps with little preparation. If things are happening on a more-or-less continuous basis, you will have plenty to talk about. Keep in mind that you can see more of the events than your audience, so description is encouraged. Describe not only the events, but also the environment. You can include sounds, smells, people's reactions, efforts to deal with the situation, and things that are changing. Paint a clear picture using descriptive terms for the size of the flames, the density of the smoke, or the rush of the floodwaters.

A harder situation is one where less is transpiring, but you're supposed to do live reports from the scene. An extreme example of this was when a man with a gun barricaded himself in a house, and nothing else happened. The police decided to wait him out. However, the station wanted regular live feeds, and the reporter struggled to find things to say. You can assume that some viewers have just tuned in, so a review of what has occurred up to the present is appropriate, and also a summary of anything else that is known. Again, you can use description of all you can observe. Possible outcomes are another direction to go with your report, but be careful about speculating too much as your remarks could be misinterpreted. If your on-air time is lengthy, it may be necessary to do a complete review, essentially repeating all that you have already said. This is an excellent time to keep your word rate down, as it will give you more time to think and will allow you to stretch the material as well. It's good practice, when you see a possible news story, to mentally list all the things you could talk about and describe in that situation. It will sharpen your observational skills and prepare you for something like the barricaded man.

Let's look at the process of preparing your field report in another way. Take a sheet of paper and divide it into four equal parts. Label each Must Use, May Use, Pad Only, or Won't Use. Gather your story and then go through it slowly, and, with each bit of information, decide in which of these four categories that item should be placed. This will help focus your thinking and make value decisions on each item. When you finish, most of your report will be waiting in the Must Use box. You only have to decide which are the most important, depending on how much time you have. Assuming that you are to do an onsite report of about 45 seconds, you would have about 135 words to work with, including your open and close, at standard delivery rate of 180 wpm. This approach will help you identify the material for your story and thinking about word economy.

For the on-location reporter, ad-lib skills are absolutely essential, and the newscaster in this situation will quickly learn that effective ad-libs require knowledge, practice, confidence, and organization. As with ad-lib commercials, you need a plan. How are you going to start? What element are you going to use as

a thread? What points are you going to cover and in what order? How are you going to conclude? Once you answer these questions, you have the basis for your notes. Reporters on location commonly make use of some pattern to present their news information. The most basic technique is a simple three-part pattern of beginning, middle, and end, as demonstrated in Video Clip 8.7. The beginning and ending follow a similar style by including the reporter's name and location. For example, many endings are along the lines of, "For WDMA News, I'm Beth Anderson at Mercy Hospital" or "From Public Square, I'm Ron Sanders … and now back to Judd and Susan." The middle part may be organized around one or more of the basic journalistic questions: who, what, where, when, why, and how.

Another technique used is to describe the scene. This begins with a general description of the conditions, such as time and weather factors. Then the scene is described in more detail. The best way to begin is to choose a direction; for example, begin at the left of the scene and move to the right, or begin from far away and move closer. Finally, the ad-lib ends on the area of action, which is described in detail. For example, if you are on the scene of a house fire, the description can include the people who are watching, the firefighters, and the condition of the house, in that order.

A third pattern or technique is to follow a chronological story line. This requires the reporter to know about the development of the story and to explain the story up to the present time. First, the reporter describes the current situation: a robbery at a convenience store. Then background information is added, such as conditions that led to the current news story. For example, at the scene of the robbery, the reporter may tell of other problems that have occurred there over the past six months. Finally, the reporter summarizes the current situation. Video Clip 8.8 shows some elements of both the descriptive and chronological techniques for the on-location reporter.

On-location reporting requires the announcer to put observation into words. Understanding the story and thinking of the main ideas, not the exact words, is necessary.

To build confidence, beginning newscasters can practice ad-libs in short segments, out loud, by describing everyday situations as they are experienced by the reporter. If time is a limitation, the focus of the story is on the most important facts for the audience to know. This determination is based on the reporter's knowledge of the target audience and an understanding of the facts. Never guess or try to tell what you don't know.

Accuracy and credibility are as important in the ad-lib situation as in any other news circumstance. No matter what approach the newscaster chooses, remember that effective ad-libbing takes preparation, practice, organization, and knowledge.

Study Figure 8.9 for an example of one way to break down a story.

A variation of the field report is becoming increasingly popular across the country. Commonly referred to as **active live**, it calls for the reporter to become more involved with the story, rather than just reporting it. Obviously, the reporter should not disrupt what is taking place, but in some way the reporter may be able to participate in it without changing its nature. Active live is more likely to apply in softer stories than in hard news.

In one case, a young woman reporter was assigned to do a story about the dangers of leaving small children and pets locked in a car on a hot summer day. Rather than just talk about it, she closed herself in a car in the sun, microphone in one hand and a large thermometer in the other. There she described how she felt in the rising heat. When she emerged after several minutes, dripping with perspiration, the thermometer reading 130 degrees, she made her point much more effectively than a straight standup would have done. Your producers will be searching for stories you can have reporter involvement, and you should be alert to possibilities as well. You could end up walking, talking, and participating all at the same time, so having a strong grip on the story you want to tell becomes critical.

PERFORMANCE TIP 8.4

Another Tip from Bill McGinty, KHQ-TV, Spokane, WA

Be creative! Be different! *Think outside the box and don't be afraid to break free from what other reporters at the other stations are doing on the same story. You'll never be first if you are constantly following. Look around you, and listen. The best stories and interviews are usually lurking on the fringe. Pay attention and take chances. For example, in Tampa, I was covering a story about a new Laundromat opening in the drug/crime-ridden neighborhood of East Tampa. The story was important because it represented a rebirth in a neighborhood where most people had simply given up on a good quality of life. It was the culmination of hard work between community activists and the police department who were both trying to improve things. The Mayor was present, so was the Police Chief as well as other dignitaries, so naturally reporters flocked to them … except one. Me. I noticed an older woman on her front porch in a rocking chair across the street, watching the whole ceremony at the Laundromat. I walked over and asked her what she thought of the event. We ended up talking to her and shooting the whole story from her view on her front porch. She talked about her 30 years living there and how it was such a nice place to live when she moved in with her family. She provided us with perspective by sharing her story of how she watched her nice neighborhood slip into a run-down/crime-ridden drug hole over the years. She even had pictures in a scrapbook of what the neighborhood used to look like 30 years ago. While the other stations put officials on TV, we put on a neighbor with a real story. Our news director loved it because it was different than what everybody else had done that day.*

8.12 AD-LIB SITUATIONS WITHIN BROADCAST NEWS

The broadcast newscaster needs to know how to ad-lib. Transitions during a newscast, such as when the newscaster turns to the weather person, are sometimes accomplished with a humorous, off-the-cuff remark. Reporters on location will also make extensive use of ad-lib skills. An important aspect of being a member of a news team is the ability to talk to your colleagues on the air, between segments. The idea is to sound informal and friendly. These ad-libs are usually planned but not written out in the news script, and

it's occasionally obvious that they lack spontaneity. Not every performer has the ability to be humorous, but some performance situations require it anyway. The fact that it is a news "team" helps, because each announcer can play off the other. The basic toss technique allows a smooth segue from one segment of the news to another. The news anchor may introduce the weather person by picking up on key words or a phrase from the news script just read. For example, "Well, the heat wave continues and Dick is here to tell us what we can expect over the next few days. Any showers in the forecast?" One concern faced by the newscaster in this type of ad-lib is how to keep it in good taste.

While situations will vary and you will have to learn to adjust, here are some guidelines to help you prepare your report:

1. Where am I? Let the audience know from where you are reporting.
2. What's going on? Present a quick overview of the situation, which will probably have to be adjusted to fit the anchor's lead-in.
3. Will the audience need any background information?
4. What's important? Interesting?
5. What may happen in the future?
6. How do I end this appropriately?

News Story

Heritage Village, a $156 million shopping "community," is having its grand opening and the traffic is backed up for a mile in all directions. All the parking places are used and the cars are circling around hoping something will open. The police have shut the gates and tempers are a little heated. People have driven from the other end of the state and an adjoining state to take part. The builders had promised 3500 parking places when their plans were approved, but there is evidence that the actual total is more in the 2600–2800 range. What's more, the employees have already taken many of the parking places. The Village employs 3500 people. People who opposed the Village before it was built have told the news media that this immense traffic jam is just what they predicted, and that neighbors can't even get out of their driveways. Representatives of the Village say that the jam is just the excitement of the opening and will calm down in a few days. The primary intersection where the shopping center is located is Richards Avenue and Cedar Road in Linville.

Consider how you would answer each of the above questions using the information in this story. To familiarize yourself with the process, you could write out what you would say in the report. Then make notes from it and practice your report aloud.

The report might go something like this:

1. Where am I?	*I'm standing in front of the main gate at Heritage Village at the corner of Cedar and Richards,*
2. What's going on?	*Where traffic is backed up for at least a mile in every direction. Today is the 156 million dollar shopping center's grand opening, and people have come from as far as the other end of the state to be here.*
3. What's important?	*Clearly there isn't enough parking. Police have closed the gates but some cars keep circling, hoping to get in.*
4. Will the audience need any background information?	*When the complex was approved by city planners, the builders promised 3500 parking places. Police tell me that there are actually only 2600 to 2800 spots, and many of those were taken by the hundreds of employees who have been hired. When the center was being considered, opponents claimed traffic would be a horrendous problem. One of the leaders of the opposition today commented, "See, it's just as we told you it would be."*
5. What may happen in the future?	*The developers claim that everything will improve as soon as the initial excitement of the opening wears off.*
6. How do I end this appropriately?	*This is John Smith reporting from a big traffic jam at Heritage Village in Linville.*

Certainly there are other ways to tell this story. You might consider how you'd go about doing the report in other ways.

FIGURE 8.9   Breaking down a story.

Amy Basista, of WCMH-TV, says,

> "Ad-libbing is huge as an anchor. You have to have chemistry with your co-anchors, with the weather forecaster, with the sports guy. You have to listen to them, know what they're talking about, and act interested. When you're going into lighter things, it's a chance to show your personality, that you have a chemistry with the people you work with."

FIGURE 8.10 The importance of ad-libbing. (Photo and statement by Amy Basista, of WCMH-TV, Columbus, OH)

To move from serious news to a more casual style is not easy and the news copy needs to be written so the jumps are not offensive to the audience. For example, an insensitive anchor might toss with, "Speaking of an outpouring of sympathy, what about that rainstorm this morning?" Tacky? You bet.

Another situation in which the news team may chitchat is when a newscast ends early—that is, the available news copy is read before the newscast time is over. The newscaster may have to make a remark or two based on the content of the current news. This type of ad-lib situation is another reason an

understanding and knowledge of the news stories of the day are important and useful.

8.13 THE INTERNET AND THE FUTURE

Most individual broadcast stations, networks, and news organizations have a presence on the Internet. For example, visit web sites like www.klas-tv.com, www.foxnews.com, or www.ap.org. Internet reporting consists mainly of research, writing copy, and some technical skills, such as knowledge of computer software like Photoshop. The focus is on the information more than on the performer. These sites integrate several news sources and present news that includes graphics, audio and video, and written copy.

However, Brooke Spectorsky, General Manager of WKYC-TV in Cleveland and a vice president of NBC describes the future as "Backpack Journalism." Others have used the term "MoJo," mobile journalism. The reality of rising competition from multiple channels and the Internet means that revenues are tougher to come by and television news crews are likely to be reduced in size. Spectorsky envisions a time in the not so distant future when the news crew consists of one person equipped with a camera and tripod, a laptop and an Internet card. The reporter will go to a story, gather the news, shoot the related footage, put the camera on the tripod and shoot the standups, then edit the resulting footage on the laptop and send it to the station via the Internet. Next the reporter would write a story about the situation and add it to his/her blog, then prepare an edited version of the video and standup for an iPod download. Following that might be a report for streaming video. If you happened to be a sports reporter covering a game, you might then go online for a live question and answer session with fans. Then it may be time to move on to the next story.

A senior on an internship spent her summer working for a newspaper's website where she chose stories to cover, shot and edited them and then did the audio portion as well. It was a smaller city, and she was mostly on her own. What does this mean for the reporter? Clearly a beginner needs to be knowledgeable and able to write, edit, and report a news story, which is in different lengths and to be able to shoot and video edit appropriate footage on a laptop and then transmit the results over the Internet. Bill McGinty of KHQ-TV in Spokane tells the story that when he applied for his first job in broadcasting, as a reporter, the manager was as interested in whether he could shoot and edit videotape as he was in his delivery. McGinty had taken production classes in college and replied that he could. He got the job. That kind of versatility will be essential for just about every new reporter going into the field.

8.14 CONCLUSIONS

Broadcast news announcing is a demanding area of work. In addition to the vocal skills required, newscasting demands an understanding and knowledge about specific legal and ethical issues (see Chapter 13). The ability to write for broadcast, to make correct news value judgments, and to understand the audience are critical to the success of a news career. In radio news, familiarity with equipment in the field is a must. For television and cable, technical skills in editing and equipment use can also be important. In addition to these skills, research, credibility, an interest in reporting, and willingness to put in long hours are the elements that combine to make a successful broadcast journalist. The announcer starting out in the news area should also realize that there are many more reporter positions available than there are anchor slots, and that most beginners will start a news announcing career as a reporter.

Self-Study

■ QUESTIONS

1. The term broadcast journalist describes an on-air performer specifically employed to deliver the news.
   a) true
   b) false
2. A multiple-car accident on the interstate would be an example of a _____ story.
   a) soft news
   b) feature news
   c) hard news
   d) timeless news
3. Which of the following is used the least to determine the news value of a story?
   a) proximity
   b) conflict
   c) audience
   d) the reporter
4. Which of the following is least likely to develop a broadcast journalist's credibility?
   a) having a good sense of geography
   b) staying current with world affairs
   c) using correct grammar and pronunciation
   d) using humor in the newscast
5. An international news wire service that a broadcast journalist may use as an information source is _____.
   a) Reuters
   b) NPR
   c) ABC
   d) VNR
6. Which quality is least likely to be associated with a successful news anchor?
   a) credibility
   b) news savvy
   c) humility
   d) good appearance
7. Writing in a conversational style includes all of the following except _____.
   a) use of contractions
   b) use of slang
   c) use of proper grammar
   d) use of simple words for attribution, such as "says" or "told"
8. Extra copy used by the newscaster to fill time is referred to as _____.
   a) pad
   b) extra copy
   c) outcue
   d) kicker story
9. The sound of a news event or the voice of a newsmaker is known as _____.
   a) a wrap
   b) a voicer
   c) a voice-over
   d) an actuality
10. All of the following describe the duties of a news anchor except _____.
   a) may produce the newscast
   b) generally stays in the studio
   c) develops a news package
   d) introduces stories in a newscast

11. The telegenic appeal of a newscaster could be lessened by all of the following except
_____.
   a) wearing eyeglasses
   b) crooked teeth
   c) wearing conservative clothing
   d) a flamboyant hairstyle

12. Which of the following is not included in the slug line of a news script?
   a) reporter's last name
   b) outcue
   c) story identification
   d) newscast time

13. The television news team member who is responsible for deciding which reporter will cover a particular story is the _____.
   a) general assignment reporter
   b) news director
   c) news producer
   d) assignment editor

14. Notices about meetings, news releases, clippings from magazines, and personal notes about upcoming events would most likely be found _____.
   a) on a beat
   b) in a future file
   c) through a wire service
   d) on an affiliation list

15. All of the following describe the duties of a general assignment reporter except
_____.
   a) reporting news on-the-scene
   b) recording a news package
   c) producing a newscast
   d) reporting breaking news live

■ ANSWERS

If You Answered A:

1a. No. A broadcast journalist gathers, writes, edits, and arranges the news, as well as reads it on-air. Newscaster is an older term that has been used to designate a news reader. (Reread 8.1.)

2a. Wrong. A breaking news story like this wouldn't be considered a soft news story. (Reread 8.2.)

3a. Incorrect. News is what is close (in proximity) to the audience either emotionally or physically. (Reread 8.2.)

4a. No. A background in local, national, and world geography provides a sense of where the news is taking place and helps build a newscaster's credibility. (Reread 8.3.)

5a. Correct. Reuters is a British international news wire service.

6a. No. Credibility is a quality associated with successful news anchors. (Reread 8.8 and 8.9.)

7a. Wrong. Conversational style includes the use of contractions. (Reread 8.5.)

8a. Correct. Additional copy, known as pad, is planned just in case the announcer needs to fill extra time.

9a. Incorrect. A wrap is a combination of an actuality and a voicer. (Reread 8.6.)

10a. Incorrect. The news anchor often also produces the news, especially at smaller stations. (Reread 8.8 and 8.9.)

11a. This is not the correct answer because eyeglasses can become a barrier between the newscaster's eyes and the viewer. (Reread 8.3.)

12a. Wrong. The reporter's last name (and often first initial) is included in the slug. (Reread 8.5.)

13a. Wrong. The general assignment reporter will cover a story, but won't determine which story he or she might cover. (Reread 8.9.)

14a. No. A beat refers to a specific area a reporter may cover, such as the environment or labor. (Reread 8.4.)

15a. No. Reporting on-the-scene is the main responsibility of the general assignment reporter. (Reread 8.10 and 8.11.)

If You Answered B:

1b. Yes, this is a false statement. While a broadcast journalist may deliver the news, the term describes an individual who also gathers, writes, edits, and arranges the news. Newscaster designates an on-air performer who just reads the news.

2b. Wrong. Feature news is another term for soft news and a breaking story like this wouldn't be considered a soft news story. (Reread 8.2.)

3b. Incorrect. News often involves reporting of conflict. (Reread 8.2.)

4b. No. A clear understanding of current affairs helps the newscaster convey a sense of authority. (Reread 8.3.)

5b. Incorrect. NPR is National Public Radio, public broadcasting for the United States, not a wire service. (Reread 8.4.)

6b. No. News savvy is a quality associated with successful news anchors. (Reread 8.8 and 8.9.)

7b. Correct. Although people use slang in everyday speech, slang should not be used in broadcast writing because the style should be slightly more formal.

8b. No. There is a specific term for extra copy and "extra copy" isn't it. (Reread 8.5 and 8.6.)

9b. Incorrect. A voicer is a report filed from the field by a radio journalist. (Reread 8.6.)

10b. Incorrect. The job of the anchor is to be in the studio rather than in the field. (Reread 8.8 and 8.9.)

11b. This is not the correct answer because crooked teeth can lessen the newscaster's telegenic appeal. (Reread 8.3.)

12b. Correct. An outcue is used to identify the last few words of an actuality and when included in a news script would not be in the slug.

13b. Wrong. The news director is in charge of the overall news operation, but usually doesn't decide which reporter covers which story. (Reread 8.9.)

14b. Yes. A future file is a device that helps a reporter organize future story ideas.

15b. No. The general assignment reporter will often put together a news package. (Reread 8.10 and 8.11.)

If You Answered C:

2c. Correct. A breaking story like this is usually a hard news story.

3c. Incorrect. News must take into account the audience for which it is intended, how significant the story is for that audience, and how many members of the audience the story will affect. (Reread 8.2.)

4c. No. Physical qualities, especially the use of the voice and correct pronunciation, add to the credibility of a broadcast news reporter. (Reread 8.3.)

5c. Incorrect. ABC is a national network and local stations may be affiliates and receive information from various services offered, but there is a better answer. (Reread 8.4.)

6c. Yes. While humility would be a nice quality for the successful news anchor to have, many see themselves as "star" performers, and this quality isn't one often exhibited.

7c. Wrong. Although people may use incorrect grammar in conversation, broadcast writing needs to follow correct rules of grammar. (Reread 8.5.)

8c. No. An outcue is written on the script and includes the last few words of a taped segment. (Reread 8.5 and 8.6.)

9c. Incorrect. Voice-over is a term used in television to describe a voice heard over a video recording. (Reread 8.6.)

10c. Correct. The development of a news package is usually the job of the general assignment reporter.

11c. This is the correct answer. Well-dressed but conservative is the rule-of-thumb for the television newscaster.

12c. Wrong. Story identification is included in the slug. (Reread 8.5.)

13c. Wrong. The news producer is responsible for the on-air style of a newscast, but usually doesn't decide which reporter covers which story. (Reread 8.9.)

14c. No. A wire service provides news from an agency such as the Associated Press. (Reread 8.4.)

15c. Yes. Some news anchors may also produce a newscast, but this is not something the news reporter does.

If You Answered D:

2d. Wrong. Soft news is usually relatively timeless, meaning that it could run today or next week and still be viable. A breaking story like this wouldn't be considered a soft news story. (Reread 8.2.)

3d. Correct. The reporter alone does not determine the news, but rather must apply news value criteria to the story.

4d. Yes. While humor may be added to a newscast, it does not contribute to credibility and may undermine a reporter if not done correctly.

5d. Incorrect. VNR is a video news release that is a public relations form of information, not a wire service. (Reread 8.4.)

6d. No. A good appearance is a quality associated with successful news anchors. (Reread 8.8 and 8.9.)

7d. Incorrect. Proper attribution in news writing should be simple for the audience to understand and for the reporter to say. (Reread 8.5.)

8d. No. A kicker story is usually the last story of a newscast and includes humor or human interest. (Reread 8.5 and 8.6.)

9d. Correct. The voice of a newsmaker is an actuality.

10d. Incorrect. Introducing stories in a newscast is one of the main duties of the news anchor. (Reread 8.8 and 8.9.)

11d. This is not the correct answer because extremes of hairstyle can lessen the newscaster's telegenic appeal. (Reread 8.3.)

12d. Wrong. The time of the newscast in which a story is used is included in the slug. (Reread 8.5.)

13d. Correct. The assignment editor has the main responsibility of deciding which reporter will cover a particular story.

14d. Incorrect. This is a list of stations that have agreements with networks. (Reread 8.4.)

15d. No. A general assignment reporter will be called upon to give live reports quite often. (Reread 8.10 and 8.11.)

Projects

■ PROJECT 1

Record radio news.

Purpose
To give you the opportunity to present a newscast in a radio setting.

Advice, Cautions, and Background
1. Use the AP News wire stories in Figures 8.1 and 8.4 for this project.
2. Your performance is to be straight news reading except for the kicker. Add a sense of humor to your delivery of the last story by smiling when you read the story.
3. Read for meaning and vary the mood with the type of story, but remember that few words should really be punched for meaning.
4. Breathing is important in reading news. Read copy with long phrases, taking a breath only between stories or at the end of a sentence.
5. Remember to use pauses; they are also important in news copy to add emphasis and meaning.
6. Use broadcast writing style for the weather segment. Keep it simple.

How to Do the Project
1. About 1 minute of news copy is provided. The kicker story will add another 15 to 30 seconds.
2. You'll need to add a weather segment of about 20 to 30 seconds in length. Type the weather copy using broadcast radio script style.
3. Add an introduction and a close. You can also add additional segues between segments (for example, "In other parts of the country today … "), but be careful of the timing if you do that. It is not a requirement to add any transitions.
4. Total time of the newscast should be 3 minutes. Timing must be within 3 seconds without going over. Mark your copy to help you read it properly.
5. Record your newscast onto a CD, MP3, or audio cassette. If tape is used, be sure it is cued at the beginning of the news before you turn it in.
6. Do not staple the news script pages—use a paper clip.
7. Turn in your news script and the recording labeled "Radio News Summary" to your instructor to receive credit for this project.

■ PROJECT 2

Record TV news.

Purpose
To give you the opportunity to co-anchor a television newscast.

Advice, Cautions, and Background
1. Your audience is your city's general audience that would be viewing a local newsbreak between segments of a network morning show. Stories you write and ad-libs you do should take this information into account.

2. Remember, ad-lib does not mean unprepared. It only means you are not reading from a script.

3. Use an introduction and closing that include your name, title of the newsbreak, and a greeting.

4. Choose stories with different emotional content so that you can demonstrate your ability to convey emotion. The last story should be an upbeat kicker.

5. Following guidelines discussed in this text, your appearance should be appropriate for the local news.

6. Timing and taking cues from the floor director will be important. Be sure to go over the correct hand signals.

How to Do the Project

1. You will work on a news team. The news team will either read from a teleprompter (if available) or use a script.

2. One anchor should plan an introduction and the other a close. These will be short, ad-libbed segments.

3. Use the copy provided by your instructor, but put it into correct television news script style.

4. Turn in a copy of the script with performance marks and phonetic spelling as needed.

5. The completed newscast should be a 5-minute morning update and be within 5 seconds of that time without going over.

■ PROJECT 3

Record on-location news.

Purpose
To give you an experience of on-location, ad-lib television news reporting.

Advice, Cautions, and Background

1. Your appearance should follow guidelines as discussed in this text.

2. You will work in groups of five or six and tape each other. One person runs the camera, while another person gives time and other cues. Hand signals are the same as in the studio, so be sure to review the signals.

3. Remember to use direct eye contact with the camera and only occasionally glance down at your notes.

How to Do the Project

1. You will ad-lib a 1-minute news story from the fact sheet in Figure 8.11. Bring a notebook and pencil.

2. Take notes from the fact sheet and organize your information. Do not write out complete sentences, just key words or phrases. Write (or print) with large letters so your notes are easy to see.

3. Begin with a slate—your name, story title, and countdown (5, 4, 3, -, -). Keep the rhythm the same as you read the numbers.

4. Introduce yourself and the story. Walk toward the camera (about three or four steps) as you introduce yourself, then give your location, and begin to explain the story.

5. Use a hand-held mic and portable video camera to record your story on-location. For this project, you will be working in front of the administration building on your campus.

6. The story should be recorded in one take.

7. Use notes, but no written script. Turn in your notes, with the recording, to your instructor.

Ad-Lib Fact Sheet

SITUATION: Fire in the Administration Building has suspended exams during final exam week. Because of the damage resulting both from the fire and the firefighters, no one is sure when exams will resume. Seniors are concerned over losing credits needed for graduation. Students are packing their bags and leaving despite receiving no official word from the administration.

YOUR LOCATION: Outside the Administration Building

BACKGROUND INFORMATION: The fire occurred yesterday afternoon. At least three students are in the hospital, with one in critical condition. Names of the students have not been released. There are rumors that the student in critical condition is the senior class president. Apparently, the fire alarms did not go off. The cause of the fire has not been determined. The president of the university and the dean of Arts and Sciences were in the building and suffered smoke inhalation. The smoke was so thick they could not find their way out and a student (name unknown) led them to safety. The administration is trying to find the student.

Building Manager Jerry Lanz says the fire is the worst in the history of the school. He urges faculty and students to call the trouble line (231-6440) if they have any information about the fire. He is unsure of the extent of damage, but is certain only the main administration offices were affected. The classroom areas and the adjacent Business School were not damaged. It is the responsibility of the city to inspect the buildings. They have not been inspected since last year. The city would like to hire additional people to work on the inspection team, but funds are limited. Pat Logan, Director of Capital Improvement for the city, said the city is aware of the inspection problem around campus and does its best. She pointed out that the city responded quickly when called to the scene and has been responsible in its efforts to give city services to the university. City Hall will not comment further.

FIGURE 8.11 Ad-lib fact sheet.

8. End your report with, "For WDMA News, this is [insert your name]." Hold the microphone and look directly at the camera for at least 5 seconds after completing the story. HOLD YOUR POSE. You will be given a cue when to end.

Practice Material

The following is a true story, modified only slightly, that was published in a major newspaper, complete with two photographs. Using the techniques discussed in the text, prepare and record a 1-minute, 15-second report on the story.

LAKE MARTIN_For generations of the E. B. Smith family, the brick outhouse behind the six-bedroom home represented the epitome of 19th-century sanitary hygiene. Four holes, no waiting, separate facilities and entrances for each gender. When Bob Johnson and his wife, Karen, bought the old Smith home in 1982, they saw the outhouse as part of the historic package that came with the home, built in 1857. It was something worth saving, even if it had long out lived its original purpose.

The Johnsons' garage burned down in January, and they wanted to rebuild a new, larger one on the outhouse site. So they decided to move the old privy instead of tearing it down.

That's when they discovered the structure was built like, well, a brick outhouse. Initially they couldn't find a contractor willing to touch the building for fear it would fall apart if moved.

After all, the 10-by-6-foot wide structure did go back nearly to the days when this hilltop community was originally settled by southern Quakers, who rejected slavery and moved north during the early 1800s. The walls were two bricks wide, nearly as hefty as the three-brick thick wall of the matching house, where local bank treasurer E. B. Smith had had a commanding view of the surrounding farm field in Jackson County.

The Johnsons rejected several options: tearing the outhouse down and rebuilding it, erecting a replica or simply building the new garage around it (as one contractor had suggested). The cost of those options seemed prohibitive. But the couple also wanted to preserve the past—a sentiment perhaps reflective of their families' century-plus presence in the area.

Bob Johnson, 54, is the third-generation owner of Johnson and Sons bakery supplies and one of 12 directors of the Lake Martin Historical Society. His mother, Joan Johnson, also a director, paid for refurbishing the outhouse with new wallpaper, paint, and floors, shortly after her son bought the house. "It's part of our community heritage and we should try to preserve the things we have," she said. "Even outhouses."

Early in March, the Johnsons finally found a contractor willing to tackle the move, Saback Excavating of Emersonville. Owner Jim Saback had some serious misgivings about the first privy project he would face in 33 years of digging home foundations and building roads. "I thought it'd be almost impossible to move and keep it from falling apart," he said.

After reinforcing the outhouse foundation with steel beams, rods, and a surrounding concrete collar, Saback took a guess and brought in an eight-ton capacity crane. The outhouse didn't budge.

He tried a 14-ton crane. No dice. Saback quickly figured he was dealing with something weighing in excess of 15 tons—the equivalent of a World War II tank. By this time, word had gotten around town, and a small crowd gathered to watch. Someone suggested the project lent a new meaning to the term Porta-John.

The eighth-grade teacher found out about it from her students, who didn't have the slightest idea what an outhouse was and seemed both fascinated and grossed out by the concept. Meanwhile, out in the Johnsons' backyard, the Saback crew put a crane on either end of the outhouse. They used a backhoe to keep one crane from tipping over and pushed against the side of the structure with a small bulldozer. It moved. One slow, torturous inch at a time. But it moved, or rather slid, all 75 feet of it, with nary a crack in the original window panes or a shift of its estimated 5400 bricks. The new site is near the Johnsons' above-ground swimming pool, where the outhouse will provide dressing rooms, and storage for pool chemicals. Karen Johnson plans to landscape it with pansies, ferns, and day lilies. Her husband is keeping mum on how much he paid for the project. "It was not unreasonable, for something like that," he said, but more than I probably should've spent, I'll guarantee you that."

As for Saback, flushed with his success, he's more than willing to move another brick outhouse, "for the same amount of money." Shortly after the outhouse project, someone called to ask him about moving an old log cabin. Saback said he would pass.

(Watch one student's first attempt at this story in Video Clip 8.9. Consider the positives and negatives of the effort.)

■ NEWS COPY

News Copy #1

1. Mostly cloudy today, with a chance of flurries this afternoon. High about 30, with tonight's low near 22.
2. Zsa Zsa Gabor gets out of jail in El Segundo, California, today, after serving a 72-hour sentence for slapping a Beverly Hills cop last year.
3. Late in the summer of 1969, not long after Neil Armstrong took his first step on the moon, the first message was sent over the Internet.
4. With resident conductor Jahja Ling conducting, the Cleveland Symphony Orchestra will present Bruckner's Symphony #8 at 8pm tonight at Severance Hall.
5. Representative James Traficant came out swinging today at a candidates' breakfast. This was Traficant's first appearance since he acknowledged he was under investigation by a federal task force for underworld ties.
6. A Kenya Airways jet carrying 169 passengers and a crew of 10 crashed into the sea last night shortly after taking off from Abidjan. Airport officials said at least nine people survived.
7. Elian Gonzales's grandmothers arrive back in Cuba this morning, but without the child they had hoped to bring home. They will be greeted by a huge, government-organized parade throughout the streets of Havana.
8. Northern Ireland's shaky new government is hanging in the balance as the province awaits a report today on whether the Irish Republican Army has begun to disarm.
9. Feeling lonely, anxious, depressed, or bored? For some, relief comes at the shopping mall. Olivia Mellan, a Washington psychotherapist, insists some people actually get something like a chemical high from shopping.

News Copy #2

A Michigan woman has confessed to embezzling nearly 2 million dollars from the local United Way in Jackson. Jacqueline Allen-MacGregor worked at the agency for 20 years, ending up as chief of finance. Allen-MacGregor admitted to stealing the money to buy show horses. She faces up to 10 years in prison if convicted.

The number of premature births rose by more than 20% in the 1990s, according to University of Iowa doctors. The rise is partly due to more couples using fertility drugs. This causes more women to become pregnant with twins and triplets … and carrying more babies usually means they're born earlier.

Health researchers say that nearly 40% of Americans will be obese in five years. That's if we keep packing on the pounds at the present rate. You're considered obese if you're more than 30 pounds overweight, say the doctors. About 59 million people are already there. Even worse, about 65% of us are overweight to some degree. That level starts at 10 pounds more than you should be carrying. We typically add a pound or two a year and that's all it takes. Experts say you can stop this trend by just burning an extra 100 calories per day, or by cutting back on your intake by 100 calories. That's an extra one-mile walk per day or one less bottle of soda.

Thinking of calling in sick? Employees who do that too often might get fired. Employee absences have become such an epidemic that some companies are taking action. Workers with perfect attendance are getting raises. However, some companies are including attendance in performance reviews. Studies show that absenteeism costs companies an average of $789 per employee. American Airlines reports that more than 5% of its workforce is absent on an average day. Mercy Medical Center in Baltimore is firing staff who have more than seven sick episodes per year. Starmark International, in Fort Lauderdale, awards employees an extra $100 at the end of the year for each unused sick day. That's an extra $600 for perfect attendance.

The frogs are going to continue jumping in Calaveras County, California. The frog jumping contest, made famous by a Mark Twain short story, was endangered by a state law that forbids returning captured frogs to the wild. Almost 2000 frogs are captured each year for the jumping contest, and organizers feared that the California Fish and Game Department would require the destruction of the frogs in the contest. Not to worry though, the organizers found a loophole in the law that allows frogs to be released if they've been used in jumping contests.

News Copy #3

It used to be that a middle-class family lived on one income. Today, many of those families can't live on two paychecks. It isn't frivolous spending and high-priced cars, says a Harvard University study, it's the cost of what most people view as essentials—medical insurance, living in a good school district, and child care, among others. Unexpected job losses are adding to the problem, so that the number of families filing for bankruptcy has risen sharply. Credit cards are used to buy groceries and pay heating bills. Even with tight controls and credit counseling, it will take years for these families to get out of debt, even if there is no catastrophe to sink them further.

Many American companies are discovering that social consciousness is part of the cost of doing business. Pressure from the organization, People for the Ethical Treatment of Animals, has caused McDonald's, Wendy's, and Burger King to improve their treatment of cattle. Now Proctor and Gamble, Starbuck's, and Dunkin' Donuts have agreed to sell "Fair Trade Coffee," which is guaranteed to give the small growers a decent living. A number of groups are pushing hard for this action, as drops in prices paid to coffee farmers have created family crises in 50 coffee-growing countries.

Mexican police have arrested four men in connection with a tunnel that led from a Mexicali auto repair shop under the U.S.-Mexican border into Calexico, California. The 250-yard tunnel had lighting and ventilation and had probably been used to smuggle drugs and illegal immigrants into the United States.

In Lebanon, three more bodies were discovered in the ruins of two collapsed apartment buildings near Beirut over the weekend. Twenty-seven people were injured when two adjacent four-story buildings came crumbling down early Saturday morning. The owner of the buildings was arrested by authorities as he was caught trying to leave the country.

The deadly Ebola virus continues to spread in Uganda, as confirmation of the disease came from a third district of the country yesterday. The new case was found in MAS-in-dee, 11 miles north of the country's capital. So far, 106 people have died from the current outbreak.

A mortar bomb was discovered Saturday night in County Fer-man-ah-gan, a small community southwest of Belfast, in Northern Ireland. Four men were arrested in connection with the bomb. No group has yet claimed responsibility for the planned bombing, though the police are watching the Irish Republican Army closely. It is the first case of attempted violence since the cease-fire was reestablished.

Blowing snow and poor visibility have prevented the rescue of an ill American at the South Pole Research Base. The rescue attempt has been hampered by temperature approaching minus 100 degrees and strong, erratic winds. The next attempt will depend on improvement in the weather conditions. The ill American is in need of surgery.

Leftist rebels have kidnapped eight foreign tourists in the mountainous region north of Bogata, Colombia. The rebels finance their activities with the ransoms paid to release such victims. Colombia has the highest kidnapping rate in the world. Nearly 3000 people are abducted each year. Some individuals have been held for years. At present, the group is holding dozens of prisoners, including a former presidential candidate and three American contractors captured when their plane crashed in rebel territory.

Rangers at the Mammoth Cave National Park in Kentucky have a new problem—ginseng poachers. The medical root can bring $350 a pound and individuals from considerable distances are sneaking onto the grounds to dig up the valuable roots.

The federal government wants you to walk more. It's supporting a national walking program designed to get you to cut one hundred calories a day. In an attack on the nation's obesity problem, the program, called America on the Move, seeks to get millions to wear inexpensive step counters. The goal is to get you to walk an additional 2000 steps per day, which is the equivalent of about one mile. That mile will burn an extra 100 calories. There's a push to make people more aware of weight as a health issue so they'll start walking, exercising more, and eating less. Researchers also tell government health officials that the public needs more education on how to use the product label, which describes the calories and other factors in the food we eat.

Not too keen about wearing a necktie? Well, here's a new argument to use when you don't want that thing to put a choke hold on you. British researchers have found that a tight necktie increases the blood pressure in the eyes—that's a leading cause of glaucoma, a disease that damages the optic nerve and can result in the loss of vision.

A J. D. Powers survey finds that big-name cars with steep prices and world-class images—the Mercedes, BMW's, Cadillacs, and Jaguars of the world-are more likely to spend time in the repair shop than many cheaper cars. The study asked over 100,000 owners of cars less than three years old whether their service visits were for repairs or maintenance. Nine of the 13 luxury brands scored worse than the industry average of 35 percent. While some respondents may have confused the difference between repairs and maintenance, the results are still significant. The director of auto testing for Consumer Reports says European luxury brands have suffered as the manufacturers have focused on making new types of vehicles like SUV's or sought ways to cut costs.

America's expanding girth is showing up in a new location—the coffin business. It seems that a lot of people no longer fit in the standard casket, which is 24 inches wide. When Keith and Juliane Davis started Goliath Casket Company in the late 1980s, they sold about one "triple wide" coffin, their largest product, per year. Now they're shipping four or five of these oversize beauties per month. The "triple wide" is forty-four inches across and designed to handle up to 700 pounds. Cemetery operators have started increasing plot size, too. Looks like the Davis family has found a growth industry, as their business is increasing about 20 percent each year.

■ TELEPROMPTER SCRIPT FOR VIDEO CLIP 8.4

Good afternoon. It's (say day and date) and this is your hourly News Break. I'm (say your name).

1. President Bush announced a new Mideast peace initiative Tuesday in which he urged Israel to end its offensive against militants, and called Palestinian leader Yasser Arafat's efforts to prevent terrorism a failure. Bush said he is sending Secretary of State Colin Powell to the region next week to implement plans for a cease-fire and move on accords for Palestinian statehood. He also condemned the rash of suicide bombings by Palestinians in recent weeks. "They're not martyrs, they're murderers," he said, adding that Arafat has betrayed the hopes of his people by missing opportunities for peace. Prime Minister Ariel Sharon, in a meeting with Bush's envoy, Anthony Zinni, reportedly backed down and agreed to let Zinni meet with Arafat.

2. The nation's five largest pilots' unions have asked President Bush to intercede personally to let pilots arm themselves aboard commercial jets. The appeal to the president is an unprecedented show of solidarity by unions representing 114,000 airline pilots. It comes after two top Bush officials said they oppose guns in the cockpits. The unions say the new Transportation Security Administration has not moved fast enough to establish a firearms training program for pilots who want to carry guns. Some aviation experts say guns would create new hazards such as accidental discharge or thefts. The pilots' unions say a training program would address those concerns and that lethal force is the only certain way to stop hijackers.

3. A Taliban fighter held captive at Guantanamo Bay, Cuba, is expected to be moved to a U.S. Naval base in Virginia, because authorities believe he may be a U.S. citizen. The Pentagon said Yasser Esam Hamdi, whose birth certificate indicates he was born in Baton Rouge, could be moved to the Navy base at Norfolk, Virginia, as soon as today. Moving Hamdi to the base makes it easier to charge him in an ordinary federal court, rather than the military tribunals that will be used to try non-U.S. citizens who are Taliban or Al Qaeda fighters. It also will make it easier for him to assert the right to a speedy trial and to challenge unlimited pretrial detention. Apparently Hamdi's parents were working in the United States when he was born and moved back to Saudi Arabia when he was a toddler.

4. A fuel leak has forced NASA to postpone Thursday's launch of the space shuttle Atlantis, delaying a space station construction program. The hydrogen fuel could be seen in a NASA videotape, streaming out in white clouds of gas and dissipating into the air. The seven astronauts were hours away from boarding Atlantis, and had not begun to suit up. Liftoff was postponed until at least Sunday. Atlantis is due to deliver the newest piece of the space station, an elaborate 44-foot girder. The mission is to last 11 days and includes four space walks.

Now it's time for a look at the weather, so here's (say weatherperson's name).

5. Washington Wizards superstar Michael Jordan woke up Tuesday morning in Milwaukee and decided that it's time to let his surgically-repaired knee heal. Jordan will miss the rest of the NBA season, but said that he plans to return next season. Jordan was put on the injured list and returned to Washington. He had arthroscopic surgery February 27th, and has played as a reserve since returning March 20th. Wearing a therapeutic sock that covered his right leg, Jordan scored only two points Monday in 12 minutes of play against the Lakers. The Wizards have seven games remaining and are three games out of the last playoff spot in the East.

6. Golfers and suburban park lovers, take heart: the government is addressing your goose problem. Faced with a population explosion among non-migratory Canada geese, the U.S. Fish and Wildlife Service is proposing to give the state wildlife agencies broad authority to reduce the flocks that nest and live in the lower 48 states year round. That would make it easier for states and local communities to destroy eggs and nests and expand hunting. The goal is to reduce, by about 25%, the approximately 2.7 million geese that nest in the lower

48 states. That would alleviate some of the aesthetic, health, and safety problems caused by birds that have adapted to suburban golf courses, subdivisions, office parks and airports. In some areas, goose populations are growing at 14% a year. Without controls, the national total could more than double in the next decade.

That's the news update at 3pm. Our next news break will be at 5. Please join us then. I'm (say your name).

■ TELEPROMPTER SCRIPT FOR VIDEO CLIP 8.5

Good afternoon and welcome to the Hourly News Update I'm (say your name) with the latest headlines.

President Clinton told reporters yesterday that a top financial regulator should not have been invited to a coffee arranged by the Democratic National Committee for bankers who have contributed to the party. The president said, "Mistakes were made" in pursuit of campaign contributions. He did not specify the errors he had in mind and his phrasing left responsibility for the matter unclear.

Benazir Bhutto lost a bid to regain office when Pakistan's highest court ruled yesterday that her ousted government was corrupt. New elections will be held as planned on Monday. Bhutto's government was accused of sanctioning hit squads that targeted members of the opposition's political party.

Witnesses say a Learjet's pilot was apparently trying to avoid a school and homes before the plane crashed into an apartment building in Elgin, Illinois. Both crew members were killed. The plane was being used in a National Guard war game.

A new poll finds most Americans want welfare reform, but not at the expense of the poor

Nearly 60% of those responding to the New York Times/C-B-S poll say they would be willing to pay more taxes if the government creates jobs to get people off welfare.

Controversial ex-Vice President Spiro T. Agnew died yesterday of undisclosed causes. Agnew was the little-known governor of Maryland when Richard Nixon picked him as his running mate in 1968. The conservative Vice President made a name for himself with his colorful phraseology such as when he described the media as "Nattering nabobs of negativism." He resigned from office after pleading no contest to one count of income tax evasion.

King Hussein of Jordan is dead. King Hussein led his country for 46 years and was a leader in Middle East peace talks. His eldest son, Prince Abdullah, is the new regent for this tiny Middle East country. World leaders attending the funeral in Amman include Boris Yeltsin of Russia, Benjamin Netanyahu of Israel, and U.S. Presidents Clinton, Carter, Ford, and Bush. The king died of complications from Non-Hodgkin's Lymphoma. He was 62.

And finally, there is a new weapon in the age-old battle between man and mosquito. Two scientists in New Delhi say garlic does the trick. They've discovered garlic not only helps stimulate the human immune system and kills bacteria, a little spray kills the mosquito, too. However, at the dosage they're recommending, it could kill your social life as well.

CHAPTER NINE

MUSIC ANNOUNCING

9.1 INTRODUCTION

In many broadcast performance situations, the announcer is working from a script. For example, the news anchor has news copy to read and the voice-over announcer has a commercial script to follow. However, there are times when the announcer will be ad-libbing what he or she is saying. Of all the broadcast performers, the music announcer or radio disc jockey, more than anyone else, uses the ability to talk spontaneously.

According to recent FCC broadcast station totals, there are 13,837 radio stations in the United States, and in the current *Broadcasting & Cable Yearbook* most of these are listed as music format stations. Add to this the satellite radio music channels and the hundreds of Internet "radio" stations, and you have a lot of potential "homes" for the music announcer. This chapter mainly looks at radio music announcers (like the one shown in Figure 9.1), the environment in which they work, and the various types of station formats DJs can expect to encounter. The chapter closes with a look at some other types of music announcers: the video jockey (or VJ—the music television version of the disc jockey), the Internet disc jockey (or Net-J), and the satellite music DJ.

9.2 THE DUTIES OF THE RADIO ANNOUNCER

Most people think the job of radio disc jockey is a much simpler task than it really is. The typical listener imagines the DJ merely introducing a song, lounging around while it plays, and then introducing the next song. While radio announcers do introduce recorded music, they also often present news, sports, and weather information, read commercials, interview guests, provide information on community events, and ad-lib on a variety of topics of interest to their listeners. The modern radio announcer is a key element of a

FIGURE 9.1 Las Vegas radio announcer Kim Linzy, host of the program "Morning Jazz With Kim Linzy," in the KUNV 91.5 FM studio. (Image courtesy of KUNV and Ms. Linzy.)

station's overall sound and is expected to both attract and entertain listeners. As noted in an earlier chapter, the DJ is also often working combo or operating his or her own equipment while announcing and is responsible for a number of "behind-the-scene" chores.

The major radio announcer duties can be remembered by putting them into four "p" categories: preparation and production (which occur off-air), along with performance and procedural duties (which occur on-air). **Preparation** includes all the chores an announcer needs to do *prior* to actually going on the air. While some preparation occurs immediately before an actual on-air shift, it also means working on the next day's material after you come off the air. This can include pulling music, commercials, and other supporting on-air materials; preparing and rehearsing on-air bits; and obtaining information from a variety of sources, such as wire services, joke books, the Internet, and trade publications. Top-quality announcers usually think in terms of one hour of preparation for each hour they will be on the air.

Production refers to the fact that most radio announcers do more than just their on-air performance. Typically, an announcer may be on-air for a four-hour shift and may have **production studio** duties for the other four hours of the work day. Production work may include recording commercials that the station will be airing later, producing promotional spots for the station, or recording "bits" that the announcer may use on the next day's program.

Performance relates to the actual talent portion of being a radio announcer—ad-libbing or reading commercials, liners, song introductions, time checks, weather, community events, interviews, and all the other regular announcing chores. Later in this chapter you'll learn about some performance styles that are appropriate for various radio station formats.

Procedural duties relate to operating the studio equipment and are what actually gets the programming on the air. In addition to playing CDs or music files, the announcer will probably have to take transmitter readings, record network feeds, and maybe even answer the telephone. The best rule of thumb for the announcer in this area is to expect the unexpected. Things will go wrong on a regular basis while operating broadcast equipment. However, if you plan on this and have an idea of what you will do when something happens, in most instances the average listener will never realize that something has gone awry. In most radio situations, you will be expected to run a **tight board**, which means that the equipment must be operated correctly as you move smoothly from one on-air event to the next, with no dead air in between. One final note here: radio announcing duties are often inversely proportional to market size. In other words, in a small market situation, you'll do everything noted above and more. In a larger market, it's likely you can concentrate more on the performance portion of the announcer job, as you'll probably have help in the preparation, production, and procedural areas.

9.3 DEVELOPING THE ABILITY TO AD-LIB

While it's true that impromptu announcing is not scripted, that shouldn't be taken to mean that it's not prepared or even rehearsed to some extent. Most announcers, even when ad-libbing, have planned the basic content of what they are going to say. They know they are going to talk about point A, then point B, and so on, and they know the delivery style they're going to use to convey the material to the listener. What they

don't know is the exact words they'll use to do all of this. That's a proficiency that will develop in time, but you can help hone your ad-libbing skills by adhering to a couple of simple rules.

First, know the subject you're talking about and highlight things that will interest your listeners. Radio announcers often talk about the music they play. At one time, announcers merely looked at the **liner notes** on the back of a record album to get information for ad-libbing something about the music they were playing, but that is rarely enough today. When ad-libbing, look for interesting tidbits beyond the simple song title and artist information that your listeners might want to know. For example, is there any significant meaning to the song or album title? Who wrote the song—the artist or perhaps another known performer? Has this artist written anything that has been performed by another well-known artist? Is the artist performing in your area anytime soon? Do any prominent guest artists play on this particular song or album? In general, if you were listening to an announcer talking about a particular artist, what would be interesting to know about that artist?

This means that you, as the radio announcer, need to be knowledgeable about the music business. Make a habit of reading trade magazines like *Billboard*, or *Radio & Records*, subscribe to online services like FMQB.com (Friday Morning Quarterback), and look at popular press publications like *Rolling Stone* or *Spin*. Check websites that provide information about music celebrities. For example, most recording artists maintain their own websites or are prominently featured in record label sites. Most search engines, such as Google, will take you to thousands of pages that lead to information on song titles or artists, music trivia, and similar details. Your local bookstore's "performing arts" section will have a selection of books about music—there are compilations of number-one hits, one-hit wonders, musical encyclopedias, and biographies of many recording artists.

However, every ad-lib can't be about the music, so how do you develop material for general talk? Follow the same techniques as for developing musical knowledge: read, read, and read some more. Almanacs such as *Chase's Calendar of Events* provide a wealth of material on events that happened and are happening on a particular day, whose celebrity birthday it is, and much more. Trivia books and texts like *The Guinness Book of World Records* are useful for ad-lib material. And if you're serious about being an on-air personality, begin building a personal notebook of possible items to ad-lib about. As you read newspapers and magazines, whenever you see an interesting item, cut it out and paste it into your notebook. Papers and magazines often use short, oddball items along the lines of "The average great white shark weighs ..." to fill up a column or page. Some announcers have accumulated thousands of items like these that they categorize and then work into an appropriate ad-lib. Again, the Internet has a number of sites dedicated to radio "show prep" that can provide you with helpful general material for an interesting ad-lib. For example, a few show prep sites include radiojock.com, preplinks.com, radio411.com, and audiopros.com. Many others can be found with a simple Internet search. As noted in the first chapter, having a broad-based, general education as part of your academic background will also help you be conversant on any number of topics.

Now that you have something to ad-lib about, the second important point is that you must learn how to deliver that ad-lib, and that means learning to edit yourself. The two best rules for editing ad-lib material are 1) shorter is better and 2) if in doubt, leave it out! Even the most experienced announcers sometimes make the biggest ad-libbing mistake—rambling on and on and on! There's an old radio story that one station had an electronic device to limit rambling—an automatic shut-off on the microphone if the speaker went on too long! How much time an announcer can actually ad-lib is often limited by station policy that can range from "no ad-libbing" to "unlimited," but in most cases it will be a fairly brief segment. Good ad-lib technique says that before you open your mouth, you should know exactly what the point is you're going to make, how you're going to do so as quickly as possible, and how you're going to cleanly end the ad-lib. Most broadcast ad-libs develop in three stages: the hook, the detail, and the stinger. Whatever you say first—designed to capture the listener's attention—is the hook. Then you provide some specific details to elaborate or set up the bit. Finally, you offer a climactic sentence or punch line—the stinger— which is the payoff for the whole ad-lib and what the listener is going to remember most. Because of its importance, it probably should be thought of first, even though it's given last. Remember, you must know how to end the bit before you ever begin!

PERFORMANCE TIP 9.1

The PREP Formula

Unlike the announcing we hear so often on radio today, true professional announcing is a craft. And like all crafts— learning to play guitar, for example—announcing can be distilled into a series of repeatable, perfectible steps. In the same way the beginning guitarist doesn't launch instantly into mind-spinning pyrotechnics, a young announcer starts by learning the fundamentals that underpin his craft. Once those have been drilled into mental muscle memory, the real creative excellence can begin.

   An important note: the process that follows has nothing to do with any particular music format. I've been an announcer and a coach in music formats from heavy metal to classical and I've learned that, when you get the big picture, you see that there is no such thing as a jazz style, a college style, a rock style. There are only communication fundamentals that work no matter where you happen to work. These include preparation, rehearsal, editing, and performance. This specific sequence makes a memorable acronym called **PREP**. Let's go through each step.

Preparation. Announcing is an acting job. But rather than read someone else's script, the announcer creates his or her own material by gathering information from music, media, culture, and life itself. Before entering the studio, the prepared announcer has his or her show blocked out. Not every tiny detail—there is always room for improvisation—but the road map is clear. The prepared announcer knows the listener, the listener's values, and what makes the listener tick. The prepared announcer knows the music (or other) format and the station's marketing objectives. The prepared announcer knows his guests, his anecdotal material, the "temperature" of the audience, and the market on that particular day. All of this preparation happens "offstage," before he or she ever walks into the studio.

Rehearsal. Only amateurs believe that rehearsal inhibits spontaneity. Professionals respect their audience and rehearse their voice breaks off-mic so that their performance on-mic will be brief, bright, smooth, natural, and personable. They practice the art of planned spontaneity so that even their most carefully-scripted bits sound fresh and off the top of their head. Rehearsing twice is ideal. While the music plays, practice your next voice break out loud. Not in your head, but aloud. Any bugs in your thinking or speech will become apparent to you. Then speak your break again a second time and notice that you're smoother now, but still fresh. The third time, go live.

Editing. Less is more, they say, and they're right. The world is awash in information so learn to deliver yours in brief, compelling, and memorable doses. Every voice break can be improved by using fewer, more powerful words. You can pack an encyclopedia into thirty seconds if you eliminate unnecessary chatter and focus on real substance. You can condense a two hour movie into a twenty word headline: "Kansas girl bumps her head and visits far-away land, where she learns that there's no place like home." Leave the details for your novel. Brevity works best for radio.

Performance. You are not a person alone in a studio full of blinking electronics talking to a faceless crowd that you can't see. It just seems that way. Announcing is a one-to-one performance art and works just like live theater. So channel your adrenaline, get psyched to perform, and then deliver the goods. Great radio performers are like stage actors—highly aware of and stimulated by their audiences. But instead of talking to a group, they focus their communication on one listener at a time. When they make eye contact with one listener in this way, all staginess and fake "DJ-isms" disappear. All plural references to the audience go away. It's just me and you, the only two people in the radio universe.

Now that you have the PREP foundation, here is a short list of things to do and things to avoid.
    Whatever you do:

1. Always prepare. The harder you work outside the studio, the more you look like a genius when the red light goes on.
2. Always make eye contact. Visualize one listener and speak directly to that person in the same tone you would use when you're talking to a close friend.
3. Always be yourself and be real. What you say matters much more than how you sound. Think of the difference between models and actors. Actors are (or seem) real; models just look good.
4. Always edit your speech and use fewer, more powerful words to achieve a bigger impact.
5. Always air-check your show and review it with a supportive coach. It's the best way to improve your craft.

Whatever you do, don't:

1. Imitate anybody else. When you imitate, you're just a copy of the original. When you are yourself, you ARE the original.
2. Think that it's all about you. It's not. It's all about the listeners. Make them the stars and they will give you all the love you need.
3. Do the same thing the same way every time. That's boring.
4. Become self-conscious when you make a mistake. When it happens, which it will, stabilize quickly and move forward. Your error will be forgotten in a moment.
5. Forget that this is a performance. You're on stage. Get up for it.
    One final word play and we'll leave the acronyms alone. LORE stands for, "Learn Once, Repeat Everywhere." Learn the PREP formula—Prepare, Rehearse, Edit, Perform—and whether or not you make radio announcing your life's work, you can apply this formula to every speech and every live presentation you make for the rest of your life, wherever your career path may lead you."

    John Silliman Dodge has a 25-year career that spans and integrates music, media, and management. He has been a program director for both stations and networks from coast to coast. Currently, John is a talent coach and consultant who conducts performance workshops on the art and science of creative radio communications. He is also program director for All Classical 89.9 KBPS-FM in Portland. John can be reached at john@sillimandodge.com or visit www.sillimandodge.com.

FIGURE 9.2

9.4 HOW TO BE AN EFFECTIVE MUSIC ANNOUNCER

You can't really learn to be an effective radio announcer from reading a single section of a textbook, or for that matter even from reading the whole book. It will take some time to develop your personality, announcing style, and skills in reading or ad-libbing material. Utilizing the PREP formula presented above is a good start, and here are a few more items to consider that will keep you pointed in the right direction. Half of them relate to good equipment operation and the other half apply directly to your on-air performance.

First, always strive for consistent sound levels. You should not have volume levels that are all over the place. For example, don't introduce a song and have your microphone at a volume of 5, and then start playing the song at a volume of 10. The arbitrary numbers in this example are simply meant to illustrate that you can't have one level indicator twice as high as the other. Watch the VU meters on your audio console to keep volume levels consistent. Watch your mic-to-mouth distance, too. There is a tendency for beginners to lose track of the microphone, as shown in Figure 9.3. With all the other things going on in the studio, such as cueing up music or recording network feeds, announcers sometimes forget about the microphone. If you get your

mouth too far from the microphone, not only do you lose the volume of your voice, but you pick up too much background noise or studio ambiance. If you notice a lower level in your headphones, you might begin to speak more loudly to compensate, and suddenly you're in that situation of talking at the listener. If you get off to the side of the microphone, you could well get out of the microphone's pickup pattern. In any of these instances, you're detracting from your ability to communicate with the listener and you should obviously avoid that.

A more subjective task is to keep a proper balance when mixing two sounds, such as your voice and background music. In most instances, your voice must be the dominant sound; however, the background can't be too low or you'll lose the effect of having it there in the first place. Many beginning announcers tend to run background music too high because they aren't sure of their voices and use the background to cover them a bit. This is a mistake and should be avoided. But you can't really use the VU meters to judge this because you often have only one set of meters and two sounds going through the audio board. You must therefore use your ears and careful judgment to create a good balance between two sounds when you're mixing them.

Finally, good equipment operation requires that you make smooth transitions from song to song, or

FIGURE 9.3 When you don't "stay on mic," you're detracting from your ability to communicate with the listener!

from talk segments to songs. Most of the **transitions** in radio are either segues or cross-fades. To **cross-fade** between two songs, you'd fade out, or lower the volume of, the end of one song as you fade in, or raise the volume of, the beginning of the next song. There will be a brief period of time when both songs are playing together, so take care with songs that you cross-fade because not all songs mix well together. A **segue** is an instant change from the end of one song to the beginning of the next, with no overlap, but also no pause between the two songs. The best segues happen when the first song ends cold—that is, has a natural ending rather than a fade-out. The second song should also have a fairly up-tempo and quick start, rather than a slower, fade-in beginning. Listen to Audio Track 9.1 to hear the difference between a cross-fade and a segue. Good announcers really think about how they move from one song to another and make sure that their transitions are smooth and sound good.

To be a good radio announcer requires expert equipment operation, but that's not enough—you must also pay attention to your actual on-air performance. Never talk over song vocals. Radio announcers often talk up the introduction of a song, that is, they speak over the 10 to 30 seconds of instrumental at the start of the song before the vocal begins. That's good radio practice and it's a real skill to finish your ad-lib a split second before the song vocal begins. However, it's terrible radio practice to step on the vocal or not be done talking as the vocal starts. In most instances, you just can't have two vocal sounds on-air at the same time; about the only time this works is at the end of a song, as it fades out. Here, announcers often come on to back-announce the song title and artist information. As long as the song volume is kept in the background, this is acceptable.

You should also work to match the mood of your talk to the mood of the music you are playing. For example, you shouldn't use a frenetic vocal style to introduce a soft ballad. It makes a lot more sense to soften your delivery style, maybe even lower your voice to slightly above a whisper, to match the soft beginning of a love song. Put a chuckle into your voice when introducing a novelty song, and go up-tempo to introduce the latest number one rock hit. Your announcing style should flow with the music—it should all sound like a single element and not separate, discrete components one after the other. In general, think of three speaking levels—private, public, and personal. Private is very soft speech; the voice you might use to tell a secret when you are very close to someone.

Public speech is much louder; the voice you'd use if you were giving a speech to a group of people. Personal speech is an in-between, moderate volume level, the voice you use when you're just having a conversation with someone. It's the best voice level for good radio communication. You're not making love to your listener, so there's no need for your private voice, and you don't want to shout at your listeners with your public voice. So just use your personal voice and talk as you do when you're talking with a friend. Remember, most people are alone when they're listening to the radio; it's just you and a single listener (of course, multiplied many time over), so speak as if you are talking to that one person.

Finally, the best performance skill you can learn early on is to always project a positive, enthusiastic attitude. Good announcers sound like they are having fun on the air and therefore we enjoy listening to them. Even when you are having a bad day or aren't feeling well, once the microphone is on, you need to be on. Avoid being a sarcastic know-it-all or an insincere charmer or a boring song introducer—there really isn't a place for them in radio announcing. You'll find the better approach is to be yourself and to develop a warm, friendly style.

9.5 RADIO PROGRAM FORMATS

The Winter 2008 Station Information Form from Arbitron (radio's leading ratings research firm) lists about 50 major radio format categories, from active rock and adult contemporary to urban oldies and variety, as shown in Figure 9.4. *Broadcasting & Cable Yearbook 2007* recognizes 90 radio formats, and on satellite radio there are hundreds of channels of music, news, sports, and entertainment covering many of these same formats. When you take into account subcategories or fragmented versions of some of these major formats, the actual number of radio formats balloons from there. In fact, the Internet radio network, Live365.com, lists over 250, including such esoteric formats as acid jazz, emo, garage rock, and trip hop.

While we usually think of a radio station's music as its format, we know that there are also nonmusical formats. The term format really means the arrangement of all the programming elements that a station presents. It's the music played, but also the news, weather, and other information given, the number of commercials aired, the jingles and station promos, contests and listener requests, announcer ad-libs, and so on. For most radio station formats, every item that

ARBITRON

SPRING 2008
FORMATS

80s Hits	Easy Listening	Rhythmic Contemporary Hit Radio
Active Rock	Educational	Rhythmic Oldies
Adult Contemporary (AC)	Family Hits	Soft AC
Adults Hits	Gospel	Southern Gospel
Adult Standards/MOR	Hot AC	Spanish Adult Hits
Album Adult Alternative (AAA)	Jazz	Spanish Contemporary
Album Oriented Rock (AOR)	Latino Urban	Spanish News/Talk
All News	Mexican Regional	Spanish Oldies
All Sports	Modern AC	Spanish Religious
Alternative	New AC (NAC)/Smooth Jazz	Spanish Tropical
Children's Radio	New Country	Spanish Variety
Classical	News/Talk/Information	Talk/Personality
Classic Country	Nostalgia	Tejano
Classic Hits	Oldies	Urban AC
Classic Rock	Other	Urban Contemporary
Contemporary Christian	Pop Contemporary Hit Radio	Urban Oldies
Contemporary Inspirational	Religious	Variety
Country	Rhythmic AC	World Ethnic

FIGURE 9.4 Radio station format categories recognized by Arbitron. (Reprinted with permission from the Arbitron Company.)

is aired each hour of the broadcast day is carefully programmed to present a specific sound for that station. For example, computer programs are used to generate a music **playlist**. The station's music can be rotated throughout the broadcast day following a number of parameters the program director (PD) or music director (MD) sets up, such as how often an individual song is played. The announcers merely follow the playlist. Music and other programming elements are often shown using a hot clock, like the one in Figure 9.5. The hot clock is a depiction of the station's format for a one-hour period. Music, commercials, jingles, news, and all the other elements that make up the station's format are placed around the clock to let the announcer know when during the hour each element should be played. Much of this same information may be listed in a station program log, but the hot clock is a more visual representation of the station's programming. Most stations would vary their hot clock slightly for different dayparts. If you seriously want to be a radio announcer, you'll need to continue learning about formats and programming beyond this text, but to help you develop an on-air delivery approach, the next few sections look at some of the most popular radio formats and announcing styles that seem to fit well with them. (Remember, it was noted in

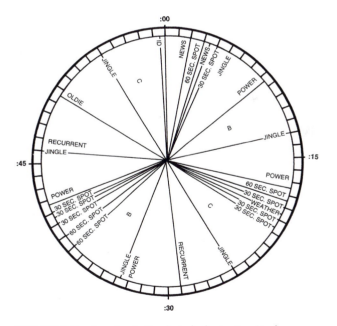

FIGURE 9.5 A radio station hot clock gives a visual representation of the station's programming for a one-hour period.

Performance Tip 9.1, that many of the basic announcing skills will transcend any one specific format and gaining those skills will put you on the track to just being a good announcer.)

9.6 ADULT CONTEMPORARY

The adult contemporary (AC) format is one of the most popular programming formats in radio today. It will be found in almost every radio market and a good portion of the AC audience listens at work place locations. Various versions of the basic format are also known as **soft rock**, **hot AC**, **light rock**, or **modern AC**, and feature current pop and rock music with some older songs mixed in. Light AC stations tend to play more easygoing music, while hot AC stations play more up-tempo and more new rock/pop releases. There are no strict rules about this, so a station labeled "soft rock" may well play the same music another station calls "adult contemporary." In any case, AC music is usually inoffensive or "safe," meaning there is no rap or harder rock included. On soft-rock stations, older releases are often limited to music that came out no more than fifteen years ago. Established artists like Celine Dion, Phil Collins, or Matchbox Twenty have been joined by newer AC stars like James Blunt, Kelly Clarkson, or Lifehouse and are presented in longer **music sweeps** broken up by three or four **spot set** breaks each hour. The target audience for an AC format is general listeners, primarily 18- to 35-year olds, and leans toward a strong female appeal with an emphasis on softer ballad type songs. Most adult contemporary stations, in addition to their music mix, offer listeners a good amount of information, such as short news briefs, weather, time, and traffic, especially during drive time periods. The overall tempo of adult contemporary formats is most often a medium pace, and the announcer's style should match this. Most announcers on AC stations are expected to project a friendly personality and take on a "companionship" role. Their announcing style should convey a feeling of chatting with the listeners and providing them with necessary information, rather than announcing.

9.7 CONTEMPORARY HIT RADIO

Contemporary or current hit radio (CHR) is a descendent of the Top-40 format, which was popular from the early days of rock 'n' roll to the 1980s. The CHR music mix features a hefty number of chart-topping artists such as Sean Paul, Justin Timberlake, Panic! At The Disco, Fergie, Kanye West, The Pussycat Dolls, Nickelback, and Rihanna. Of course, the artists vary from year to year, depending on who has the "current" hits. Whether singles or album cuts, the music is presented in a rotation that has the top pop, rock, and R&B songs repeating as frequently as every 90 minutes. Most stations select songs based on charts published in

Billboard, Radio & Records, or similar trade publications, along with surveys of local record sales and even phone requests. Since some hit songs can stay on the charts more than 30 weeks, current popular music usually means songs released within the last year. The primary audience for CHR is 12- to 24-year-olds, with teens being the most important segment. The pace of most CHR stations is fast, frantic, and frenzied. In fact, some stations "pitch up" the music, that is, they actually raise the pitch of the music slightly so that it sounds "livelier" and "brighter," but isn't noticeably off-speed. The CHR DJ needs to present this high energy, upbeat style, and he or she will be expected to run a tight board, because most CHR stations won't tolerate the slightest bit of dead air. While some CHR announcers develop a true celebrity personality, others may not do much more than read liner cards—short station slogans or image lines, or station promotional announcements usually prepared by the program director. The announcer will also have to be knowledgeable about the music played, because most CHR listeners are true fans of these artists and will quickly spot someone who is just faking it on-air. Listen to Audio Clip 9.2 to get a feel for the sound of the contemporary hit radio station.

9.8 COUNTRY

At one time, most country music stations were called "country and western," had a very "twangy" sound to their music and announcers, and catered to a rural lifestyle most prevalent in sections of the southern and western parts of the United States. However, today's modern country format is often a far cry from this, with a rocking sound that has a wide-ranging appeal. In fact, there are more than 2000 country, classic country and new country format stations, according to Arbitron's Radio Today 2007 report. Contemporary country stations feature a tight format delivered at a moderate pace that appeals to a primary audience of 25- to 54-year-olds. Key artists include Brad Paisley, Kenny Chesney, Carrie Underwood, Shania Twain, Rascal Flatts, Toby Keith, Brooks and Dunn, and Keith Urban. Country announcers usually have a bright, cheery style and have an active interest in the music they play. While they don't need a "good old country boy" demeanor, country DJs are usually very down-to-earth and convey a neighborly feeling in their on-air work. Kelsi Jordan at Calgary's Country 105—CKRY explains what you have to do to be a good country music DJ in Performance Tip 9.2. Listen to Audio Clip 9.3 to hear the sound of the contemporary country radio station.

PERFORMANCE TIP 9.2

Country Announcing

Three things—first, "Be REAL!" You'll hear this a million times when you're starting out on-air because it's so important. Country listeners are incredibly loyal and include you in their life, like a friend. But they can spot a phony, which makes it impossible to build any kind of relationship. Being "real" is crucial—look at the success of real personalities like Oprah, Regis Philbin, and Howard Stern. The second thing to remember is something my program director says all the time—"you're paid to talk, but it's equally important to listen!" *Listen* to your co-host, your interviewer, callers you put on the air, everyone! When you listen, you make others the star of the show and it'll be bigger and better than you can imagine. Don't always be thinking about your next witty comment, or you'll lose track of what's happening, and lose the moment. Besides that, my co-host Mookie is a very talented radio guy, and I don't *want* to miss anything he says. And finally, get involved in your community as much as possible. Emcee charity events, do the sideline announcing at football games, or volunteer for the dunk tank at a local fundraiser. Name recognition is key—so get your name out there. Believe me, judging sexy young firefighters for our Calgary "Hot Stuff" charity calendar was a tough chore, but it's all part of the job!!!

FIGURE 9.6

Kelsi Jordan has been in radio since 1990, and has co-hosted the afternoon drive show at Country 105 FM in Calgary since 1995. She won the 2003 Calgary White Hat Award for "Media Person of the Year"—and fully credits her dog, Mooch, for helping her snag this honor. (Not really, but Mooch wanted a name mention in this book!)

9.9 SMOOTH JAZZ

A blend of easygoing popular music and lighter jazz vocals helps define the **smooth jazz** format. Often called **new adult contemporary** (NAC), this format also utilizes a good number of contemporary jazz instrumental tracks and has an overall mid-tempo pace, which produces a mellow, unobtrusive mood for the listener. The primary audience for smooth jazz is adults, 35 to 55 years old (and older). Core artists include Spyro Grya, Dave Koz, Norah Jones, Michael McDonald, Kenny G, Sade, Luther Vandross, David Sandborn, Steely Dan, and Diana Krall. An announcer on a smooth jazz station would be expected to have a mature-sounding, warm, mellow voice and a fairly low-key style. Often the announcing chores are relatively simple, with short song introductions and basic time and temperature information given between long music sweeps.

9.10 ROCK

Rock radio stations can range from album rock to classic rock to contemporary rock, with stations often playing very similar music. The **AOR format**, or album-oriented rock, developed as a backlash to Top 40. Rather than having frenetic-paced DJs play hit singles from a tight playlist, AOR stations feature laid-back announcers playing an eclectic mix of past and present rock album cuts. AOR developed from the 1960s underground rock and 1970s progressive rock stations. The primary audience for rock music stations is 12- to 34-year-olds, especially male listeners. The classic rock format features the most popular rock songs from the 1960s to the 1990s, and they are usually played in long music sweeps. Artists like the Rolling Stones, Bob Seger, Led Zeppelin, Ozzy Osborne, The Who, Pink Floyd, Bob Dylan, and Eric Clapton get plenty of airplay on these stations, and many contemporary rock stations also have added newer artists to their rotation such as the Black Crowes, Velvet Revolver, Marilyn Manson, Blink 182, Kid Rock, Limp Bizkit, and Pearl Jam. Rock announcers still display a relaxed, conversational style, and the rock DJ often is expected to understand the lifestyle of the listeners and be able to ad-lib about common experiences.

9.11 NEWS/TALK/INFORMATION

While not a music format, this format is still programmed by a fairly large number of radio stations. There are various combinations of radio stations that fall under the N/T/I format—some are **all news**, some **all-talk**, but many are a blend of both. Almost all News/

Talk/Information stations are found on the AM radio band, but over the years, a number of them have developed on FM. Typically, these stations are news heavy during the drive times and more talk during the midday and evening time slots. News only stations often feature a rotation of about 10 to 20 minutes of breaking news, local and national news, along with sports, entertainment, weather and traffic, and feature segments. Talk-only stations often feature nationally syndicated shows such as *The Rush Limbaugh Show, The Laura Ingraham Show,* or *The Sean Hannity Show* along with local call-in segments. N/T/I radio is frequently a fusion of local announcers plus national programming that is delivered via satellite. News/Talk/Information formats appeal to an older audience, where the average listener is 58 years old and almost all listeners are over 25 years of age. The N/T/I announcer needs to be very well-read and is expected to have an interest in current events. He or she will need to have strong interviewing skills and be able to ad-lib on a variety of topics.

9.12 URBAN CONTEMPORARY

Urban contemporary (UC) is a format name that covers stations playing music dominated by black artists and other programming elements of interest to the young urban community. About two-thirds of the UC listening audience is under 35 years of age and more than 75% are African-American. Music styles like rap, hip-hop, rhythm and blues, soul, disco, and contemporary pop can all be part of the mix. Many of the artists are also heard on CHR- and AC-format stations, in fact, Urban AC is a subformat of Urban Contemporary. Key urban contemporary artists include Ne-Yo, Mary J. Blige, 50 Cent, Lil Jon, Nas, Jennifer Lopez, Kirk Franklin, Alicia Keys, Notorious BIG, and Snoop Dog. Much like CHR and AC stations, the primary audience for the UC format is teens and 18- to 35-year-olds. The UC DJ would need to be knowledgeable about the music, and most are expected to be fairly upbeat and festive in their delivery style.

9.13 OLDIES

Radio stations that program rock music from the late '50s to the late '60s are using an **oldies** format. Whether they are AM or FM stations, they mimic the sound of the popular AM stations that had their heyday in the '60s. Some stations expand their music library to include music from the '70s and early 1980s. A few stations concentrate on just one musical era, and another variation is the "Jammin' Oldies" format, which features rhythm and blues and Motown oldies from the late '60s and 1970s.

In any case, the oldies format has immense appeal to the huge baby boomer population that originally grew up with this music. Oldies stations appeal equally to both men and women in the 45- to 64-year-old age bracket, but a surprising number of younger listeners also tune in. Rock 'n' roll pioneers like Elvis Presley, the Beatles, Chuck Berry, the Beach Boys, the Four Seasons, and British Invasion and Motown artists get prominent airplay on oldies-format stations. Most oldies announcers need an in-depth knowledge of the music to relate ad-libs to the songs and artists played. The oldies DJ also needs to develop a good rapport with his or her listeners, as most oldies stations make heavy use of requests, dedications, contests, and other listener call-ins.

9.14 ALTERNATIVE

The alternative format can also be known as new rock, modern rock, or progressive rock. It's a format that came to the forefront during the late 1980s and early 1990s. One of its developing influences was college radio stations that were willing to introduce new rock bands and artists like U2, R.E.M., and the Talking Heads before commercial radio would. Most of the music on modern rock stations is less than a year old and often comes from the influence of "punk," "grunge," and "metal" styles. Artists such as Foo Fighters, Kid Rock, Queens of the Stone Age, Linkin Park, Static X, Korn, Alice In Chains, Sum 41, and Marilyn Manson get maximum exposure on alternative stations. Many of these artists also find airplay on some CHR or AOR stations once they establish some hits. This format appeals primarily to the 18- to 34-year-old listener; however, that group is divided into two distinct generations—Gen X (25- to 34-year-old listeners) and Gen Y (18- to 24-year-old listeners). The modern rock format must serve both generations, and some ratings show that that can be a difficult task. Alternative announcers often have a brash style—a little bit caustic, a little bit unconventional, a little bit cutting edge. Since the whole image of the format is to present alternative music, the announcers try to fit into that same mold. However, as an increasing number of alternative artists have found acceptance by a wider audience, many alternative stations and announcers have sounded more and more like traditional rock formats. Listen to Audio Track 9.4 to get a feel for the sound of the alternative radio station and read Performance Tip 9.3 to get some advice about being an alternative announcer.

PERFORMANCE TIP 9.3

Alternative Music Announcing

Most important, love and live the life style of whatever your passion may be—whether it's rock, classic rock or even sports broadcasting. Not only loving the music that you play, but being a student of it, will allow you to understand the artist and music which will help you convey your message and sound like you're part of this music world. Another aspect that is very important is being "you" on air. For instance, I have a little East Coast attitude and like to be edgy and push the envelope. You could be more laid-back; whatever category you fall in, roll with it! One thing you need to realize is listeners will eventually figure you out if you're being a fake. You will have thousands of people that will be able to relate with you, in some sort of way, no matter what personal traits you present on air.

Know your audience, this is huge! This is also why I say live the life style. Just picture yourself trying to get your message across about "Zombie" (Rob Zombie) coming to town for a show to a senior citizen. They wouldn't have a clue...they use different terminologies, slang and lingo just like you and I do. They would think you were talking about some monster film coming to town. Knowing who you're speaking to will allow you to get the message across. For me, the thing that works the easiest is to just picture hanging and talking among your friends at a party.

The last advice ... get out in the public as much as possible. Listeners love this probably the most; they get to see you and feel closer to you, almost like a friend. Yes, you'll always have your 'groupies' and listeners that may be a little station crazy, but they will be a part of your success. This also allows you to become more than just that "voice" coming out of their radio and gives them the chance to interact with you on a more personal level.

FIGURE 9.7

Eric Dionne started his radio career soon after high school in his home town of Boston at a free-form radio station (basically making coffee trips), but then trekked across the country to see new things in Las Vegas. He attended UNLV where he had his own show, "Nocturnal Rebelun," spinning all spectrums from Hardcore to Punk to Classic Rock on the university station. He received the call from X 107.5 FM, a local modern rock station in Vegas, where he still continues to create havoc on the air waves!

9.15 CLASSICAL MUSIC ANNOUNCING

This is not one of the major radio station formats; however, it is a unique format from both a programming and announcing perspective, and that's why it is being included here. According to Arbitron's publication,

"Radio Today: How America Listens To Radio" (2007 Edition) there are only around 300 radio stations programming classical music and most of these are public, noncommercial stations. Despite the small number of stations that program classical music, they do maintain an intensely loyal audience that is heavily composed of listeners with higher-than average income and educational levels. Some classical stations have been very successful because certain advertisers want to reach this audience. Other classical music stations are noncommercial and don't look to advertisers for financial support. In either case, classical stations typically offer a variety of instrumental and vocal music from the classical music folio. While shorter pieces or segments are played, often symphonies, operas, or other works are aired in their entirety. Listen to Audio Track 9.5 to hear a classical radio station announcer.

In most circumstances, the music is the primary attraction for listeners to classical music stations. The announcer takes on a secondary role. Still, the announcer will be expected to provide information about the selections being played. In addition to the title of the piece and the composer, classical music announcers often include the orchestra (artist) name, the conductor, the soloist, and the record label. Some background information about the piece may also be given. Most classical music announcers are expected to convey an authoritative tone and often have a delivery style that is more formal than any other type of announcer. If you want to be a classical music announcer, you must bring three key skills to the position: First, you must have an extensive knowledge of classical music. You can't fake this—you must really know, enjoy, and appreciate this style of music. Second, you should have a background in basic musical theory. Classical selections are often described in terms of tempo, dynamics (loudness or softness), and other musical characteristics that require correct pronunciation and understanding by the announcer. Finally, since most of the names of composers and musical selections will be foreign, a classical music announcer must be well versed in foreign pronunciation (See Performance Tip 9.4). German, Russian, Italian, French, Japanese, and many other foreign languages will be the basis for many of the words and phrases the classical announcer will have to utilize in his or her on-air announcing. While you can memorize correct pronunciations, it will sound more natural and be much easier if you actually have a strong foreign language background. Obviously, not everyone who would make a good radio announcer would make a good classical music announcer, but if you have the skills and the interest, it might be just your cup of tea.

PERFORMANCE TIP 9.4

Classical Music Pronunciation Help

If you're thinking of becoming a classical music announcer, you may want to check out a website put together by Chris Wendl. It's at www.pronunciationguide.org and offers a "guide for classical radio announcers." In the late 1990s, Wendl was a Classical Music Director for the Harvard student-run radio station, WHRB. He built his guide (and eventually the website) from some existing guides and reference books to help amateur (student) classical radio announcers. The purpose of the website "is to teach speakers of North American English how to pronounce other languages—particularly those that are useful in discussing classical music—with a respectable degree of confidence and correctness." The website explains that last part and also his "antiperfection manifesto" where it is sometimes better, for radio purposes, to use a slightly Anglicized pronunciation than, say, an authentic German pronunciation. The website text provides a visual guide for correct pronunciation and there are many audio examples (in mp3 files) so you can hear the suggested pronunciation.

9.16 ANNOUNCING ACCORDING TO DAYPART

Regardless of what format you may be working with, to a degree, your announcing style will need to match the time of day when you are on the air. The radio broadcast day is broken into five key dayparts: morning drive, mid-day, afternoon drive, evening, and all-night. Formatted radio stations are looking for a consistent sound throughout the broadcast day, but subtle differences in announcing styles will be evident.

Morning drive, from approximately 6 AM to 10 AM, is the most listened to daypart when considering the entire radio audience. Listeners typically tune in for music, information, news, and to be entertained. Because of this, the morning drive announcer is often the highest-paid announcer on the station staff. It's not unusual for the morning drive shift to be filled with a team of announcers: often, a lead announcer and one or two sidekicks—what is referred to as the "morning zoo" concept. Certainly morning drive announcers are expected to be amusing and entertaining, but they also frequently talk more than other announcers because they are giving out a lot of information as they play their music. Time checks, weather updates, traffic conditions, and regular news supplement the ad-libbed bits, station promos, and contests that fill the nonmusical segments of the morning drive shift. Even in a tightly formatted situation, the morning drive DJ will have more freedom to "break" format than any other announcer.

The mid-day time slot is usually from 10 AM to 3 PM, and the whole emphasis of the program switches from announcing to playing more music. While many people listen to the radio at work and in their cars at this time of day, the majority of the audience is at home and that audience is still predominantly female. The mid-day announcer is expected to have a warm, friendly, charming style and, compared to the morning drive announcer, should have a fairly laid-back approach.

Similar to morning drive, the afternoon drive slot (3 PM to 7 PM) is once again up-tempo and the announcer style should reflect this. Information such as weather and traffic conditions is important, but not as important as it was during morning drive. The afternoon drive audience, in addition to the in-auto listeners, is supplemented by teens getting home from school. Both the music and the announcer need to appeal to this dual audience. Often, afternoon announcers will promote evening activities and take on an attitude that the work (or school) day is over and it's time to play.

The evening announcer works a 7 PM to midnight on-air shift, during which a big part of the radio audience moves to television, especially the adult listener. The evening program is generally more up-tempo than the afternoon drive time because the audience is younger. Most of the adult radio audience has now shifted to watching television. A heavy reliance on request lines is often employed in this daypart, and the announcer needs to develop a good audience rapport to keep the listener involved with the station.

From midnight until 6 AM is the domain of the all-night or overnight DJ. This is a fairly dead time for radio, so there are few commercials or other nonmusical elements programmed. Long music sweeps are common and news or public affairs programs often fill a large part of this time slot. Beginning announcers frequently get their first time slots in this daypart because if mistakes are made on-air, it isn't necessarily fatal for either the station or the announcer. The announcing chores are kept simple, and if there is a style of announcing, it is that the DJ tries to relate to others listening who are also all-nighters.

9.17 ANNOUNCING FOR SATELLITE RADIO

In the early 2000s, two satellite-delivered radio services began offering programming in the United States— XM Satellite Radio and Sirius Satellite Radio. In 2008, the FCC allowed these two companies to merge into one satellite radio service (Sirius XM Radio). This service offers hundreds of digital channels of music, sports, news, talk, comedy and information for a basic monthly subscription fee of around $13.00 . Music channels run the full spectrum of musical styles, from pop and rock to country, jazz, and classical, and everything in between. Many channels are commercial-free and some run a limited amount of commercial content to help keep subscription prices low. Other programming includes specialty shows, such as "The Howard Stern Show" and "Theme Time Radio Show With Bob Dylan". From a radio announcer's viewpoint, satellite radio offers the possibility of an announcing job. A portion of the Sirius studio complex is shown in Figure 9.8. While satellite radio is not standard in cars or homes yet, many autos do include this option and home receiver sales have

FIGURE 9.8 Studios for satellite radio feature digital equipment and a pleasant studio environment. (Image courtesy of Sirius Satellite Radio.)

shown growth so satellite radio does compete with traditional radio for listeners. However, because of huge start-up costs and continuing programming costs, satellite radio has not done well financially.

An announcing position with a satellite radio service would require the usual skills of a broadcast announcer. You'd also be expected to be well-versed in the specific music format the position entails and, because many of their formats are automated, you'd need to understand voice-tracking. To be more than a jukebox, you'd need to add to the musical mix a great radio personality, good production skills, and creative radio programming. Satellite radio has advertised job positions in the industry trade publications, and has utilize websites to promote career opportunities with the company. While there may seem to be fewer announcing jobs in traditional radio these days, there are also new opportunities arising all the time, and the astute radio announcer does not overlook the possibility of being an announcer for satellite radio.

9.18   THE MUSIC VIDEO JOCKEY

A television music announcer counterpart to the disc jockey is the music video jockey. Before the early 1980s, such a performance position didn't exist, but with the advent of MTV and other music video channels on cable television, the video jockey ("VJ") came into being. Hired to introduce videos, interview performers, and give music news, this new breed of broadcast performer, for the most part, was a young, fresh, "hip" talent. Since there were no "historical" performers to emulate, the VJs developed a style of their own. Like radio DJs, most were passionate about the music, well-versed in ad-lib skills, and had a delivery style that appeared natural even though they often could not see the music videos and had to fake their reactions to them. Names like Kennedy, Carson Daly, Daisy Fuentes, and Carmen Electra were well-known as successful music video jockeys, and many have become more entertainment celebrity than broadcast announcer. For example, while Carson Daly (see Figure 9.9) became famous as host of MTV's *Total Request Live*, he's currently host of NBC's late night television show, *Last Call with Carson Daly*.

Music video channels, like MTV, have had open trials to find their next VJ star. Personality and charisma usually take precedence over broadcast performance,

FIGURE 9.9 *Carson Daly is the former host of MTV's "TRL" and current host of NBC's Last Call with Carson Daly. (Photo courtesy of Andrew Eccles and MTV Networks.)*

but the VJ talent still must possess the ability to effectively communicate with the audience, and that means having a degree of skill in all of the areas mentioned in this chapter. Today, MTV has put less importance on music videos and more on reality and pop culture programming aimed at the youth market. Still, MTV and other music channels offer the possibility of announcing opportunities.

9.19   THE INTERNET DISC JOCKEY

Another development in music announcing is the performance position of the Internet disc jockey or Net-J. Many enterprising webcasters have begun their own radio stations "broadcasting" strictly on the Internet. There are several heavy metal stations that serve an audience that is often ignored by traditional radio, but other stations program CHR, alternative, or other typical radio formats. It should be noted that the majority of announcers on these amateur stations have no training as broadcast announcers and the quality of the stations' programming can range from painfully mediocre to quite professional. However, if the number of stations continues to grow and the public comes to see the Internet as another form of "radio," the opportunities for the professional music announcer on commercial Internet stations will increase. You can find hundreds of Internet radio stations by going to www.live365.com.

PERFORMANCE TIP 9.5

Doing a DJ Show

Your First DJ Show: Things to Think About

Your first DJ show is more likely to be an assignment to be turned in, rather than an actual air show.

1. What is going to be your source of music? Some schools will have a library that is available to you. In other situations, it will be up to you. In many situations, you will be required to only use the music that the station has in its library, but you are free to choose the selections you want to play. In other situations, you may have to use a smaller music playlist and you will have no choice what music you play … it will be computer generated and you merely follow the list song after song. If you have some type of specialty music show, it is possible that you will need to have your own music and you will be expected to build your show around your personal music library.

2. How will the music be played? Again there will be different situations. Will you be able to use CDs? MP3s? Many stations are now playing all their music from some type of computer system, so essentially you are playing computer files. There may be a music library on the computer or accessed through the computer and you probably have a way to add additional songs into the library. Other stations still play music directly from CD, using two or three CD players to segue and cross fade from song to song. Most broadcast CD players will also play songs stored as MP3 files.

3. What facilities are available? Can you transition from one recording format to another? Will you have more than one CD machine to use? Actual broadcast facilities can vary widely, especially at the college station level. But at the least, you have some type of audio board or mixer, one or two microphones, and several playback and recording devices. You should become familiar with what's available to you and make sure which formats your station will support (CD, audio files, etc.). In almost all cases, you'll be able to play song after song using multiple machines and possibility moving from one format to another, such as CD to MP3 to CD, etc.

4. Do you want to have the experience of using multiple CD players, or is it required to use them? Some student DJs plan their show in advance and actually burn the songs they are going to play on one or two CDs in sequence. This can save a lot of effort getting songs ready to play, but may lose some of the "liveness" of the show. Many other DJs like the idea of putting the show together "on the fly"—assembling the various elements as they go along … while one song plays they plan what song they'll go with next and how to get from one song to the next.

5. You may want to arrange to get some practice in the audio studio before you schedule your production. Know how to adjust levels, start and stop machines and read the VU meter. Practice is important for the beginner. You'd really like to get to the point that the equipment operation is "automatic"—you don't even have to think what you're doing, but you do it all correctly. That comes with time. Just be sure you know how to adjust levels and maintain good, constant volumes (*watch the VU meters!*). Of course, you need to know the basic operation of each piece of equipment.

6. What music format are you going to use? Do you know enough about it to be able to talk about the bands and the musicians? Do you have a good selection of music to choose from? Your radio show should be more than just playing music back to back. That's a jukebox. Make sure you can talk about the music you're playing …. the artists, the song writers, give the listener some interesting tidbits to go with the music. And make sure you've thought about the music … is it just random songs … or have you built a show around a theme …or all females artists or all ballads or something like that.

7. Having chosen your songs, what order are you going to play them in? Why? Give some thought to the ordering of your songs. Usually, it is moving from fast to medium to slower to medium to fast. Try to avoid "train wrecks"— two songs back to back that just don't fit, for example a hard, guitar thumping rocker immediately into a ballad. Ouch! That doesn't work. If you talk between songs, you can make this type of transition, but think about the songs you'll play and why you go from one to the other.

8. How are you going to open your show? You can start with a greeting or the name of the show or some appropriate piece of music, but since this is a DJ show, you probably shouldn't start by playing a whole song without identifying yourself or the program. Some radio shows begin (and end) with a standard "theme song." That lets the listeners know your particular show is about to begin. It might be an instrument piece over which you begin the show with a "greeting" or opening of some kind. Or it may be a vocal (or portion of a vocal) that starts the

show and then you come on and do your opening segment. If you have a specialty music show, your opening should tell the listener what the show is all about.

9. Since this is related to a performance course, your instructor will probably expect you do a reasonable amount of talking, so there may be a ban on playing more than one song without a break. Do you have something interesting to say about each song or the musicians? Will you be back announcing, that is giving information about the artists or songs at the end of the song? If your program is somewhat "personality radio" in style, you should plan on talking frequently, and maybe even talking after each song. Make sure you have interesting things to say. Sometimes talk breaks are also done at the front of a song as an introduction.

10. You may be expected to do an ad-lib about music, give a weather report, and read some commercials during your show. How much time will you need for that? Remember ad-lib material is rarely completely "off the cuff"—have an idea of what you're going to say even if it's not scripted out. Weather information is usually fairly brief, maybe 30 seconds or so. Most radio commercials are either 30 or 60 seconds in length.

11. You'll probably be expected to finish on time, so give some thought to how you will do that. You could introduce your last song, say good-bye, play it until the time is up and then fade it. You could have a little material to talk about if your last song will end with a small amount of time to go, but have a plan. More student shows end poorly than start poorly. You have a definite clock ending, in that your show only goes so long and ends when the next show begins. But choose a good song to end with, and know how you're going to say "good-bye" to the listeners. Some DJs do their last talk segment before their last song, then just play that song to the show's end. If you back-timed properly, it will end exactly when your show should end. Other DJs play the last song and save some time to say good-bye after it finishes. Make sure you have enough to say, to fill whatever time you've left yourself. If you run out of material, you're stuck with "dead air" and that's just not allowed. If you think you're getting stuck, maybe "promo" the next show that is coming up to fill up that extra time.

9.20 CONCLUSIONS

In broadcasting, ad-lib announcing is never as spontaneous as you might imagine. Even when announcers don't have a script to read, they usually have planned what they want to say. The key to ad-libbing is knowing the subject you're talking about and being able to edit your comments. Radio announcers do more ad-libbing than most other broadcast performers. The radio announcer also does more work than most people imagine. Announcer duties fall under the general categories of preparation, production, performance, and procedural duties or equipment operation. Most radio announcers are employed at a music format radio station, and their announcing style should match the format and daypart in which they are working. The relatively new performance positions of music video jockey (VJ), satellite radio announcer, and Internet radio DJ (or "Net-J") hold the promise of new opportunities for the music announcer.

CHAPTER NINE

Self-Study

■ QUESTIONS

1. Most radio announcers, when ad-libbing, are speaking completely "off-the-cuff."
   a) true
   b) false

2. Which of the following is the least effective way an announcer could develop ad-lib material for the music he or she is playing?
   a) check Internet sites
   b) read trade magazines
   c) check CD liner notes
   d) read artist biographies

3. The biggest mistake announcers make when ad-libbing is rambling on and on.
   a) true
   b) false

4. Which of the following is not an on-air performance duty of the radio announcer?
   a) ad-lib a song introduction
   b) record a commercial
   c) read a community event announcement
   d) conduct an interview

5. In which radio format would we most likely hear an energetic, upbeat announcer operating a tight board?
   a) AC
   b) alternative
   c) CHR
   d) smooth jazz

6. Which radio format is least likely to have a large teen component to its target audience?
   a) urban contemporary
   b) album-oriented rock
   c) contemporary hit radio
   d) oldies

7. Which announcer skill is least important for a classical music announcer?
   a) ability to run a tight board
   b) extensive knowledge of the music
   c) being well-versed in foreign pronunciation
   d) basic understanding of music theory

8. Which daypart is most likely to feature an announcer team rather than a single announcer?
   a) morning drive
   b) mid-day
   c) afternoon drive
   d) evening

9. To talk up the beginning of a song means to ad-lib title/artist information first, then segue into the start of the song.
   a) true
   b) false

10. For the music video jockey, personality and charisma often take precedence over actual broadcast performance skills; however, the VJ still must possess the ability to ad-lib and effectively communicate with the audience.
    a) true
    b) false

11. The "ability to run a tight board" falls under which category when considering the duties of the broadcast announcer?
    a) preparation
    b) production
    c) performance
    d) procedural duties

12. Which speaking level should radio announcers use for good communication with their listeners?
    a) private
    b) public
    c) intimate
    d) personal

13. Radio announcing duties are often inversely proportional to market size.
    a) true
    b) false

14. Which of the following is not one of the stages of development for most broadcast ad-libs?
    a) stinger
    b) segue
    c) detail
    d) hook

15. Which radio format is most likely to feature a caustic and unconventional announcing style?
    a) urban contemporary
    b) oldies
    c) modern rock
    d) country

16. Announcing fundamentals can be distilled into a series of repeatable steps as illustrated by the PREP formula. What does the "E" in the PREP formula refer to?
    a) enthusiasm
    b) educating
    c) enhancement
    d) editing

17. Good announcers usually think in terms of 30 minutes of preparation for each hour they will be on the air.
    a) true
    b) false

18. Which of the following would be something that a good announcer should do?
    a) Think that it's all about you.
    b) Air-check your show and review it.
    c) Do the same thing the same way every time.
    d) Become self-conscious when you make a mistake.

19. Radio's leading research firm, Arbitron, recognizes about how many major radio format categories?
    a) 50
    b) 90
    c) 250
    d) 300

20. Which radio format has been known to "pitch up" music so that it sounds "livelier" and "brighter?"
    a) AC
    b) AOR
    c) UC
    d) CHR

■ ANSWERS

If You Answered A:

1a. No. While they might not know the exact words they'll use, most radio announcers have planned the basic content of what they are going to say even when ad-libbing. (Reread 9.1 and 9.3.)

2a. Wrong. There are many Internet sites that could provide information about recording artists; some are even operated by the artists themselves. (Reread 9.3.)

3a. Correct. This is a true statement because even experienced radio announcers sometimes forget the best rules of editing ad-libs: shorter is better and, if in doubt, leave it out.

4a. No. The on-air performance relates to the actual talent portion of being a radio announcer, such as ad-libbing a song introduction. (Reread 9.2.)

5a. No. AC announcers usually present a friendly, companionship style. (Reread 9.6, 9.7, 9.9, and 9.14.)

6a. No. UC stations appeal to teens and 18- to 35-year-olds. (Reread 9.7, 9.10, 9.12, and 9.13.)

7a. Correct. Classical stations are slower paced and often air long musical selections that wouldn't require intense equipment operation.

8a. Yes. Morning drive often uses an announcer team, usually a lead announcer and one or two sidekicks.

9a. Wrong. Ad-libbing title/artist information over the instrumental beginning of a song and then stopping just before the vocal begins is a talk-up, so this is not a true statement. (Reread 9.4.)

10a. Yes. This is a true statement because personality and charisma are important for the VJ, but so are performance skills, such as the ability to ad-lib and effectively communicate with the audience.

11a. No. While you might utilize some equipment prior to going on-air, preparation usually means gathering materials for later use. (Reread 9.2.)

12a. Wrong. This is a soft speaking level used to tell a secret and isn't the best for radio announcing. (Reread 9.4.)

13a. Correct. In a larger radio market, you may well have help, such as an engineer or board operator, to handle some of the announcer duties.

14a. No. The stinger is the punch-line of an ad-lib. (Reread 9.3 and 9.4.)

15a. No. UC announcers usually have a fairly upbeat and festive style. (Reread 9.8, 9.12, 9.13, and 9.14.)

16a. No. Enthusiasm is a quality we often like announcers to display, but in this case, it is not part of the PREP formula. (Reread Performance Tip 9.1.)

17a. Wrong. This is a false statement because most announcers will spend as much time preparing for a show as the show length; in other words, one hour of preparation for each hour on air. (Reread 9.2.)

18a. No. It's all about the listener. Make them the stars and they will give you all the love you need. (Reread Performance Tip 9.1.)

19a. Correct. From active rock to variety, Arbitron's Station Information Form lists about 50 radio formats.

20a. No. This is not a common practice at adult contemporary radio stations. (Reread 9.6, 9.7, 9.10, and 9.12.)

If You Answered B:

1b. Yes. This is a false statement because most radio announcers, even when ad-libbing, have planned the basic content of what they are going to say.

2b. Wrong. Trade publications like *Billboard* or *Radio & Records* are good sources of ad-lib material about recording artists. (Reread 9.3.)

3b. Wrong. This is a true statement as even experienced radio announcers forget the best rules of editing ad-libs: Shorter is better and, if in doubt, leave it out. (Reread 9.3.)

4b. Yes. Recording a commercial would normally be a production duty of the radio announcer.

5b. No. Alternative announcers tend to be brash and a bit quirky and are less likely to worry about perfect equipment operation than many of the other formats. (Reread 9.6, 9.7, 9.9, and 9.14.)

6b. No. AOR stations appeal to 12- to 34-year-olds, especially young males. (Reread 9.7, 9.10, 9.12, and 9.13.)

7b. Wrong. Extensive knowledge of the music is a requirement of the good classical music announcer. (Reread 9.15.)

8b. No. Since the emphasis is really on the music during the mid-day time slot, there wouldn't be much need for an announcer team. (Reread 9.16.)

9b. Correct. To ad-lib title/artist information first and then segue into the start of a song is a straight song introduction, not a talk-up.

10b. No. A music video jockey must have personality and charisma, but also performance skills such as the ability to ad-lib and effectively communicate with the audience, so this is a true statement. (Reread 9.18.)

11b. No. You certainly utilize broadcast equipment when doing production work, but running a tight board isn't usually associated with the production studio. There is a better answer. (Reread 9.2.)

12b. Wrong. This is a louder voice level used to give a speech and isn't the best for radio announcing. (Reread 9.4.)

13b. Wrong. In a small radio market, the announcer probably handles all of the typical announcer duties, but in a larger market he or she is likely to have assistance. (Reread 9.2.)

14b. Yes. A segue is an instantaneous transition from one song to another.

15b. No. Oldies announcers generally develop a good rapport with their listeners. (Reread 9.8, 9.12, 9.13, and 9.14.)

16b. No. Some announcing can be educating to the listener, but in this case, it is not part of the PREP formula. (Reread Performance Tip 9.1.)

17b. Correct. This is a false statement because most announcers think in terms of one hour or preparation for each hour of on air announcing.

18b. Yes. Always air check your show and review it with a supportive coach. It's the best way to improve your craft.

19b. Wrong. You may be getting confused with the format list in *Broadcasting & Cable Yearbook*. (Reread 9.5.)

20b. No. This is not a common practice at album-oriented rock radio stations. (Reread 9.6, 9.7, 9.10, and 9.12.)

If You Answered C:

2c. Correct. While you might find some information here, it's often not much more than title, artist, and songwriter information.

4c. No. The on-air performance relates to the actual talent portion of being a radio announcer, such as reading a community event announcement. (Reread 9.2.)

5c. Yes. An energetic, upbeat announcer style and tight board operation best describe the CHR announcer.

6c. No. Teens are the most important segment of the CHR station's primary audience of 12- to 24-year-olds. (Reread 9.7, 9.10, 9.12, and 9.13.)

7c. Wrong. Being well versed in foreign pronunciation is required of the good classical music announcer. (Reread 9.15.)

8c. No. Afternoon drive usually features a single announcer. (Reread 9.16.)

11c. No. The performance aspect of the broadcast announcer centers on ad-libbing and reading scripts more than equipment operation. (Reread 9.2.)

12c. Wrong. This is the same as a private speaking voice and isn't the best for radio announcing. (Reread 9.4.)

14c. No. The detail is additional information which elaborates and sets up the ad-lib. (Reread 9.3 and 9.4.)

15c. Yes. The modern rock announcer is often as "alternative" as the music he or she plays.

16c. Wrong. The "E" in the PREP formula doesn't refer to "enhancement." (Reread Performance Tip 9.1.)

18c. No. That's boring. (Reread Performance Tip 9.1.)

19c. Wrong. You may be getting confused with the format list at Live365.com. (Reread 9.5.)

20c. No. This is not a common practice at urban contemporary radio stations. (Reread 9.6, 9.7, 9.10, and 9.12.)

If You Answered D:

2d. Wrong. Music encyclopedias and biographies of recording artists are excellent sources of ad-lib material about the music an announcer is playing. (Reread 9.3.)

4d. No. The on-air performance relates to the actual talent portion of being a radio announcer, such as conducting an interview with a recording artist. (Reread 9.2.)

5d. No. As the name implies, a smooth jazz announcer usually presents a mellow, low-key style. (Reread 9.6, 9.7, 9.9, and 9.14.)

6d. Yes. The name says it all. Oldie stations appeal to 25- to 54-year-olds who want to hear the music they enjoyed when they were teens.

7d. Wrong. A basic understanding of music theory is a requirement of the good classical music announcer. (Reread 9.15.)

8d. No. The evening time slot usually features a single announcer. (Reread 9.16.)

11d. Yes. The procedure category of announcer duties directly refers to equipment operation and running a tight board refers to smooth transitions from event to event with no dead air.

12d. Correct. This is a moderate speaking level used when you're just talking to someone and it works best for good radio communication.

14d. No. The hook is the beginning of an ad-lib which captures the listener's attention. (Reread 9.3 and 9.4.)

15d. No. Country announcers usually convey a down-to-earth, neighborly feeling on-air. (Reread 9.8, 9.12, 9.13, and 9.14.)

16d. Correct. The "E" in the PREP formula refers to editing. Most announcing can be improved by using fewer, more powerful words.

18d. No. When mistakes happen, stabilize quickly and move forward. Your error will be forgotten in a few moments. (Reread Performance Tip 9.1.)

19d. Wrong. You may be getting confused with the total channels of music, news, sports, and entertainment offered by satellite radio. (Reread 9.5.)

20d. Yes. Some contemporary hit radio stations have been known to raise the pitch of music slightly to make it sound "brighter."

Projects

■ PROJECT 1

Ad-lib song introductions.

Purpose
To give you an opportunity to research several recording artists and then ad-lib song introductions for them.

Notes
1. This project assumes you have an understanding of how to operate the equipment in a radio studio.
2. You'll need several CDs to complete this project.

How to Do the Project
1. Select five popular recording artists. Make sure you have access to CDs by these artists.
2. Choose two songs for each artist that you will be introducing in the project.
3. Now research the artists to find material that you can use to ad-lib your song introductions.
4. Check the Internet, trade publications (if you have access to them), and other sources to gather some interesting information about the artists. Remember, you're looking for something unique or entertaining about the artist or the specific song that you will be introducing.
5. Do not write out exactly what you will be saying, but note key points so you remember what you want to include.
6. Set up a CD player, a microphone, and an audio recorder so that you can record your song introductions.
7. Begin recording and ad-lib an introduction for one of the songs. For each artist, one song introduction should be a talk-up and one should be a straight song intro.
8. After the introduction, let about 30 seconds of the song play, and then fade it out. Pause your recorder.
9. Record another song introduction and continue in this manner until you have completed all 10.
10. Label the recording "Song Ad-libs" and make sure you put your name on the recording.
11. Turn the recording in to your instructor to receive credit for this project.

■ PROJECT 2

Record a disc jockey show.

Purpose
To enable you to develop skills as a music radio announcer.

Notes
1. Select one of the formats presented in this chapter as the basis for this project.
2. Remember, you'll need to slightly adjust your announcing style to be appropriate for the format that you choose. For example, a CHR announcer may be upbeat and energetic, while a smooth jazz announcer can be mellow and laid-back.

3. You may want to listen to a local radio station that uses this format to get an idea of the music played, announcer styles, pacing, and so forth.

4. It is assumed that you can operate the equipment in a radio studio before you attempt this project.

How to Do the Project

1. Select some appropriate music for the format that you've chosen. You'll probably need six to eight songs.

2. Plan to include some non-music elements in your program—commercials, public service announcements, weather information, and news, at least. You can use any of the material in the text or write your own, but it should be realistic and sound like something we would actually hear on the radio.

3. Write out a "program log" listing the order of the elements you are going to include in your program.

4. Record the program in real time; in other words, don't stop or pause the recorder once you begin. Play the songs all the way through so the program flows like an actual radio show.

5. Remember, your announcer style and music should be appropriate for the format. Your ad-lib material should make sense for the target audience of this format. In every facet, your program should simulate this radio format.

6. Listen to the recording when you are finished. If you're not pleased with the final product, do it again.

7. If the project is good enough, label the recording with your name and "Disc Jockey Project."

8. Turn in the completed recording to the instructor to receive credit for this project.

■ PROJECT 3

Compare traditional radio, Internet radio, and satellite radio.

Purpose
To give you an opportunity to investigate different "radio" services that offer an employment possibility for the radio announcer.

Notes
1. This project requires you to monitor various radio services and obtain material through the Internet.

2. Prepare a list of questions you want to answer before you begin your research.

3. You can use any radio format for this project, but you might find some type of "rock" format works best.

How to Do the Project

1. Listen to at least one hour of a local radio station. Avoid syndicated shows or periods when the station might be automated. You should be listening when there is a live, local announcer on the air. Note the call letters, frequency, and any slogans the station uses, as well as the time when you are listening. You can also obtain additional information about the station if they have a website.

2. Keep a log of the music played, commercials aired, contests, news, or other nonmusical items you hear. Note the announcer's style—what he or she says to introduce songs, comedy bits, or general information given during the time that you are listening.

3. Now use any "search engine" to find an Internet-only radio service that uses the same format as the radio station you listened to. Don't listen to a traditional radio station that is just

streaming their programming on the Web; you want to find a "station" that is only available through the Internet.

4. Listen for a minimum of one hour (note the time), and keep a log as you did for the local radio station. Note the "call letters" or name of the Internet station, its URL, and any slogans the service uses.

5. Next, listen to at least one hour of satellite radio.

6. If you do not know someone who is a subscriber, you might be able to listen to the service at a local audio store, or you can go to the service's website and you should be able to monitor some of their formats via the Internet.

7. As you did before, keep a log of your monitoring activity. Note the satellite service name, what format you listened to (remember, it should be the same or similar to the radio station and Internet station you listened to), and any slogans it uses, as well as, the time when you listened.

8. Even if you listen to the station through a satellite-capable radio, visit the service's website to obtain additional background information about satellite radio.

9. Finally, organize your material into an informative report that compares the three "radio" services. Try to address the following:

   a. How are they the same or similar and how are they different? Compare things like how each service approaches its format, what commercials are aired, and what role the announcer seems to have.

   b. Which station did you enjoy listening to the most and why?

   c. Which station would you most like to be an announcer for and why?

   d. What conclusions can you draw about these "radio" services?

10. Label the paper "Radio Announcer Report" and make sure you put your name on it.

11. Turn the report and log sheets in to your instructor to receive credit for this project.

CHAPTER TEN

SPORTS ANNOUNCING

10.1 INTRODUCTION

One area of broadcast performance that holds much attraction for many young people is that of sports broadcasting. While many opportunities exist, there is also plenty of competition. However, sports programming is increasingly popular with broadcast and cable stations because of the audience it attracts, and more and more channels are becoming available as digital service takes hold. This means that opportunities for the prepared, capable person who is willing to work hard will likely increase in the next few years. The sports announcing field has many segments—from sports reporter, to sports anchors, to play-by-play, to color, to sports talk host, with additional variations along the way.

10.2 SPORTS ANNOUNCING

The field of sports announcing seems to offer glamour and excitement, and there are very few sportscasters who would claim to dislike their occupation. The opportunity to hobnob with star athletes and work in beautiful stadiums, arenas, and fields seems to offer the dream occupation. However, it can also mean long hours and considerable travel, often to places you've been to many times before. The field is very competitive and there will be many applicants for every available job position. Sportscasting can be broken into several categories. With some variations, these are sports reporting, sports talk, play-by-play announcing, and event color and analysis. At major events, the broadcast announcing team may include three or more individuals, with extra reporters on the sidelines, but it is more common to have just two main announcers. Some sportscasters are employed by stations, networks, and cable companies; some by the teams themselves; and some operate on a freelance basis, going wherever the opportunity presents itself.

When considering the opportunities in sports broadcasting, it is encouraging to realize that the growth of cable broadcasting has resulted in much wider coverage of sporting events. Because of ESPN (Entertainment and Sports Programming Network) and other cable channels, many additional events are now covered that wouldn't have been in the past. As competition between broadcasters and cablecasters grows, cable's drive to make virtually any game available to a pay-per-view audience means that coverage and opportunities should grow in the future. When we think of sports broadcasting, we may first think of the national telecasts of major sports events where the broadcasters themselves have become famous, but as with other jobs in broadcasting, the bulk of the career opportunities is likely to be at the lower levels. Many colleges do radio and television broadcasts of their sports events, and some high schools do, too, particularly those private schools that use sports success as a recruiting tool. Some carry additional sporting events on the Internet, a situation where beginners may get an opportunity. Some public television stations have a continuing policy of covering high school sports that are ignored by other stations. While these are often broadcast on a delayed basis, additional opportunities for experience and exposure are there for the sports broadcast performer.

10.3 SPORTS REPORTING

Sports reporting provides many opportunities in broadcasting as a whole, as most television stations will have one or more reporters who are expected to gather sports news and deliver it on the air, as shown in Video Clip 10.1. Most sports news reports are given in the evening, although brief summaries of daytime events may be cut in, if there is sufficient local interest. Radio stations also often include brief sports reports as a part of their regular news segments. The frequency and length of these will vary considerably with the station format and policy. There are a number of successful all-sports radio stations that broadcast vast amounts of sports information and offer numerous sports reporting opportunities.

A sports reporter's duties are many and the demands heavy, yet the job can be most satisfying as well. In terms of general requirements, perhaps the first is to realize that many of your audience members may be nearly expert on the sport in question and will not tolerate mistakes or ignorance. A good sports reporter will need a strong interest in the field and an in-depth knowledge of sports. General reporters may get away with covering events that don't particularly interest them, but there are always fans who will tune in to sports reports, so an enthusiasm for what you are doing is vital.

If you look at pictures from team sports events, you will see hundreds of excited people, some who have even gone so far as to paint their faces with team colors, don outlandish costumes or hats, and design elaborate posters and signs to support their team. These fans are not going to be responsive to a sports reporter who seems bored. On the other hand, a few sports reporters have carried enthusiasm to the extreme. Some seem to be in a perpetual state of excitement, shouting and waving their arms, while others work at a lesser degree of exertion, but nonetheless project a high level of excitement. The proper degree of energy is a vital commodity in sports reporting for many reasons. First, it provides some of the personality that makes you appealing on the air. You need to convince your audience that you are excited about what you are reporting. Second, it carries you through what can be a very demanding day. Going to sports banquets and press conferences can be enjoyable, but can also become wearisome.

In addition to reporting the news of sports, the reporter should remember that there is a big element of entertainment involved as well. Listening to some pros in action will reveal wisecracking, stories, favorite expressions of exuberance, and sometimes stunts to provide entertainment. For example, one young reporter did a series of stories by participating on various high school teams during the practice seasons and then reporting on his experiences. This was done with the coaches' approval, but his teammates thought he was a transfer from another school. This unique approach provided some interesting angles, and the reporter is still on the air many years later. Some reporters set out to become a "character," which can make them very recognizable and perhaps successful, but an act can be difficult to sustain and can limit advancement and opportunities to branch out. Listen to a sports feature by Lisa Brooks on Audio Clip 10.1.

A sports reporter should expect a steady diet of the following: attend a variety of sporting events, do pre- and post-game interviews, track the progress of other key teams, and note the accomplishments and failures of both the home and opposing players. It means regularly reading sports publications such as *The Sporting News* and *Sports Illustrated*, plus the daily newspapers of the cities where key opposing teams are located. There will be team and award banquets to attend, where you might get a good interview with a visiting guest speaker who was once a star in that particular sport. Teams and schools frequently call press conferences to make announcements, make coaches and players available for interviews on a regular basis, and provide an annual *press book* of player and team statistics.

In addition, you will spend time watching televised games from other places and working the telephones, gathering news, or setting up and confirming special interviews. In every case, it is essential that you keep good notes, whether at an event or during an interview, so that you'll have accurate and firsthand material for your reports. For statistics, the Internet has become a prime source. There is probably more information there than you will ever need, but it's reassuring to have it when you're on the air.

One of the potentially exciting duties of the sports reporter is interviewing star athletes and coaches. This may occur as part of a media day, a press conference, or as a few moments of individual time you've been able to arrange. Remember that, while giving interviews is a normal part of the work of these individuals, they are often tired or stressed and their patience can be short. Also keep in mind that they have heard the same standard questions hundreds of times and may be weary of repeating the same answers. This is a time to really do your homework, and be up-to-date on their accomplishments and failures. Try to find out some personal interests of theirs that will separate you from the other questioners, and strive to plan questions that will be a little out of the ordinary. The players, coaches, and your audience will appreciate it. It could also mark you as someone with potential to move to a higher level.

There is one unwritten rule that you should keep in mind: Never ask a pitcher for an interview when it's his day to start, unless he makes an offer. In most cases, starters are mentally preparing and do not want to be distracted. The same rule applies to quarterbacks before a football game. Other participants in virtually any sport tend to focus themselves before the event, and it isn't appropriate to interrupt them. On other occasions, they can be very cooperative, but they have other commitments, so don't prolong the interview unless they seem to want to continue. Remember that many of them have families, and may want to get home, particularly when they play a sport where they are on the road frequently.

Some interviews can be arranged for times other than immediately after the event. These can often be longer and more relaxed, and if you're prepared, they can be most enjoyable. Athletes are also individuals with other interests and activities, so questions about these and causes they are supporting can yield discussions that reveal the personality of the sports figure and will be interesting to your audience. Viewers and listeners want to feel that they really know the person. The way you handle yourself can do much to make the meeting a success. You need to earn the respect of the athletes, who are professionals or at least are highly skilled at what they do. They realize that you have a job to do and will respect you if you are prompt, prepared, and businesslike.

Athletes' personalities will vary, and some may test you with difficult responses or put-ons to see how you handle the situation. They work under pressure all the time and may want to see how you deal with it. Poise, patience, and preparation will help to win their respect and get you a quality interview. If they choose to be difficult throughout, that may become your story. Remember, not every sports personality is known for being pleasant.

When preparing for and conducting interviews, maximum preparation is critical. First, you may be doing it several days before a game, yet will be using bites from the recording right up to game time. You'll need fresh material for each day. Second, you will want to carefully log all your clips and save the recording as remarks made may have more meaning some time in the future, in connection with coaching changes, player trades, and other incidents.

Names are always a challenge in the sports field. There are Japanese athletes playing major league baseball, Samoans in the National Football League, Lithuanians in the National Basketball Association, and individuals from around the world in many other sports—a trend that is likely to continue. You can't fumble the names. You must get the pronunciations correct every time or lose your credibility with the fans. Historically, few sportscasters of the "character" variety could get away with mangling a name, but those announcers are rare and not worth copying.

In both radio and television, your station will either be a part of a network or subscribe to one or more sports services that will provide you with audio and

FIGURE 10.1   *A sportscaster interviews a player for a later report.*

video feeds. These will need to be viewed and then edited down to fit the stories you are planning. Daily assignments will vary, particularly with the size of the market, the existence of local school and professional teams, and management's attitude toward sports as a marketable commodity. A sports reporter at a radio station might be expected to do eight or ten reports of 1 to 3 minutes per day. Some would be live and others recorded to permit you to get out into the field. A smaller television station could expect two or three 5-minute reports, perhaps at 5, 6, and 11 PM. At a larger television station, you could be expected to cover one event, perhaps calling in the story for the sports anchor to deliver or doing a live report from the scene. If it's a big event, there could be more than one event cut in, but in most cases it will be a post-event report. Frequently, you will be expected to include some highlights on tape that you narrate live or provide from a recorded postgame interview. In every case, accuracy, details, and color are essential. Listen to another Lisa Brooks sports feature on Audio Clip 10.2.

10.4 WHAT A SPORTS REPORTER COVERS

While the demands of coverage will vary with the sport, the community, and station policy, a sports reporter will be expected to handle a wide range of events. One of the key elements is the need to gather and keep current on a wide variety of statistics. Many sports fans follow statistics closely, get excited over them, and expect you to provide the latest and most complete data. Fans will expect information on game conditions, injuries, slumps, league standings, and even the statistical fact known as *games back*, which indicates how many games the home team must win and the opponents must lose to get the locals into first place. You'll need the stars' accomplishments, the progress and contributions of new members of the team, and even how certain players have done against particular opponents. In your notes, you will be looking to catch the flavor of the event and those factors that contributed to a win or a loss. Those factors may immediately influence a team or player's statistics, and you'll need to note any significant changes that result. (Listen to the use of statistics on a pre-game show on Audio Clip 10.3)

Looking to the future, computer online services and other all-sports media are going further into statistics. Today it is possible to electronically call up virtually any bit of data on any team or athlete. A sports statistician, though not an on-the-air personality in most cases, may find a niche as a supplier of data, perhaps with an occasional on-air appearance as well.

Further, although you may be specializing in sports, keep in mind that you are a reporter. That means using all the reporter's tools such as recognizing a story opportunity, pursuing it, locating sources, checking facts, and writing it in an interesting and informative manner. Just don't overdo it to the extent we see from the overeager reporter in Figure 10.2.

The importance of writing cannot be overlooked. Even though it may seem that much of sports reporting is ad-lib, only the live coverage of an event will be unscripted. Continued polishing of your writing skills is essential. Excellent writing has gotten beginners jobs in sports over more experienced people whose writing skills are not outstanding. In your writing, you will be faced with the reality that the events you are covering may not have ended yet and could change dramatically before they are over. Over-plan your segments by writing more than you will need, and consider how you can rewrite if an event finishes early, runs long, or experiences a dramatic change. An event you were counting on for a significant segment of your report may not work out as you had expected. If this happens, what story will you go to instead? Is it written and ready to go?

CHAPTER TEN

FIGURE 10.2 Overeager sports reporter.

Part of your duties will include recording actualities and sound bites to go with your reports. In the field, you may be using a good-quality audio recorder and microphone for radio or have a video camera person with you for television. Don't trust your memory; take plenty of notes, including the time and the score at different moments so you can redevelop the flow of the action later on. Your camera operator should provide you with frequent shots of the scoreboard, where you can find the time and score at that moment. Keep a program with you while you are working. Check for any changes in numbers and never rely solely on the public address announcer for information; they get it wrong sometimes, too. You'll be looking to get audio, video, and facts on the key moments of the game: the winning home run, long touchdown pass, or last-second jump shot. Back at the station, you will not only be reviewing the material you gathered, but going through feeds from other sources covering events in other parts of the country for highlights to use. This means being continuously aware of the big games around the country and the times when they should be over.

10.5 THE SPORTS ANCHOR

At many stations, the sports reporter may also present the news on the air. At some larger organizations, there may be a sports director who doubles as the sports anchor or main on-air talent, delivering stories fed in by reporters. Often the director will be covering stories, as well as handing out assignments and anchoring the sports segments of the broadcasts. The anchor is faced with dealing with all of the challenges of reporting, plus the pressure of assembling the report, combining feeds and reports from national as well as local sources. Sports anchors can be working the telephones right up to the last minute, getting scores and incorporating them into the report. During big events, they may slip off-camera during the show to get last-minute results, or have someone pass them the latest information while they are on-air. This can mean interpreting and integrating this latest report, without a misstep or loss of composure, while you are reporting something else and taking all the required cues.

One of the problems faced by both reporters and anchors is how to keep the delivery of scores interesting. The professional leagues have grown to the point that there may be 10 or more scores to cover on a particular broadcast. If the report is on college football, there may be at least 20 games of interest. The challenge is to describe the victory of one team over another in an interesting way, while keeping it brief. You can't say, "the Angels beat the Tigers 4 to 3, the Reds beat the Cardinals 6 to 1," and so on. It quickly gets dull. This has caused sportscasters to go to great lengths to come up with different verbs to describe one team or individual's victory over another.

The best technique is to first consider the magnitude of the victory. One-sided wins could be described with words like slammed, overpowered, ran away from, demolished, or annihilated. Close wins could be squeaked by, slipped by, escaped with a win over, or got past. Verbs with some tie-in to the sport are also a good choice. A football team might "smash" or "crush" another, a baseball team that stole several bases in its victory may have "run away from" its opponent, or a hockey team may have "slashed" its way to victory. Beyond that are verbs like bested, upset, topped, overcame, and outscored, which are not as colorful but will wear well if not overused.

Variety is the key, and even though the audience may be aware of what you're doing, it's better than hearing the word "beat" 25 times in a row. Building a list of action verbs to draw on is a good way to prepare, so that you won't be struggling to think of a new one when the story is due in a few minutes. Copy these various words right on your script. Don't count on your memory to come up with something new while you're on the air. Just writing "Angels 4, Tigers 3, and Reds 6, Cards 1" can leave you repeating the same verb over and over. Be careful not to overuse the more dramatic words such as "smashed," as they quickly become as boring as "beat."

As with the sports reporter, energy, enthusiasm, and knowledge are essential for the sports anchor. In addition, many stations expect their sports anchors, like the one shown in Video Clip 10.2, to be a bit more of a "character." This could mean dressing so that you don't look like a news anchor, appearing a bit more relaxed and informal, and, on occasion, being the subject of a little kidding as a part of the station's effort to make the news personalities more human and appealing. It's a part of the job and may give you an opportunity to get off a quick joke or clever remark. However, as you venture into this territory, it is better to be a bit conservative, as your enthusiasm and cleverness can get you into trouble. You need to be particularly careful not to insult your colleagues or in any way degrade them in the public eye, or you will make enemies that could affect your career for a long time to come. When starting out, being too "clever" or "crazy" can be a distraction. Save the wild material for that time in your career when you are well established.

FIGURE 10.3 A sportscaster checks his monitors. (Photo by Paul S. Clapp.)

10.6 PLAY-BY-PLAY AND PLAY ANALYSIS

One aspect of sports reporting that is attractive to many beginners is play-by-play (PBP).

The idea of traveling with the teams and getting to associate with the players seems particularly exciting. However, there are many different levels of play-by-play and the workload associated with them varies considerably. You may be employed by a station, by a network, by the sports team itself, or by a cable company, plus colleges and schools. In addition, it is quite possible that any of these organizations will employ you on a game-by-game basis. In some cases, you will be expected to be neutral, and that's probably the best approach for the beginning play-by-play announcer. In other situations, particularly if your employer is the team, you may be expected to openly favor your employer's squad. Showing home-team bias is known as being a "homer," and while it is not uncommon, it can detract from your credibility, as you can become known as the sports person who gives only "approved" information about the team. This becomes an issue when things are not going well with a team or with specific players, and you're always reporting a "positive spin" on things. It's better to be in a position to just report the action, good or bad, and be frank about the situation when it's bad.

The time required to prepare for a broadcast can vary extensively. Traveling with a minor league baseball team, you could be expected to broadcast six games in five days and then hit the road again for a repeat performance for several months at a time. If you were employed to do college football, you might do ten games over three months, with a week to get ready between each game. However, for most beginning sportscasters, you will not be with just one organization. The chances are you may have two or three teams which contract for your services. This can mean a lot of travel. It is quite possible that you have a game in Milwaukee one night, Orlando the next, and Omaha the night after that. That means a steady diet of airports, rental cars, tight schedules, and nights with little sleep. Still you will need to project an enthusiastic image in every case. Hopefully, you will be working with one of the teams at each event on a regular basis, so you will not have to learn that team's players and information. It's a business and you need to treat it that way. One person who can be of great assistance is each team's sports information director. Commonly call SIDs, they can usually help with your needs for the broadcast, and perhaps on places to stay, restaurants, and other local information. Get to know them. Part of their job is to be helpful, and as long as your requests aren't ridiculous, they probably will. Don't forget to give thanks. You may need them again.

The key duties of the PBP announcer are preparation and calling the action. One of the realities of sports such as baseball and football is that there can be fairly lengthy moments when there is little or no action. This is the time when your preparation can pay off. Plenty of research on the players, the coaches, and team accomplishments, along with anecdotes and records, will help fill the time. If you only use half the material you've gathered, you will know that you filled the time and provided interesting information to your listeners or viewers. The baseball rain delay is perhaps the toughest, as it can last for an hour or more, with nothing to report except how hard it is raining, whether it appears to be clearing, and what you may have learned from a call to the weather bureau. With luck, you may be able to arrange an interview or two to help fill the time. At some games, sympathetic sports directors or other team officials may visit your booth to be interviewed, knowing that you could be struggling. Particularly with the availability of good portable computers, building a file of information to carry with you can be valuable. Some sportscasters subscribe to newspapers from rival cities so they can have access to what the opposition is saying. Certainly the local papers would be a source of information in every town you visit, and many of them have websites where electronic editions can be found.

For many beginning announcers, a full day of preparation for each hour of game broadcast would be an appropriate ratio. Announcers with more experience and more familiarity with the teams and players might cut some of that preparation time, but every sports announcer knows that being ready is vital. One veteran sportscaster, Jim Donovan, has stated that he devotes four hours a week to just learning names and numbers. Cable television cooking star, Emeril Lagasse, has a rule of P's that is remarkably appropriate for the PBP announcer: "prior proper planning prevents poor performance." All the preparation is to get you ready to cover the action of the game. The chances are that your first opportunities will come from radio, because many smaller stations cover both local high school and college games. PBP specialist, Al Pawlowski, states that radio is the best place to start.

Radio and television reporting are quite different from one another, in some ways nearly opposite, as you can tell by comparing Video Clip 10.3 and Audio Track 10.4. In radio, you are the eyes of your listeners. You must paint a word picture of what is going on, with a good portion being descriptive of the environment. Consider all the elements that go into that picture: the weather, the wind and degree of sunshine, the condition of the field, the size and energy of the crowd. In baseball, you may describe the behavior of the pitcher, how he is reacting to the course of events, what pitches he is throwing, and how they are working. The batter's behavior also is material for description, as are the placement and movement of the various fielders. Listen to Pawlowski calling part of Major League Soccer game on Audio Clip 10.5.

PERFORMANCE TIP 10.1

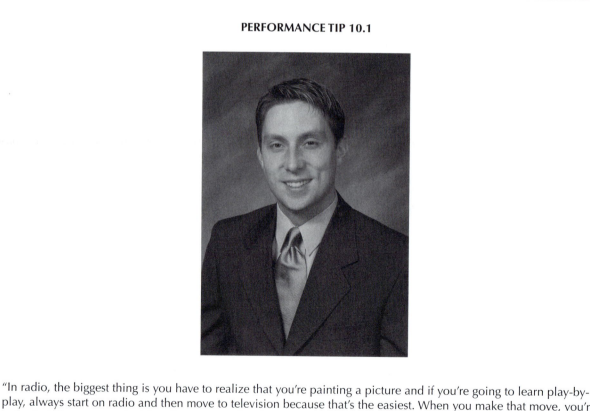

"In radio, the biggest thing is you have to realize that you're painting a picture and if you're going to learn play-by-play, always start on radio and then move to television because that's the easiest. When you make that move, you're going to talk more on television than you need to, but it's easier than when you start doing play-by-play on television and then move to radio"

Al Pawlowski does play-by-play for ESPN, Major League Soccer, and Cleveland State University Basketball.

Perhaps the most amazing example of radio description occurred in the 1930s and early 1940s before sports radio networks developed. Sportscasters recreated entire games working in an empty studio from nothing but a basic description received over a teletype machine. These broadcasters could take the information that "the next pitch was a ball, low," and recreate all sorts of pitcher, batter, and crowd behavior. They even had crowd sounds they could use and a stick to thump when the batter hit the ball. With all the action in front of you, a little thought and planning should provide plenty of material.

Television presents a different situation, because the audience can see what is going on. In this case, the amount of talk from the announcer is reduced and focuses on those aspects that may not be as evident to the viewer. In football, use short phrases to identify the ball carrier and other key players and the action going on outside the screen, such as a receiver breaking loose behind the defense. Your job is to supplement the information the viewer is getting from the screen, not repeat it. Pawlowski says that if you don't know what to say, it's probably better to say nothing, as the scene is there in front of the audience anyway. Many times there will be more talk between plays, as you fill the audience in on developments. In case of injuries, be careful of your statements. Never guess at an injured player's condition or speculate about the injury if the situation looks serious. Remember that the player probably has family and friends looking on. You don't want to exaggerate an injury or belittle a potentially bad situation.

Trying to pick out football uniform numbers from a distance, particularly in bad weather, can result in many corrections, which will make you look incompetent. Talk about the play, but wait for a clear view of the player before identifying him. In college and professional sports, you are almost certain to have "spotters," representatives from the two teams, or assistants who work with you on a regular basis, who will help you with identifications. However, in the minor leagues and many other situations, you may well be on your own. Wait until you have the facts and then present the information.

One of your primary tools when doing play-by-play, whether you have spotters or are working by yourself, is your spotting board. While there is no standard format and you can construct it to fit your tastes, there are certain things you will probably want on it. Boards commonly have pockets for slips of stiff paper, each with the name and number of a player. Often these are arranged so that the pockets are in the same layout as the team in action. In football, this would mean seven pockets vertically for the line and four for the backfield. The slips could be color coded to remind you which team the individual plays for. Beyond that, you might want to add the age, height, weight, and such additional tidbits as school attended, years in the league, and some highlight or unique item about the player. The slips should be big enough to read easily, and also permit the quick change of names to cover substitutions. The spotting board is most valuable for football, as there are a large number of players and the people on the field change often. Particularly for football, you might want to make your board two-sided—offense on one side and defense on the other.

Having a spotter or some sort of assistance is valuable, so there is someone to be alert to substitutions. Your spotter will probably point to the names of the key players at any given moment so you won't have to search for them. Getting the information right and promptly is essential, so it's wise to develop a plan with your spotter(s) as to how you want to proceed. You're calling the game, so think of what works best for you. In sports such as soccer and baseball, where there are fewer player changes, you may want to approach it differently. Al Pawlowski, who reports MISL indoor soccer, prefers a full roster list, in numerical order. He marks the starters and makes notes on the margin. He finds that he can glance down and get a name when he needs it, rather than trying to keep a spotting board up-to-date. The idea, however you approach it, is to get the information quickly without having to search a program or your notes for it. Listen to Pawlowski do a portion of an MISL soccer game on Audio Clip 10.5.

PERFORMANCE TIP 10.2

Al Pawlowski on calling basketball

In radio you're using action verbs and descriptive adjectives to paint the best picture you can, but on TV, the audience can see it all. If a beginning TV PBP person has the discipline (because your natural urge is to talk) just say the name of the players, and nothing else at first. You will sound polished and get the idea. Instead of "Daniel Gibson passes the ball to LeBron James. James dribbles in and shoots the 15-footer ... GOOD!" It could be as simple as "Gibson ... LeBron ... Good!" Of course more words can be added here and there as you progress, but learning how to back off first will give you the feel for a TV PBP game versus a radio call.

You can listen to Al Pawlowski giving two examples of radio basketball calls by going to Audio Tracks 10.6 and 10.7.

Part of your preparation should be getting to know the names and numbers of the players so you don't have to grope for them. If you work regularly for one team, you have a head start on that group, so you can devote most of your efforts to the visitors. Getting the names right, even if it means calling the sports information director of the visiting team, is important. Otherwise you run the risk of embarrassing yourself and your employer. An extreme example of this occurred when an inexperienced color announcer mispronounced the name of one of the schools throughout an entire tournament playoff game. The more time you invest in preparation, the smoother and more professional you will sound, and that can open doors for you.

Certainly, you will need to know the rules and strategies of the sport you are covering. Before the beginning of the season, or when you are moving to a sport you haven't covered in a while, it's critical that you learn and get clearly in mind all rule changes that may have been made since you last broadcast the sport. Particularly in football, there are changes almost every season, and the rules for the pros may differ from those in college ball. Don't let yourself be caught in the embarrassing situation of explaining a rule, when half your audience will know you're out-of-date.

After all the preparation, it comes time to do the game. Arriving early is essential, as it will give you time to check on any late developments and avoid the panic of a car breakdown or getting caught in traffic. Dress like a professional. Even if you're doing radio, how you look will significantly affect your acceptance by the coaches, players, and other pros. When your announcing is underway, go ahead and show some excitement and energy. This should be easy since you enjoy sports.

One of the first rules for covering a game is to give the score often. All sorts of devices have been developed to remind sportscasters of this, but listeners still complain that there is too much time between score reports. When you're busy, that time will seem like a flash, so fit the score in often. The location of the ball is another element to mention often, as are other popular statistics, such as which "down" it is and distance to go, in football. One of the factors to remember is that your audience isn't all listening continuously. People are tuning in and out all through the game, so two minutes is probably more than you should wait before giving the score. Some facts you may need to announce at the beginning of every play.

Another fact the audience wants is the time remaining in the game, inning, or period, if time is an element in the event. Frequently do a recap of major occurrences so that the audience will know how scores were obtained, about injuries that removed players, and outstanding plays that should be remembered. Particularly in football, and occasionally in baseball, soccer, and hockey, formations will need to be described. Football, even at the high school level, uses a variety of lineups, which can change with every play. Although the formation may be visible on the screen, the shot will be wide, so take the opportunity to note where key players are located on the field. Phrases like "at the top of your screen" will help your viewers locate the player. There is so much substitution in football that most of it is ignored by broadcasters, unless a significant player is entering or leaving the game or a previously injured player is returning. There is enough going on that you will need to decide which items are worth including.

Among all your other duties, you must also keep an eye on the program monitor, which should be in front of you or very near. This will help you coordinate your remarks with what the audience is seeing, and on occasion will help you because a close-up of a situation will be available. It will also help you judge what you need to comment on, because you will have an idea of the area covered by the shot and what can be seen clearly by the audience. You will know where more verbal description is necessary and how much needs to be said. If you are using an IFB system, your producer may give you cues as to the shot or call your attention to something on which you need to comment.

FIGURE 10.4 The announcers and camera operators team up for smooth game coverage. (Photo by Paul S. Clapp.)

Still another challenge is that, in most situations, you may be expected to deliver live commercials between plays and note the sponsors of certain segments of the show. You could have the Jones Market kickoff and the Sam's Diner Halftime Report. These may be fed to you on 3 × 5 cards by a producer working behind you, or be given to you in a stack at the start of the game, and you would then be expected to add them in as the game proceeds. Your tone will need to turn a bit more serious for those moments, and the delivery should be a professional one. As soon as you finish, you must shift gears again and get into the excitement of the game.

Energy, enthusiasm, and excitement are an important part of what a PBP person provides, but they are tools you should use with care. In most sports, there are routine moments where some energy is still called for, but you should scale your reaction to the significance of the moment. A home run by either side when the score is 6 to 1, deserves an acknowledgment of the accomplishment, with a comment on the number of home runs the player has for the season, but should not elicit the same level of enthusiasm as the reaction to a game-winning homer at the bottom of the ninth. Projecting excitement adds to your appeal, but ration it according to the moment. You lose credibility if you get excited over everything. Have a range you apply according to the magnitude of the occurrence.

Some sportscasters develop pet phrases that they use with some regularity. These become part of their "trademark." This is a tough area for the beginner, as it can easily sound forced or foolish. Instead of trying to create something, listen to your air checks for any phrase that you have repeated and that sounds natural. You might try using the phrase a little more often and see if it works, but be critical and honest with yourself. Repeated phrases bring up the matter of cliches, or phrases that are used so often that they become boring or funny. For a beginner who has not gathered much experience, falling back on these repeated phrases will be very easy, but they can make you sound amateurish. Work to do your descriptions without leaning too much on them.

One aspect that can be overlooked is that there are occasions where your presence becomes a factor. This is particularly true with golf, where a broadcast booth is often situated near the green. Tradition demands that the audience be quiet when someone is putting. Your voice, even in what you feel is a whisper, may be annoying to all. Plan your material so that you are ready to pause as the player prepares, and don't speak again until the stroke is over. This will mark you as

a professional and will avoid the glares and possible complaints that otherwise could result. A similar situation could develop with tennis if your broadcast table is near the court. Here you'll want to pause as a player prepares to serve. Once the action is underway, you should be safe, although there shouldn't be a lot to say, assuming you're doing television.

One last bit of advice. Every year it seems that there are incidents where a PBP or a sideline reporter makes some remark that is inappropriate or actually offensive. You must think before you speak. It isn't always easy, but a rash remark can get you quickly suspended or fired. It's particularly dangerous in the heat of an exciting moment or the boredom of a lot of time to fill, but it can have a huge influence on your career.

Color/Analysis

The role of color commentator or event analyst has become the most difficult for an individual trained in broadcasting to enter, as more and more former athletes and coaches are being used as the analysts, on the assumption that they bring an insider's view and a deeper understanding of subtleties of the sport than a non-participant would. In this situation, the color-caster can be more the star than the person doing the PBP. Certainly, game analysis at the network level is almost always covered by a former player or coach; however, many announcers doing college or high school sports events are able to provide the "color" for their play-by-play partner. If you're working alone, as may often occur at minor league events, you'll be expected to do your own color, so know your sport.

There aren't a lot of hard-and-fast rules regarding play analysis. However, remember that you're part of an announcing team and your key responsibility is to supplement the information that the PBP announcer is giving, as you can hear in Audio Track 10.8. Don't just repeat what has already been said. If the play-by-play has just described a long pass from the quarterback to the tight end, your job would be to explain how the end got behind the defenders. While you would normally have something to say after most plays and during official time-outs, don't feel you have to make some analysis after every play. In fact, some PBP announcers will cue you when they want you to speak, and otherwise expect you to remain silent. When you're making comments, make sure you finish talking as the next play starts so you don't "step on" the beginning of the play-by-play.

A PBP and the color announcer can disagree on events during a game, as long as it's done amicably.

However, try to avoid correcting the PBP announcer on-air. It's better to jot a note or wait until a commercial break to alert your partner about a slip of the tongue and let him/her correct it when the action resumes. There may be times, however, such as a misidentified player, when an immediate correction is called for, and you may need to do so as diplomatically as possible. Most PBP and color announcers build up a rapport after many games together and develop an easy and natural style of working in tandem.

10.7 SPORTS TALK HOST

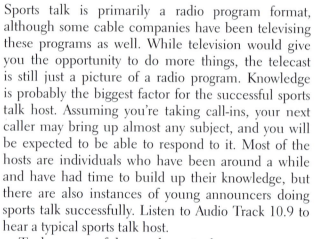

Sports talk is primarily a radio program format, although some cable companies have been televising these programs as well. While television would give you the opportunity to do more things, the telecast is still just a picture of a radio program. Knowledge is probably the biggest factor for the successful sports talk host. Assuming you're taking call-ins, your next caller may bring up almost any subject, and you will be expected to be able to respond to it. Most of the hosts are individuals who have been around a while and have had time to build up their knowledge, but there are also instances of young announcers doing sports talk successfully. Listen to Audio Track 10.9 to hear a typical sports talk host.

To be successful, you have to be an expert on what's going on in sports. That means lots of reading of national papers, sports magazines, and the newspapers in other key cities. With the Internet, there is no excuse for not having the information. As mentioned, most major newspapers have online editions and there are many other useful sites as well. This information will give you topics for your show. As sports/talk host Dave Grendzynski says, "You're always looking, reading, listening to other shows, and watching games on television. You never know where your next idea will come from. Listen to people, what they are talking about. That's what you should have on your show."

Come in to each show with a list of things you want to talk about, knowing that things could go in a completely different direction. Have a foundation, but don't force yourself to stick to it. Often shows begin with something of a monologue, where the host comments on a variety of issues and lists things that will be brought up in the course of the show. Plan for variety, since it helps build a bigger audience. Perhaps there are some people out there who aren't that interested in college football, but will stay with you as you've "teased" a discussion on golf.

There are lots of egos in broadcasting, but a sports talk show is about people, not the host. Avoid berating your callers or embarrassing them. Not all will be as sharp as you are and they may occasionally say something you think is stupid. Remember, there are many sports shows on the air and you can't afford to lose any audience, or your show may disappear. Give them a chance to talk. Don't be abrupt with them. Obviously, callers will come in many types. Some will try to dominate, some will make no sense, some will want to go off in another direction when you're focusing on one sport or event, and some just want to be disruptive or hear themselves on the radio. They may want to brag about what they pulled off on your show. You almost certainly will have a "dump" button, which cuts the caller off, but unless they're into foul language, a good way to handle it is to make a response to their remarks and in the process, cut the connection. By the time you've finished your reaction, it will seem natural to go on to another caller. Sometimes you may get two callers who have different positions on some matter and you'll want to put them both on the air at the same time to debate the point. You stay on the line, too, as a moderator, and perhaps act as referee to keep things under control. It can make for an interesting show.

Not only do you need to have a good grasp of sports history, but you must continuously be adding to your knowledge of popular events everywhere. Callers will want to talk about the effect of the trade of players and its implications. Some hosts let the callers propose trades and then analyze whether they would make sense. This requires a strong knowledge of the abilities of many athletes on many teams.

Some shows will have two hosts, and this can make it easier for you. The other host will give you a break, be someone to interact with, and may know something you don't or think of something you haven't. Typically, your partner will try to take a position that is different from yours on many topics, so that you can have a lively discussion. In some cases, you'll work as equals, and in others, one may take the lead, setting up a topic that the other will then comment on. Both of you will jump in when you get to the phone segment. Again, you'll want to start with a list of topics to discuss and probably decide who will initiate each one. One aspiring sports talk host started a show with a buddy on the campus radio station. It drew an audience and a commercial station soon picked it up.

Grendzynski says that, while preparation is vital, his motto is "I and A"—"Improvise and Adapt." It may be that you receive word of an injury to a major athlete, such as an NFL starting quarterback, during the show. Certainly, the discussion will want to shift to the implications this has for the team and the league. A classic example of I and A came during the massive blackout in the summer of 2003. A sports talk host was doing his show when the lights went out all over the East. A generator kept him on the air. He shifted to discussing the power failure, and for the next several hours, became one of the key figures in keeping everyone calm and up-to-date. He took many calls reporting where the power was on or off, the location of water problems where major pumps in the metropolitan system were not working, and anything else the callers wanted to talk about related to the situation. The newspapers the next day called it some of the best work he had ever done.

PERFORMANCE TIP 10.3

Dave Grendzynski, sports talk host

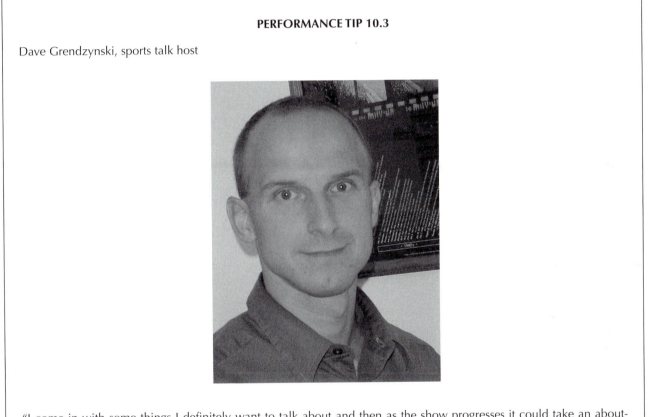

"I come in with some things I definitely want to talk about and then as the show progresses it could take an about-face. You format it in a way so that you have a foundation, but any good sports talk host doesn't stick to that foundation, you're only hurting yourself if you do."

Some of your callers will be regulars, calling almost daily to comment on something. Grendzynski says he's delighted to have them, as they are reliable when no one else is calling. He even started giving callers nicknames, such as "Westside Mike," to give them a special identity. Other callers began adopting their own names, so that a bit of camaraderie developed. He is always glad to have first-time callers and welcomes them with a sort of musical salute. Promotion is part of the task as well, so you might award T-shirts with the name of your show, the station, and some motto on it, to spread the word about your work. In addition, you might consider doing remotes from sports bars and other locations, where you can get to meet your audience, promote your show, and learn more about what people want to discuss.

10.8 CONCLUSIONS

Sports reporting, in its many forms, can make for an exciting and fulfilling career in broadcasting. However, it is one that appeals to many people and the competition for each opening is fierce. It is not uncommon to find friends competing for the same job. The preparation for a sports reporting or anchoring career begins while you're still in school and never ends. Every game can present new situations and challenges. The more you know about the field, the better your chances when an opening occurs. Take every opportunity to gain experience, no matter how inconsequential the event. Continuously critique your work. Veteran pros record and review everything they do, and this is something you can do to improve as well.

Self-Study

■ QUESTIONS

1. All of the following are general requirements to become a sports reporter except _____.
    a) strong interest in the field
    b) depth of knowledge about the sport
    c) energy
    d) development of a "character" or an act
2. There are more jobs today in sports reporting than there were 10 years ago.
    a) true
    b) false
3. The sports anchor may want to build a list of action verbs to present the sports scores because _____.
    a) the audience expects it
    b) it is important to use variety to avoid being dull
    c) each score should have a verb that has a tie-in to the sport
    d) it is important to use dramatic words as much as possible
4. A "homer" is _____.
    a) a team mascot
    b) a local sports team
    c) a play-by-play announcer who favors the home team
    d) a sports anchor on a local station
5. All of the following describe television play-by-play announcing techniques except _____.
    a) short phrases to identify players
    b) reports of action occurring off-screen
    c) supplementing information seen on-screen
    d) repetition of information appearing on-screen
6. The most difficult announcing job to enter for a person trained in broadcasting is _____.
    a) sports anchor
    b) color commentator
    c) play-by-play announcer
    d) sports reporter
7. Enthusiasm, ability to deal with whatever comes up, knowledge of sports history, interviewing sports figures live, keeping control, and keeping your cool—these are qualities that best describe the job of _____.
    a) sports reporter
    b) sports anchor
    c) color announcer
    d) sports talk host
8. Which of the following is the biggest factor for the successful sports talk host?
    a) enough ego to be the star of the show
    b) ability to handle prank telephone callers
    c) ability to deliver live commercials
    d) in-depth knowledge of sports
9. Which of the following would probably not offer an employment opportunity for a sports announcer?
    a) TV network
    b) sports team
    c) freelance basis
    d) these all offer sportscaster employment opportunities

10. What is one of the best places for a sports reporter to glean team statistics?
    a) team media guide
    b) team Internet site
    c) Sports Illustrated
    d) post-game press conference

11. As a sports reporter, you should never ask a star athlete a question he or she can't readily answer so you don't embarrass them in any fashion.
    a) true
    b) false

12. A beginning sports play-by-play announcer might easily find him or herself devoting how much time to game preparation?
    a) 1 hour of preparation for each hour of game broadcast
    b) 4 hours of preparation for each hour of game broadcast
    c) 1 day of preparation for each hour of game broadcast
    d) 4 days of preparation for each hour of game broadcast

13. One good rule of play-by-play announcing is not to speculate about an injured player's condition.
    a) true
    b) false

14. Which of the following is the most important responsibility of the color or play analysis announcer?
    a) make some analysis after each play called by the PBP announcer
    b) supplement information the PBP announcer gives
    c) never disagree with events noted by the PBP announcer
    d) correct the PBP announcer if he or she makes an on-air mistake

15. A good sports talk host will discourage any regular telephone callers, as they usually monopolize the program.
    a) true
    b) false

■ ANSWERS

If You Answered A:

1a. No. A strong interest in sports is an essential requirement and helps to prevent the sports reporter from sounding bored. (Reread 10.3.)

2a. Correct. The growth of cable television, especially, has expanded sports broadcasting opportunities, so this is a true statement.

3a. No. The audience is important, but they want and expect accuracy more than anything else, so there's a better answer. (Reread 10.5.)

4a. No. A homer is an announcer who favors the home team; a team mascot would be expected to do so. (Reread 10.6.)

5a. No. A television sports announcer should use short phrases. (Reread 10.6.)

6a. No. There are job opportunities for the sports anchor. (Reread 10.2 and 10.6.)

7a. Incorrect. Although enthusiasm is a must for any announcing job and some of the other qualities related to a sports reporter, there is a better answer. (Reread 10.4 and 10.7.)

8a. No. While there are lots of egos in broadcasting, a sports talk show is about the audience, not the host. There is a better answer. (Reread 10.7.)

9a. Wrong. TV networks, large and small, offer employment opportunities for sports announcers. (Reread 10.2.)

10a. No. This certainly is a valuable compilation of team facts and figures that a sports reporter will use, but in modern sportscasting, there is another, better source of statistics. (Reread 10.3.)

11a. Wrong. This is not a true statement and just the opposite is likely true. Athletes are asked standard questions all the time and become weary of repeating the same answers. A good sports reporter strives to plan questions that will be a little different. (Reread 10.3.)

12a. No. You need more preparation time than this. (Reread 10.6.)

13a. Correct. This is a true statement because you don't want to exaggerate an injury or belittle a bad situation. Good sports announcers wait until they have the facts before presenting any injury information.

14a. No. Talking after every play is not necessary and some PBP announcers will actually cue the color announcer for their comments. (Reread 10.6.)

15a. No. This is not a true statement because regular callers are reliable and can provide comment when no one else is calling. Of course, like all callers, there may be times when you have to cut the connections. (Reread 10.7.)

If You Answered B:

1b. No. Sports fans expect the sports reporter to have a great deal of knowledge in this field. (Reread 10.3.)

2b. Incorrect. Cable television has led to more sports reporting jobs than ever before, so this is a true statement. (Reread 10.2.)

3b. Yes. The key to an effective delivery is word choice, and variety will help the announcer to avoid sounding bored.

4b. No. A homer is an announcer who favors the home team; it is not used to describe the actual local team. (Reread 10.6.)

5b. No. A television sports announcer should report action that occurs off-screen as well as what is shown on-screen. (Reread 10.6.)

6b. Yes. Not that a broadcaster couldn't do it, but usually former athletes and coaches are hired to handle the color commentary job.

7b. Incorrect. Although enthusiasm is a must for any announcing job and some of the other qualities related to a sports anchor, there is a better answer. (Reread 10.5 and 10.7.)

8b. No. While you may have to handle prank calls, it's part of the everyday sports talk show host's job. There is a better answer. (Reread 10.7.)

9b. Wrong. Often sports announcers are hired by sports teams themselves. (Reread 10.2.)

10b. Yes. Most teams websites include an electronic media guide that provides the most accurate and up-to-date statistics on the team and players.

11b. Correct. This is a false statement because asking standard questions will get you the same "pat" answers. Good sports reporters strive to plan questions that will be a little different.

12b. No. You need this amount of time just to learn the players names and numbers. (Reread 10.6.)

13b. Wrong. Good sports announcers wait for the facts before presenting any injury information so they don't exaggerate an injury or belittle a bad situation. (Reread 10.6.)

14b. Yes. The color announcer should not just repeat what the PBP announcer has said, but rather supplement whatever information has already been given.

15b. Yes. Most sports talk hosts are delighted with regular callers because they are reliable and provide comment when no one else is calling.

If You Answered C:

1c. No. Energy helps the sports reporter develop an appealing on-air personality. (Reread 10.3.)

3c. No. Verbs that have a logical sports tie-in can be used occasionally, but can also be annoying if overdone, so there is a better answer. (Reread 10.5.)

4c. Yes. A homer is an announcer (in this case, a PBP announcer) who favors the home team. It's not good broadcast practice, but may be required in some circumstances.

5c. No. A television sports announcer should supplement what on-screen information is given. (Reread 10.6.)

6c. No. There are job opportunities for play-by-play announcers. (Reread 10.2 and 10.6.)

7c. No. Although enthusiasm is a must for any announcing job, and some of the other qualities related to a color announcer, there is a better answer. (Reread 10.6 and 10.7.)

8c. No. While you may have to occasionally read an occasional live commercial, most of it will be prerecorded. There is a better answer. (Reread 10.2.)

9c. Wrong. Some sportscasters operate on a freelance basis, going to whatever employment opportunity comes up. (Reread 10.2.)

10c. No. While sports reporters read various sports publications, these won't provide comprehensive team statistics. (Reread 10.3.)

12c. Yes. A full day of preparation for each hour of game broadcasting would be the appropriate amount.

14c. No. A PBP and a color announcer can disagree on events during a broadcast, as long as its done amicably. (Reread 10.6.)

If You Answered D:

1d. Correct. Developing a "character" or "act" could make the sports reporter recognizable, but can limit advancement and certainly isn't required.

3d. No. Overly dramatic copy can become annoying to the audience, so there is a better answer. (Reread 10.5.)

4d. No. A homer is an announcer who favors the home team. Local sports anchors usually don't show this type of bias; it's more likely to be seen in a PBP announcer. (Reread 10.6.)

5d. Yes. The television sports announcer does not need to repeat exactly what is on the screen and what the audience obviously already knows.

6d. No. There are job opportunities for sports reporters. (Reread 10.2 and 10.6.)

7d. Correct. These qualities best describe the demanding work of a sports talk show host.

8d. Yes. To be successful, a sports talk host must be an expert on what's going on in sports.

9d. Correct. Sportscasters are employed by stations, networks, cable companies, sports teams, and on a freelance basis.

10d. No. Most post-game press conferences give sports reporters some information regarding a just finished event, but it doesn't offer any comprehensive statistics. (Reread 10.3.)

12d. No. This would be excessive and you'd probably not have enough days between broadcasts for this much preparation. (Reread 10.6.)

14d. No. The color announcer should try to avoid correcting a slip of the tongue by the PBP announcer on-air, if possible. Unless the situation calls for an immediate correction. Wait for a break or hand the PBP announcer a note and let him/her make the correction. (Reread 10.6.)

Projects

■ PROJECT 1

Be a radio sports PBP announcer.

Purpose
To practice preparation and calling the action of a sports team.

Notes
1. Remember that preparation is key to becoming a good play-by-play announcer.
2. Preparation includes knowing the rules of the game, the names of players and coaches, and interesting facts about both teams.
3. Organizing information on note cards or in a notebook will help you find information quickly and fill in the time when the action is slow.
4. Radio listeners are not accustomed to dead air.

How to Do the Project
1. Choose one of your school's athletic teams.
2. Prepare material for play-by-play announcing of a home game.
3. Using a portable recorder and microphone, sit off to the side at the game and record 10 minutes of yourself announcing the play-by-play of the game.
4. Listen to your recording and write a critique based on the material in this chapter.
5. Turn in your recording, your critique, and your notes of preparation to the instructor to receive credit for this assignment.

■ PROJECT 2

Watch a sports broadcast.

Purpose
To learn more about sports play-by-play and color commentary by analyzing a network-level broadcast.

Notes
1. This project is set up to monitor a football broadcast; however, you could modify it for another sport with your instructor's approval.
2. While the project could be accomplished in real time, you may want to record the game to better analyze what you see.
3. Start your recording once the actual game has begun, skipping the pre-game material.

How to Do the Project
1. Record 30 to 40 minutes of a network football broadcast.
2. Watch and analyze the broadcast by answering the following:
   a. Did the announcer's energy and enthusiasm seem to match the actions of the game? Give an example.

  b. Was it obvious that the color announcer was a former player or coach?

  c. Did the PBP announcer use a "pet phrase" during the broadcast? Explain.

  d. How many times was the score given? How often was the time remaining mentioned?

  e. Besides calling the action of the game, what information about the team or individual players was given? Give several examples.

  f. How much statistical information was given? Give an example.

  g. If there were injuries, how did the announcers handle them?

  h. Did the color announcer provide a comment after every play?

  i. Did the announcers ever "step on" each other's comments?

  j. Did either announcer have to read a live commercial or promotional spot during the broadcast?

  k. Did either announcer correct the other on a mistake, or did they correct themselves?

   1. Was a sideline announcer involved in the broadcast? How did he or she contribute to the broadcast?

   2. Provide an overall summary and give your opinion of the effectiveness of the broadcast.

   3. Make sure your paper is a finished, polished project—misspellings or errors in grammar will count against your score.

   4. Do not put your paper in a plastic binder or cover; rather, put a simple title page at the front that includes your name and the title, "Sports Broadcast".

   5. Attach a blank page at the end for comments from your instructor.

   6. Turn in the finished paper to your instructor to receive credit for completing the project.

■ PROJECT 3

Prepare for a sports/talk show.

Purpose
To understand the preparation involved in hosting a sports/talk radio program.

Notes

1. Review Section 6.10 and the "Live Standup" portion of Section 8.11 on ad-lib techniques. Although these are written for commercials and news, the principles are the same in this situation.

2. Your objective is to prepare to do the "monologue" portion of a sports/talk show, which often starts that type of program, and sets the stage for at least some of the later elements.

3. The segment will be an ad-lib of at least 10 minutes and not more than 12 minutes. At the end of the ad-lib, you will announce that it is time to take your first telephone call.

4. The project can be done for either a radio or a television show.

How to Do the Project

1. Using local and national newspapers, sports magazines such as *Sports Illustrated*, and other sources, identify several timely and appropriate topics that you would like to use as the core of your program.

2. Research these topics so you are prepared to talk about them at some length. Five topics would be the maximum for the segment, but four would be better in demonstrating that you can research, develop, and sustain a topic.

3. Gather appropriate statistics and anecdotes to enliven your presentation. Plan some statements and questions that should trigger caller responses.

4. Prepare your notes, planning how you will start, the sequence of the topics, and the order of the points and ideas you will present.

5. As this is presumed to be live, you will have only one take, but off mic you can practice your open or any other part you wish.

6. Determine how you will end each segment and how you will conclude when it's time to take phone calls.

7. Record the segment in the facilities designated by your instructor. Label the tape "Sports/Talk Ad-lib" and turn it in for credit for the project.

CHAPTER ELEVEN

SPECIALTY ANNOUNCING

11.1 INTRODUCTION

While performance areas that include the newscaster, the radio and commercial announcer, and the interviewer make up the bulk of the opportunities for on-air talent, several other fields of performance announcing deserve some attention. These include weather, financial, feature, multimedia narration, and on-air sales announcing. Each has its special requirements and attractions; however, each also relies on the basic performance principles examined earlier in this text. To be successful in any specialty area requires an ability to master some basic skills and techniques as well as a passion for being successful in that specific area of announcing.

11.2 WEATHER REPORTING

Weather reporting has evolved considerably since the early days of radio and television. The early supposition was that weather was boring and had to be covered as quickly as possible in radio, or enhanced in television with some distraction. The field became characterized by screwballs, clowns, and extremely attractive young women who may or may not have had any weather training. While weather is still broadcast as short segments in radio, it receives more attention and is broadcast more frequently on many television stations. Certain segments of the population, such as farmers and resort area operators, have always had a serious interest in weather. In addition, the nation has become much more conscious of the potential for sudden, serious storms and the value of broadcasts about them. Stations expend considerable energy and time keeping their audiences current on the weather. When major summer thunderstorms, with the potential for tornadoes, approach, stations have been known to drop regular programming to give minute-by-minute reports for long periods. Stations have invested large sums of money in sophisticated radar systems to enable them to display all the latest weather developments. As listeners and viewers have grown more interested and knowledgeable, weather reporting has become an acceptable professional career for a young broadcaster (see Video Clip 11.1). The existence and success of The Weather Channel, a 24-hour cable channel devoted exclusively to weather, emphasizes that point.

If an opportunity presents itself to do weather, you should devote as much effort as possible to rapidly become knowledgeable, as many in the audience will spot errors of ignorance. It should be emphasized that individuals with little or no weather training do get opportunities and pursue them successfully. The American Meteorological Society (AMS) maintains standards for recognizing weathercasters and awards "seals of approval" to those who are properly trained. The AMS Seal of Approval is given to television and radio forecasters who have a degree in meteorology or have completed 12 credit hours in atmospheric or related sciences. For television, the weathercaster must submit a recording that is reviewed by a board of professional meteorologists. A satisfactory rating must be earned in four areas: technical competence, informational value, explanatory value, and communication skills. Another organization, the National Weather Association (NWA), also awards a Seal of Approval after two years of full-time or three years of part-time on-air experience, submission of a recording, and passing a written exam. Both the AMS and NWA Seals of Approval must be renewed annually. Some stations go to considerable lengths to promote the fact that their weathercasters have the seal, while others simply ignore the fact that theirs do not. Knowledge of weather reporting can be an extra asset for any young announcer seeking a job in broadcasting. Obtaining an AMS or NWA Seal of Approval should be done as soon as possible by those interested in a weathercasting career, to show credibility and to be a stronger contender in a competitive job market.

In addition to locally developed reports, the U.S. National Weather Service provides continuous information via telephone lines and computer links. With satellite dishes and the Internet, it is possible to access satellite images of cloud patterns and storms from around the world. Commercial weather information services such as Accu-Weather and Colorgraphics have developed, which, for a fee, will provide a station with anything from basic information and weather maps to gorgeous graphics and animated charts. Radio stations can obtain complete, localized reports, wherein the reporter identifies him or herself with the community purchasing the service and includes references to local situations or landmarks. In addition, the Associated Press and other news wire services supply their subscribers with considerable weather data, which forms the basis of many radio reports.

Today, particularly in television, stations like to develop their own weathercasters as one of their stable of personalities. An individual may be associated with the same station for many years as its resident weather expert. While some of the "character" types of weathercasters still exist, and a young announcer who can be funny, on occasion, may have an advantage, the field favors a personable, but serious reporter. These solid individuals are the ones who are called upon when storms and severe conditions threaten. Any weathercaster who has been operating with a flip manner during normal conditions will need to shelve that style when things get critical. The audience knows the flippancy is an act and will welcome it back when the weather calms down again. Making jokes about tornado damage can land you on the street very quickly. This is just common sense.

Weather reporting comes with a variety of terms, many of which are not familiar to the average new graduate. There is a vocabulary to be learned and applied. While most reports focus more on simple explanations for the viewer, you will need to know these terms and their meanings in preparing your report. A list of common terms can be found in Figure 11.1. Some computer skill is also desirable, as many of the graphics sources are accessed by computer. Furthermore, larger stations will have their own systems for generating maps and illustrations. In many cases this will include animations as part of the graphic.

11.3 THE CHROMA-KEY SYSTEM FOR WEATHER

One of the more challenging experiences for the beginning TV weather person is working with the chroma-key system, which was mentioned earlier in

---

COMMON WEATHER TERMS

Anemometer—A device used for measuring wind speed. One type consists of three small cups on a center shaft. These catch the wind and rotate on the shaft, their speed being related to the speed of the wind that is turning them. The shaft is connected to a device similar to a speedometer.

Atmospheric Pressure—The weight of the air above any point. This considers the air all the way out to the edge of space. The pressure varies with heating and cooling. Changes in atmospheric pressure are often indicative of the approach of a change in the weather.

Barometer—A device for measuring atmospheric pressure. One type utilizes a thin glass tube about three feet long that is filled with mercury. The higher the air pressure, the more mercury is forced up into the tube. Therefore air pressure is often reported in inches of mercury, although that term is omitted and the report states only that the air pressure is 29.9 or 30.2, for example. Because mercury is dangerous, other devices are used, but the reports still utilize the "inches of mercury" system.

Barometric Pressure—Another term for atmospheric pressure.

Celsius—A temperature measurement commonly used in Europe and often used by American weather reporters. In this scale, water freezes at 0 degrees and boils at 100 degrees.

Discomfort Index—This is the reverse of the wind chill factor. It combines the temperature and humidity to give a measurement of the uncomfortable combination of high temperature and high humidity in the summertime.

Front—The leading edge of a weather change. The temperature usually differs on the two sides of the front. If the difference is significant, there can be sudden and severe weather changes, often accompanied by high winds. In the summertime, there may well be thunderstorms and even tornadoes associated with the change. Fronts are often identified as warm or cold, indicating the type of change they are bringing.

Hail—Pieces of ice, often in nearly round shapes, associated primarily with thunderstorms and tornadoes. Most frequently, these are about one-half inch or less in diameter, but in severe storms, hailstones can grow to several inches in diameter.

FIGURE 11.1 Common weather terms

These can cause considerable damage, injury, and even death. An equivalent example might be a baseball delivered at 90 miles per hour.

High—This term is used to refer to an area of high atmospheric pressure. Highs are usually associated with clear or clearing weather. The winds revolve around a high in a clockwise direction. A high to the north usually brings cooler weather to the area to the east and below its location. A high in the south brings warmer weather to the area to the west and north of it.

Humidity—The amount of moisture in the air. Warm air is capable of carrying large amounts of moisture while colder air carries less. Warm air that does not have associated high humidity, as in the desert, is often called "dry heat." High humidity tends to result in an uncomfortable condition, since perspiration does not evaporate rapidly, giving the body a "sticky" feeling. Dry, cold air can accelerate the evaporation of perspiration, increasing the "chilly" feeling a person may have in the winter.

Hurricane—Contrasted with tornadoes, which may do damage in a fairly localized area, hurricanes can be very large. These are born as tropical storms over warm ocean waters and may be up to several hundred miles in diameter. Hurricanes are made up of winds that rotate about a center or "eye." They are most dangerous in the southeastern part of the United States, but the storms, when they come ashore, can travel hundreds of miles inland and still do damage. In addition to high winds, they carry large amounts of water, so that flash flooding can be a danger in any community in their path. Along the shore, they can drive large amounts of water up onto the beaches, giving the impression of a very high tide. The most dangerous time is when the eye of the storm comes ashore, as it can be accompanied by a "storm surge" or great wall of water that has been known to wash large boats as far as three miles inland.

Isobar—Lines on a weather map that connect points that have the same atmospheric pressure. These are often used in television weather broadcasts to illustrate extremes of pressure.

Isotherm—Lines on a weather map that connect points that have the same temperature. These are commonly used to indicate the high and low temperatures a region is likely to experience.

Jet Stream—A "river" of high-speed winds that circle the earth at a height of approximately 5–10 miles. The wind speeds approach 200 mph. These winds can have considerable effect on weather as they frequently control the paths of storms. They can also cause cold weather to move south in the winter, or hold the cold in the north. The path of the jet stream can vary considerably, sometimes almost following the U.S.-Canadian border and other times swinging north to Alaska and south into Arizona.

Low—An area of low atmospheric pressure. Its winds revolve in a counterclockwise direction. Its effects are the reverse of the high, bringing cooler weather to the south and west of it when it is in the north, and warmer air to the east and north when it is in the south. Lows are usually associated with worsening weather. The lower the barometric pressure, the more dangerous the accompanying storm.

Sleet—A mixture of rain and snow, which can become dangerous, as its presence suggests that the air temperature is very near freezing. Road surfaces can go from wet, but safe, to a glaze of ice very quickly. Motorists often refer to this as "black ice," as it is nearly invisible on the road.

Squall Line-A group of thunderstorms moving together in a front. These can become particularly dangerous, since their power can combine—resulting in a super cell, or enlarged, very powerful storm.

Thunderhead—A cloud formation usually associated with a potential thunderstorm. It rises much higher than most other clouds and occasionally may look like the head and shoulders of a man. Sometimes thunderheads will rise so high that the winds of the jet stream cause the top of the cloud to be pulled away, giving it an "anvil top."

Tornado—An intense, though localized, storm characterized by very strong, rapidly rotating winds, which usually develop in association with large thunderstorms. These winds can form a funnel-like cloud, which drops down from the storm clouds above and touches the ground. As the winds can be spinning at 200 mph or more, they are very destructive. Tornadoes can be amazingly selective, striking one side of the street while leaving the other side untouched. Some funnels may be less than 10 feet in diameter, while others have been recorded at more than a quarter mile in width. In some cases, tornadoes have traveled in groups for considerable distances, while others have touched the ground for only a few seconds. The majority of tornadoes

FIGURE 11.1 Continued   **FIGURE 11.1** Continued

occur in the U.S. Midwest, but they can develop nearly anywhere.

Wind chill—A number calculated by weather forecasters that combines the temperature with the wind speed. In the winter, the degree to which persons experience discomfort from the cold is a combination of both factors. A strong wind on a cold day can result in a wind chill factor well below the actual temperature. This is an effective way of describing conditions to the public.

FIGURE 11.1 Continued

FIGURE 11.2 AND 11.3 Weathercaster Holly Strano, WKYC-TV, Cleveland, gestures to an empty green screen while to the right, the audience sees her with the added chroma-key information. (Photos courtesy of Holly Strano.)

this text. Many people realize that the weather maps behind a television reporter are not really there, that the reporters work by looking at off-camera monitors that show their image superimposed on the maps. The problem arises because we are accustomed to mirror images. When looking into a mirror, if we move a hand to the right, the image moves its hand in the same direction. However, if you will think a moment, that mirror person is actually moving his or her hand to the left. By contrast, a television image is "real" image. If you move your hand to the right, the image moves its hand to its right also, which is the opposite from what you are used to. This can create difficulties when you are trying to point to a specific place on a map that isn't there, by looking at the picture on the monitor. Boston and Los Angeles will seem to be on the wrong sides, and even pointing to Chicago can be difficult. Practice will help, but don't try to be too exact until you get skilled at this. Gesturing with an open hand is preferable to pointing with a finger, as it will reduce the possibility of pointing to one city while mentioning another.

The chroma-key is an electronic system in which the cameras are modified so that they do not see one color, usually green, formerly blue. Any color could be used, but green is most common. The electronics insert the image from another source into the blank area. With weather reporting, this is usually a map or graphic from a computer or still-image storer. The reporter stands in front of the green or blue screen and points to the various significant elements, but there is actually nothing on that surface. Usually there are monitors placed on either side of the weather set and probably out in front as well. The announcer points to the appropriate spot by watching the monitor, as shown in Video Clip 11.2. To the audience, it looks as if the weathercaster is pointing at the weather map itself.

With practice, you can become quite adept at pointing at the right spot while judging your position from the monitor. Work on developing a mental image of the layout. With your back to the screen, Boston is to your left and San Francisco is to your right. With some work you can anticipate where most of the cities will be. The gestures, of course, have to be done smoothly while delivering your report in whatever style you have chosen. Don't try to be too specific at first. An open hand rather than a single finger pointing will reduce the potential for misdirection. You can even spread the fingers a little to improve your changes of being on target. One other caution for the beginner: the chroma system reacts to green or blue anywhere on the screen, so a pair of green slacks could disappear from the screen, leaving you with a map instead of legs (review Video Clip 3.5). An all-blue outfit could result in your head and hands floating around on the

FIGURE 11.4 *Pointing when using the chroma-key system can be tricky.*

map as you give your report. It is your responsibility to wear the correct clothing. Chroma screens were originally always blue, but it was discovered that, on tighter shots, the chroma scene could sometimes be visible in the eyes of a blue-eyed reporter. As chroma was used in news reporting for many years, there were situations where war footage could be seen in the reporter's eyes. Green chroma was then developed.

11.4 WEATHER REPORTING STYLES

Weather reporters present a range of personalities across the country; however, there are at least three qualities that are common to all weathercasters: seeming to be involved and interested in what they are doing, showing some energy without becoming a caricature, and relating to their audience. In most cases, as a weathercaster, you can be reasonably informal in your greeting and remarks. Unless the weather is truly bad, use your smile. Project some charm. Basically, you are sharing the same weather as your audience, so you can comment on the heat, the cold, or the rain

as one who is also suffering through it or enjoying it. Further, remember your audience is down that glass tube we call a lens. Staying connected with the audience is critical and eye contact will be a big factor. Don't get so attached to your side monitors that you forget your audience is out front. Look at the monitors when you are about to point out a city or region, but get back to the camera quickly. This is a time to be reasonably animated, depending on your persona. Certainly use your hands and face to support what you are saying, but don't get into rocking or moving around. Keep yourself balanced and stable. You may need to change sides once during your report, or move across the area to get to a different spot on the map, but limit your movement. Don't turn your back on your audience. Finally, watch your word rate. In this situation going at high speed usually will detract from your presentation.

While radio weather reports are usually read, either from the wire service or copy that was written for the occasion, television reports will be largely ad-libbed, perhaps with the assistance of some cue cards. You'll have your maps and charts to prompt you, but a plan as to how you will approach your report is essential. One example might be to first, comment on current local conditions, then review the national scene, and finally return to make your local forecast. When covering the national map, present your material in some sort of geographic order, so that you are not bouncing all over the map. Since so much of our reading goes left to right, starting on the West Coast and moving eastward is one logical option. However, if there is a major weather event, such as a hurricane or tornado, you'll want to go to that first, but remember to be aware of what the news reporters are covering, so that you won't wind up duplicating. If you find yourself covering a significant local storm, such as a big thunderstorm that threatens to generate tornados, be sure to stay calm and don't say anything to alarm the viewers, unless you have a true emergency. You could warn your audience to take cover or lay in some supplies, but be sure not to exaggerate.

Plan in detail what you're going to cover and especially how you're going to conclude the report. A summary sentence or two is often the best solution, but have it in mind. Don't expect to create it on the spot. Be particularly alert, as it is easy to slip into the "uh" filler in this situation. Furthermore, you should have the report clearly in mind for those occasions when the technology fails you, which it inevitably will. Being able to continue with an interesting, clear

> Here's a hypothetical report, so let's make it a nice day.
>
> *Good afternoon, I'm Jane Smith. Isn't this a great day? It's 76 degrees and sunny with a five mile an hour breeze coming from the southwest. Looking around the country, we find that they have sunshine in Seattle also, something that doesn't happen too often there. San Francisco and Los Angeles are also clear. There is a front moving west from the Rockies that will bring some much needed rain to the Arkansas, Kansas and Nebraska area. Further east it's mostly clear skies. It's 76 in New York and 74 in Boston. Looking ahead, we're going to have more good weather tomorrow. There will be showers tonight but they will have cleared by 8 am. The low tonight should be about 61 and the high tomorrow should be 77. I'll be back with another update at 6 pm.*
>
> That report should take you about 45 seconds.

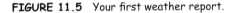

FIGURE 11.5 Your first weather report.

report, verbally visualizing the weather conditions when your map system fails, will mark you as a pro and someone who has the poise and preparation to succeed. As usual, the pros make it look easy. You will find it is a bit of a challenge to ad-lib an interesting, clear report, keeping track of all the aspects you want to cover. A card sitting on the monitors on either side could list key temperatures across the country to prompt you and also help you remember where you were going next. The writing should be big and clear and simple enough for you can read it in a glance. As with other ad-lib projects, students often underestimate how much they need to do to get ready. Say your report completely and aloud, off camera somewhere, several times, as part of your preparation. As a final reminder, remember to hold when you finish your report or do something appropriate. Immediately starting for the news desk can leave the director with an empty screen. Take a look at "Your First Weather Report, Figure 11.5.

As if you didn't have enough to think about, there is one other factor to keep in mind. Many stations use the weather reports as the "variable element" in the total news show. If something runs long or a story breaks, you could be asked to reduce your report to thirty seconds … just before you go on. Some graphic systems are set so that you can't skip over any of them. Another time, a live field report may fall through and the producer asks you to add a full minute, just as you are about to begin. Always give a thought to how you would handle these challenges when planning your reports.

Weaving in various local community names helps make everyone feel a part of the report. You may want to arrange with a few members of your audience to call in reports from their neighborhoods, if your coverage area is large. You may need to furnish them with a good thermometer and perhaps other simple weather devices, but it shouldn't be expensive. To further relate to the audience and boost your community standing, you could be active in the support of some local charitable event, or even create an occasional segment about pets needing homes.

Many stations, in an effort to make the news team seem more human, will expect some chatter, usually at the end of the report, sometimes referred to as "Happy Talk." This could come in the form of a question or comment from an anchor, such as, "Do you think it will clear for the game Saturday?" or "Will I be able to get in a round of golf before the storm hits?" You'll be expected to make a pleasant and interesting response, so again, some advance discussion of a topic can be helpful.

Special weather conditions may give you the opportunity to do more extensive reports that could evolve into a feature or short documentary. Depending on your location, you could be called upon to do an in-depth story on tornado safety, the upcoming hurricane season, or the impact on your community of prolonged drought or flooding. A portion of this report would be gathered in the field and could involve a series of interviews. Larger stations may have several weather reporters, some of whom will be sent into the field during major weather events. It is not improbable that you could find yourself reporting in the midst of a raging snowstorm or other disaster. In this case, you become both a reporter and a weather expert, describing conditions while at the same time analyzing the information and projecting probable developments. As stations compete for attention, weather reports from the field have become very common. Conditions for the big game, parade, or other event will be reported from the site as well as from the studio. Reporting skills, in addition to weather skills, will make you more valuable to the station.

Weather reporting has progressed from being something of a sideshow to being a respected science. Reporters are called on for specific information, interpretation, and analysis. Weather reporting now uses extensive animation and computer graphics. Some of those are drawn from national sources, but many will be prepared in-house so that they will be completely current and local. Travelers will be interested in the projected weather for common destination cities like New York, Chicago, and Los Angeles, but the majority will want to know what to expect locally for the next two or three days. For those who find it attractive and are willing to acquire the necessary knowledge and skills, weather forecasting and reporting can be a rewarding specialized career.

11.5 FINANCIAL REPORTING

Over the past 20 years, Americans have become much more conscious of the financial markets. Self-directed individual retirement accounts (IRAs) and 401(k) plans have caused thousands to invest significant portions of their retirement money in the stock market. This has resulted in a greater awareness of stocks and bonds and what they are doing each day. In response, three nearly full-time cable channels have emerged that are devoted to the subject, as well as streaming video feeds over the Internet that deal with the latest information on financial developments. In addition, many radio and television news reports are placing greater emphasis on the markets, and this trend will probably continue. While this is a specialized field, it is one that many find interesting.

For general reporting of financial news, a student needs to know about the elements that are most interesting to the public and how to interpret them. For full-time anchoring on a cable channel, knowledge of economics and experience in the stock market, as well as news writing and reporting skills, are essential. This also means reading newspapers and other financial news daily to keep up with all that is happening in the world of finance. An additional media position is the financial commentator, which involves specialized knowledge and is usually held by someone with

considerable work in the markets who has migrated to performance to use this experience.

Many of the continuing shows are two hours long and combine long segments read from the teleprompter plus interviews with experts, both in the studio and via satellite links. These interviews are ad-libbed, perhaps with some prepared questions as starters. The reporter/anchor will need to be able to understand and interpret the guest's statements and ask meaningful questions. Often the host must screen guests' remarks for jargon that would be beyond the knowledge of typical viewers, and ask follow-up questions to clarify. In some cases, the host will ask questions to which he or she knows the answers; however, these questions must be posed in a sincere way, so they don't seem staged or forced. Good interpersonal skills are essential as well, as some guests may try to pontificate or run on at great length and must be cut off. Some executives being interviewed may try to become public relations agents for their company or mask problems their company is having. In these cases, the financial reporter has to ask the hard questions and recognize that the speaker is avoiding them.

Many things influence the movements of stock prices, particularly news events. A good understanding of the world's political and economic structure will come into play. When big events happen, nationally or internationally, stock prices can move rapidly up or down and the number of viewers of a financial program can rise quickly. A rapidly dropping stock market is of major concern to thousands of people, for it means the loss of great sums of money. While light banter is generally acceptable when times are tranquil, a dropping market calls for calm reporting with no evidence of "scare" remarks or other comments that could cause the audience undue anguish.

Financial commentators have great influence with their audience. The recommendation of a stock can cause it to rise significantly in a short time. A negative comment can cost investors millions. It is an area where the individual has a tremendous responsibility to be careful of remarks and avoid any hint of favoritism. Furthermore, unscrupulous individuals exist who have tried to influence the announcers to speak favorably of a stock, even to the extent of offering gifts, trips, and outright bribes. Accepting anything like this is a quick way to destroy a career. In recent years we have seen the arrival of hosts who openly recommend particular stocks on the air. These have proven to be popular. However, the hosts are not allowed to have any investment in those stocks or, at least, must acknowledge that they do.

Talking about the market every day, hearing tips and recommendations, and perhaps knowing people who have made a great deal of money in stocks, presents a great temptation to dabble in the stock market yourself. Your station will have rules concerning this, but it is an area loaded with danger. If you purchase a stock and then seem to be making favorable remarks about it on the air, you can be accused of "touting" the stock so that the price will rise, making a profit for yourself. This is both unethical and illegal. Careers have been destroyed in this manner and it isn't worth the risk. If you're doing market reporting, there are appropriate ways you can still invest; but get some good legal advice before you begin.

11.6 WHAT A FINANCIAL REPORTER COVERS

What you include in a financial report will first be determined by the amount of time you have. When only a brief period is set aside for stock reports, the first choice to cover would be the Dow Jones Average. Actually, the Dow Jones Company issues three averages—the Industrials, the Transportation, and the Utilities—but for most people, the preference is for the Industrials. This is a number derived from the selling prices of 30 major stocks, such as IBM, GE, and General Motors. Listeners will want to know the current figure and the amount of change since the end of the previous business day. In addition, they will want to know if the change is an increase in price or a decrease.

A second popular average is the S&P 500, put out by Standard and Poor's, which includes 500 companies. Some experts view the S&P as a better gauge, even though most people still prefer the Dow. Here again, the latest number and the amount and direction of change are what is desired. The third popular average is the NASDAQ (pronounced "Naz-dak"), which

stands for National Association of Securities Dealers Automatic Quotations. This is a separate, computer-based operation and deals primarily, but not exclusively, in smaller and cheaper stocks. Many people who do not have much money to invest prefer this exchange because of the lower prices. Here again, the latest number and the amount and direction of change are desired. Check Figure 11.7 for a report example.

FIGURE 11.6 Get your symbols straight.

(Here is an example of how a stock market report might go.)

Good afternoon, this is your 3 pm stock market report. The Dow Jones Industrials are up ten points to 13 thousand, five hundred, forty one, the S and P average is up two points at 13 hundred twenty two. Looking at some widely held stocks, IBM is up fifty cents to one hundred, twenty-four dollars and forty cents, General Electric is at 33 dollars and twenty cents, up ten cents and Microsoft is unchanged at 31 dollars and forty-four cents, while General Motors is down thirty cents at 15 fifty two. I'll be back in one hour with another update.

(That report should take you just about thirty seconds and covers the points the average investor wants to know.)

FIGURE 11.7 Your first stock market report.

If additional time is available for your report, the next step would be to list the current prices and the changes in price for several widely owned stocks such as IBM, GE, or Microsoft. As usual, give the current price and the amount and direction of change. If your city has a major company that is a big employer, listeners and viewers will be interested in this as well, as many companies pay benefits in the form of stock, so you could be speaking to many stockholders.

On the stock exchange and the Internet, stocks are identified by two, three, four, and occasionally five letter codes. Some are quite obvious, such as GE and IBM. Others are not. Dupont is DD and Union Pacific Railroad is UNP. Can you figure out what MSFT and INTC are?

Your wire service, such as the Associated Press, will provide you with regular reports, but they are not likely to list the specific local stocks you need. In that case, you can call a local stockbroker for the latest information, or there are numerous Internet sites where the information can be obtained at no charge. One source is www.CNNmoney.com, where you can get information on any stock. Or, you could set up an "account" there, listing the stocks you report on regularly. You don't need to own them. This way you would access the ones you need in one stroke. Still longer reports will probably be drawn from your wire service. Look for the stories that seem to have the widest implications or some local connection. Avoid showing excitement over any company reports, as it might appear that you are encouraging listeners to buy or sell the stock. Deliver the reports in a calm but energetic voice. If the markets are taking a serious fall, reduce your energy but remain unemotional. Listeners will be upset enough without you adding to it.

11.7 FEATURE SPECIALIST

Some stations have a person who is responsible for preparing what might be thought of as novelty features. These are segments that can be included in a newscast or omitted, depending on the time available, or they can have a regular schedule. Some are essentially video field trips. One station for many years ran a feature series called "One-Tank Trips," in which the same host would take you to places around the state such as an historical site or tourist attraction. The angle was that these were all within the distance you could drive and return using one tank of gasoline. The fact that the host used a very small car, which probably got excellent gas mileage, was incidental. It gave the station an opportunity to promote state attractions and offer a little change of pace as well. Another such feature was known as "Del's Folks," and it highlighted individuals and small businesses in the coverage area. The host, Del, even had a decal he gave to those he interviewed, which people proudly displayed after he had visited. This provided a vehicle for recognizing accomplishments, good works, and unusual circumstances. Still another feature was known as "Outside the Box." It appeared on a cable channel devoted to financial matters and was intended to provide a lighter moment to mix with the more serious coverage of the stock market. The host occasionally donned a crazy costume and visited unusual locations or businesses. In this case, he was expected to develop something that had some degree of humor to it, covering activities that otherwise would not show up on the channel. For many of these hosts, they had other off-camera duties such as advertising sales or scriptwriting, and this was virtually all of the on-camera time they got.

The host of a specialty feature must have considerable rapport with the audience and be an interesting person to know. You only have a few moments to connect with your audience, to establish your topic, and get to some interesting aspects. Most of these segments are recorded in advance, but some are done live, or live with video cut in. Jim Sislo is a television time salesman who does a segment known as the Sislo Kid, which deals with new innovations in technology (Figure 11.8). He identifies his audience as individuals who are not particularly knowledgeable about the field. He has three minutes, every other Thursday, to inform and entertain his audience. Jim looks for gadgets that are interesting, entertaining, and inexpensive. He also knows that the gadget must be something that can be presented simply. As a feature specialist, deciding who your audience will be and what kind of subject matter you will cover is a good place to start. As with other good performers, Jim spends considerable time in planning and preparation, and still has to be prepared for things to go wrong. You can hear one of his experiences on Audio Clip 11.1.

Jim prefers to prerecord his segments whenever possible, although he has gone live many times. Since the length of his segment is rather fixed and some seconds are lost to a produced opening, he has to plan carefully. His general formula is to allocate a little time to his greeting and topic introduction, then focus on two or three points related to the subject, and then quickly build to some sort of strong, sometimes comedic, ending. Since he has been a professional magician since childhood, he often draws on that knowledge to add a

"The performance aspect is important because that's the delivery, but the preplanning is really what takes a lot of the time and a lot of work."

FIGURE 11.8 Jim Sislo, media salesman and specialty feature host, WEWS-TV, Cleveland, Ohio. (Photo courtesy of Jim Sislo.)

little flair. His magic work has also given him experience with performance and public appearances, which has contributed to his success and illustrates that any kind of performance experience can be valuable.

Jim finds that manufacturers are more than willing to provide items for his use. Many contact him. However, when he makes the contact himself, he invites them to visit his section of the station's website to establish his credibility. A key point to remember is that he returns the items after use, as ethical issues could come into play, and he does not want to jeopardize his credibility. Still, Jim sees himself as a salesman and enjoys his "real" job, but is grateful to have been invited to be a feature specialist, too.

11.8 HOST SELLING

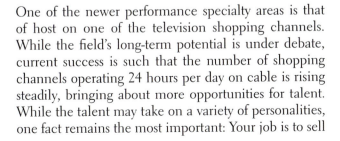

One of the newer performance specialty areas is that of host on one of the television shopping channels. While the field's long-term potential is under debate, current success is such that the number of shopping channels operating 24 hours per day on cable is rising steadily, bringing about more opportunities for talent. While the talent may take on a variety of personalities, one fact remains the most important: Your job is to sell

as much of the product as possible. While brief digressions into humor or nostalgia are acceptable, the focus must always be on sales. In terms of skills, the ability to ad-lib for prolonged periods is essential. During any given period, usually one or two hours, you will be offering items that have some common element, such as jewelry, cookware, women's clothing, or sports memorabilia. You will need to chat about the items, be enthusiastic about them, and describe them in interesting ways without showing any strain or loss of excitement. Through it all, you will need to regularly mention the product number to be used for ordering, and the price, which, of course, is a bargain. In some situations, you may also be pushing how little time is left for the viewers to get their orders placed. Watch a student make a sales presentation in Video Clip 11.3

Certainly this is an area where the gift of gab is almost a necessity. At least initially, the chances are that you will specialize in the type of items you present. It could be just jewelry—perhaps just gold jewelry—or it could be electronic devices, like GPS receivers or organizers. Except for the occasional sports souvenirs, tools, or auto supply shows, where more of your audience will be men, you can assume that the majority of your audience will be women. Consider the image you should present. Certainly it should be friendly, sincere, interesting, and knowledgeable. You will want to seem like someone who is up-to-date on fashions and fads, a little sophisticated, but not so much so that the audience feels disconnected from you. Be someone they feel could be their friend, someone they can admire without being over-awed.

If your audience is able to relate to you, they will support you with purchases and calls that management will not miss in rating your work. In many cases, you will also regularly field live calls from customers during the show. QVC has a "testimonial" line for those who want to say how much they like the items on sale at the moment, and talk with the hostess as well. You'll need to be interested in the caller, but know that you must keep it brief while being conversational and friendly. You also will be quizzing them on what item they bought and why, as well as subtly seeking a statement about how great this or some product is. It is probable that some callers will be "gushy," thrilled at the chance to talk with you. Be prepared to politely thank them for their kindness and then get back to the product. Be on guard for callers who are headed off the deep end, with some other purpose for being on the air, or who are just so excited they can't control themselves.

When a group of items is to be offered, you will have a briefing session with your buyers who will go over the products' characteristics, advantages, and applications. These are the talking points you will focus on, although any related personal experiences or general knowledge will be useful. Becoming somewhat expert on a subject, such as gold, can give you material to supplement the information you've been given. Using or wearing the items can give you personal experiences to draw on, which often pleases the audience. You'll prepare or be given a set of note cards, which will be inconspicuously placed where you can refer to them. You will only be able to glance at them while you're talking, so learn them well.

Although this is sales, it is also entertainment. The product is the start, but you are the host, ringmaster, and consultant. Your acting ability will come in handy, as you will need to project excitement over many items while chatting and sharing tips and experiences. Jokes should always be on you, never on the product, the organization, or the customer. Occasionally you will have guests, usually people who have developed a product line they are promoting. Some will be skilled on the air, while others will need help. As is true for the host of any talk show, it's your job to keep the show on track, be aware of the time, the objectives and other demands of the business, and make your guest look as appealing and successful as possible. Further, it is common for the host to wear clothing that is being sold, so you could be called upon to do some fast changes, getting into new outfits during a promo or recorded product review.

Clearly, the goal of preparation for such a program is knowledge, knowledge, knowledge. The more you know about the products, the manufacturers, the applications, and the interesting little sidelights, the easier it will be to talk enthusiastically and at length about them. Your own hobbies or areas of interest, like cooking, cameras, jewelry making, or collecting, can give you a place to start. Since much of what is offered is clothing, a current knowledge of fashion and fashion trends will be a big asset. Your increasing expertise, combined with your speaking ability and presentation, could yield an interesting performance opportunity. Don't rely entirely on your ability to talk. Support yourself with as much research, facts, and even trivia as possible. You may not always use them, but if you don't, it probably means that everything went smoothly. Being caught with nothing to say except endless repetition for several minutes is a painful experience. Unfortunately, it's also a time when it's easy to lapse into fillers. Figure 11.9 will give you some ideas to consider as you prepare.

At least one of the television shopping channels, QVC, has held open auditions for on-air salespeople. The pool of several hundred applicants ranged from amateur actors to professional broadcasters, and included many with no experience at all. The candidates were given about two minutes to sell a product, something they had brought with them, or something given to them by QVC. The successful salespeople could sell the product with an easy conversation rather than a fact-filled sales pitch. According to QVC Vice President Jack Comstock, "You've got to have that ability to really talk to the camera as if it truly was your best friend."

11.9 THE VOICE-OVER AND NARRATION

A voice-over is any situation in television where something other than the announcer is seen on the screen while his or her voice is heard. Review Video Clip 6.1 to see one example of a voice-over commercial. We see examples frequently in commercials, news reports, documentaries, and public service announcements (PSAs). For the announcer at a radio or television station, extra income may result from freelance opportunities to do voice-overs. In addition, there are many individuals who make good incomes doing voice-over work as a profession. It is a career where age and looks are not factors. There are voice-over specialists, male and female, of all ages, from their early 20s to their 80s. The primary requirements include a good voice, the ability to read copy effectively, the responsibility to show up on time ready to work, and a willingness to promote yourself and respond quickly to opportunities.

Learning to do voice-over work can begin while you're still in school and can continue after graduation through workshops and coaching. Theatrical training would be an additional asset. Some people focus on one aspect of the field, frequently commercials, while others expand their skills with character voices and work with animation. At the professional level, the talent will probably have an agent, but may still need to go to auditions or at least submit samples of work, as this field is very competitive. (Review Lisa Brooks's comments in Figure 6.5) Audition recordings are an important element. These are usually only two to three minutes long, beginning with a short segment of your natural voice and then presenting snippets from six to eight commercials that show your ability to do a variety of vocal styles. These should show different attitudes, energy levels, and characters. The segments are run together without pauses, as producers

---

Planning a sales presentation

Begin with the understanding that it's not nearly as easy as it looks. Although in some cases the sales object may be provided, we'll assume it's your job to bring something to sell. Take a little time making your selection. Just grabbing a coffee mug or a hoodie can leave you scrambling for material. Make a list of talking points, qualities, uses, values, style, and beauty implications. Don't just think about them, write them out. This will be your cue list. If you can't come up with about eight points, perhaps you should consider something else. We'll assume your presentation is four minutes.

Think about any problems displaying the item. You may have a counter to work behind and you can place the object there. Assuming you have two cameras, one may be designated as "your camera." This is the one you talk to all the time, even when the other is on a close-up of your item. Next, select a spot where you will place things for the close-ups. If your item has several parts, show each individually, by moving one to that spot and then back to the group after the shot is finished. You will have to watch the tally lights to know when "your camera" is back on. Don't line things up like a wall in front of you. Check the quality of the close-ups. Do they show what you want? Practice pointing to key spots. Avoid holding up the objects as it rarely works out well.

When you get the cue to start, show your smile and do your best to keep it there. Unless you have specific instructions, you can start as if this is the beginning of your segments, or just another item in an on-going sequence. You could do a greeting or just say "our next item is..." Watch your rate. This is a situation where it is easy to speed up and that only works against you. You want to be charming and enthusiastic, but not over the top. Don't overdo it. Begin by stating what you are selling, the identifying number and the price. You could slip in "only" when stating the cost.

Maintaining the smile, launch into your first sales point and include something personal about why you like it. " I really like this____." Include phrases about what a great price it is, how it is sure to generate compliments (if that fits), how it will expand your "collection," (even jeans and sweats can be collected.) Then move on to another characteristic, trying to use positive words about beauty, value, style, ease of use, and comfort. Be involved, gesture, use your face, project an image that you're having a wonderful time, just sharing a great find. Periodically mention the item number and the price. In most cases the phone number will be on the screen. If not, include that too. If you're adequately prepared, you won't have to resort to a lot of repeating, but you can wind up your last thirty seconds with a review of the key points, ending with something like "So call now!"

FIGURE 11.9 *Your first sales presentation.*

are always short of time and will give you only a few seconds to convince them you are the best choice. Listen to Audio Track 6.2 to hear a portion of a voice-over performer's audition tape. Today, professional voice-over specialists are producing their own CDs on which they group examples of their different types of work, so that producers can go immediately to the type of voice that they are seeking. They will also have an opportunity to hear all the other skills the talent can offer as well.

PERFORMANCE TIP 11.1

Job Opportunities from Lisa Brooks

The opportunities in voice-over have grown in recent years. Videogames, web-site voices, podcasts, and Internet radio all use voice-overs. Pay range depends on the client, the job and the number of lines. Even something as basic as voicemail can be a source of income. One actress I know goes to a major corporation regularly, where she updates the voicemail. She walks into the studio, says "For Tom Smith, press 67." and walks out with a paycheck. Not glamorous, but it pays the bills.

11.10 DEVELOPING VOICE-OVER SKILLS

Most of the more challenging voice-over situations are encountered in television and film work because you are not only seeking to present the copy in the best manner, but you are also coordinating your delivery to the visual portion of the program. Timing is again a critical element. Frequently the voice portions are mixed with segments of music, recorded statements on-camera, and assorted sound effects. As with the donut commercial, getting in and out at the right moment is the challenge. While editing and time compression have made this a bit easier, you can't assume these tools will be available. Particularly in the area of animation, you may record the audio track before the visual production begins. Still there may be timing instructions you will have to follow.

If you are doing a voice for existing visuals, the first step, after you have gotten familiar with the copy, is to examine the pictures to which you will be recording. Clearly identify the points where you must begin and end each segment. Realistically, in a longer piece there may be 20 or 30 of these spots, commonly called *in points* and *out points*. In each, look for a shot change, a body movement, a word, a note of music, or anything that will cue you as to when to start your next segment. Obviously, this cue needs to be very near your start point. Write these on your script, close to the appropriate line. Likewise, become very familiar with the visual elements that will be seen while you are reading. You will need a cue that tells you that you are a few seconds from the end of the visual segment, so that you can make minor adjustments in pace to finish that portion on time. This of course means that you are not only concerned about pronunciation, inflection, mood, and all the other elements of performance, but where you are in the video as well. Again, this skill is primarily the result of practice and concentration. It is done daily by hundreds of professionals and is something you can master as well.

Some producers will give you extensive instructions as to what they want, and others will want you to read the copy with little or no coaching. They then may seek adjustments in your delivery, asking for more or less energy, enthusiasm, emphasis, or speed. Listen carefully to their comments and instructions. It will help you get into their mindset so you can meet their needs. One of the important elements is to hear and feel the desired characteristics so that you can sustain them throughout the session and even recreate them if you are called back for additional work at a later time.

11.11 VOICE CHARACTERIZATIONS

In addition to using your natural speaking voice as a media performer, you may be able to offer another form of announcing by doing voice characterizations. Many people have made careers out of providing the voices for cartoon characters. One of the most famous of these performers was Mel Blanc. In the early part of his career, he was most closely associated with Jack Benny's radio program where he was featured in various roles such as Professor LeBlanc (Benny's violin teacher) and the sputtering engine of Benny's Maxwell automobile. He is probably better known to a younger generation as the cartoon voices for Warner Brothers, including Bugs Bunny, Daffy Duck, Porky Pig, Elmer Fudd, Sylvester and Tweety, Pepe Le Pew, and Yosemite Sam. In the 1988 film, *Who Framed Roger Rabbit?* he recreated many of these voices. He also worked for Hanna-Barbera productions and did the voices of Barney Rubble and Dino the dinosaur on *The Flintstones*. It was said that his voice was heard more times, in more places, for more years than any other in broadcast history.

Voice-overs for cartoons have also become popular jobs for Hollywood actors. They are hired for their names and well-known voices rather than for any exceptional ability to do character voices. Walt Disney Productions has made many of these films, such as *Beauty and the Beast* with Angela Lansbury as Mrs. Potts, and Robin Williams as the genie in *Aladdin*. While the typical performer may not become the voice of a well-known cartoon character, it is possible he or she will use a fake foreign dialect or character voice at some time. Figure 11.10 shows one possible setup.

Commercials, especially, often take advantage of a performer's ability to create an unusual voice. You've probably heard commercials that center on a Dracula-type voice, a Southern belle, an Irish brogue, or any number of other specific speech styles. There is one rule of thumb regarding these types of character voices: If you can't do them well, don't do them at all. The mistake many beginning announcers make is that they only approximate the actual voice style when trying to affect a character voice, and then drop in and out of character as they are reading the script. The voices need to be practiced and tested over time to reach a professional level. Doing voices can be a good career, but it certainly is no shortcut. If you develop the ability to mimic various vocal styles and create voices, it can lead to additional performance work that wouldn't be available to you based on your normal style of speaking.

FIGURE 11.10 Voicing animation.

Michael Cardamone is co-host of a daily live production on WKYC-TV, Cleveland, entitled Good Company. He was a communications major in college, but got into television in an unusual way. He was chosen as a cast member of the reality show, Average Joe 2: Hawaii. After the production was complete, he was a frequent guest on a Cleveland talk show, Studio 3. Eventually he filled in as a guest host and when a new longer show was developed he was asked to continue as a co-host, handling some segments alone.

FIGURE 11.11 Michael Cardamone.

11.12 PROGRAM HOSTING

Some students dream of hosting their own show, whether it be an interview, panel, sports, or game format. Although "hosting" might not be viewed as a specialty, there are numerous individuals who do primarily that, and make a career of it. Again, it is often done so well that there is the illusion that anyone can do it. An analysis of the roles and responsibilities are in many ways, a summation of all the different bits of advice already covered in this text.

First, if you are the host, you are going to be a visible person, and everyone will be watching to see how you conduct yourself. Host Michael Cardamone (Figure 11.11) says that "You have to realize that you are in the public eye, so that the things you do, even at a local level will be under scrutiny, whether it's in the studio or outside. Even at a restaurant you will always have to be careful what you say and do."

As host of a local interview show, Cardamone says he goes to his guests first and tries to make them more comfortable, since some of them will be nervous. "I just sit there and have a nice conversation, even crack some jokes to make sure they are comfortable with me."

Again at a local level, you may well be working without a teleprompter, which will call on all your ad-libbing skills. Cardamone stresses that you must think before you speak. One aspect students overlook is the language you use with your friends outside the studio. Cardamone says, "You have to be very careful in ad-lib conversations as foul words can slip out and you could lose your job." Students with serious performance goals should consider this in their conversations. It might be wise to work on getting such words out of your habit patterns.

Whether you are hosting an entire show, or just a segment, you are largely responsible for the direction and flow of what goes on. This means being aware of everything around you, so you are ready to go to the item, deal with a delay, help a guest or co-panelist who is having difficulty, avoiding any surprises for the director, and generally doing what is needed to get a good show on the air. Every show will have unplanned moments, even emergencies. How you react to them and how you resolve them will have a big impact on your reputation in the field. Keep cool, do what's needed and be part of the solution, not the problem.

Regardless of what type of show you are doing, there probably will be audience criticism. Cardamone says, "You have to have a tough skin. Everyone who watches the show has an opinion. You can't please everyone who watches. You have to realize that you may get more criticism than praise. If you are a female, there are women out there who won't like the way you look, or the way you dress, or they are mad because you are on TV and they aren't. The Internet has made it easier for the audience to send criticism."

In many situations, you will be the most experienced person on the set. That could mean supporting someone with a nervous attack, calming someone who gets too excited or upset, and keeping everyone on the subject. One author of this text once directed a 15-minute live interview show where the guest froze as the show hit the air. The skilled host had to not only ask the questions, but also paraphrased likely answers to which the panicked guest then struggled to nod "yes" or "no." It was done so skillfully that many people did not realize the guest never spoke.

Clearly, ad-libbing ability will be a major asset. You will need to speak clearly and apropriately regardless of what develops. It is something that you can practice to improve your skills. On a regular basis, select a topic, situation or a bit of information and record yourself talking about it. Strive for a professional sound, with good projection and freedom from stumbles, long pauses and fillers. Give yourself a time goal. Set out to speak in an interesting way for at least three minutes on any topic you give yourself. Keep the rate down and the enthusiasm at an appropriate level. Be entertaining. Critique yourself seriously and have others listen as well. Is your rate good? Speaking a bit slower gives you more time to think. Are the "ahs" or "and ahs" sneaking in? Do you hear any repeated inflection patterns? Finally, commercial television offers you the opportunity to study individuals who are experts. Analyze what they are doing. Listen to and critique a student's effort to do a four-minute ad-lib on Audio Clip 11.2.

If you do your television job well, you will likely be asked to be the master/mistress of ceremony for banquets and other special occasions, which may generate some additional income, and certainly can contribute to your stature in the community. It could also lead to opportunities like appearing in corporate videos, which can be financially pleasing, and can contribute to an exciting career. One thing to remember is that you have a great opportunity to study professional hosts at work, just with your television watching. Whether it's Jimmy Kimmel or David Letterman, or any other pro, consider what they are doing, how they are handling situations and how they present themselves. You could learn a lot.

11.13 CONCLUSIONS

Specialty announcing can offer an interesting entry into the field of media performance. Most of the skills employed by any broadcast performer will be called upon, but you will also need to develop some specialized skills and knowledge. The weathercaster needs meteorology training. The financial reporter needs an understanding of the stock market. The shopping channel host must know the products and techniques of this type of selling. The specialty features person must be creative and personable and, at times, humorous. The voice-over specialist needs to develop a wide variety of styles and deliveries. These examples should not be seen as the only specialty announcing areas either. Movie show host, consumer reporter, and industrial media narrator, to name a few, are other broadcast performance opportunities to pursue.

Self-Study

■ QUESTIONS

1. The main difficulty for the performer in working with a chroma-key effect is _____.
   a) movement is awkward since it is not a mirror image
   b) maps are difficult to see
   c) the blue color of the background makes the talent look pale
   d) choice of clothing

2. Skills for general reporting of financial news include all of the following except _____.
   a) knowledge of economics
   b) knowledge about the workings of the stock market
   c) experience in news writing and reporting
   d) an AMS Seal of Approval

3. An important skill for a host of a shopping channel is _____.
   a) familiarity with NASDAQ or the S&P 500
   b) the ability to develop a "character" or an act
   c) the ability to ad-lib for long periods of time
   d) experience in writing and performing

4. Which voice characterization announcer was famous for creating the voices of Bugs Bunny, Yosemite Sam, and many other Warner Brothers cartoon characters?
   a) Robin Williams
   b) Angela Lansbury
   c) Mel Blanc
   d) Jim Sislo

5. As a host of a shopping channel, you should not know too much about the product you're selling so as you talk about it, it will be fresh and exciting to you.
   a) true
   b) false

6. An isotherm is any situation in television where something other than the announcer is seen on the screen while his or her voice is heard.
   a) true
   b) false

7. Which specialty announcer is least likely to have to clarify jargon in the normal performance of his or her job?
   a) weathercaster
   b) financial reporter
   c) shopping channel host
   d) voice characterization announcer

8. All television weathercasters are required to receive a "seal of approval" from the American Meteorological Society (AMS).
   a) true
   b) false

9. Which of the following is not a common weathercasting term?
   a) isobar
   b) PSA
   c) squall line
   d) anemometer

10. Which of the following is not something the majority of weathercasters do when reporting the weather?
    a) create an unusual character voice or foreign dialect
    b) seem to be involved and interested in what they're doing
    c) show some energy without being a caricature
    d) relate to their audience

11. As a financial reporter talking about the stock market daily and hearing tips or recommendations, you should plan on investing in the market as a part of your job.
    a) true
    b) false

12. A financial reporter would be least likely to include which of the following in his or her nightly report?
    a) current Dow Jones averages
    b) current S&P 500 data
    c) current NASDAQ average
    d) current Discomfort Index

13. As an announcer selling a product on television, regardless of the personality you employ, what is your most important task?
    a) to accurately describe the product being sold
    b) to ad-lib about the product being sold
    c) to sell as much of the product as possible
    d) to talk with purchasers of the product

14. For which announcer specialty are age and on-camera looks least important?
    a) weathercaster
    b) financial reporter
    c) host selling
    d) voice-over narrator

15. The mistake many beginning announcers make when trying to carry off a fake foreign dialect is that they drop in and out of "character" as they are reading the script.
    a) true
    b) false

■ ANSWERS

If You Answered A:

1a. Correct. Most people will need some practice before their movement becomes smooth when using a chroma-key effect.

2a. No. Economics is an essential knowledge base for a financial news announcer. (Reread 11.4 and 11.5.)

3a. No. NASDAQ and S&P 500 are references to knowledge needed by a financial reporter. (Reread 11.4 and 11.5.)

4a. No. Although Robin Williams has done some voice characterization work, including the genie in *Aladdin*, this isn't the correct answer. (Reread 11.10.)

5a. Wrong. This is not a true statement. Being unfamiliar with a product more likely will lead to problems with your description of it. (Reread 11.7.)

6a. No. This is not true. An isotherm is defined by lines on a weather map that connect points having the same temperature. (Review Figure 11.1 and reread 11.2.)

7a. No. For the weathercaster, there are many jargon terms that can come up and require further explanation. (Reread 11.2.)

8a. No. This is not a true statement. While it is unlikely to be the case in modern television, weathercasters are not required to have any weather training at all. (Reread 11.2.)

9a. No. This describes lines on a weather map that connect points having the same atmospheric pressure. (Review Figure 11.1 and reread 11.2.)

10a. Correct. This is something more appropriate for the voice characterization announcer who may be providing a cartoon voice.

11a. This statement is neither true nor false, but an area an announcer must be very careful with. Your employer will most likely have guidelines concerning this and any attempt to "tout" a stock you own would be unethical and illegal. A smart financial reporter would seek legal advice before investing, if he or she chooses to do so. (Reread 11.4.)

12a. No. Most financial reporters will include Dow Jones averages, especially the Industrials. (Reread 11.5.)

13a. No. While you will need to describe the product and its features, there is a better answer. (Reread 11.7.)

14a. Wrong. As politically incorrect as it may be, age and on-screen appearance can come into play for the weathercaster. (Reread 11.2.)

15a. Yes. This is a true statement. The other main problem is the announcer can only approximate the actual vocal style.

If You Answered B:

1b. No. Maps are seen off to the side of the set on television monitors and are easy to see with peripheral vision. (Reread 11.3.)

2b. No. Understanding the stock market is an essential knowledge base for a financial news announcer. (Reread 11.4 and 11.5.)

3b. No. Developing a "character" or an "act" is a reference to the characteristics of some sports announcers. (Reread 11.4 and 11.5.)

4b. No. Although Angela Lansbury has done some voice characterization work, including Mrs. Potts in *Beauty and the Beast*, this isn't the correct answer. (Reread 11.10.)

5b. Correct. This statement is false. The more you know about a product, the manufacturer, its applications, and interesting sidelights, the easier it is to talk enthusiastically and at length about the product.

6b. Yes. This is a false statement. A voice-over is any situation in TV where something other than the announcer is seen on screen while his or her voice is heard.

7b. No. For the financial reporter, there are many jargon terms that can come up and require further explanation. (Reread 11.4.)

8b. Yes. This is a false statement. Weathercasters are not required to have any weather training, but most do have a degree in meteorology or course work in that area and an AMS Seal of Approval does recognize certain standards of weathercasting.

9b. Yes. This is the abbreviation for a public service announcement.

10b. Wrong. Most weathercasters seem to be actually involved and interested in weather-casting. (Reread 11.2 and 11.3.)

11b. This statement is neither true nor false, but an area an announcer must be very careful. Your employer will most likely have guidelines concerning this and any attempt to "tout" a stock you own would be unethical and illegal. A smart financial reporter would seek legal advice before investing, if he or she chooses to do so. (Reread 11.4.)

12b. No. Most financial reporters will include the Standard and Poor's 500 latest number along with the amount and direction of change. (Reread 11.4 and 11.5.)

13b. No. While you will often ad-lib about the product for extended periods, there is a better answer. (Reread 11.7.)

14b. Wrong. As politically incorrect as it may be, age and on-screen appearance can come into play for the financial reporter. (Reread 11.4.)

15b. No. This statement is not false. Beginning announcers can usually only approximate a foreign accent and often drop in and out of the dialect when reading a script. (Reread 11.10.)

If You Answered C:

1c. No. The blue color for chroma reacts with the color of the clothing you may wear, but not your skin tone. (Reread 11.3.)

2c. No. News writing and reporting skills are essential because the role of the financial reporter is similar to that of any news reporter. (Reread 11.4 and 11.5.)

3c. Yes. The selling of products is done from fact sheets on cards and the announcer must ad-lib the information, often for extended periods of time.

4c. Yes. It's been said that Mel Blanc's voice characterization has been heard more times, in more places, for more years than any other in broadcast history.

7c. Not a bad guess, but often jargon terms can come up when describing a specific product's features. (Reread 11.7.)

9c. No. This describes a group of thunderstorms moving together in a front. (Review Figure 11.1 and reread 11.2.)

10c. Wrong. Most weathercasters show energy and enthusiasm in their weathercasting without becoming caricatures. (Reread 11.2 and 11.3.)

12c. No. The NASDAQ (National Association of Securities Dealers Automatic Quotations) is another popular average given in financial reports. (Reread 11.4 and 11.5.)

13c. Yes. Your job as host or hostess is to sell as much of the product as possible and all your other skills ultimately focus on sales.

14c. Wrong. As politically incorrect as it may be, age and on-screen appearance can come into play for the host or hostess selling a product. (Reread 11.7.)

If You Answered D:

1d. No. Choice of clothing is always an important consideration for television, and especially if you are using a chroma-key effect. (Reread 11.3.)

2d. Correct. The AMS seal is important to a weathercaster, but not a financial reporter.

3d. No. Writing and performance skills will be useful, but there is a better answer. (Reread 11.4 and 11.5.)

4d. No. Jim Sislo was a TV host of a specialty feature on new innovations in technology. (Reread 11.6.)

7d. Yes. Many voice characterizations are for cartoon characters and rarely would lead to jargon in the broadcast; certainly less often than the other choices.

9d. No. This is a device for measuring wind speed. (Review Figure 11.1 and reread 11.2.)

10d. Wrong. Most weathercasters relate to their audience and develop a friendly rapport during their weathercasting. (Reread 11.2 and 11.3.)

12d. Yes. This is a weathercaster term which measures the uncomfortable combination of high temperature and high humidity in summertime.

13d. No. While you will talk with purchasers of the product and often seek testimonials from them, there is a better answer. (Reread 11.7.)

14d. Correct. The focus is on the voice only for the narrator or voice-over announcer.

Projects

■ PROJECT 1

Be a television host selling on a shopping channel.

Purpose
To practice ad-libbing using a soft-sell style in the format of a television shopping channel.

Notes
1. Ad-libbing requires preparation and knowledge about the subject.
2. Ad-libbing requires proper use of English grammar and pronunciation.
3. Selling requires the announcer to understand the advantages of the product.
4. Energy levels must remain high during the entire time of the ad-lib without becoming a hard sell.
5. Ad-lib material should be delivered in a conversational and friendly manner.
6. Remember to include an element of entertainment and use acting skills when necessary.
7. Repetition is key to being a good salesperson.

How to Do the Project
1. Choose two products that are related, such as two pieces of jewelry or two pieces of clothing.
2. For each of the products, prepare a list of positive qualities that the audience would be interested in.
3. Prepare a comparative price and a product number for each item.
4. Following the procedures developed by your instructor, record your ad-lib.
5. Using a soft-sell approach, ad-lib for about three minutes about each product, one after the other, with no break in between.
6. Include the use of gestures when selling the products. Be sure to handle them following the guidelines in Chapters 3 and 6.
7. Turn in your list of product qualities and the recording to your instructor to receive credit for this project.

■ PROJECT 2

Record a voice-over public service announcement.

Purpose
To enable you to practice the skills necessary for a good voice-over announcer.

Notes
1. Review Section 11.9 on voice-over and narration announcing.
2. Timing will be very important, so practice reading the script to the video several times before you attempt to record the project.
3. You may need to have a television crew work with you to record this project, so your instructor may schedule this as a class assignment.

How to Do the Project

1. Use the television script provided in Figure 11.12, and record the voice-over audio to match the pace of the video.
2. The video is provided on the DVD that is part of this text. It is track 11.3.
3. To record the project, you will need to set up your studio or equipment so that you can see the video on a TV screen while you are recording both the video and audio on some type of video recorder.
4. There are various ways to accomplish this, so utilize whatever setup works best for your situation.
5. The key to this project is matching your vocal work with the transitions from one video scene to another.
6. You may need to record your performance several times before you get the timing down correctly.
7. While working on your timing, don't forget the vocal performance for delivering the announcement. Match your tone and mood to the script.
8. Turn in the recording to the instructor to receive credit for the project.

SEAT BELT PSA

VIDEO	AUDIO
Seat Belts Save Lives	Seat belts save lives—everyone knows that
Question marks	So why do so many people continue not to wear them?
Confined?	Well, some people say that seat belts make them feel confined.
Wheelchair?	I wonder if they ever considered how confining a wheelchair is.
Happy Birthday!!	Seat belts are the best way to ensure that you'll see the next Christmas and your friend's birthday, plus many other wonderful things.
Insurance!	Wearing your seat belt is like buying car insurance.
Whew!!	You hope you'll never need it, but it's sure nice to have it when something happens.

FIGURE 11.12 Television script for a public service announcement.

■ PROJECT 3

Record a stock market report for television.

Purpose

To enable you to experience the preparation and delivery of the terminology associated with presenting reports on the status of the stock market.

INFORMATION FOR STOCK REPORT

Closing Prices

Dow Jones Industrials: 9751, up 17.5
NASDAQ: 1755, up 2.4
S&P 500 Index: 1022, up 2.4
Number of shares traded on the New York Stock Exchange: 1,517,000,000 (average day)
Number of shares traded on NASDAQ: 1,821,000,000 (average day)
521 stocks advanced, 478 declined, and 341 were unchanged on the NASDAQ
21 new highs and 16 new lows in stock prices

Closing prices of widely held stocks

IBM: 97.57, up $.05
GE: 22.12, down $.12
Microsoft: 21.25, up $.14
ExxonMobil: 77.67, down $.20
Intel: 19.05, up $.52
General Motors: 5.85, down $.26
TimeWarner: 13.30, unchanged
Dell: 14.76, up $.50
Union Pacific Railroad: 57.75, unchanged
Citigroup: 7.78, up $.15
Viacom: 17.46, up $.35
Ounce of gold: $812, up $1.00
Barrel of oil: $71.97, up $.10

FIGURE 11.13   Stock market data.

Notes
1. Review the sections of this chapter related to financial reporting.
2. Use the information provided to prepare a one-minute stock report for TV.
3. You can prepare a simple notecard to assist you.
4. You will need to plan some ad-lib material to provide an introduction and closing for the segment, as well as transitions between items in your report.

How to Do the Project
1. Select whatever material from Figure 11.12 you feel is appropriate for your report
2. Direct your performance to the camera lens. Concentrate on variations in pitch and pace, word emphasis, vocal quality, timing, and energy.
3. Dress appropriately for a television performance.
4. Present the report in a friendly but serious, positive manner.
5. Record the report in the studio as if it were being done live, i.e., it should be recorded as a single take.
6. Turn in your notecard with the finished recording.
7. Label the recording "Stock Market Report," and turn it in to the instructor to receive credit for this project.

CHAPTER TWELVE

LEGAL AND ETHICAL ISSUES FOR MASS MEDIA PERFORMERS

12.1 INTRODUCTION

A broadcast performer may face a number of basic ethical dilemmas and legal decisions. For example, DJs may have to decide whether or not to play a certain song with questionable lyrics, or voice-over announcers may have to decide if they can do a commercial for a product they are morally opposed to, such as fur coats or condoms. A sports reporter may be offered free tickets to professional or college sports events.

Following legal statutes is usually not a question of whether a performer will or won't engage in illegal activity, but often is a case of not being aware of a specific regulation or perhaps misinterpreting a rule. On the other hand, making ethical decisions is not easy and often involves careful thought and consideration. To make it more complicated, ethical decisions can vary because of time of day or geographic location and the issues can change over time. A song played at 1:00 a.m. may not be acceptable at 3:00 p.m. An announcer's comments that are acceptable in New York City may not be acceptable in Topeka, Kansas. News-gathering practices that were not acceptable in the 1980s may be acceptable in the 21st century. Some live music and webcasts may have few guidelines. Whether considering an ethical or legal issue, self-regulation by broadcast performers occurs constantly and informally as they make decisions on a daily basis about what to say or not say and how to conduct themselves in their jobs.

Ethics are the good (or bad) behaviors practiced by individuals that are based on moral codes. Society expects moral conduct even if it is not spelled out by the law. For broadcast performers, ethical behavior is often explained in professional codes of conduct or by guidelines spelled out in a station employee handbook. Generally, codes of conduct encourage high standards for performers, and ethical behavior is of even greater concern in the media because we recognize the influence that media may have on people, especially children.

If continued ethical misbehavior occurs, the public begins to mistrust the media, and this leads to many serious concerns about the role of the media in society.

Ethical codes encourage fairness in news and contests, avoidance of excessive sex and violence in programming, and making certain not to broadcast derisive words or misleading information, to mention just a few items. These codes have no legal force and, generally, no penalty for failure to comply. On the other hand, legal behavior is based on standards as developed by governmental agencies, such as the courts or the FCC. While FCC regulations are applied throughout the United States, other laws vary from state to state and nation to nation. Federal guidelines were developed to apply to over-the-air broadcasting not cable or online. Today, with cable television and radio pervasive media sources, application of legal and ethical guidelines can be even more ambiguous. Laws and regulations affect various aspects of the media business. For example, the broadcast journalist needs to have a basic understanding of the laws that are associated with the gathering and reporting of news. Also, radio announcers need to be aware of the legal necessity of properly announcing station identification and EAS notification. Violation of legal statutes can result in sanctions for a station that range from a simple inquiry to a fine to a loss of station license and, for an individual performer, to possible loss of employment. This chapter surveys some of the most common ethical and legal areas that may cause the beginning broadcast performer difficulties.

12.2 CODES OF ETHICAL STANDARDS

As noted earlier, some broadcast performers (and stations) are committed to various codes of ethics developed by professional organizations. For example, many broadcast journalists follow the voluntary standards developed by the Radio-Television News Directors Association (RTNDA) (shown in Figure 12.1). However,

**CODE OF ETHICS AND PROFESSIONAL
CONDUCT RADIO-TELEVISION NEWS
DIRECTORS ASSOCIATION**

The Radio-Television News Directors Association, wishing to foster the highest professional standards of electronic journalism, promote public understanding of and confidence in electronic journalism, and strengthen principles of journalistic freedom to gather and disseminate information, establishes this Code of Ethics and Professional Conduct.

PREAMBLE

Professional electronic journalists should operate as trustees of the public, seek the truth, report it fairly and with integrity and independence, and stand accountable for their actions.

PUBLIC TRUST: Professional electronic journalists should recognize that their first obligation is to the public.

Professional electronic journalists should:

* Understand that any commitment other than service to the public undermines trust and credibility.
* Recognize that service in the public interest creates an obligation to reflect the diversity of the community and guard against oversimplification of issues or events.
* Provide a full range of information to enable the public to make enlightened decisions.
* Fight to ensure that the public's business is conducted in public.

TRUTH: Professional electronic journalists should pursue truth aggressively and present the news accurately, in context, and as complete as possible.

Professional electronic journalists should:

* Continuously seek the truth.
* Resist distortions that obscure the importance of events.
* Clearly disclose the origin of information and label all material provided by outsiders.

Professional electronic journalists should not:

* Report anything known to be false.
* Manipulate images or sounds in any way that is misleading.
* Plagiarize.
* Present images or sounds that are reenacted without informing the public.

FAIRNESS: Professional electronic journalists should present the news fairly and impartially, placing primary value on significance and relevance.

Professional electronic journalist's should: APPENDIX A

* Treat all subjects of news coverage with respect and dignity, showing particular compassion to victims of crime or tragedy.
* Exercise special care when children are involved in a story and give children greater privacy protection than adults.
* Seek to understand the diversity of their community and inform the public without bias or stereotype.
* Present a diversity of expressions, opinions, and ideas in context.
* Present analytical reporting based on professional perspective, not personal bias.
* Respect the right to a fair trial.

INTEGRITY: Professional electronic journalists should present the news with integrity and decency, avoiding real or perceived conflicts of interest, and respect the dignity and intelligence of the audience as well as the subjects of news.

FIGURE 12.1 *Many broadcast performers in the news area subscribe to the RTNDA Code of Ethics. (Copyright by Radio-Television News Directors Association, reprinted by permission of RTNDA.)*

Professional electronic journalists should:

 * Identify sources whenever possible. Confidential sources should be used only when it is clearly in the
   public interest to gather or convey important information or when a person providing information might
   be harmed. Journalists should keep all commitments to protect a confidential source.
 * Clearly label opinion and commentary.
 * Guard against extended coverage of events or individuals that fail to significantly advance a story,
   place the event in context, or add to the public knowledge.
 * Refrain from contacting participants in violent situations while the situation is in progress.
 * Use technological tools with skill and thoughtfulness, avoiding techniques that skew facts, distort
   reality, or sensationalize events.
 * Use surreptitious news-gathering techniques, including hidden cameras or microphones, only if there
   is no other way to obtain stories of significant public importance and only if the technique is explained
   to the audience.
 * Disseminate the private transmission of other news organizations only with permission.

Professional electronic journalists should not:

 * Pay news sources that have a vested interest in a story.
 * Accept gifts, favors, or compensation from those who might seek to influence coverage.
 * Engage in activities that may compromise their integrity or independence.

INDEPENDENCE: Professional electronic journalists should defend the independence of all journalists from
those seeking influence or control over news content.

Professional electronic journalists should:

 * Gather and report news without fear or favor, and vigorously resist undue influence from any outside
   forces, including advertisers, sources, story subjects, powerful individuals, and special interest groups.
 * Seek to intimidate those who gather and disseminate the news.
 * Determine news content solely through editorial judgment and not as the result of outside influence.
 * Resist any self-interest or peer pressure that might erode journalistic duty and service to the public.
 * Recognize that sponsorship of news will not be used in any way to determine, restrict, or manipu-
   late content.

ACCOUNTABILITY: Professional electronic journalists should recognize that they are accountable for their
actions to the public, the profession, and themselves.

Professional electronic journalists should:

 * Actively encourage adherence to these standards by all journalists and their employers.
 * Respond to public concerns. Investigate complaints and correct errors promptly and with as much
   prominence as the original report.
 * Explain journalistic processes to the public, especially when practices spark questions or controversy.
 * Recognize that professional electronic journalists are duty-bound to conduct themselves ethically.
 * Refrain from ordering or encouraging courses of action that would force employees to commit an
   unethical act.
 * Carefully listen to employees who raise ethical objections and create environments in which such
   objections and discussions are encouraged.
 * Seek support for and opportunities to train employees in ethical decision-making.

In meeting its responsibilities to the profession of electronic journalism, RTNDA has created this code to
identify important issues, to serve as a guide for its members, to facilitate self scrutiny, and to shape future debate.

FIGURE 12.1 Continued

there is no actual enforcement of these standards, and recent years have shown that these codes are not always followed by reporters. The two main unions that represent performers, SAG (Screen Actors Guild) and AFTRA (American Federation of Television and Radio Artists), have no specific code of ethics. The guidelines for membership in these unions include an understanding that members will accept jobs from union employers and will complete the job as contracted.

12.3 PAYOLA AND PLUGOLA

The acceptance of money in return for playing songs on the air is known as **payola** and is illegal. If a disc jockey is caught accepting money to influence program selection or content, he or she can be fined or even imprisoned, and the station can also be sanctioned.

Many radio stations require their announcers to sign a form stating that they understand what payola/plugola is and will not participate in any such scheme. **Plugola** is the free promotion of a product or service in which the announcer has a financial interest or from which the announcer receives some benefit. For example, an announcer ad-libs about a restaurant throughout his or her air shift in return for a free meal each evening at the restaurant. Reading or playing a commercial that has been paid for, even if the announcer has a financial interest, is not illegal. A rather blatant example could be heard on the old Don Imus show on MSNBC. He made frequent references to a salsa product that his brother produced and which Imus admitted he was part owner. Because the company that produced the salsa bought commercial time, no legal guidelines were violated. However, the ethical concerns should be obvious.

12.4 STAGED NEWS

News coverage can be manipulated by altering or falsifying events through the use of techniques such as staging or reenactments. Not only is it contrary to FCC regulations, but it's unethical as well. The ethical concerns here go to the very heart of the role of a journalist. The journalist should observe, record, and report news events. His or her role is not to change, alter, manipulate, or influence the news by staging events that did not occur or by reenacting events not observed. A journalist should never stage a news event; an example would be if the journalist asked several passersby on the street to join a protest group so it would look like more people were involved and result in a better visual. One of the most famous instances of staging took place in the late 1960s when a Chicago TV station showed a "pot party" at Northwestern University as part of a story on marijuana usage. Unfortunately, it turned out that the reporter had set up and staged the party to get the desired footage.

The reporter should not become part of the story. Again, his or her job is to observe and report, not to participate. However, reenacting events may not always be unethical.

For example, if you are doing a story on fire safety, you may ask a firefighter to recheck a smoke alarm or reenter a room so you can have that action for editing the video. Reenactments should be used sparingly and always identified as such when used. Finally, good judgment and common sense should be used when considering a news reenactment.

12.5 HOAXES AND PRANKS

Competition sometimes leads to unethical or even illegal actions. For example, a Cleveland radio station's coverage of a live Howard Stern broadcast was interrupted when a competing station cut their broadcast cables during the performance. In 1990, the FCC established guidelines to fine stations up to $250,000 for broadcasting a hoax. This occurred after two LA DJs faked a murder confession on the air that led to a nationwide police search for a nonexistent murderer. The FCC "hoax" rule prohibits stations from airing

"*Everyone will try to give you gifts, dinners, clothes, tickets to the game. Don't take any of that because eventually it will come back to haunt you. Always pay for things.*"

— Amy Basista, WCMH-TV, Columbus, OH

FIGURE 12.2 A pro's thoughts on gifts.

false information concerning a "crime or catastrophe" under any of the following conditions: first, the broadcaster knows the information is false; second, the broadcaster could foresee that the broadcast would cause substantial public harm; and third, the broadcast actually does cause such harm.

Several radio stations flirted with violating this regulation when they broadcast prank commentary about older $20 bills becoming worthless within a few hours after the new twenties were first introduced.

12.6 PAYMENT FOR NEWS STORIES

Some journalists say that *checkbook journalism* is unethical, jeopardizes the credibility of the news organization, and makes the information obtained suspect. Others say that payment may be appropriate under some conditions. Most news organizations say that paid consultants must be identified as such in the story, such as experts in specialties like medicine or economics. If such identification is hidden or glossed over, the audience may begin to suspect bias or lack of objectivity on the part of the reporter or news organization, and this can have serious consequences.

The influence of publications such as *The National Enquirer*, that regularly pay for stories, especially about celebrities, has affected what is acceptable in the professions and the public. Recently, there seems to be less concern over the issue. However, any serious journalist needs to remember that paying for stories is considered a serious breach of the news process.

12.7 POLITICAL COVERAGE

Another concern relates to the modern political campaign. Politicians frequently use "spin doctors" to generate comments and opinions. These spokespeople provide a highly partisan, one-sided voice or "spin" on an issue. Candidates often avoid reporters and prefer to speak to friendly audiences. Rather than just accept this biased version of the issue, it is the job of the journalist to question this type of information and sometimes to seek alternative sources to provide balance in reporting.

A recent development in political coverage relates to the role of family members in the reporting on a political figure or candidate. The family of the 2008 Republican vice-presidential nominee, Sarah Palin, became part of the new stories. That coverage was deemed inappropriate by most legitimate news organizations.

12.8 SPORTS COVERAGE

As sports coverage has increased on cable television and a global audience for sports has emerged, there is increased awareness and concern over ethical issues in sports journalism. In 2008, UNESCO organized a conference in China for Chinese sports journalists who will cover the 29th Olympic games in 2008. The Conference, "Ethical Standards in Sports Journalism," included issues related to doping and other highly controversial issues in international sporting events. Sports reporters may not think they need to adhere to the same ethical standards as news reporters since sports may be considered a fun or leisure subject. All reporters have a special obligation to the public to uphold the highest in ethical standards no matter what the area of coverage.

The Associated Press Sports Editors (APSE) (http://apse.dallasnews.com/main/codeofethics.html) has developed ethical guidelines for newspaper sports reporters. These guidelines suggest that sports reporters should not serve as official scorers at baseball games, should not write for league or team media guides, should not accepts free tickets or memberships. APSE also suggests that sports reporters should follow their own newspaper's ethical guidelines. Other issues that sports reporters may face include gambling and voting in sports polls. Sports reporters appearing on electronic media should follow similar guidelines and always follow the ethical standards established by the organization for which you work.

12.9 SENSATIONALISM

Reporting rumor or innuendo and the use of footage of a sensational nature are on the rise. This is partly because of the increased competition for the news audience that has resulted from the expansion of news outlets on cable television. Stories should be kept in perspective and a context for them should always be included. It may be exciting to see close-ups of upset union protesters, but that should be balanced by long shots and reactions of people passing by who may not be interested in the protest. This is also part of the role of the observer. The use of sensationalism covers not only stories that have sexual or violent aspects. Recently, a local television station was reporting an ambulance accident and showed close-ups of the injured man's head and face three times during the story. This was totally unnecessary for the report and actually was quite gruesome. The competition for viewers and ratings in a system based on the advertising dollar increases the likelihood that this will be a continuing issue.

A related issue is the development of **infotainment**. This is a term that is used to describe the merging of entertainment and information. In this circumstance, broadcast journalism has become sensationalized with the use of audio and video manipulation and fewer stories that are "journalistically pure," that is, objective and newsworthy. Stations spend time providing entertainment that is packaged as news, and the audience increasingly finds little difference between the two. The hiring of news reporters and anchors that look good but have little or no journalistic training is also a concern and contributes to the public perception that stations are more interested in providing good TV rather than good journalism.

12.10 CONFLICT OF INTEREST

Many reporters want to be involved in their own communities, particularly in small markets, yet need to be objective because they will be reporting on their community. Some journalists work part-time outside of news. This may obstruct balance or fairness if the companies they work for are involved in news stories. Also, advertising clients want to be shown in a positive light. It helps the reporters' credibility if they avoid being identified with a particular side of an issue and make an effort to present all sides. It is best not to cover stories in which the reporter has a vested interest. If a conflict of interest becomes obvious, the reporter should either leave one or the other job, or disqualify him or herself from stories involving the conflict.

12.11 PRIVACY

It is generally recognized that people have the right to be left alone. Issues of privacy are a growing concern in the age of technology, where unauthorized people have access to so much information via computers. Invasion of privacy can occur when a reporter interrupts the solitude or personal privacy of another individual. This is usually covered by state law. A reporter can avoid problems by obtaining consent, avoiding private spaces, and using public property to record interviews. Recording telephone calls and using hidden cameras or microphones are other potential problems. Obtaining prior consent on tape from all involved is the best way to avoid problems. Public disclosure of private facts that are not newsworthy, if you do not have permission to reveal them, is a possible invasion of privacy. Public figures may not be included in this category as easily because they do surrender some of

their privacy rights due to the issue of public trust. The higher the public office, the closer the permissible scrutiny of private facts. Coverage of a subject's youthful indiscretions now is a regular part of a story. Bill Clinton admitted he smoked marijuana, but did not "inhale." George W. Bush was repeatedly asked about his use of alcohol in college. Barak Obama admitted during the 2008 presidential campaign that he experimented with drugs in college. A reporter must always consider what effect a person's past life experiences may have on their ability to do the job but the story should not become mere gossip.

A special type of invasion of privacy may occur when a news story presents information that creates an inaccurate impression about a person's character, often called "false light." This could happen when a reporter tries to sensationalize or otherwise embellish a story to make it more dramatic. This also means that the reporter should be careful in using file footage. Be sure that the date or an indication of the source of the footage is clearly shown if it is used onscreen. Stations usually place a small insert on the screen that says "File Footage."

12.12 LIBEL AND SLANDER

Defamation is a false statement that damages the character or reputation of a person or a group of people. It may be spoken, which is referred to as slander, or written, which is referred to as libel. Most states include slander in their libel laws. A reporter needs to be aware of the specific laws in each state, but some general guidelines can help the reporter know the limits of what is appropriate. For libel to occur, the statement must be published. Broadcasting (oral statements or pictures) is considered publication because libel occurs if a third party hears of the statement. The statement must also be false and clearly be about the person who believes he or she has been libeled. The person who has claimed to be libeled must also show that the statement has damaged his or her reputation and that the statement was published due to the negligence of the reporter or station, In other words, that malice was intended and that the reporter knew the statement to be false but broadcast (published) it anyway.

As a reporter, you need to verify all facts and comments and be precise in your reporting duties. Be sure to be accurate about names and titles. Keep your personal opinion to yourself. It is a good idea to record on tape the correct spelling and pronunciation of the names of all people interviewed. Sometimes written consent forms may be used. If you are unsure what to do, ask the news director, station management, or legal consultant. If you do face a libel charge, common defenses include the truth of the statement in question (which may be difficult to prove in court), consent from the persons involved, privileged statements (made during an official proceeding), or expiration of the statute of limitations. Each state sets its own rules and guidelines.

12.13   CONTESTS AND LOTTERIES

Ratings are a driving force in the broadcasting business; no radio or television personality will succeed unless the public is interested in listening to or viewing his or her programs. This pressure to succeed may cause performers to engage in illegal or unethical behavior. A favorite device used to gain an audience, especially during a ratings period, is a contest. Contests are popular and are legal as long as they don't become lotteries. The FCC considers a contest to be a lottery if all three of these elements are present: prize (something of value), consideration (such as an entry fee charged to participate), and chance (winner chosen by random selection). Obviously, with most contests there is a prize and the winner is selected by chance, but usually, to avoid being a lottery, the contest is open to all with "no purchase necessary" or any other type of consideration. As long as one of the elements of a lottery is not present, then it is not a lottery. With the exception of state-run lotteries and some charitable organization activities, stations cannot broadcast lottery information. Many stations have additional guidelines for conducting any contest or promotion. Ethical concerns about contests involve the actual odds of someone winning, the actual value of the prize in relation to its stated value, and the timing of the promotion when these contests occur during ratings periods.

Other techniques to capture an audience include sensational subjects (such as an in-depth story on porn shops) and the use of obscenities. Sometimes new technology is used to establish a station's credibility and boost ratings. Recently, advanced weather equipment has made competition more intense to provide the most current information first. However, the overuse of such equipment, when unnecessary, could cause panic in the public. Such equipment should never be used more as a ratings tool than to warn the public of a true weather emergency.

12.14   PROTECTION OF SOURCES

A reporter should know how to handle requests for confidentiality, anonymity, or privacy when requested by news sources. Subpoenas, newsroom searches, and shield laws are all areas an informed reporter needs to understand. A subpoena is an official order by the court for information or to testify concerning a case. Congress passed the Privacy Protection Act of 1980 to prohibit federal and state searches of newsrooms and reporters' homes in all but a few limited circumstances (when it is related to a crime, will prevent death or serious bodily injury, or might prevent a breach of national security). Material protected includes original and edited video and audio tape, notes, drafts of work, outtakes, and photographs. Forty-nine states and the District of Columbia recognize the reporter's privilege of protection of sources and have shield laws to further protect the journalist from having to divulge sources of information. However, there is no uniform protection that applies to federal cases. RTNDA advocates the development of a federal shield law. Reporters can spend time in jail for contempt of court when they refuse to turn over documents or reveal sources of information. Reporters may be held in contempt of court for disobeying court orders or using material that ridicules the court or obstructs justice. Federal and state laws apply and may carry a fine, a jail sentence, or both. Judith Miller of *The New York Times* served 85 days in jail rather than reveal the source of her information on the Valerie Plame case. Two *San Francisco Chronicle* reporters were sentenced to prison for refusing to reveal sources about illegal distribution of steroids to major league baseball players. Fines recently imposed on journalists by a U.S. District Court judge went from $500 a day for the first week to $1000 a day for the second week and $5000 thereafter until the reporter appeared before the judge again.

12.15   ACCESS TO GOVERNMENT INFORMATION

The federal **Freedom of Information Act** establishes a procedure for obtaining government documents and restricts the government's ability to withhold information from the public. Also, every state has laws governing access to official meetings and records. These are referred to as sunshine laws and vary from state to state.

12.16 FAIRNESS DOCTRINE

In 1987, the FCC voted to eliminate the Fairness Doctrine, which obligated broadcasters to address "controversial issues of public importance" and provide reasonable time for contrasting points of view. Although numerous appeals have been made to reinstate the doctrine, it seems a moot point as most stations seem to make a reasonable effort to follow this principle on a voluntary basis. One aspect of this regulation that is still enforced is the personal attack rule. This requires that a station offer free time for an individual to speak in his or her own defense, when that person's honesty, integrity, or character has been attacked on the air during a discussion of a controversial issue of public importance. Editorials and documentaries are not exempt from this rule, although bona fide news interviews, on-the-spot news coverage, and newscasts are exempt.

12.17 SECTION 315

Journalists and other broadcast performers have a special obligation in regard to political broadcasts. The Communications Act of 1934 has a special paragraph, Section 315, which explains the obligations of broadcasters to provide equal opportunities to all political candidates. If a legally qualified political candidate appears on the station, equal time must be given to all other legally qualified candidates for that office. Appearances that are exempt from this law include newscasts, interviews, documentaries, or other news reports that include political candidates. If a broadcast performer, such as a weatherperson, becomes a political candidate, the station that employs the performer faces a dilemma, because the station would be obligated to provide equal time to other candidates whenever the weather person was seen or heard on radio or TV. When Ronald Reagan (an actor-turned-politician) was campaigning for the presidency, his old movies were not aired so that stations would not have to give other candidates comparable free airtime.

12.18 COPYRIGHT

A famous entertainer has died and you want to use some videotape of his singing. A local sports team has won a championship game and the video was on another network and you want to use the footage. Your station does a movie review and wants to show highlights from the film. All of these situations involve copyright, and permission is needed from the copyright holder to use this material. Creative works are protected by copyright for 50 years after the death of the author/creator. The author can be an individual or a company. The author or creator of the work may not hold the copyright. Rights and ownership can be given or sold to another individual or company. Permission must be obtained from the owner of the copyrighted material. Generally, material provided from a news service has already received clearance. There are two exceptions to copyright: public domain and fair use. Material that is old enough to no longer be under copyright protection is in the public domain and may be used without concern for violation of the copyright license. Fair use includes using copyrighted material for a very brief moment or for educational purposes.

12.19 PROFANITY, INDECENCY, AND OBSCENITY

Profane, indecent, and obscene broadcasts are all outlawed by the U.S. Criminal Code, and the FCC has the responsibility of enforcing these regulations. Profanity is defined as the irreverent use of the name of God. In practice, the FCC rarely fines a station for mild swearing, either by an on-air performer or contained in song lyrics or other programming. Indecency involves broadcasting language or material that describes sexual or excretory organs or activities in terms that would be deemed patently offensive based on the standards of the community. Indecency has been an area of much concern for broadcasters. In the 1990s, the FCC fined Infinity Broadcasting almost $2 million because of sexual and excretory remarks made on the air by shock jock Howard Stern. Although Infinity originally fought this ruling, they eventually paid the fine. Indecent broadcasting receives limited First Amendment protection and is not entirely banned.

The FCC recognizes a time period late at night, when children are not likely to be in the audience, for the airing of indecent material. Currently, midnight to 6:00 a.m. is considered safe harbor for this material, according to the FCC. Obscenity is more extreme than indecency. To be obscene, broadcast material must meet a three-pronged test based on the *Miller v. California* court decision (1973). Something is obscene if 1) an average person finds that the material appeals to prurient interests, based on community standards; 2) the material describes sexual conduct specifically defined by law in a patently offensive manner; and 3) the material lacks serious literary, artistic, political, or scientific value. Obscenity has been less of a problem because broadcasters have tried to avoid indecent programs and, therefore, have not aired programming that reaches the level of obscene material. Broadcasters also realize that obscene speech is not protected by the First Amendment and cannot be broadcast under any circumstances. However, radio disc jockeys and video disc jockeys may encounter the problem because of lyric content of some of today's songs.

Cable TV may also come under more scrutiny in this area; cable regulations do not necessarily prevent the airing of indecent material, because cable TV is not broadcast to the general public. Viewers must make a conscious decision to subscribe to the cable service to see the programming. However, cable TV is still prohibited from airing obscene material because it is not protected by the Constitution; cable law allows cable stations to refuse to air programs they consider indecent on their leased-access channels.

12.20 ETHICAL AND LEGAL ISSUES FOR "ONLINE PERFORMERS"

The basic legal and ethical issues that have been discussed thus far are also applicable to the world of "online performers." This section will provide a brief update of three areas that may be of particular interest to performers.

Many codes of ethics currently exist and these must now be applied to online issues. Most codes include guidelines regarding accuracy, disclosure, acceptance of gifts (don't), and fairness. These principles apply in any medium. Additional principles may be added for areas related only to that medium, such as clear identification of site sponsorship if links are supplied by advertisers. (See Figure 12.3, Online Ethics Guidelines by the American Society of Magazine Editors.)

As mentioned earlier in this section, shield laws exist to protect journalists and their sources. However, an emerging problem is what is the definition of a journalist. Prior to the development of online news and web logs, a journalist was someone who gathered the news for a news organization. Today, virtually anyone can gather news and "report" it on a personal webpage. The emergence of cell phones capable of taking pictures results in bloggers not only telling the audience what is going on but also showing them in real time what is occurring.

As "blogs" have become more popular they challenge the traditional role of journalists. Reporters who maintain their own "blogs" may jeopardize their careers. There is already one case of a reporter who was let go when it was discovered he ran his own blog at night and reported for a traditional medium during the day. Federal courts have ruled that maintaining a personal website does not grant someone the privileges of a journalist. This is very important to remember specially in regards to the laws that protect journalists such as shield laws and the **Privacy Protection Act**. Newspapers have begun to develop policy for blogs that allow for personal expression but protect the newspaper's interest. Liz Allen of the *Erie Times News* has suggestions about personal blogging that can be found on the Poynter Institute website (www.Poynter.org). In general, if a reporter keeps a personal blog, the employer should know and the reporter should ask for guidelines or a blogging policy. If directives don't exist, it is safe to follow the general principle that you would never post anything on a blog that you would not say out loud. Other policies guidelines may include no discussion about stories in development, nothing that puts the newspaper in a negative light, nothing about sources and nothing that would cause you or your colleague's embarrassment. Social networking has blurred the lines between the professional and personal world. Young media professionals must learn to balance the technology that is available and what is possible to do with professional behavior that is both ethical and legal. Although AEJMC and RTNDA have addressed these issues at conferences and on their websites, no formal policy exists. Two websites that may be helpful that address blogging ethics are blogethics2004. blogspot.com and cyberjournalist.net. The latter site based its Blogger's Code of Ethics on the Society of Professional Journalists Code of Ethics and includes the following: be honest and fair, minimize harm, and be accountable. Performers must be aware that credibility is important to success and blogging without a personal code of ethics may cause difficulty in a career.

Copyright laws for Internet work are similar to those in the traditional business world. Although the laws (or statutes) may not change, the interpretation of those laws by the courts updates the protection of copyright laws to cover individuals whose work is online. Because the Internet has resulted in many new problems, the law is somewhat uncertain. Areas that are especially important to the performer are music, video streaming, the development of web pages, and electronic publishing. The battle over the right to access music files using Napster and similar programs was just the beginning of a long struggle to determine rights on the Internet.

ONLINE ETHICS GUIDELINES— AMERICAN SOCIETY OF MAGAZINE EDITORS

Credibility is the key to the success of all digital-media businesses with an editorial component. Users must trust the advice and information given, just as they do the offline brands. While linking and other technologies can greatly enhance the user experience, the distinction between independent editorial content and paid promo information should remain clear.

Thus we recommend the following standards (subject to change as the medium evolves):

1. The home pages and all subsequent pages of a publication's website should display the publication's name and logo prominently, in order to clarify who controls the content of the site.
2. All online pages should clearly distinguish between editorial and advertising or sponsored content. If any content comes from any source other than the editors, it should be clearly labeled. A magazine's name or logo should not be used in a way that suggests editorial endorsement of an advertiser. The site's sponsorship policies should be clearly noted, either in text accompanying the article or in a disclosure page (see item 8), to clarify that the sponsor had no input regarding content.
3. Hypertext links that appear within the editorial content of a site, including those within graphics, should be at the discretion of the editors. If links are paid for by advertisers that should be disclosed to users.
4. Special advertising or "Advertorial" features should be labeled as such.
5. To protect the brand, editors/producers should not permit their content to be on an advertiser's site without an explanation of the relationship (e.g., Reprinted with permission).
6. E-commerce commissions and other affiliate fees should be reported on a disclosure page, so users can see that the content is credible and free of commercial influence. Exact fees need not be mentioned, of course, but users who are concerned about underlying business relationships can thus be reassured.
7. Advertisers or e-commerce partners should not receive preferential treatment in search engines, price comparisons, and other applications presented under the content provider's brand. An editorial site should not try to vouch for others that it may offer.
8. A website should respect the privacy of its users. If a site intends to collect information about its visitors-whether the data will be disseminated to third parties or not—it must offer users a chance to decline if they choose, through an "opt-out" option. As part of its privacy policy, the site should explain its use of cookies and other data collection methods and tell what it intends to do with the information it gleans. Potential benefits to the user—broader site access, better personalization, features, etc. should be presented as well.

FIGURE 12.3 Online ethics.

12.21 CONCLUSIONS

Codes of conduct encourage high ethical standards for broadcast performers. This is justified because of the great influence that the media have on society. Legal and ethical guidelines and standards are constantly changing, especially for Internet use. This means that an important responsibility of a broadcast performer is to be aware of current standards of performance. Ignorance is no excuse for unethical or illegal behavior. The consequences of unethical or illegal behavior may affect fellow performers, the station owners, the general public, and the individual announcer. In addition, performers must decide what ethical standards are important to them and realize that they may have to make choices that could even result in losing a job.

Self Study

■ QUESTIONS

1. The acceptance of money for playing songs is known as:
   a) plugola
   b) payola
   c) checkbook journalism
   d) a prank

2. Codes of ethics developed by professional organizations such as the RTDNA are voluntary.
   a) true
   b) false

3. For libel to occur, the statement must
   a) be published
   b) damage the reputation of a person
   c) be known by the reporter to be false
   d) all of the above must happen for libel to occur

4. If reporters work for a company that is the subject of a story, this may be considered
   a) false light
   b) slander
   c) conflict of interest
   d) payment for a news story

5. Contests are often used to gain an audience and are
   a) considered illegal
   b) considered legal if they don't become lotteries
   c) a conflict of interest for the announcer
   d) considered infotainment

6. All of the following are a defense for libel except:
   a) the statement is true
   b) consent from the person to state a fact
   c) a privileged statement
   d) damage to reputation

7. The Privacy Protection Act of 1980 prohibits
   a) all federal and state searches of newsrooms
   b) all federal and state searches of reporters' homes
   c) searches of newsrooms in all but a few circumstances
   d) reporters from being arrested

8. Which of the following is NOT helpful to reporters to gain access to information?
   a) Freedom of Information Act
   b) Sunshine Laws
   c) Privacy Protection Act
   d) state laws that permit access to official meetings

9. Although the Fairness Doctrine is no longer in effect, one aspect of it is still binding, the personal attack rule. Under which of the following circumstances does the rule apply?
   a) bona fide news interviews
   b) editorials
   c) on-the-spot news coverage
   d) newscasts

10. A special obligation for stations for political broadcasts in the Communications Act is known as:
    a) Section 315
    b) Fairness Doctrine
    c) conflict of interest
    d) public domain

11. The obligation of the station under Sec. 315 is
   a) equal time to all legally qualified candidates
   b) equal time for candidates to speak in their defense if attacked
   c) free time to all legally qualified candidates
   d) free time for contrasting points of view
12. One exception to copyright protection is material that is old. This material is considered
   a) to be fair use
   b) in the public domain
   c) in a safe harbor
   d) a shield law
13. Irreverant use of the name of God on radio or television is
   a) profanity
   b) indecency
   c) obscenity
   d) illegal
14. Indecent broadcasts receives limited protection under the First Amendment and is not entirely banned
   a) true
   b) false
15. Online journalism is given exceptions to the traditional journalism of radio and television and most Codes of Ethics do not apply.
   a) true
   b) false

■ ANSWERS

If You Answered A:

1a. Incorrect. Plugola is the free announcement of a product or service in which the announcer receives some benefit. (Reread 12.3.)

2a. Correct. Codes of Ethics are completely voluntary but are strongly encouraged by organizations and expected by the public.

3a. No. This is only one of the conditions for libel to occur. (Reread 12.12.)

4a. No. False light is a type of invasion of privacy. (Reread 12.11.)

5a. No. They are only illegal if they become lotteries. (Reread 12.13)

6a. Incorrect. This is one of the defenses for libel. (Reread 12.12.)

7a. No. Searches are permitted if related to a crime, to prevent death or serious injury or to prevent a breach of national security. (Reread 12.14.)

8a. No. The act establishes a procedure to obtain government documents. (Reread 12.14.)

9a. Incorrect. Bone fide news interviews are exempt from this rule. (Reread 12.16.)

10a. Correct. The special paragraph in the Communications Act of 1934 is known as Section 315.

11a. Yes. This is the rule of Sec 315.

12a. No. Fair use allows for copyrighted material to be used for a brief moment or for educational purposes. (Reread 12.18.)

13a. Yes. This is the correct definition.

14a. Correct. Some limits are imposed by the safe harbor concept.

15a. Incorrect. Although online journalism is affected by blogs and other nontraditional sources of news and facts, journalists are still expected to uphold Codes of Ethics. (Reread 12.20.)

If You Answered B:

1b. Correct. Payola is the acceptance of money to play a song and is illegal.

2b. Wrong. Codes of Ethics do not have the force of law but the expectations of society to act in a responsible manner. (Reread 12.1.)

3b. Incorrect. Libel damages a person's reputation but is only one of the conditions for libel to occur. (Reread 12.12.)

4b. No. Slander is a spoken statement that damages a person's reputation. (Reread 12.12.)

5b. Correct. Contests are legal if they are not lotteries.

6b. Incorrect. This is one of the defenses for libel. (Reread 12.12.)

7b. No. Searches are permitted if related to a crime, to prevent death or serious injury, or to prevent a breach of national security. (Reread 12.14.)

8b. No. Every state has sunshine laws so reporters can access official meetings and records. (Reread 12.14.)

9b. Correct. A station would need to offer free time to an individual if that person's honesty, integrity or character had been attacked during an editorial or documentary.

10b. Incorrect. The Fairness Doctrine applies to personal attacks on anyone, not just a politician. It does not have to do with equal opportunity. (Reread 12.16.)

11b. No. This refers to the Fairness Doctrine. (Reread 12.16.)

12b. Yes. Material no longer under copyright is considered in the public domain and may be freely used.

13b. No. This is a definition of language or material that describes sexual or excretory organs or activities that may be deemed offensive based on the standards of the community. (Reread 12.19.)

14b. Incorrect. First Amendment protection does apply to indecent material in a limited way. (Reread 12.19.)

15b. Incorrect. All journalists, no matter what medium they use, are expected to uphold standards of moral conduct as described in Codes of Professional Ethics. (Reread 12.20.)

If You Answered C:

1c. Wrong. Checkbook journalism occurs when a journalist pays for a story. (Reread 12.6.)

3c. Incorrect. For libel to occur, the reporter must know the information is false, but it is only one of the conditions of libel. (Reread 12.12.)

4c. Correct. This could cause the reporter to not present fair and balanced information and situations where this may happen should be avoided.

5c. No. There is no conflict of interest inherent in a contest. (Reread 12.13.)

6c. No. This is one of the defenses for libel. (Reread 12.12.)

7c. Correct. The circumstances are: information related to a crime, to prevent death or serious injury, or to prevent a breach of national security.

8c. Correct. This Act helps the reporter to protect sources of information, not to gain access to information.

9c. No. On the spot news coverage is exempt from the Fairness Doctrine. (Reread 12.16.)

10c. Incorrect. Conflict of Interest occurs when a reporter is in a situation that may be difficult to be fair and balanced in a story, for example if they work part time for a company they are reporting about. (Reread 12.10.)

11c. No. Sec 315 only requires stations to offer equal opportunity. Politicians still have to pay for their time on air. (Reread 12.17.)

12c. Incorrect. Safe harbor refers from midnight to 6:00am, a time when children are not likely to hear indecent material. (Reread 12.19.)

13c. Wrong. Obscenity is more extreme than indecency and must meet three criteria. (Reread 12.19.)

If You Answered D:

1d. Incorrect. A prank is when an announcer knowingly broadcasts false information that may cause harm even if it is done as a joke. (Reread 12.15.)

3d. Yes. This is the correct answer because a, b, and c must all happen for libel to occur.

4d. No. Payment of a news story is considered check book journalism. (Reread 12.6.)

5d. Incorrect. Infotainment is the combination of news and entertainment. A game is entertaining and used to increase the audience. (Reread 12.19 and 12.13.)

6d. Correct. If there is damage to a person's reputation, libel has occurred and there is no defense.

7d. No. Reporters can still be arrested for contempt of court or obstruction of justice. (Reread 12.14.)

8d. Incorrect. States have laws so that reporters can access information. (Reread 12.15.)

9d. No. Newscasts are exempt from the Fairness Doctrine. (Reread 12.16.)

10d. Incorrect. The Public Domain refers to the status of copyrighted material. (Reread 12.18.)

11d. No. This refers to the Fairness Doctrine. (Reread 12.16.)

12d. No. Shield laws protect a reporter's sources. (Reread 12.14.)

13d. Incorrect. Limited use is permitted and the FCC rarely fines a station for mild swearing. (Reread 12.19.)

Projects

■ PROJECT 1

Purpose
To think and discuss an ethical media issue and the implications for personal responsibility.

Notes
Be sure to understand the meaning of slander and defamation of character. Sometimes legal and ethical issues are intermingled in decision making. Although what you do may not be illegal, it may not be ethical. Check the codes of conduct for broadcaster announcers. Also, check the regulations for over the air broadcasters and cable/internet broadcasters.

How to Do the Project
Read the case study below and write a two-page response. Be prepared to discuss in small groups in class.

You have been hired by a small radio station to do a morning drive-time program. Primarily you do updates on weather and traffic. Recently you have been very upset because the morning DJ you work with is very insulting to you off-air. He describes your on-air voice as too thin and not professional. You decide that because you are new you cannot confront him because you may lose your job. You decide the only way to vent your feelings is to discuss the situation on your blog. Your boss discovers your comments and is afraid that the station will be sued for slander. No one else at the station seems to be aware of your comments. How do you defend your actions? Is this slander? Would your answer change if you worked on Internet radio?

■ PROJECT 2

Purpose
To discuss a legal media issue and understand the implications of your actions as a reporter.

Notes
Look up the Privacy Protection Act of 1980 prior to writing your response. If time allows, talk to a local investigative reporter to understand the local laws (if any) and to gain an understanding of a reporter's legal responsibilities.

How to Do the Project
Read the case study below and write a two-page response. Be prepared to discuss in small groups in class.

You are an investigative reporter working for a local television station. You have been looking into the selling of drugs, especially to teenagers near some of the local high schools. You have two very good sources and have promised them complete protection as you are aware that if their names were known, their lives would be in danger. In the process of researching your story, you uncover some evidence that implicates a terrorist group in the selling of the drugs to fund overseas terrorism against the United States government. This information is not relevant to your story and you do not intend to use the information in your three-part series that will be broadcast soon. Prior to the broadcast, you are subpoenaed to reveal the sources of your information regarding the terrorist group. Are you protected by law from revealing your sources? The terrorist group is located outside of the continental United States. What do you do? Do you have any ethical obligations in this situation?

■ PROJECT 3

Purpose
To discuss the legal obligations of television stations under the Fairness Doctrine and Sec. 315.

Notes
Be sure to review both the Fairness Doctrine and Sec. 315. If there is time, discuss these guidelines with a local station manager or media lawyer. Be sure that you understand the difference between what is required by law and what might be expected by the viewer.

How to Do the Project
Read the case study below and write a two-page response. Be prepared to discuss in small groups in class.

You are a station manager and have decided to run for a local office. Although you are not on the air every day, you occasionally will broadcast, and you do decide what stories will be covered. Most of your on-air work is interviews with local community leaders on Saturday or Sunday. These programs do not have high ratings but you feel they are important for the local community. Should you resign from your job? Is there a conflict of interest? Does the station have any obligations to the other candidates? What if you worked on a cable television station? Would the guidelines change?

■ PROJECT 4

Purpose
To discuss the ethical dilemmas faced by electronic journalists based on real incidents that occurred in the media. Both cases were adapted from *Media Ethics Magazine* (www.mediaethicsmagazine.com). Used by permission.

Notes
Both of the following situations described are based on real incidents that happened in the United States and in Europe. Both had as their purpose some perceived good for the public and both helped increase the rating of the television network. Consider both the legal and ethical concerns of airing programs with these competing concerns.

How to Do the Project
Read the case study below and write a two-page response. Be prepared to discuss in small groups in class. Consider the following questions: Should journalists make news or report it? How do incidents as described below effect media credibility? Are there limits as to what a reporter should do even if there is some good to the public that may occur?

NBC's *To Catch a Predator* sets up sting operations to attract and expose pedophiles using Internet chat rooms to meet potential victims. A city manager in Texas was fired for permitting NBC to tape a show in the community. During the sting operation, an assistant prosecutor in a neighboring county committed suicide when it was revealed that he was one of those who allegedly engaged in explicit online chat with an adult posing as a 13 year old boy. Although potential pedophiles were uncovered, the local district attorney refused to prosecute any of the cases because they were organized by the media and not law enforcement professionals.

A Dutch television reality show, *The Big Donor*, announced that it would feature an ailing woman, who would select one of three contestants to receive her kidneys when she died. The program had very high ratings. The government called for the show's cancellation. The network claimed that running the show would increase public awareness of the need for transplant organs. A few minutes before the end of the show, the producers announced that it was a hoax. The donor was an actress and the potential recipients were in on the hoax. One of the directors said they had worked on the hoax for a year but never thought it would be a "runaway success."

CHAPTER THIRTEEN

BEGINNING AN ANNOUNCING CAREER

13.1 INTRODUCTION

This chapter is designed to help you land that first job in the broadcast performance area. (See Performance Tip 13.1 for some worthwhile advice.) Even if you've had some experience as an announcer, the techniques mentioned here can assist you when you want to move to a better position. If you are a beginner, first take stock of why you want to get into this field. If you're looking for a high-paying job or stardom, it isn't going to happen, at least not at first. Entry-level pay in broadcasting is modest at best. It's true that you could make tremendous sums of money at some point in your career, and that's the lure for many people who head into the talent aspect of broadcasting. Be realistic, though; when you're an untried performer, you'll be at the low end of the pay scale. Typical salary figures for an entry level position were presented in Chapter 1, if you need to refresh your memory. As a novice, you'll also get the unglamorous task of working those odd hours the established talent doesn't want. Someone is going to work Christmas Day, New Year's Eve, or every overnight shift, and most likely it will be you. Most beginning performers aren't going to start out in New York, Chicago, Los Angeles, or, for that matter, any **major market**. Most entry-level jobs in broadcasting are found in small and medium markets. Although there are always exceptions, you'll probably have to work your way into a larger-market position. Sure, there is some glamour to being an on-air personality, even at the smallest station, but you aren't going to become a major celebrity immediately. And remember, broadcasting is a one-to-one medium; what the audience really wants the performer to be is a companion and friend, not a superstar.

One other thing you should not be looking for in broadcasting is job security. Many performers lose broadcast jobs through no fault of their own because consultants suggest a different personality or new owners want to "sweep" out the old staff. It's something to

be aware of, but not something you should lose sleep over—if you do, chances are you shouldn't be heading into the broadcast performance area. What you *should* be looking for is the fun and challenge and reward of being in the broadcast business. You should feel that no other job is going to be as enjoyable as being a broadcast performer. You also should be willing to devote yourself to preparing thoroughly for getting a job and being persistent until you do. Getting that first job in broadcasting will probably be the hardest one you ever secure. There is a lot of competition for entry-level jobs, and the qualities that separate one candidate from another are often minor. You will need to work hard and put yourself in the best possible light to stand out in the crowd and get a potential employer interested in you. It will be tremendously helpful if you have some basic steps to follow before you begin the job search. Remember, the best person for a job isn't always hired, but the best-*prepared* person almost always is. To begin looking for a performance job, you will need these key items: a resume and cover letter (if mailing the resume out), an air check or demo recording, and a contact list.

13.2 WRITING YOUR RESUME

Your resume will highlight your qualifications and stress the experience that you have gained so far in your career. It's the written portion of how you will be judged and is as important as your demo recording. If you don't engage your prospective employers' attention with your resume, you won't have the chance to impress them with your air check or a personal interview! If you are looking for your first job, you will not have an extensive resume; in fact, a single page should suffice. Only under rare circumstances should your resume exceed two pages. Don't make the beginner mistake of padding your resume with every possible thing you can think of. Make your resume complete, but don't tell your life story! It should go without saying that this document should be typed and absolutely

---

PERFORMANCE TIP 13.1

Getting Your First Job in Broadcasting

"The avenues of getting your first job in broadcasting vary greatly depending on the route you take to get into the business. The best way to go about it, if you are able, is to go to college, take as many broadcasting courses as possible and work on the college radio and TV station as much as you can. Then when you graduate, find a nice small market station where you can learn on the air and grow. I know, I know, you and everyone else want to start off in a major market. It sounds great, but that is NOT what you want. You would be expected to be perfect all the time. It would be like trying to jump in a NASCAR for the first time and race 500 miles at 200 miles an hour without crashing. Not gonna happen. If you can't go to college, consider career broadcasting school. You don't get the all-around education there that you would in college, but you would get a highly focused radio/TV program, giving you the basics to work with. Again, you want to take that and get a job at a small market station where you can learn and move up.

I've been asked many times, "Do I really need to go to school to get a broadcasting job?" The answer is no, but it sure helps. These days you almost have to have some education to get into TV, because there is a lot more equipment to learn about. It's a little easier in radio. I got my first job when I was 16 years old with no previous experience. How? I showed the program director that I was completely serious about doing a great job, and that I was willing to work any shift offered, and work as hard as it took to get better every time I went on the air. Do not think you are entitled to anything, you must earn it. The most important part of getting your first job in broadcasting is believing you can do it. Then you get to prove it."

Chris Schneider has worked on the air in Dallas, Los Angeles, Chicago, Cincinnati, and London for ESPN, the BBC, and CBS, and other great companies. He is joined by big-name colleagues like Bob Costas, Chris Berman, and Larry King in his book *Starting Your Career In Broadcasting* and speaks all over the world about "The Keys To Broadcasting Success," "Funny Stories From Broadcasting Greats," and "Funny Stories and Lesson's Learned from Sports Legends". Chris would be happy to answer your questions at his website www.radioactivespeaking.com.

---

free from any mistakes. Computer word processing makes this easy, but it is amazing how many resumes are received that contain typos, misspellings, erasures, and other defects that greatly detract from any other content on the resume. In most cases, such resumes immediately eliminate the candidates from further consideration for the job. Those who won't take the time and effort to look up the spelling of a word or give any kind of thought to what they want to put on their resume probably don't deserve to get the job. If you feel you do deserve a job, then put the appropriate effort into your resume.

The first rule of putting together a resume is that there are no standard models to follow. Many resources can be found in the library or on the Internet, and computer programs are available that will help you put one together. There are also commercial companies that will, for a fee, help you prepare your resume. Unlike resume-writing services, your university career center may assist you for no charge. Whatever approach you take to putting together your resume, make sure the layout is neat and easy to read. Use regular margins and spacing. You'll be judged as much on your resume presentation as you will on the information it contains. Figure 13.1 shows one approach to putting together a resume. Use 20-pound paper (with a watermark)

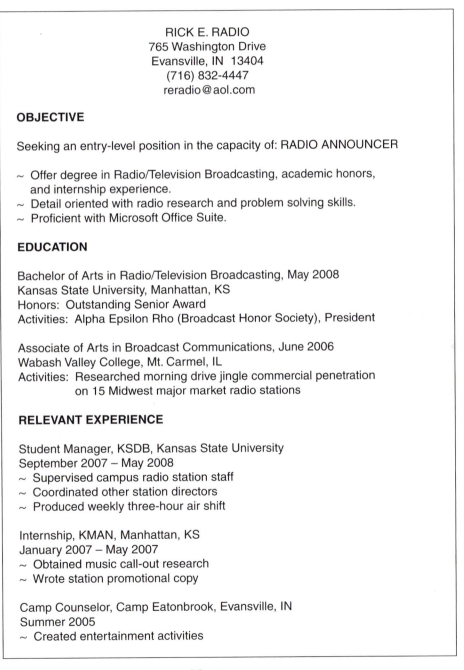

RICK E. RADIO
765 Washington Drive
Evansville, IN 13404
(716) 832-4447
reradio@aol.com

OBJECTIVE

Seeking an entry-level position in the capacity of: RADIO ANNOUNCER

~ Offer degree in Radio/Television Broadcasting, academic honors, and internship experience.
~ Detail oriented with radio research and problem solving skills.
~ Proficient with Microsoft Office Suite.

EDUCATION

Bachelor of Arts in Radio/Television Broadcasting, May 2008
Kansas State University, Manhattan, KS
Honors: Outstanding Senior Award
Activities: Alpha Epsilon Rho (Broadcast Honor Society), President

Associate of Arts in Broadcast Communications, June 2006
Wabash Valley College, Mt. Carmel, IL
Activities: Researched morning drive jingle commercial penetration
                   on 15 Midwest major market radio stations

RELEVANT EXPERIENCE

Student Manager, KSDB, Kansas State University
September 2007 – May 2008
~ Supervised campus radio station staff
~ Coordinated other station directors
~ Produced weekly three-hour air shift

Internship, KMAN, Manhattan, KS
January 2007 – May 2007
~ Obtained music call-out research
~ Wrote station promotional copy

Camp Counselor, Camp Eatonbrook, Evansville, IN
Summer 2005
~ Created entertainment activities

FIGURE 13.1 The modern resume often employs a qualifications summary.

in white, cream, or light grey. The font employed should be fairly conservative, such as Ariel or Times New Roman, and sized to 11 or 12 point. The modern resume must be neatly packaged, provide the reader with your pertinent data, and separate you from all the other candidates.

Your personal information should include your name, address, phone number and e-mail. Because "snail mail" is used less often, your address is no longer as important as your phone number or e-mail, but make sure you employ a professional user name on your e-mail. A general manager may not be comfortable responding to "BigStud@aol.com" or "SquirrellyEyes@yahoo.com." If you have a website that includes professional information, you could also include it. This vital data is usually placed as the heading for the resume. There are several different approaches; just make it neat and easy to read. You should also make it as easy as possible for someone to get in touch with you. Don't use your school address if it is exam week and you'll be going home in a few days, and don't give your home phone number if you're going to be at school for the next three months. However, you might decide to give both. Avoid nicknames on a resume; however, if you use an air name in addition to your real name, put it in parentheses after your real name. Don't make the embarrassing mistake of putting your real name on a resume and cover letter and only an air name on an air check. If they get separated, it could cost you a job opportunity.

For the modern resume, the objective statement has given way to a "qualifications summary." While the objective statement only told what *you* wanted (such as an entry-level job position or room for advancement), the qualifications summary also tells what you *can do for the employer*. It shouldn't be more than a few concise phrases. Use specific skills that you can bring for each job you apply for, such as shown in Figure 13.1.

Your educational background should show academic work in reverse chronological order. If you've completed your undergraduate work, leave off your high school work. Highlight any honors or scholarships and make sure you include what schools you've attended and when, your major field of study, and what degrees you've earned. If your grade point average (GPA) was above 3.5, it is probably worthwhile to include it. Remember, your college degree is important, and most employers are looking for you to demonstrate a broad-based knowledge along with good communication skills. If your educational background is not extensive, you might want to list some specific courses, especially those that make evident your broadcast

or communication skills. If you've done associate's work prior to your undergraduate schooling, or graduate work after, don't forget to include it. You might also include, as a subcategory, any relevant campus or community activities that you were involved with. This can be especially important if you held a position of leadership in a particular organization or received some distinction as a member. If you are looking for an entry-level job, in most cases you would put your educational background before your work experience; however, if you've been in the business a few years, it makes more sense to put your work experience first and then your educational background.

For many broadcast positions, your work experience is the most important section of your resume and could well mean the difference between getting a job and not getting it. Even if your work history is quite limited, this is your opportunity to highlight what you have done and what you can offer to an employer. List all your previous employers and dates of employment, along with your job titles, duties, and responsibilities. When mentioning your responsibilities, use action words where appropriate— "supervised," "completed," "organized," "developed," "achieved," and similar words convey a sense of ability and accomplishment. Work experience is normally given in reverse chronological order, so list your most recent position first. Don't forget to include working for the campus media, internships, and part-time jobs, especially if they're relevant to a broadcast position. Being station manager at the campus radio station probably carries more weight than flipping burgers at McDonald's, but if that fast-food job helped you pay your own way through college and you can convey that information, that will also say a lot about you to a prospective employer. Use whatever employment background you have to your best advantage.

You might also want to include a section for your other skills, if you haven't mentioned them in your qualifications summary. For example, if you are fluent in a foreign language and it might be a plus for a particular job, or you held a leadership position with a volunteer organization, you may want to note it here. If you're highly skilled with numerous computer software programs, you could list them, and even participation in athletics may be noted here to show either leadership qualities or that you are a team player.

The trend for the modern resume is that you can entirely eliminate any mention of references because it's assumed you have them and you will be asked for them. So, make sure you do in fact have two or three names ready to supply if you are asked for them. A good practice is to put your references on a separate piece of paper that matches your resume. You can then easily present them whenever asked to do so. You should be able to give your potential employer the name, business address, telephone number, and e-mail address of people who have agreed to supply a reference on your behalf. Make sure you have talked with your references in advance, and that they are both willing and qualified to speak positively about your character, work habits, and abilities. If you are recently out of school, your professors are usually willing to provide references, but if you skipped half their classes and turned in several assignments late, you might not get the reference you're looking for! Use your good judgment and only ask someone who knows your character and what you've done in school or at a job, and with whom you've established at least some type of relationship. It's best if you can give a variety of references, like a teacher and a couple of different employers. If you've worked for or studied under someone who has a recognizable name in the broadcast field, so much the better. However, don't just drop a name; this person must be someone who knows you well enough to evaluate your qualifications.

For most radio or audio-only jobs, it is not necessary to include a photograph with your resume. In fact, if the prospective employer has a bias against a certain body type, hairstyle, or facial feature, you could make a negative impression with your photo even before you can say "hello." That old expression about a "face for radio" is correct—your personal appearance isn't the key element that will get you hired because your vocal style is what they are interested in. For television or video talent positions, appearance takes on a more crucial role. You'll definitely be appraised in your demo recording; however, for most broadcast performance jobs, don't include a photo as part of your resume. The exception here would be for television commercial jobs where a specific "character" is being sought and a photo will be required. The best photo would be a color shot in the 8- by 10-inch format; however, black and white is perfectly acceptable. Don't use your graduation pictures and avoid art photos that stress composition over content. A straightforward professional photo is best and should include your name and contact information on the back. Always make sure the photo is current. An employer can feel deceived if your personal appearance is startlingly different from your photo.

Remember, your resume is your opportunity to sell yourself even before a prospective employer has seen or talked with you. You should also be aware that most employment situations are really screening out processes. Employers are looking for reasons why they shouldn't hire someone. Don't let your resume knock you out of the picture; rather, it should procure a meeting between you and the station at which you'd like to work. There are a half-dozen problems that continually creep up on resumes and keep unwary applicants from getting jobs. These include resumes that are too long, contain exaggerated claims, contain errors, lack specific details, don't list accomplishments, and do contain irrelevant information. Remember, resumes for broadcast positions should be kept to one page. Also, do not ever be untruthful on your resume—don't claim to be an experienced camera operator if you've only had one "Introduction to Television" class. It should also go without saying that your resume should be mistake-free and neatness does count. Remember to list specific job duties and accomplishments using action words, and include the information that is most relevant to the job you are trying to obtain. The bottom line here is that you don't want to do anything that gets in the way of your having the best chance of getting the job. Figure 13.2 shows another approach to putting together a resume.

13.3 ELECTRONIC RESUMES

Because of the number of applicants applying for a position, or to just speed up the job search process, some employers are asking job applicants to send a resume via e-mail, post a resume on a website, or submit a resume that is going to be computer scanned for content. So in addition to your paper resume, you may also need an electronic version. The basic purpose of the resume—to get you a job interview—doesn't change, but the format must be structured to fit the technology employed. In this case, content is going to be more important than style.

For an electronic resume that is going to be sent by e-mail or posted on the Internet, you can use your standard resume, but you should "save" a copy as an ASCII (American Standard Code for Information Interchange), RTF (Rich Text Format), or any other plain-text file. For the most part, this will eliminate any elaborate formatting and allow the resume to be accurately read by any computer, but you will probably have to do some editing on the electronic version. For one thing, the word-wrap feature usually isn't recognized, so you might have to shorten a few lines. Bold type, italics, and underlining won't come

Tonya S. Television

CAMPUS:
P.O. Box 49628
San Jose, CA 95122
(408) 297-1682
t.television@sjsu.edu
(until June 2008)

PERMANENT:
2038 N. Irwin Avenue
Santa Cruz, CA 95060
(408) 458-1985

E-mail Address:
tontel@gmail.com

SUMMARY:
- ~ Weather coordinator internship with KNTV
- ~ Magna Cum Laude graduate with BA in Mass Communications
- ~ Proficient with HTML, MS Office, Windows Vista and the Internet
- ~ Fluent in Spanish

EDUCATION:
Bachelor of Arts in Mass Communications, May 2008
San Jose State University
Graduated Magna Cum Laude with a GPA of 3.6

Courses taken included:
Writing for Broadcast Media Ethics
Television Studio Production Broadcast Management
Introduction to Computer Graphics Video Editing and ENG
Advanced Television and News Production

EXPERIENCE:
Floor Director, KICU-TV, 2007 – Present
San Jose, California
- ~ Production team member for weekday "Live On Five" newscast
- ~ Production Assistant for "San Jose Speaks" weekly talk show

Weathercaster, "San Jose Scene," Campus TV Program, 2005 – 2007
- ~ Lead weathercaster for nightly newscast
- ~ Substitute news anchor

Internship, KNTV, San Jose, California, 2004–2005
- ~ Coordinated station's "Know Your Weather Facts" school program

ACTIVITIES:
Vice President, Student Council, 2006–2007
President, Future Writers of America, Student Chapter, 2005 – 2006

FIGURE 13.2 Your resume should be mistake-free and neatness does count.

through on the plain-text, electronic version, but you can emphasize items by using capitol letters, the plus sign, or an asterisk. A good test is to send an e-mail to yourself that contains the electronic resume in the body of the message. If it doesn't look good to you, make changes until it does. When you send it to an employer, include your cover letter and resume in the text of one single e-mail. Most employers don't like attachments because of the possibility of a computer virus or potential problems in opening them.

A few companies may let you know your resume is going to be scanned or read by optical character recognition (OCR) software which will analyze your resume to match keywords in your education, experience, and skills with the qualities being sought. Again, you can start with your standard resume, but you will need to format it appropriately and give some thought to the keywords you should be sure to include. A careful reading of the job announcement or just an understanding of industry "buzzwords" for this type of job can be helpful. Figure 13.3 shows one possible format for an electronic resume. Note that your name should be the only thing on the first line, that you should include a keyword summary along with typical resume sections, and that you should never staple or fold a resume that is going to be scanned.

```
CHARLES T. CABLE
    134 Lincoln Street
    Syracuse, New York 13244
    315-443-6832
    ccable@yahoo.com

KEYWORD SUMMARY
    * B.A. Television-Radio-Film, 2008
    * Cable programming, promotional events
    * Television production, customer service

EDUCATION
    Bachelor of Arts, Television-Radio-Film, 2008
    Syracuse University
    S.I. Newhouse School of Public Communications
    Minor: Business Communications
    GPA: 3.4/4.0

EXPERIENCE
    Production Assistant
    Empire Sports Network, 2007 - Present
    * Produce live studio broadcast
    * Perform staging, lighting, and audio setup

Customer Service Representative
    Adelphia Cable, summers, 2004 – 2007
    * Explain services, features, options and rates
    * Handle trouble calls
    * Perform credit information checks
    * Maintain customer database

Associate Producer
    COW-TV, Syracuse University, 2002 - Present
    (Collegiate Original Works Television)
    * Develop program concepts
    * Organize all aspects of final production

    ++ Willing to relocate ++
```

FIGURE 13.3 One possible format for a resume that will be scanned.

13.4 ADDING A COVER LETTER

Unless you are delivering it in person, you will also need to include a cover letter when you mail out your resume. Don't make the mistake of just sending an air check and resume in a package with nothing else, and don't make the mistake of using a form letter with your demo and resume. That's one of the quickest ways to have your material make its way to the circular file—most program directors and managers won't consider an application that employs a photocopied cover letter. It conveys the message that the package they've received is just one of a mass mailing you're sending to lots of stations and that you're not really interested in this individual station. The letter you send should be neatly typed and presented in a businesslike manner. Keep it short (one page), but it should convey your interest in the job, make a positive impression, and thank the reader for listening to or viewing your air check. Give as much attention to the cover letter as you do to the resume. The letter is going to be read first and will give the prospective employer his or her very first impression of you as a candidate for the position. Like the resume, there is no standard form for a cover letter; however, Figure 13.4 shows one possible approach.

Always personalize the letter. If you're responding to a "help wanted" ad, you probably have a name to reply to. If not, look up the correct name. Most key personnel names can be found in a station's listing in the *Broadcasting & Cable Yearbook*, but be aware that even the current issue of this publication is quickly outdated. You might do better to check the station's website, but to be sure, call the station and check for the correct full name and spelling of the current position holder. If you're applying to a blind ad, avoid using "Dear Sir" as some Program Directors (of either sex) will deem this politically incorrect, and avoid "To Whom It May Concern," as this has the same effect as sending a photocopied letter. If you just can't find the appropriate name, at least send your letter addressed to the correct position, as in "Dear Program Director," or avoid a title altogether and use a simple "Hello" to open your letter, although this may be a little too informal for some situations.

The first paragraph explains why you are writing so reference the job position you're applying for and express your interest in it. If you found the job in a *Radio & Records* listing or were told about it by a colleague in the business, mention this here. Always include in this paragraph a sentence that expresses your desire to be considered for the job and give a little information about yourself.

```
                                                                        Rick E. Radio
                                                                 765 Washington Drive
                                                                   Evansville, IN 13404
                                                                    reradio@aol.com

June 17, 2008


Mr. John Hackett
Program Director
WLHM-FM
Box 93854
Logansport, IN 46947


Dear Mr. Hackett:

    Please consider me for the position of evening announcer as posted on the WLHM-FM
website this June 15th. This opportunity is very appealing to me and I believe my educational
background and experience will nicely complement the duties of this entry level position.

    Having just graduated from Kansas State University, I have not yet held a professional
position in radio. However, I have been on-air at KSDB, the campus station, for the past three
years with a weekly radio show. This experience has allowed me to develop an attention-getting
radio personality that listeners seem to enjoy. During the past year, I have been station manager
and have been responsible for the day-to-day operation of our facility. I have strong leadership
skills and can work well with both management and co-workers. As requested, an MP3 air
check and resume are enclosed for your consideration.

    Please give me an opportunity to answer any questions you may have in mind about my
qualifications for this position. During the day, I can be reached at (716) 832-5547; otherwise,
please use the number listed on my resume. Thank you for your time and  consideration. I will
call you next week to follow up. I look forward to speaking with you about this job position.


Best Regards,

Rick E. Radio

Rick E. Radio
```

FIGURE 13.4 *A sample cover letter.*

The second paragraph should highlight your current professional status or a special qualification for the position, and reference the resume and demo recording you are enclosing. Explain how your background fits the job position and tell what contribution you can make or why they should be interested in you. If you're currently working in broadcasting and mention what you are doing, you probably also need to mention why you're leaving that position and applying for this job. If you're a beginner, don't apply for a major-market position—it will be readily apparent you are unqualified to work in that particular market size, and your lack of judgment will be noted as much as your weak qualifications. If you apply for a job position that is essentially the same as the job you currently hold, you may get labeled a "drifter"—someone who

moves from job to job on a regular basis and someone most stations don't want to invest in as an employee. Lateral moves usually don't advance a career, so try to apply for a job that is truly a better position—perhaps a larger market situation or a move from announcer to announcer/music director—something that is positive for your broadcast performance career. Close this paragraph by noting that you have enclosed an air check and resume with the cover letter.

An optional third paragraph might make some significant reference to the station or market where the position is located; however, never be insincere here. Don't say that you'd love to work there because you know it's the most exciting radio market in the country—that sounds patronizing. However, if there is some personal reason why you'd like to work at this station, you might note it. Even if you don't use this section in your cover letter, you should know something about the market where the position is. Make sure you really are interested in the market and the station before you actually apply there. Don't apply for jobs just to see if you could get hired.

The last paragraph of a cover letter should reiterate your interest in the job, provide additional contact information, and include thanks for the employer's consideration of you for the position. This is where you are essentially asking for an interview. If you have an additional phone number or easy way to be reached other than what is on your resume, include it. You might want to initiate a follow-up by including a sentence like, "I will call you next week to see if you have received my materials and to further discuss this job opportunity." Finally, common sense and courtesy tell you to conclude this paragraph with a simple thank you for taking the time to consider you. Remember that your cover letter should complement your resume and not just provide the same information that it contains.

13.5 MAKING YOUR AIR CHECK OR DEMO RECORDING

Most of the job-seeking techniques mentioned in this chapter are as appropriate for a radio position as for a television position. However, your demo recording will either be a CD recording or audio file for radio or a videotape or DVD recording for television.

For Radio
A demo recording for radio is a telescoped air check. It should be short—three to five minutes at most. Put it on compact disc because most program directors prefer this format and can readily play them. You should put your audition demo onto a CD as an MP3, WAV, or other common audio format, as this is currently the best method. This will provide the best quality and will make it easy for the PD to listen to your effort. You can custom label the CD and make an attractive package that stands out. Although air checks used to be submitted on reel-to-reel tape or cassette, these formats are rarely used anymore. It is also possible to put an air check on a conventional computer disk or you may be asked to just e-mail it to the station. Use an MP3 or other compressed audio format and make absolutely sure it will readily play back on typical computer audio players, such as RealPlayer or Windows Media Player.

The audition should be telescoped because the PD doesn't need to hear the music or spots you didn't produce. Edit out most of it, leaving just enough to get the feel of the break that leads into or follows the music. The best air check is a tape of an actual on-air broadcast. You can do that if you currently are on-air, but if you are a beginner you may need to simulate an on-air performance in the production studio. The key here is that you record your whole performance in real time. Don't try to telescope as you are recording, because it's almost impossible to produce a typical show if you are doing a break, starting a CD, stopping the recording, and so on. Instead, let the recording roll, play the songs all the way through, and telescope it when you have completed the show. Most PDs want to hear consecutive breaks, too, so don't "cherry pick" just the best breaks and leave out the others. Many beginners produce audition recordings that feature one great break, one great song introduction, one great spot—what is called the "sampler" approach. Remember, the purpose of a demo is to present how you sound every day. If you only put on your absolutely best performances, you really won't be able to duplicate that with your typical work. However, when you do telescope, don't use the first couple of breaks. It takes a while to get into the flow of a program and early breaks are often a bit awkward. Listen for a great break to start with and then continue from there.

The actual content of the air check, for an announcer position, should be about a half-dozen breaks, followed by some examples of your production work, followed by a short newscast. You can leave out the newscast if you know the station has separate news announcers, but it's not a bad idea to show you can read something other than a short liner card or spot announcement. The most important point about a demo is that you will only have 15 to 30 seconds to capture the interest of the listener. Make the first break your best because you must dazzle them immediately. Most PDs won't listen to the second break if that first impression doesn't grab their attention. It should go without saying that the board work heard on the audition recording must be top notch. There is no excuse for sloppy equipment operation on an air check. You can produce a demo recording with a "neutral" format, such as adult contemporary, that will work for most other radio formats, or you can make an individual air check in the format of the station where you are applying for a job. What doesn't work well is to send a country station a demo recorded in a hard rock format, so use some common sense here when you make your recording. Listen to Audio Tracks 13.1 and 13.2 to hear examples of a radio audition recording.

If you are applying for a different type of radio performance job, you need to adjust your demo appropriately. For example, if you're looking for a news job, the first thing on your recording needs to be a newscast or report. It still needs to be a grabber! Include an actual newscast, but keep it short. Telescope commercials, reports by other reporters, and actualities, but make sure the content of the stories can be followed. Include a variety of story types. Don't just read fire and fatality stories; include a budget story, a courthouse story, and a soft news or feature story. It's an asset to be versatile in the styles of news stories you can properly read, so show that you are. Make sure the news you use is current; don't send out a news demo that was recorded six months ago. An audition recording for a specialty announcing position, such as a play-by-play announcer or voice-over announcer, would be put together in a similar manner. You would select material that best showed your skills with that specific type of announcing.

For Television

A **video audition recording** is also a compilation of your work. It can be longer than an audio demo, but generally 6 to 8 minutes is long enough. Record some of your best performances onto a DVD or VHS, but remember that you need to be able to duplicate this level of performance on a day-in, day-out basis. The recording should be geared to the position you are applying for and, like an audio demo, your best material should be at the beginning of the tape. A good rule of thumb is to assume you will have just 30 seconds or less to impress the viewer of your audition. You have to sell your skills and at least arouse some interest before a closer look will be taken at your style and abilities; otherwise your demo recording will be ejected and your audition will be over. At the beginning of your videotape or DVD, don't put on color bars or tone—this isn't a "for broadcast" production and it wastes time and annoys many program directors. Also avoid using any type of on-camera biography where you appear on-screen and say something like, "Hello, I'm Tonya Television and I really want to work for your station. What follows is an example of my work." However, do put down a simple slate at the head of the recording. A graphic screen with your name, address, telephone number, and e-mail address is good insurance in case your resume and other materials get separated from your demo.

Many audition recordings are begun with a montage of four or five clips. These short excerpts from complete stories shown later in your tape are designed to show you in action right away and should highlight your best efforts. Then, think in terms of three different types of items. If you are applying for a news position, you could include a short newscast from an anchor desk, an on-the-scene stand-up report at a fire, and an interview segment with a local politician. Try to show versatility in delivering different styles of news stories, as you would with an audio demo. However, if the job position is specifically for a consumer reporter, you must show that you can do that type of reporting first. It's a good idea to include the recording contents on a rundown sheet. Type or print what's on the recording in what order and how long it runs, and put this on an index card that can be taped inside the tape or disk box. Don't put a rundown sheet on the actual tape or disk because it can't be read while the media is playing. Remember to make your audition a quality production—pay attention to your clothing, lighting, audio quality, and all the other details, just as you would in an actual performance situation. Always check every recording you make before you send it out to be sure you have good audio, lighting, and other production values. There's no point in sending out a poor quality demo recording, for it will just be thrown away with little consideration. Remember to cue up your recording to the beginning also. Video Clip 13.1 shows one example of a television audition recording.

Make sure your audition material presentation is professional. Put your name, address, phone number, and e-mail address on both the case and the actual tape or disk. Don't just write your name on a piece of masking tape with a pen or marker, either—use a neatly typed or printed label. Since demos are often stacked up before they are played, it's not a bad idea to make sure the tape or disk is labeled on the side, as well as the top, so it can be seen easily in a stack of other audition recordings.

You should also give some thought to putting together a unique package—something that really stands out. One enterprising announcer sent his audition tape in on CD, but put it in a SONY Walkman CD player! It was all ready to be listened to by the PD, who ended up with a new CD player. While such an approach may be too extreme (and too expensive), it certainly made his air check stand out from all the others received for that job position. Another prospective news reporter tucked her demo in a box of individually wrapped candies. You can bet the news director gave at least a passing thought to her audition every time one of those candies was eaten. A unique package and a good audition aren't necessarily going to get you a job, but if they like what they see or hear, it will get you in the station's door and they will probably ask to see or hear more or have you do some additional live performance.

One final word about your demo: whether it's a tape or a disk, don't expect it to be mailed back to you unless you include a self-addressed envelope with the appropriate return postage. From time to time you will run into a news director or program director who will take the time, effort, and expense of returning audition recordings, but most will not. If it's a re-recordable medium, many PDs use air checks they receive to air check their current staff, recording over your efforts. If you're a beginning broadcaster looking for that first job or looking to move up a level from your current job, you will need to plan for this expense as part of your job search effort.

PERFORMANCE TIP 13.2

On-Air Job Hunting Tips

Mark Stiles, Sports Director

WOHL, Lima, OH

Make sure your resume/tape is solid and stands out. There are lots of different ways to do your tape, but I would say your best bet is to make sure you're on camera early and often. They want to see you and they don't want to wait long to do it. How do you stand out? Unfortunately, having a good tape is not enough. Hopefully, there will be an opening at a station near you. This is a huge advantage because stations love having on-air staff from the area. If this is the case, stress your knowledge of the area in your cover letter and consider just driving to the station to drop it off. Do it early in the day though. Nothing is worse than having someone show up an hour before the next newscast. Once you've landed that small-market job, your next plan is to get out of there. Use the first six months to a year to soak in the job, learn the basics of the trade, and work all the extra hours they want. After that period, start looking for stories that would look good on your tape. Let's be honest, you want to do your best and make a good impression at your first job, but it's really about learning the business and making a tape. And, oh yeah, learn to live frugally!

13.6 DEVELOPING A CONTACT LIST

A contact list is merely an inventory of people you can call on to see if they have a job opening or know someone else who may have a job open that you would be interested in. If this is the first broadcast job you've ever looked for, your contact list is going to be fairly slim, but it needn't be empty. If you've worked at an internship in school, you've got one or two of the best initial contacts you could have. Many students obtain entry level jobs at the same station or company where they held an internship. Even if they don't have a position open, these people are contacts you can call on, and perhaps they can suggest someone else to check with about a job position. Did any of your broadcast classes have a guest speaker from the industry? Did you get a business card (or at least a name and telephone number) from that speaker? If not, you missed a chance to add a name to your contact list. If someone took the time to speak to a class of students, he or she is already sympathetic to beginners, and just might have, or know of someone who has an entry-level position open. Make and develop contacts while you are still in school and don't overlook any chance you get to network. Why not call on some of the local broadcast stations? This may be less productive in the larger markets, but small-market stations often look for talent right out of school, and you shouldn't overlook your own hometown station.

Of course, you'll be checking the trade publications (or their web sites) for job listings. *Broadcasting & Cable, Radio & Records,* and *FMQB* (Friday Morning Quarterback) all list performance jobs. Many of these employers will be looking for more experience than you have at first, but sometimes a listing will specify that it's an entry-level job. The trade publications also often carry ads for employment services. These companies offer lists of jobs in the broadcast business for a fee. Often the listings are just a compilation of jobs from various other sources, but it is another possibility you may want to look into, although you will probably have to subscribe to the service or list for a minimum period of time. Check the Internet for broadcast sites that might list job openings. Check with your state broadcast association, especially if it has student memberships. Don't forget the job placement office, career center, or alumni office at your school if you are a recent graduate. While broadcast positions don't often make it to the job placement office, it is another source to check. See if any alumni are in the business, because they are often willing to support students from their alma mater. At the very least, they should be willing to talk with you, and if they don't have any positions available, they may know someone else who does. Finding a broadcast job is a job, so plan on working hard and checking every possible source for an open position.

If you've been in the business awhile, you should have been keeping a regularly updated contact list. As colleagues leave your station and head to different stations, stay in touch with them. Network, network, network! A radio management position came about for one of the authors because he'd stayed in touch with a fellow announcer from his first radio job, some two years after both had headed out to different stations. If you attend broadcast conventions, make contacts with other broadcasters at all levels—announcers, PDs, managers, industry representatives—each one is a contact. Don't be shy at these gatherings. It will be to your advantage to talk with as many people as possible. You never know who could lead you to another job.

Broadcasting is really a small business. It's amazing how one person can quickly get to know a lot of other people in this industry. And that brings to mind an important point about this business: don't ever burn any bridges if you can help it. Try to leave every position on good terms with your old employers. In fact, always be a class act and leave on better terms than they might have shown you. You can be sure that old employer knows many people in the business and maybe even someone with whom you are trying to get a new job. Leaving a broadcast job on unfriendly terms can come back to hurt you later on and could cost you the possibility of getting a job you really want.

A contact list can just be scribbled on paper, or put into a computer database, or maybe you will want to make up some index cards with the key information. Make sure you have a name and title of the contact, his or her phone, fax, and e-mail, and the company address. You probably also should note how you met this person or obtained his or her name. Just try to keep the list current and keep adding to it over the years. While it takes a little effort, it will all pay off when job-search time comes around.

13.7 INTERVIEWING FOR A JOB

You made the right contact and have found an open position that you'd really like to have. You sent out a cover letter, resume, and audition recording, and you've been asked to come for a job interview. You're halfway home to getting that job, but the next step is just as important to getting hired as anything else you've done so far. The job interview is your chance to prove your suitability for the position, but it's also a chance to lose the job if you don't make the right impression. Because of this, most job interviews will make you, at one end of the scale, a little bit anxious or nervous and, at the other end of the scale, totally stressed out. However, that need not be the case if you concentrate on two key aspects of the job interview process: preparation and presentation—what you do before you get to the interview and how you act during the interview will determine your success.

The bulk of your preparation is to anticipate questions you might be asked and practice how you will answer them. There are several questions that you can be pretty sure will be broached during the course of most interviews. While your interview will most likely start with some casual banter designed to ease you (and the interviewer) into conversation, you will quickly start answering those questions. First, be prepared to talk about your specific skills and accomplishments. You need to be able to briefly describe ways you've helped improve the stations at which you've previously worked. This is an excellent chance to distinguish yourself from other candidates, so practice what you would say out loud so you don't stumble or leave out details during the actual interview. If you're applying for that first job, you need to draw on experiences you've gained with part-time work, campus media, or internships. Be careful if you're asked something like, "Tell me about yourself." That's pretty broad-based and you could end up rambling on and on, which could cost you the job. Organize your thoughts and give one or two pertinent items about yourself and your skills. You may be asked, "What are your strengths?" or another variation of this, "What can you do for us?" In either case, you should be able to relate your strongest qualities and how those qualities will best fit with the station and the job that is open. You most likely will also be asked, "What are your weaknesses?" You might try to skirt around this one with a humorous response like, "I don't sing very well." However, you need to judge the circumstances of the interview before trying any humor as it may be very inappropriate. You might also try a response like, "I spend too much time at the station," because most radio people won't really see a workaholic attitude as a weakness. Of course, this should be an honest statement and not just something you are saying. If you are pressed to provide something else, you do need to come up with a weakness, but try to temper it with a follow-up that shows you are working on improving that weakness.

You will often be asked, "Why do you want to work for this station?" or "Why should I hire you?" You should have looked into the station and market when you put together your cover letter and if you can match some of your skills to specific characteristics of the station, you should have no problem answering this type of question. However, be careful if you're asked something like, "What do you think of the station you are currently working for?" as this type of question is designed to see if you are having trouble with other employers. Don't say anything negative

about another station (even if it is justified). Try to focus your response on your desire for career advancement, to work in a larger market, or to develop new skills. If your current position is being phased out due to new ownership and consolidation, that happens a lot in the broadcast business and there wouldn't be anything wrong with stating that fact. If you are between jobs, be prepared to answer this question: "Why did you leave your last employer?"

Questions like, "What are your career goals?" or "Where do you want to be five years from now?" are fairly typical, so know how you will answer something along these lines. Also be ready to respond to questions like, "How well do you work under pressure?" or "What makes you think you're a top-level talent?"

It's possible that somewhere near the end of the interview you'll be asked, "What are your salary requirements?" This is another one to be careful with. Don't ever give your minimum salary figure because you will not be able to move up from that figure once a prospective employer knows it. The best response to this type of question is to ask if there is a salary range for the job. You, obviously, will have in mind a minimum figure that you would take in order to accept the job. Of course, you must also consider the entire compensation package. Most stations are going to offer a salary and some benefits.

You need to consider all the perks of the job, such as health benefits, vacation time, and bonuses, which often make a lower salary figure adequate. Of course, if this is an entry-level position at a small-market station, you should understand that the station probably can afford to pay only a modest salary for the position. The time will come—and it can happen quickly— when you will be given more responsibility in your job and you will earn a better paycheck.

Remember, there is never a guarantee that you will land a job, but if you're well prepared you will put yourself ahead of many of the other candidates. Now, how you actually present yourself during the interview will complete the interview process, and there are several do's and do not's to keep in mind. First, arrive just a little early so you can compose your thoughts and relax a bit before the process begins, but if you must be late for some unavoidable reason, make certain to take the time to call the station and let them know. Candidates have lost out on jobs by arriving late without calling. There are very few acceptable reasons for being tardy to a job interview, so just don't ever be late if you can possibly help it. Never take anyone with you to a job interview; the prospective employer is

FIGURE 13.5 Most broadcast executives are fairly conservative, so a job interview isn't the place to push the envelope—a professional appearance will be to your advantage.

only interested in you, and having a couple of friends waiting around the station lobby is not acceptable. Dress neatly and be well groomed to present a professional appearance—first impressions are extremely important. Remember, most broadcast executives are fairly conservative, so a job interview is not the place to push the fashion or hairstyle envelope. It will be to your advantage to also lean toward the conservative side.

Make sure you've brought along a pen that works, because you may be requested to fill out an application form and asking to borrow a pen will not make the right impression. Even though much of the information is duplicated on your resume, many employers require you to fill out an employment application because it standardizes the information they have on all the candidates for the job. It's possible the station is also collecting some voluntary ethnic heritage information on the form for federal or state government equal-employment record keeping, which is

completely optional. Filling out an application also allows a station to see how well you follow directions and how legible your writing is, so if you're asked to fill out an employment application, do so carefully and with a smile.

During the course of the interview, avoid negative or defensive body language. Shake hands firmly with your interviewer and extend a cordial greeting. Don't cross your arms on your chest or lean back in your chair away from the person you are talking with, because these postures convey a defensive or disinterested attitude. Don't smoke during an interview, even if you normally do and even if the interviewer does. Don't make any exaggerated facial expressions, but by all means maintain good eye contact throughout the interview. Good interviewers pay attention to your mannerisms, and so should you.

If you've planned for the interview as already noted, you will have no trouble with the questions that are posed to you. Answer them in a positive, confident manner. Attitude is very important, especially for those entry-level jobs where many of the candidates have little experience and fairly equal backgrounds. You will also have the chance to ask questions about the station. Not only are you being interviewed to be considered for a job position, you are also considering the station as a potential place of employment. Forget questions along the lines of "How much do I make?" and "How many vacation days do I get?" Those hardly convey a professional image. Ask questions that will give you specific information about the job position and about the station's operation. "What problems might I encounter in this job?" or "What are the long-term goals of this station?" are good examples. You could also ask, "What are the main responsibilities of this position?" or "What would a typical day be like?" if those topics did not get covered elsewhere in the interview. In follow-up discussion to one of your questions, be sure to watch for an opportunity to relate one of your strengths to the station's operation. And remember, if you don't ask any questions during the interview, it can easily communicate a lack of interest on your part. You might even think of a question or two beforehand that you can ask at the end of the interview.

At some point, usually after about 30 minutes, but sometimes as long as 90 minutes, your job interview will come to an end. Watch for a cue to gracefully exit from an interview. For example, the interviewer may have been taking notes and finally puts down the pen and sets aside the pad, signaling that it's time to

Rick E. Radio
765 Washington Drive
Evansville, IN 13404
reradio@aol.com

July 8, 2008

Mr. John Hackett
WLHM-FM
Box 93854
Logansport, IN 46947

Dear Mr. Hackett:

It was a pleasure talking with you last week about WLHM and the evening announcer position that you currently have open. I appreciate the courtesy you've shown me and I'd like to assure you I'm still eager to be considered for the position.

I look forward to hearing from you in the near future.

Sincerely,

Rick E. Radio

Rick E. Radio

FIGURE 13.6 *A thank-you letter is a courtesy, and it puts your name in front of the person who may hire you once again.*

wrap it up. At this point, depending on how you were perceived as a candidate for the position, you may be told the station is actively interested in you. However, people are rarely hired on the spot, so try to be patient because appearing overanxious can lead them to offer the job to another candidate. Most likely you will be told that you are being considered along with other candidates and that the station needs a little time to select the best person for the position.

After an interview, even one you felt didn't go very well, always send a letter expressing your appreciation for being considered for the position. Thank the interviewer for talking with you and express your continued interest in the job (assuming you are still interested) and ask for it again. Many job candidates do not send a thank you, and as one of the few who do, you will stand out. Not only is this type of letter a business courtesy, but it once again puts your name in front of the person who might be hiring you. A typical thank you letter is shown in Figure 13.6. If you haven't heard anything two weeks after your interview, it is appropriate to call the PD or person you interviewed with to check on the status of the job position. Chances are

you will not get a positive response at this point, but sometimes stations take longer than they anticipate in selecting the person they are going to hire.

13.8 RESPONDING TO A JOB OFFER

Most broadcast people feel relieved when an interview is over and usually have a feeling about how it went. If you feel all did not go well, try to learn from the experience. If you are told you did not get the job, and you feel comfortable doing so, ask what your weakest qualities were. Perhaps another candidate had more experience or perhaps your personality just didn't click with the interviewers. If the weaknesses they describe are skills you can improve on, do so, and consider rewriting the description of your abilities on your resume.

On the other hand, if everything went in your favor and you are offered the position, congratulations! If it's an entry-level job, you may receive a verbal job offer. However, it's best to get something in writing, so ask if they will send you a written offer letter. Make sure all the terms of your employment are specified, including your salary figure, benefits, and start date. Most likely you will be given a week or two to accept the offer, although it could be shorter. Be sure to respond to the offer letter before the last possible due date. If you decide not to accept the offer, let the station know as soon as possible so that they can move to their second choice or start a new search. That's professionalism and it establishes a positive relationship in case you do business with this station at a later time. If there is something in the offer letter that is different from what was discussed at the interview, contact the station immediately. Honest mistakes do happen from time to time and it's best to clear them up immediately and not the day before your response is due. If the station declines to send you a written agreement, be cautious. You can write a letter to the station that states your understanding of the particulars of the job. Ask the station to confirm your agreement and don't do anything until they do. If you have a current radio job, it's always prudent not to resign until you have a written offer from your new employer. Otherwise, you could find yourself without any job if the prospective employer reconsiders at the last moment. Accepting the job is the last step in a long process that you've put a lot of effort into, but it should be handled as professionally and with as much care as you've taken with every previous step.

13.9 UNIONS, AGENTS, AND CONTRACTS

If you're landing an entry-level position in broadcasting, you probably won't have any dealings with a union. Most small-market stations are not union shops; however, as you advance in your broadcast career you may become employed at a station that will require you to join a union. The primary talent union in broadcasting is **AFTRA**—the American Federation of Television and Radio Artists. **The Screen Actors Guild** (SAG) and the **National Association of Broadcast Employees and Technicians-Communications Workers of America** (NABET-CWA) are two other unions that may represent some aspects of a broadcast performer's career. You don't have to belong to a union to initially work at a union station, but you will be required to do so after a short grace period. The main advantage of belonging to a talent union is that it will establish a minimum salary level, hours and working conditions, and recording and residual fees for your job position. Disadvantages include paying union dues and being fairly restricted in

what you can and cannot do at the station because of specific job duties outlined in the union contract.

If you are a beginner in the broadcast performance area, you probably don't need an agent either (see Performance Tip 13.3). However, you may reach a time in your career when it makes sense to have one. A talent agent acts on your behalf for a percentage of your salary, so obviously, you need to be making a sizable amount to be willing to give up part of it. The agent can find you job positions, negotiate salary and benefit deals, and in general, act as a buffer between you and station management. A good agent will more than pay his or her own way by getting you better deals than you could obtain on your own or handling any hassles with management that might come up. But remember, agents only come into play at a certain level of broadcasting and many broadcast performers have had a great career without ever working with an agent.

Employment contracts usually are not a factor for entry-level employment. Most smaller stations just do not use them. Many medium- and larger-market stations do, however, and you may be asked to sign one as a condition of your employment. Most talent agreements are for one to three years and stipulate the terms of employment. While contracts usually specify the length of employment, it is not uncommon for broadcast talent to leave one station for another before their contract has expired. Most stations will allow you to do this as long as you are moving to another market. Many talent contracts have a "non-compete" clause that would prevent you from going to a station within the same market while you were still under contract. AFTRA and other talent unions fight against such clauses and they are illegal in some states. In addition, like many legal documents, talent contracts are subject to negotiation. In general, contracts are good because they specify your salary and how you will receive raises or renegotiate salary, your working hours and conditions, and how you can or cannot be dismissed from the position. Of course, you shouldn't enter into a contract without having your agent or legal representative look it over carefully.

13.10 LOSING THAT FIRST JOB: A FACT OF BROADCAST PERFORMANCE LIFE

Being in the broadcast business, especially the talent side of it, almost guarantees that at some point in your

PERFORMANCE TIP 13.3

Do You Need an Agent?

Whether you need an agent or the use of a headhunter is a personal choice and there are pros and cons to each. Talent agents are usually former news directors and other assorted news professionals who charge you to make your tape and then send it out. If they get you a job, they can take anywhere from 5% to 10% of your pay. Usually, the bigger the salary, the less they take. Personally, I'm not a big fan of agents. In the late 1990s, I had one for a while, but he did nothing for me. Every move and every contract I negotiated, I did myself.

Agents make you feel that you are their only client; and although it's a nice feeling, it's not entirely true. When I worked at the CBS station in a major market, the News Director would often set out a big box of tapes for anyone to take for personal use after he was done watching them. These were old resume tapes sent by people and agents and I noticed the same agent usually sent more than one person for a job opening. Think about it, why wouldn't they? If the news director is looking for a "blonde haired blue-eyed woman with 5 years experience," the agent will send those people who fit that description. If an agent tells you this does not happen, they are not being truthful. Every news director I know says they look at all their tapes, not just the ones sent by an agency. Leaving Reno, Nevada, I had five offers, three of them were major markets and I got them without an agent.

However, I know people who swear by agents, but they also admit, they don't want the hassle of doing the job search themselves. Do your research on these agencies and talk to as many people as you can, both with and without agents. It's never a good idea to give money before they get you a job. My recommendation is to keep your money in your pocket, and push your own tape. If you're good, you'll move on without an agent. You do not need an agent to get your first job, you just need to hustle and be willing to move to any state. Try TVJOBS.COM, it lists broadcast jobs for entry level and is perhaps the 21st century way to see what's available.

I do suggest that you send your tapes to the major broadcast headhunters, like Talent Dynamics in Dallas, Texas. These places ask you to pay a one-time processing fee, less than $100.00. In exchange, they put your tape in their "Talent Library." TV stations and news directors pay them to go and view the tapes in the library. I got my job in Reno because the news director saw my work at a headhunter agency. This is the best way to put your work out there for large groups of stations to see.

Bill McGinty is an anchor at KHQ-TV in Spokane, WA. He moved there in 2006 after working as a general assignment reporter and weekend anchor at WTSP in Tampa. He has received four Emmys, two Edward R. Murrow Awards for excellence in broadcast journalism and first place in Florida's Associated Press awards. He has covered many major events, including the space shuttle Columbia disaster and the aftermath of several hurricanes.

PERFORMANCE TIP 13.4

Losing a Broadcast Job

Nathan Tannenbaum, Host/Anchor K-DAWN Morning News

KDWN AM720 Las Vegas, NV

Like most in similar situations it's usually not a complete surprise, but that doesn't make it any more pleasant. The butterflies were churning in my stomach. My palms were clammy and I remember beads of sweat appearing here and there despite my best efforts to appear relaxed as I found myself in that uncomfortable meeting in the boss's office. And there he was, at times leaning back in his big leather chair behind the desk, at times intently leaning forward, arms crossed on the desk. The decision, he was saying, had nothing to do with my on-air performance. "Oh, good," I thought. "But you're still basically firing me, right?" I didn't say that out loud. They were simply—drum roll, please—moving in a different direction.

Of course, it had everything to do with how I was doing my job, but somehow that wasn't something on the list of terminable offenses in my contract. Although—as with most contracts that appear weighted toward the employer—they probably could have just cut me off. The variation of "It's just not working out" that I got was an option to keep working at the station, but to take another shift and train my replacement, which, with my ego firmly intact, I actually considered. It wasn't until conversations with my wife and other close friends that I decided to walk away (the station was kind enough to let me think it over for an evening—a luxury many don't get). And I had another excellent option tilting my thought process which, again, many don't: I had a contract with 10 months remaining—and they agreed to buy me out.

I had lots of friends in the building and their unanimous chorus of "I can't believe it! You're one of the best people the station's got! What are they thinking?" made me feel a little better, but it still hurt. No matter what anyone says to you in this situation, no matter how much you believe in yourself and your abilities, it's just about impossible to avoid the feeling that somehow you're a failure—and that maybe, just maybe, all those people who told you you're not cut out for broadcasting were right.

Whether you do, in fact, get out of the business; whether you're on the air across the street the next day (depending on the market you're in and contracts with non-compete clauses); or, whether you're "on the beach" for a while before getting back on the air, the best way I found to get over the feeling of rejection was simply: time. You find—sooner or later—that life most definitely isn't all about that job you thought was so great when you first got it. It may have a lot going for it, but there's another one out there for you somewhere. Someone else will see the good you have to offer and you'll have another chance to get out there and give it all you've got."

Nate has been a disc jockey, reporter, weathercaster, and anchor at radio and TV stations from Indiana to Colorado to Las Vegas, Nevada, where he was named "Best TV Weathercaster" six years in a row in the *Las Vegas Review-Journal's* annual "Best Of Las Vegas Reader's Poll." He's been married to a synchronized swimmer since 1992 and their 8-year-old son is intent on being a Major League Baseball player.

career you will lose your job. In fact, many broadcasters who've been around for a while would say you really haven't been in the business until you have been fired. Broadcast performers live a precarious life—format changes result in different talent requirements, new station owners bring in all new personnel, or ratings figures fall, leading to on-air changes. The end result is that dismissals are inevitable. Losing a job in this business seems to come with the territory and, fortunately, getting fired in broadcasting does not carry the stigma that it does in other fields. Of course, a constant track record of getting let go from station after station is not a good sign to future employers. Performance Tip 13.4 offers some insight on losing that first broadcast job, as does the rest of this section.

So if you do lose your job, what do you do? First, don't take it personally. It's not you as a human being who is being fired. It may have been how you did your job or how you presented yourself on the air, or it may have been through no fault of your own that you now find yourself unemployed. Try not to internalize it, and remember that it has happened to some of the best talent in broadcasting. Yes, it will be a shock to you. Most broadcast performers don't think they will ever leave a job in this fashion and rarely see it coming when it does. It's hard to do, but again, the initial rule of being handed a pink slip is to try not to take it personally.

Second, get ready to put together some patience with a great deal of persistence. You will need to begin a job search utilizing all the tools mentioned earlier in this chapter. Dig out your contact list. Friends and acquaintances in the business can be your best shot at landing another job in a short period of time. Check with Program Directors you know. Have you worked with any consultants? Can you touch base with other talent you've crossed paths with? Network these contacts to see if anyone has or knows of a position that would be right for you. Of course, as soon as you use your contact list, you need to update your resume and make sure you have a quality demo ready to go. The best rule of thumb here is that you should always have a current air check available. Good talent will air check themselves very frequently and will keep their best air check material ready to go at any time. If your resume and cover letter are in a computer file, updating them will be fairly easy. Your job-hunting package should be ready to send out as soon as you make the right contact.

There are two other things you should realize about being between jobs. First, you must realize that the next job may require you to relocate. The younger you are, the easier that will be, because as you put down roots in a community it becomes harder and harder to leave. However, broadcasting is a transient business and you may find that you have no choice but to move to wherever the next job is. Second, to keep your emotions in check over losing a job, try to keep as busy as possible. Job hunting will take up some of your time, but you should also look into part-time work. Perhaps there are voice-over jobs that you can pick up, maybe you can do some freelance consulting for smaller stations in your area, or maybe you can just use the time to look into other opportunities. For many in this field, broadcasting is the only business they can ever see themselves working in, and while they might be frustrated with their current situation, they love the business and can only consider getting back into it as soon as possible. For a few others, this may be the time to get out of broadcasting altogether. As a performer, you've picked up a few skills and these may now come into play as you contemplate a new career track. Here are some possible scenarios for a career switch.

Most performers have a better-than-average voice and an excellent command of the language, and they like to talk. Those are ingredients that can make a superior salesperson. It doesn't have to be radio sales; it could be almost any field. If a sales position isn't appealing, public relations is another area that broadcast performers can fit into quite nicely. If you enjoy writing and are good at it, you could be a copy writer in the ad business, or a feature writer at a trade publication. There's also the music industry to consider as a record rep or, depending on your educational background, you might consider teaching. Many broadcasters, with a bachelor's degree and some solid experience, can teach in the broadcast field at the community college level. You may even consider going back to school and getting an advanced degree, which could open even more teaching possibilities. Of course, if you're really considering a new career path, the best time to prepare new required skills would be while you still have a job. That could make the transition from broadcasting to a new field much smoother and make you as a job seeker seem a whole lot less desperate to land that new job.

PERFORMANCE TIP 13.5

One person's experience with a job search

Brittany Soeder

WCJB, Gainesville, FL

A Beginner's Job Search

"A long wait is worth doing something you love for the rest of your life." Soeder

This quote I repeated in my head daily... from May 2007 until April 1st 2008—the day I signed a 2-year contract for the job of a lifetime!

Looking back … my one-year wait went by quickly. Growing up as a competitive figure skater, I learned that hard work and patience is key. While performing and being interviewed for skating, I made the decision to someday be a reporter.

I also loved the excitement of cheerleading for my high school, university, and Cleveland Indians teams. One night as I was cheering on the Indians, we went into a suite and there sat Stefani "Sissy" Schaefer, one of Cleveland's best anchors. We talked, got along great and she invited me to see what she does at WEWS, Newschannel 5, the ABC affiliate in Cleveland.

After visiting her on set and seeing the positive impact she had, I was "hooked" and wanted to be in the business. Sissy began teaching me how to succeed in one of the hardest businesses. One of her basic rules was simply treat others how you want to be treated.

I landed my first internship at WEWS and loved every minute of it. I was a news intern, but did more than your average intern. I never wanted to leave work! I went out with reporters daily and studied their every move. When the first semester ended, I begged my boss to keep me for the next semester and it worked! That next half of the year was when I really gained my experience. My first big story, interviewing Jerry Springer for the Dancing with the Stars tour. I showed up with my photog, went backstage with all of the stars of the tour and realized that I was on my way! As I stood next to the BBC reporters and ABC reporters in awe...I remembered. I had to interview Jerry Springer! They finished their interviews and then it was me, the intern interviewing him, in front of internationally known reporters. I got through it and ended up doing a good job. After that I was set to interview anyone! Some of my following stories involved everything from crime scenes to interviewing LeBron James. I couldn't wait to start. I soon learned that it would take a lot longer than expected. The resume tape was done and graduation was around the corner, I felt invincible...I will start right after school reporting on huge stories ... I was so wrong!

After sending out at least 40 tapes, I got my first bite! My first audition was at a news station in Erie, PA. I left thinking *I definitely got that job*. But, I needed more experience and didn't get the job. I was devastated, but had other things lined up. I then auditioned in Lima, OH...still nothing. My biggest audition was when my former colleagues at WEWS offered me a try for the traffic reporter job. I couldn't help but think WOW this is it! As morning anchor Paul Kiska led my audition, I had nothing but good feelings about it! They wanted me to have, yet again, more experience. Paul urged me to try for a smaller market.

I send out 10 more tapes, made a ton of follow up calls and then finally got another bite! In the beginning of March 2008, Brett Buell called me from the Gainesville, Florida, station WCJB TV20. After several phone interviews he put out the offer and I accepted! I was excited, but I was nervous. I had grown up in Cleveland my whole life, even going only 20 minutes away for college! I cried, celebrated, and worried for the next month as I left the only place I knew. I knew it was for the best, but there were so many questions.

When I arrived in Gainesville, everything fell right into place. I had never visited the city before moving down and did practically everything for the move via phone and internet. The staff welcomed me, even letting me stay with some of them for a month until my place was ready! It took a little time to get into the swing of things, but then I was sent on my first big story.

My news director, Brett, rode along with me to one of the biggest stories our area had seen in a long time. A nation-wide Amber Alert went out for a 15-year old from Putnam County, Florida. There was also a brutal murder of an innocent old man in the same area. The two ended up being tied together. It turned out the 15-year-old had taken off with her 22-year-old boyfriend after killing the old man for his car. They were both wanted for first-degree murder, and it was my story! Another great story required me to wear a bulletproof vest! I got up early and rode along with one of the Sheriff's lieutenants nabbing criminals that had active warrants out for their arrest. The stories keep coming, and I am ready for whatever comes next.

13.11 CONCLUSIONS

Obtaining a performing job in broadcasting is not an easy task. There are many talented competitors out there who will want the same job you do. However, you should not give up what you want to do because of this. Use the tips and techniques presented in this chapter to put together job-seeking materials that clearly show your skills and achievements and are polished and well-packaged. Such materials can greatly increase your chances of landing that entry-level job or advancing you to a better position in the broadcast performance area. Remember, if you never try for the job you want, you'll never know if you could have gotten it. If you get turned down for the job you want, find another job you like and keep trying.

Self-Study

■ QUESTIONS

1. When putting together a modern resume, which type of information is most likely not included?
   a) personal information
   b) job objective
   c) work experience
   d) educational background

2. Which of the following is least likely to be a characteristic of an entry-level job in the broadcast performance area?
   a) modest pay
   b) small-market job position
   c) odd working hours
   d) secure job position

3. The best way to handle references on a resume is to simply put down that "references are available upon request."
   a) true
   b) false

4. Since you are going into the media, a photograph should always be included as part of your resume.
   a) true
   b) false

5. When responding to a "blind" help-wanted ad, which greeting in your cover letter would be the best choice?
   a) Dear Sir:
   b) Hello,
   c) Dear Program Director:
   d) To Whom It May Concern:

6. Which technique should you follow when producing an audition recording for a radio DJ position?
   a) "cherry pick" only your best breaks
   b) begin with a newscast to show you can read more than liner cards
   c) send out your demo as inexpensively as possible because you'll be sending out a lot of them
   d) send out a 3- to 5-minute telescoped version of an actual on-air performance

7. All of the following are good techniques for job interviewing except which one?
   a) practice beforehand answering questions that might be asked of you during the interview
   b) dress flamboyantly because you will be going into show business and you want to make a flashy first impression
   c) maintain good eye contact throughout the interview
   d) send a letter after the interview to thank the interviewer for talking with you and considering you for the position

8. The primary talent union for radio and television performers is AFTER—the American Federation for Television, Entertainment, and Radio.
   a) true
   b) false

9. One reality of working in the broadcast performance field is the inevitability of losing a job, often related to changes in ownership or format rather than incompetent talent. Which of the following statements about losing a broadcast job is true?
   a) Now that you have some experience, it will be relatively easy to find another broadcast position.
   b) If you have a contract with a non-compete clause, you will not be able to take another broadcast job until the contract expires.
   c) It's important to try not to take the firing personally and keep your emotions in check as you look for another job.
   d) It's important not to lose time in a job search, so begin sending out applications even if you use an old resume and demo for a while.
10. All of the following are good sources for a contact list except _____.
    a) the Internet
    b) guest speakers from your classes in college
    c) trade publications
    d) an agent
11. Campus experiences, such as internships and work with campus media, should be omitted from the work experience section of your resume because they are not real work that you were being paid to perform.
    a) true
    b) false
12. When preparing an audition recording for television, you should _____.
    a) save your best work for the end of the demo
    b) make the demo no longer than 10 minutes
    c) include samples of many different types of your work, like news, interviews, sports, weather, and commercials
    d) include complete programs
13. All of the following are common problems with resumes except _____.
    a) resumes that are too long
    b) resumes that contain distortions
    c) resumes that are too short
    d) resumes that contain misspellings
14. The first item put on a demo recording for television would be _____
    a) color bars and tone
    b) an on-camera bio
    c) a montage of your best work
    d) an identification slate
15. If you are given a verbal job offer for an entry-level position, you should immediately accept it to show your interest in the job.
    a) true
    b) false
16. Which type of information is unique to an electronic resume designed for computer scanning?
    a) work experience
    b) keyword summary
    c) educational background
    d) personal information
17. On-air performers who have lost a job sometimes consider a career change, and because of skills they've gained are well suited to some job fields. In which area would a broadcast performer be least likely to be successful without much further education?
    a) salesperson
    b) trade publication writer
    c) teacher
    d) financial planner

18. Non-compete clauses that prevent broadcast performers from working in the same market for a number of months after they have been fired from or resigned from a job are illegal.

   a) true

   b) false

19. It's possible, in a job interview, that you'll be asked, "What are your salary requirements?" What is the best response?

   a) give a figure and make it clear you can't work for less

   b) give a high figure and assume you will be offered less

   c) first ask if there is a salary range for the position and see if your minimum figure falls within it

   d) say you'll take anything because you just want the job

20. Don't expect audition materials for broadcast performance jobs to be mailed back to you unless you include a self-addressed envelope with return postage.

   a) true

   b) false

■ ANSWERS

If You Answered A:

1a. Wrong. A resume will always include personal data, like your name, address, e-mail, and phone number. (Reread 13.2.)

2a. No. This is true as most entry-level positions in broadcasting pay modest starting salaries. (Reread 13.1.)

3a. No. While noting "references are available" is an option for adding references to a resume, it isn't necessarily the best. (Reread 13.2.)

4a. No. Photographs should be considered optional. If you're applying for a radio job, they're not really relevant. In any case, you should remember a photo can help or hinder your chances of getting a job. (Reread 13.2.)

5a. No. Many would find a "Dear Sir" greeting to be sexist. (Reread 13.4.)

6a. No. This "sampler" approach really isn't representative of your typical work and most program directors want to hear consecutive breaks, not "best of" breaks. (Reread 13.5.)

7a. Wrong. In preparing for an interview, you should always anticipate what questions may be asked of you and how you would respond to them. (Reread 13.7.)

8a. No. The main talent union for radio and television is AFTRA, not AFTER. (Reread 13.9.)

9a. Wrong. No matter how much experience you have, finding a job in broadcasting is never easy and will require hard work, patience, and persistence. (Reread 13.10.)

10a. No. Many state broadcast associations have web sites that list job openings, and other broadcast resource sites could provide you with information about a performance job position. (Reread 13.6.)

11a. No. Any broadcast experience on campus is important to include, especially if you are just beginning your career. (Reread 13.2.)

12a. Wrong. The ends of audition recordings are often never seen. Put your best work first, as Program Directors usually stop viewing within less than a minute if they don't see something that catches their attention. (Reread 13.5.)

13a. Resumes that are too long are a common problem. Most resumes should be one page long. (Reread 13.2.)

14a. No. Most Program Directors would prefer color bars and tone left off audition recording. (Reread 13.5.)

15a. No. It's better practice to ask for a written offer letter or you can write an understanding of the offer and ask them to confirm it. (Reread 13.8.)

16a. No. A listing of your employment history is usually a part of all types of resumes. (Reread 13.2 and review Figure 13.3.)

17a. Broadcast performers are usually gifted talkers with an excellent ability to ad-lib and can make good sales people. (Reread 13.10.)

18a. No. While some states have banned non-compete clauses and talent unions fight against them, they are still used in some broadcast employment situations. (Reread 13.9.)

19a. No. Once you provide a minimum figure you'll not get any more than that. (Reread 13.8.)

20a. Correct. Audition demos are not normally returned and this is usually noted in job announcements.

If You Answered B:

1b. Correct. On a modern resume, the job objective has been replaced by a qualifications summary.

2b. No. Most entry-level jobs are in smaller markets, so this is true. (Reread 13.1.)

3b. Yes. This is a false statement because noting "references are available" isn't necessarily the best option for adding references to your resume. Just list your reference names and contact information on a separate sheet of paper that matches your resume; then you can provide it at any time you're asked for them.

4b. Yes. This is a false statement because photos are optional and can help or hinder your chance of getting a job. They may be required for a television position, but rarely for radio jobs.

5b. The "Hello" greeting isn't a bad second choice, but could be a little too informal, and there is a better choice. (Reread 13.4.)

6b. Not for a DJ position. If you do include a short newscast, put it after your song introductions and ad-lib material. (Reread 13.5.)

7b. Correct. Dress neatly and conservatively for a job interview.

8b. This is a false statement since the union is AFTRA—the American Federation of Television and Radio Artists.

9b. No. A non-compete clause will not come into play if you are fired from a position. If you leave on your own, such a clause may prevent you from working in that particular market for a specific period of time, but you can always find a job in another market or wait out the time period. (Reread 13.10.)

10b. No. Guest speakers are often interested in helping new talent and may know of a job position that is available. (Reread 13.6.)

11b. Yes. This is a false statement. You should include whatever work experience you've gained in school to your best advantage. Internships and college media positions may not carry the same weight as an actual job, but they are important and may be the only experience an entry-level job seeker has.

12b. Correct. Audition demos, both for radio and television, need to be short and concise.

13b. Resumes that contain distortions are a common problem. Your resume must be truthful and cannot contain exaggerations or lies. (Reread 13.2.)

14b. No. It is not good practice to put either on-camera or voice-over biographies on an audition recording. (Reread 13.5.)

15b. Yes. This is a false statement because it's better to get something in writing. If the station won't send a written offer, be cautious about taking the job.

16b. Yes. A listing of keywords associated with your qualifications and the job position will assure that your resume is properly scanned and selected.

17b. Broadcast performers often have strong writing skills with an understanding of the industry and can make good writers for trade publications or advertising agencies. (Reread 13.10.)

18b. This statement is false since such non-compete clauses are still used in some broadcast employment situations.

19b. No. If your figure is out of the question, you may not be considered further for the position. (Reread 13.8.)

20b. Wrong. This is a true statement. (Reread 13.5.)

If You Answered C:

1c. Wrong. A resume will always include some type of work experience; in fact, it is often the most important section of your resume. (Reread 13.2.)

2c. No. This is true; as a beginning performer, you can be sure you will work the odd hours. (Reread 13.1.)

5c. Yes. If you don't have a name to respond to, at least address your cover letter to the appropriate position, such as "Dear Program Director."

6c. You may well send out a lot of demos, but avoid the absolutely least expensive route as it may not convey the image about you or your work that you're trying to. (Reread 13.5.)

7c. Wrong. Good eye contact should occur during an interview. (Reread 13.7.)

9c. Correct. Many broadcast professionals consider firings a part of paying your dues in the business. Don't take it personally, begin a new job search, and consider part-time work to keep busy or even a job in another field.

10c. No. Many trade publications list job positions that are available and can be an important addition to your contact list. (Reread 13.6.)

12c. Wrong. Audition demos should be made for the specific performance position you are applying for and should show your best work for that position. (Reread 13.5.)

13c. This is the correct answer. Rarely is a short resume a problem.

14c. No. While these are often included early in an audition recording, sometimes even first, there is a better answer. (Reread 13.4.)

16c. No. A listing of your educational background is usually a part of all types of resumes. (Reread 13.2 and review Figure 13.3.)

17c. Broadcast performers often have an excellent understanding of the industry and can make good teachers in this area. Of course, a college degree is usually required. (Reread 13.10.)

19c. Yes. The best approach is usually to try to get a salary range for the position.

If You Answered D:

1d. Wrong. A resume will always include your educational background. (Reread 13.2.)

2d. Yes. Broadcasting positions, especially performance ones, are not stable. There are many reasons why performers lose jobs, making this choice least likely to be true.

5d. No. A " To Whom It May Concern" greeting gives the impression that you're just mass mailing your materials all over the country. (Reread 13.4.)

6d. Yes. An audio audition recording should be a 3- to 5-minute telescoped version of an actual on-air performance.

7d. Wrong. A thank you letter after a job interview is a business courtesy. (Reread 13.6.)

9d. Wrong. No matter what the circumstances of a job search, your resume, audition demo, and other materials must be up-to-date. (Reread 13.10.)

10d. This is the correct answer. Agents are generally useful only for well-established talent. They will charge fees that can be unreasonable for new entries into the broadcast job market.

12d. Wrong. Many recordings will be viewed for a job position and there is no time to view complete programs. Edit your audition demo to include your best work in a short, concise presentation. (Reread 13.5.)

13d. Resumes that contain misspellings are a common problem. Resumes should not contain errors, typos, or misspellings. (Reread 13.2.)

14d. Yes. Put a simple graphic slate with your name, address, and phone number as the first item on your audition demo.

16d. No. Personal information, such as your address, phone, and e-mail is usually a part of all types of resumes. (Reread 13.2 and review Figure 13.3.)

17d. Of these choices, financial planning probably requires additional skills that an on-air performer has not gained in his or her broadcast career; therefore, this is the least likely area for success.

19d. No. Working for "anything" is usually not a realistic approach. (Reread 13.8.)

Projects

■ PROJECT 1

Prepare your professional resume.

Purpose
To learn how to put together a resume for broadcast performance work.

Notes

1. Remember that there is no standard form for putting together a resume; however, review Section 13.2 of this chapter to get some idea of what information should be included.
2. Your resume must be free from misspellings, typos, erasures, or any other fault that will detract from the actual content.
3. Create a layout that is neat and easy to read. Review Figures 13.1 and 13.2 to see sample resumes.
4. In most cases, your resume should be limited to a single page; use standard margins of one inch on the top, bottom, and sides.

How to Do the Project

1. Type a heading for your resume that includes your name, address, phone number, and e-mail. It should be centered on the page.
2. Below your heading, create a "qualifications summary." Use bullet points to highlight your qualifications and design a neat, easy-to-read section. Use the job announcement in Figure 13.7 to help focus your qualifications.
3. Now create an "Educational Background" section. List your most recent schooling first. Remember, if you're just getting out of college, do not include high school information. Give dates, degrees earned, honors, and other highlights of your academic achievements.
4. "Work Experience" should be your next section. Under this title, list your various jobs, again in reverse chronological order. Remember to include internships and positions at campus media outlets. Give dates and your job responsibilities using "action words" to explain what you did at each job.
5. On a separate sheet of paper list three references. Give name, title, business address, e-mail, and telephone number for each person. Make sure you have talked to your references and you know they can speak about your qualifications, attitude, and skills and have agreed to do so.
6. You should now have a completed one-page resume plus a one-page reference sheet. Remember, it should be mistake-free and presented with a neat, easy-to-read layout.
7. If you're using a word processor, make sure you save a copy of both documents for future use and easy updating.

■ PROJECT 2

Write a cover letter.

Purpose
To learn how to put together a cover letter to be included with a resume for broadcast performance work.

Notes
1. Remember that there is no standard form for putting together a cover letter; however, review Section 13.4 and Figure 13.4 to get some idea of what information should be included.
2. Your cover letter must be free from misspellings, typos, erasures, or any other fault that will detract from the actual content.
3. Use a typical business-letter layout that is neat and easy to read.
4. Your cover letter should be limited to a single page; use standard margins of one inch at the top, bottom, and sides.

How to Do the Project
1. Use the job position announcement in Figure 13.7 to respond to with your cover letter.
2. Personalize the letter by responding to the name given in the " help wanted" ad.
3. In the first paragraph, reference the job as it is described in the ad and express your interest in it. Assume the ad was posted on the R&R website (radioandrecords.com) "job opportunities" section.
4. Note any special qualifications you have for this position in the second paragraph. Remember to mention at the end of this paragraph that you've enclosed a resume and demo recording.
5. The third paragraph is optional, but if there is something unique about this position and you would like to work at this particular station, note it here.
6. The final paragraph should reiterate your interest in the position and include thanks for being considered for the job. It should be worded so that you are essentially asking for an interview.
7. Remember that your cover letter should complement your resume and not simply provide duplicate information.
8. If you're using a word processor, make sure you save a copy of your cover letter as a guide for others you will write, even though each will need to be personalized and updated.

HELP WANTED PROGRAMMING

Seeking announcer for overnights at new FM station in central Ohio. Previous broadcast experience is helpful, but not required. Must be comfortable with Classic Rock format, have working knowledge of studio operations, and demonstrate good production skills. Digital skills a plus. College degree preferred. Excellent living and working environment. We are looking for someone who wants to grow and be part of a winning team. Advancement within our organization is possible. Send resume and demo to: Paul Jones, Operations Director, WRNO Radio, The Diamond Broadcast Group, P.O. Box 41006, Columbus, OH 43215. The Diamond Broadcast Group is an equal opportunity employer and encourages women and minorities to apply.

FIGURE 13.7 Job announcement for a radio position.

■ PROJECT 3

Record an audition for radio.

Purpose
To learn how to make an air check that will become part of your job-seeking materials.

Notes
1. Review Section 13.5 and Audio Track 13.1 to get some idea of what should be included in your audition recording.
2. If possible, your air check should be an edited-down or telescoped sample of actual on-air work. However, you may have to simulate this in a production studio.
3. Try to put your best work at the beginning of the recording. If it's something unique, it will be memorable. Most potential employers won't continue to listen unless they hear something they like at the beginning.
4. The audio for this project should be recorded onto a CD-R.

How to Do the Project
1. Use the job position announcement in Figure 13.7 to build your audition tape around.
2. Plan what you intend to include in your tape. Remember, if it's an actual scoping of an on-air program, you don't necessarily want to start with the first break. Later breaks are usually stronger, so choose a later one to start with and then continue from that point.
3. If you are simulating a performance in the production studio, plan the order of your tape to make it sound as much as possible like a continuous radio show.
4. The actual content should be unique in order to highlight your talents. However, it should include about a half-dozen breaks (song introductions and ad-lib material), followed by some examples of your production work, ending with a short newscast.
5. After you've recorded and edited your demo, listen to it carefully. If it doesn't present good broadcast performance skills, redo it.
6. Make a dub of your audition recording and keep your master in a safe place.

■ PROJECT 4

Prepare an electronic resume.

Purpose
To learn how to put together a broadcast performance resume suitable for electronic delivery or posting on a website.

Notes
1. You might want to complete Project 1 before attempting this project, so that you have a regular resume to work from.
2. Remember that there is no standard form for putting together an electronic resume; however, review Section 13.3 of this chapter to get some ideas of what information should be included.
3. Save your document in a plain-text format (ASCII or RTF) so that your resume can be accurately recognized by any computer.

4. Create a layout that is neat and easy to read; remember to include a keyword summary. Review Figure 13.3 to see a sample resume.

5. Your resume should be limited to a single page; keep line length to less than 65 characters so there are no word-wrap problems.

6. Your resume must be free from any errors or faults that will detract from the actual content.

How to Do the Project

1. Type a heading for your resume that includes your name, address, phone number, and e-mail.

2. Include a keyword summary after the heading.

3. Type "Education" at the left margin. List your most recent schooling first. Remember, if you're just getting out of college, do not include high school information. Use bullet points to give dates, degrees earned, honors, and other highlights of your academic achievements.

4. Type "Experience" at the left margin. Under this title, list your various jobs, again in reverse chronological order. Remember to include internships and positions at campus media outlets. Give dates and your job responsibilities using "action words" to explain what you did at each job.

5. You should now have a completed one-page resume. Remember, it should be mistake-free and presented with a neat, easy-to-read layout. Also remember not to use boldface, italic, or underlining in this electronic version of your resume, as the plain-text format will not support it. Instead, you may want to use all caps for your headings.

6. If you're using a word processor, make sure you save a copy of your resume for future use and easy updating.

■ PROJECT 5

Record an audition for television.

Purpose
To learn how to make an audition tape for a broadcast performance job which will be part of your job-seeking materials.

Notes

1. Review Section 13.5 and Video Clip 13.1 to get some idea of what should be included in your audition tape.

2. If possible, your air check should be an edited-down or telescoped sample of actual on-air work. However, you may have to simulate some of this in a TV studio.

3. Try to put your best work at the beginning of the tape. If it's something unique, it will be memorable. Most potential employers won't continue to view your tape unless they see something they like at the beginning.

4. This project should be recorded onto a DVD or VHS tape.

How to Do the Project

1. Use the job position announcement in Figure 13.8 to build your audition tape around.

2. Plan what you intend to include in your tape, but begin the tape with a simple graphic that includes your name, address, phone, and e-mail information.

3. Next, you might consider putting on a short montage of clips showing you reporting various stories.

4. The actual content should be unique in order to highlight your talents and to address the qualities the employer is looking for. However, think it terms of three items, perhaps a stand-up news report, a feature piece, and a short newscast with you at the anchor desk.

5. After you've recorded and edited your demo, view it critically. If it doesn't present good broadcast performance skills, redo it.

6. Make a dub of your audition recording and keep your master in a safe place.

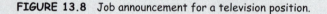

NEWS REPORTER WANTED

WVDK-TV, the FOX owned station in the Raleigh-Durham, North Carolina, market, has an immediate opening for a News Reporter. Applicants should have experience in general assignment reporting, including live ENG and satellite work, and you must be able to develop good, hard news stories as well as respond well to breaking and spot news. The ability to do features is important as well, although this is primarily a hard news position. Outstanding writing skills are required, as well as the ability to make good use of graphics and production equipment. Interested applicants should send resumes and non-returnable recordings to: Michael Striker, News Director, WVDK-TV, 411 East Lincoln Avenue, Durham, NC 27701. No telephone calls. EOE.

FIGURE 13.8 Job announcement for a television position.

APPENDIX

NEWS PRACTICE COPY

WORLD NEWS

BAGHDAD (AP) _ An Iraqi police chief and two other officers touring the site of a previous blast have been killed by a suicide bomber in Mosul.

The U.S. military says the bomber was wearing an explosives vest under an Iraqi police uniform.

An American soldier is among those who were wounded.

A police spokesman says gunman set up an ambush at the site, then as the police chief's car tried to speed away, the bomber moved in and blew himself up.

Authorities today also raised the death toll from yesterday's blast in Mosul to at least 34, with 224 others wounded.

The explosion collapsed a three-story apartment building and ravaged adjacent houses just minutes after Iraqi soldiers arrived to investigate tips about a weapons cache.

WASHINGTON (AP) _ Al-Qaida is calling for unity among Islamic militants worldwide.

A U.S. intelligence officials says the terror group has posted a new Web video urging Islamic scholars to lend their support to the group's efforts. The U.S. official says the 28-minute message is an effort to counter scholars who've been criticizing the terror group's violence as being at odds with the religion's teachings.

The video says militant groups should fight only for Islamic causes and avoid splitting into factions along national or political lines.

The U.S. official says it was posted on a well-known jihadist Web site yesterday and is not seen as a specific threat.

TOKYO (AP) _ Yesterday's stunning comeback on Wall Street has heartened investors somewhat in Asia today but there are still lingering concerns about the health of the U.S. economy.

A bellweather Hong Kong index lost value today after a seesaw ride. But stocks finished up in Japan, South Korea, Australia and the Philippines.

In roller-coaster trading Wednesday, the Dow Jones industrial average slipped as much as 323 points before skyrocketing to close up nearly 300 points for the day. The single-day turnaround is the Dow's largest in more than five years.

The American stock market bounce came a day after a major interest-rate cut by the U.S. central bank in an effort to boost the economy.

RAFAH, Egypt (AP) _ Egypt is telling the U.S. that it expects the massive exodus of Palestinians from Gaza to end today, but an American official says Egypt hasn't said exactly when the flow will be cut off.

Egyptian riot police have been directing traffic away from a Gaza border fence that was smashed yesterday by Palestinian militants. Thousands of Palestinians have continued to stream through it into Egypt to buy food, fuel cigarettes and other items that have been scarce in Gaza since Israel sealed off its border last week.

Egyptian cabbies have converged on the border region to give Palestinians rides to nearby towns to shop.

One 25-year-old Gazan says the opening will allow him to marry his 17-year-old fiancee next week because they've been able to buy the household items they need.

Israel cut off Gaza as a response to rocket attacks from Palestinian militants. It's concerned that militants and weapons could be flowing in through the wrecked border fence.

KABUL, Afghanistan (AP) _ A provincial official says at least ten people have been killed during a U.S.-led military operation in central Afghanistan.

The dead are said to include eight police officers and two villagers. Local police blame airstrikes, which they say destroyed several houses. An Afghan official says the operation also involved ground troops but there's been no coalition comment on the raid.

Because of troop shortages, U.S. and NATO forces have relied heavily on airpower in their fight with the Taliban and al-Qaida. Afghanistan's government has repeatedly protested civilian losses, and Allied commanders have accused militants of using civilians as shields.

BAGHDAD (AP) _ Angelina Jolie is in Baghdad on a mission to help Iraqi refugees.

Jolie is a U.N. goodwill ambassador. She says more needs to be done to help more than 2 million Iraqis who've had to leave their homes because of the violence.

She says the current decline in violence is a perfect time for Iraqis to return home, but she told CNN, so far, "there seems to be just a lot of talk."

Jolie spoke about the situation with the top U.S. commander in Iraq. She also has plans to meet with Iraq's prime minister and migration officials. She also took time to hang out with U.S. troops during lunch.

GENEVA (AP) _ The World Trade Organization has ruled against the European Union's import tariff for bananas, news that could be very position for Cincinnati-based Chiquita Brands.

One Wall Street analyst says the tariff costs Chiquita $1 per share each year. So, the verdict will be followed closely by the fruit company, whose shares climbed 9.2 percent in one day last year on early reports that the EU would lose a similar case.

The confidential decision was distributed earlier this week to the parties and confirmed today by trade officials.

It could open the door to millions of dollars in U.S. commercial sanctions if the tariff stays in place. The EU can still appeal.

BANGKOK, Thailand (AP) _ Oil prices in Asia rose today, adding to a rebound that started overnight as a more stable stock market calmed investors fears about the health of the U.S. economy. Light, sweet crude for March delivery rose 41 cents

to $88.52 a barrel in electronic trading on the New York Mercantile Exchange by midday in Singapore.

ANKARA, Turkey (AP) _ Turkish lawmakers have voted to approve a constitutional amendment allowing female students to enter universities wearing Islamic head scarves, a move that many secular

Turks view as an attempt to impose religion on their daily lives.

Lawmakers voted 401-110 in a preliminary vote in favor of the government's proposed amendment to the secular constitution. The government has defended its plan as a reform needed to give its citizens religious liberty and bring Turkey in line with European Union human rights guidelines.

The vast majority of Turkey's 70 million people are Muslim, but they are divided over the role of Islam in politics and daily life.

Secularists regard the head covering as a political statement and fear that lifting the ban at universities would pressure all female students to cover themselves up.

JERUSALEM (AP) _ The military says Palestinian militants launched nearly 20 rockets at Israel today after Israel yesterday cut some electricity to the Gaza Strip to try to stop such attacks.

Israel says it will continue to gradually scale back electricity to the territory until its Hamas rulers stop the rocket fire. An Israeli official says Hamas has to decide if it wants to invest in rockets with which to attack Isarel or if it wants electricity from Israel.

Israel's power cutback comes on top of its reduction of fuel supplies to the territory last month.

Human rights groups says the Israeli actions harm innocent civilians. Israel says cutting electricity and fuel is more humane than a large military operation to stop the militant rocket attacks. It says that would cause scores of civilian casualties.

ISLAMABAD, Pakistan (AP) _ Scotland Yard says Pakistani opposition leader Benazir Bhutto died as a result of a suicide bomb blast, not a gunshot.

The findings in the report released today support the Pakistani government's version of the events.

Bhutto's Pakistan People's Party immediately rejected the British conclusion and repeated its demand for a U.N. investigation.

The party says Bhutto was shot and suspects a government cover-up because Bhutto had accused political allies of President Pervez Musharraf of plotting to kill her.

The British probe also found that a single attacker both fired the shots at Bhutto and detonated the blast by blowing himself up moments later.

The death of the former prime minister sparked violent unrest across the country and forced a six-week delay in parliamentary elections, now set for February 18th.

NATIONAL NEWS

WASHINGTON (AP) _ A new study says the wide-spread use of ethanol instead of gasoline could actually increase greenhouse gas emissions.

Researchers say past studies showing the benefits of using ethanol to combat climate change didn't take into account almost certain changes in land use.

The study says farmers under economic pressure to produce biofuels will increasingly plow up more land and release much of the carbon that would have been stored in plants and soils.

And they say globally, more grasslands and forests will be converted to growing crops to replace grains lost when U.S. farmers convert land to biofuels.

Still, a group representing ethanol producers says the researchers' view of land-use changes is "simplistic" and that the study "fails to put the issue in context."

The study appears in Science magazine.

BOSTON (AP) _ There might be some scientific evidence to back up the idea of "retail therapy." A new study shows that people's spending judgment goes out the window when they're feeling down – and especially if they're a little self-absorbed.

In the study, participants who watched a sad clip about a boy's mentor dying offered to pay nearly four times as much for a bottle of water than a group that watched a not-so-sad video – about the Great Barrier Reef.

The research found that sad people were more willing to spend freely when their sadness led them to focus more on themselves. Researchers say those people were willing to pay more – presumably to feel better about themselves. And personal shoppers say they see the same thing – clients who stray from their budgets when they're feeling blue.

The study appears in the journal Psychological Science.

BURLINGTON, Vt. (AP) _ A question to consider. Just how far can authorities go when it comes to searching computers, PDA's and other devices when people cross a border? Check out the case of Sebastien Boucher, who was stopped when he tried to cross the U.S.-Canadian border. Agents who inspected his laptop say they found files that contained child pornography. But when they tried to check out the images after his arrest, they couldn't because the images were shielded by a password-protected encryption program.

The government now wants Boucher to give up the password. But if he does so, it could violate his Fifth Amendment right against self-incrimination. So far, the law is on Boucher's side. One federal judge has ruled that forcing the man to give up the password would be unconstitutional. But the government has appealed the ruling.

MILWAUKEE (AP) _ A lot of people do their banking online. But in many cases, you still have to show up at the branch or ATM when you need to deposit a check. But that may be about to change with some new technology provided through the CheckFree Corporation. The online banking service provider is out with something called Remote Deposit Capture. It's a technology that lets people scan checks through their home computers – and deposit them electronically.

The technology isn't new, it's been around for years. But until now, it has been used mainly by businesses. CheckFree said the service is available starting this week for any consumers who bank online, as long as their banks offer the ability to scan checks into the system. To use it, customers will need a scanner, a computer and an Internet connection. To "deposit" a check, users can go to their banking site, enter the amount of the check, scan both sides, do a quick review and submit it to the bank.

DETROIT (AP) _ Chrysler plans to significantly reduce its product lineup and number of dealerships as the automaker rolls out a new corporate initiative.

A Houston Chrysler-Jeep dealer says the company has told dealers it could cut its number of models by as much as half and reduce the number of dealerships selling its cars by as much as a third. It's part of an effort to boost efficiency. A Chrysler spokeswoman declined to comment. But the company says in a statement that it plans to align Jeep and Dodge product offerings under one roof.

The company says it's made no final decisions on dealerships or products. Chrysler is restructuring after a majority stake in the automaker was sold last summer to private equity firm Cerberus Capital Management.

PHILADELPHIA (AP) _ Drug maker Merck will pay $671 million to settle claims that it overcharged the government and improperly marketed drugs to doctors.

The case involves the company's two biggest drugs – the painkiller Vioxx and the cholesterol drug Zocor. Prosecutors say Merck hid deep discounts that it gave to hospitals and reported higher prices to the government, effectively charging the Medicaid program more for the drugs. Prosecutors also say Merck gave money and perks to doctors and other health-care professionals to entice them to prescribe the drugs.

Merck says the settlement doesn't mean that it's admitting any liability or wrongdoing. The drug maker says it believes its pricing, sales and marketing policies complied with all regulations.

TINLEY PARK, Ill. (AP) _ The company that owns the suburban
Chicago store where a gunman killed five women says it's offered to pay for the victims' funerals.

A spokeswoman for the Lane Bryant clothing store where the killings occurred in Tinley Park, Ill., couldn't immediately say if all the families have accepted that offer. Gayle Coolick also says the company has set up a memorial fund to provide additional financial aide to the relatives.

Meanwhile, police say their manhunt for the suspect continues. They've received more than 170 tips to a special hot line set up in the case. They add that they have more the 50 detectives on the case who've logged more than 2,000 hours on the investigation. Lane Bryant is part of the Pennsylvania-based Charming Shoppes Inc.

PITTSBURGH (AP) _ Pittsburgh is offering money to bring a Paris-like atmosphere to its downtown streets.

Using a $1 million grant from the nonprofit Colcom Foundation, the city will match funds spent by business owners who make improvements that add vibrancy to the area. The improvements could be anything from installing glass facades and outdoor seating to putting awnings or flower displays outside.

There will also be $3.5 million available to business owners who turn unused or underused upper floors into apartments.

Pittsburgh Downtown Partnership President and CEO Mike Edwards says the goal is to create a more dynamic space in the business district.

LAFAYETTE, Tenn. (AP) _ Residents in five states ravaged by tornadoes this week are still reeling. Amid widespread damage and 59 deaths, they're facing problems like looting and continued power outages. And some are still looking for missing family or friends.

The mayor of Lafayette, Tennessee, says restoring power is his number-one priority and utility workers from other areas are being called in to help.

President Bush travels to Lafayette today to assess the damage and try to offer comfort in person. He says federal aid is on the way and he's asked Americans to pray for the storm's victims.

In Atkins, Arkansas, there will be a funeral today for one family killed in the storm. A church that normally sees around 100 parishioners during a typical service is setting up television sets in the church gym for what's expected to be an overflow crowd.

KENNEDY SPACE CENTER (AP) _ The shuttle Atlantis astronauts are awake for their first full day in space. NASA woke them up with Peter Garbriel's "The Book of Love." It was dedicated to French Air Force General Leopold Eyharts (AY'-ahrts) who will stay aboard the international space station for about a month. Eyharts thanked his wife and family in English and French saying he knows yesterday was a hard day for them and he's grateful for their support.

The shuttle is carrying Europe's 2 billion dollar Columbus laboratory after two months of technical delays. It's scheduled to arrive tomorrow. European space officials both cheered and cried yesterday when Atlantis successfully lifted off from Florida, overcoming earlier fuel gauge trouble, and predictions that bad weather might delay the launch.

Japan plans to send a lab called Hope, beginning in March. It's so big, it'll take three shuttle trips to get it there. NASA faces a year 2010 deadline for completing the building of the orbiting space station and of retiring the shuttles.

PORT WENTWORTH, Ga. (AP) _ The search goes on today for six people missing after an explosion and fire at a sugar refinery in the Savannah suburb of Port Wentworth that left dozens injured. Officials have not determined what caused yesterday's explosion but say they suspect sugar dust, which can be volatile. Witnesses described widespread damage.

Savannah-Chatham County Police Chief Michael Berkow says there were 95 to 100 people believed to be working in the area of the explosion and firefighters are still battling the blaze this morning. Berkow said at least 40 people were taken to area hospitals, and some of them were airlifted to a burn center in Augusta, 130 miles up the Savannah River.

WASHINGTON (AP) _ People's confidence in the economy continues to erode. According to the RBC Cash Index, confidence dropped to a mark of 48.5 in early February, from 56.3 last month. The new reading is the worst since the index began in 2002 and surpassed the previous low reached in January.

Heightened fears about shrinking job opportunities, the housing and credit crunches and the possibility of the country falling into recession are seen as the main impetus behind the pessimism.

An increasing number of economists worry that interest cutting by the Federal Reserve and the tax rebate plan approved by Congress yesterday may not be enough to avert the first nationwide recession since 2001. Some economists believe the economy has already toppled into a recession.

Over the past year, consumer confidence has deteriorated a lot. Last February, confidence stood at a buoyant 103. The index is based on results of the international polling firm Ipsos.

KIRKWOOD, Mo. (AP) _ Police in Missouri say two police officers and three city officials attending a Kirkwood city council meeting are dead because

of a gunman who stormed the meeting and opened fire.

A reporter covering the meeting for the St. Louis Post-Dispatch tells the newspaper that the meeting had just started when the shooter rushed in and opened fire with at least one weapon.

She says the shooter started yelling about shooting the mayor while walking around and firing, hitting a police officer in the head. The reporter says the mayor was wounded. The mayor is in critical condition.

She identified the gunman as Charles Lee Thornton, who was shot and killed by police. The reporter says Thornton was often a contentious presence, as he had twice been convicted of disorderly conduct for disrupting meetings in May of 2006.

PORT WENTWORTH, Ga. (AP) _ The search goes on today for six people missing after an explosion and fire at a sugar refinery in the Savannah suburb of Port Wentworth that left dozens injured.

Officials have not determined what caused yesterday's explosion but say they suspect sugar dust, which can be volatile. Witnesses described widespread damage.

Savannah-Chatham County Police Chief Michael Berkow says there were 95 to 100 people believed to be working in the area of the explosion and firefighters are still battling the blaze this morning.

Berkow said at least 40 people were taken to area hospitals, and some of them were airlifted to a burn center in Augusta, 130 miles up the Savannah River.

NEW YORK (AP) _ Federal and state prosecutors have indicted almost the entire remaining hierarchy of New York City's Gambino crime family.

The once-powerful regime has been limping from crisis to crisis since the death of notorious boss John Gotti.

The operation announced yesterday marks one of the largest Mafia takedowns in recent memory. It seems designed to clear away the last of the "Dapper Don's" confidants, at least those not already serving time.

More than 80 people have been accused. They include a roll call of well-known gangsters in their 60s. Many have previously been imprisoned for mob-related crimes.

The allegations include skimming from unions, extorting tribute payments from construction companies, loan sharking and gambling. The charges span decades, but prosecutors say many of the illegal acts took place just in the last few years.

DAYTON, Ohio (AP) _ Jurors in Dayton are to hear closing arguments Monday in the trial of a woman accused of killing her baby in a microwave oven. The defense called 16 witnesses, but not defendant China Arnold, before resting yesterday. Judge John Kessler dismissed the jury for the weekend.

Twenty-seven-year-old Arnold has pleaded not guilty to aggravated murder in the death of 3-week-old Paris Talley in August 2005. She faces a possible death sentence if convicted.

The final two witnesses were inmates who were in the Montgomery County jail at the same time as Arnold. They refuted testimony by prosecution witnesses who'd said they heard Arnold tell another inmate that she didn't mean to kill her baby.

JACKSONVILLE, Fla. (AP) _ A former Ohio woman faces up to 20 years in prison for keeping her 17-year-old adopted son caged in her home in Jacksonville, Fla. Brenda Sullivan pleaded guilty yesterday to three counts of aggravated child abuse. Prosecutors agreed to drop lesser child-neglect charges.

At sentencing next month, prosecutors plan to call witnesses from Akron, Ohio, where Sullivan lived before moving her family to Florida.

The teen weighed 49 pounds when child welfare workers found him in 2005 in what appeared to be a cage. Sullivan told a judge at the time that Ohio authorities told her to keep the boy, who had severe medical and emotional problems, in a crib.

Sullivan's husband was also arrested but died last year while awaiting trial.

COLUMBUS, Ohio (AP) _ A federal prosecutor says former executives of a failed health care financing company misled investors and covered up hundreds of millions of dollars in misdirected payments.

Assistant U.S. attorney Douglas Squires is telling jurors that the two former owners and three senior executives of National Century Financial Enterprises on trial told investors one thing and did something different.

The government says the defendants took part in a nearly $2 billion fraud of investors that helped bring down the company based in suburban Dublin. But one defense attorney says National Century's only goal was to help doctors' offices and hospitals stay open.

Brian Dickerson portrayed a company working with a solid business model created with the help of Wall Street firms closely following National Century's operations.

HARRISBURG, Pa. (AP) _ The Harrisburg Area Community College campus is closed due to a crash involving a tractor-trailer that authorities say is carrying hazardous materials.

Dauphin County emergency dispatchers say the wreck happened on Cameron Street north of Elmerton Avenue. Officials say the tractor-trailer carrying 80 drums of corrosive materials overturned. Hazardous materials crews are on the scene, but there is no word yet whether any of the materials have spilled onto the road.

PHILADELPHIA (AP) _ Police say thieves used a car in a smash-and-grab robbery at a high-end Philadelphia clothing store. Police say two people wearing ski masks backed a car through the front window of Diesel Jeans near 15th and Walnut streets just before 6 a.m. Friday.

A security guard inside the store was told to 'freeze' while the suspects took a number of pairs of jeans and drove away. It is unclear whether the suspects were armed.

Officials estimate the two got away with $22,000 worth of merchandise. Police say they are searching for a gold or champagne colored Chevrolet.

Managers say the store was the target of smash-and-grab robberies on Dec. 10 and 12 last year. Thieves used bricks to break windows of the store before making off with $30,000 worth of clothing.

PHILADELPHIA (AP) _ Travelers are back in a terminal at Philadelphia International Airport after an evacuation while a suspicious package was checked. Airport spokeswoman Phyllis VanIstendal says an item that raised baggage checkers' suspicions early Friday has been cleared.

VanIstendal says she doesn't have details on the item. It was detected in a baggage scanner in Terminal A-East, the American-Delta terminal.

VanIstendal says she does not know now many people were affected by the evacuation about 6 a.m. But she says travelers and employees returned to the terminal in less than an hour. She still encourages travelers to check the airport's Website or their airline for possible delays.

RENO, Nev. (AP) _ The University of Nevada-Reno police chief says a missing 19-year-old woman has basically "fallen off the face of the Earth."

Brianna Denison has not been heard from for the past five days. She was last seen when she spent the night on a couch at a friend's house near the Reno campus. Denison is a student at Santa Barbara Community College in California and was home on break.

Police say they have no credible leads and consider her disappearance a kidnapping.

Appearing on NBC's "Today" show this morning, Denison's mother and aunt said she is a responsible and serious person and urged people to be on the lookout for her.

Police say Denison had been sleeping near an unlocked glass door after partying Saturday night. Friends say when they awoke Sunday morning, her clothes, purse and cell phone were there, but she ws gone.

WASHINGTON (AP) _ The number of laid-off workers filing claims for unemployment benefits has fallen for the fourth straight week. The Labor Department says new applications for unemployment benefits dropped by 1,000 last week to 301,000. That's the lowest level in four months.

The decline was unexpected. Analysts had been forecasting an increase of 19,000. The string of falling claims is a welcome sign after a December jump in the unemployment rate to 5 percent.

WASHINGTON (AP) _ New York City Mayor Michael Bloomberg is offering harsh criticism of a government stimulus plan for jump-starting the economy. Bloomberg has told a Washington meeting of the U.S. Conference of Mayors that America can't "borrow" its way out of the slump. Bipartisan leaders in Washington are hammering out a 150-billion-dollar economic boost that includes individual tax rebates of up to $800.

Bloomberg says the cash injection wouldn't be enough to save the economy because of the huge government deficits. Instead, he proposes helping homeowners who can't afford their mortgages and overhauling immigration laws to bring more workers into the country. In his words: "We have to stop turning away people that our economy needs."

The billionaire mayor is said to be considering an independent bid for the White House, but denies he's a candidate. Still, he spent part of his speech slamming Washington leadership, saying they've been "running up bills with reckless abandon."

NEW YORK (AP) _ Within a few years, a handful of rich tourists may be blasting into space for joyrides in a craft that looks like a cross between the space shuttle and a corporate jet.

British billionaire Richard Branson and the aerospace designer Burt Rutan (roo-TAN') have taken the wraps off a model of SpaceShipTwo at New York's American Museum of Natural History. Test flights begin as soon as this year.

The ship is now under construction at a hangar in the Mojave Desert. And Branson says it's "breathtakingly beautiful." About 200 prospective passengers from 30 countries have made reservations, shelling out $200,000 apiece.

FORT WORTH, Texas (AP) _ The military now says two of its planes were in an area of Texas where residents reported seeing a UFO this month.

Earlier, a spokesman had said there were no fighter jets training in the area near Stephenville – southwest of Fort Worth. Officials now say they were mistaken and want to set the record straight "in the interest of public awareness."

However, residents continue to say what they saw was no airplane. And their supporters still say the military's explanation even bolsters their claims, because several people reported seeing at least two fighter jets chasing an object.

The Texas director of the Mutual UFO Network says he finds it curious that it took officials two weeks to "'fess up," and credits "the heat from the publicity." The group took more than 50 reports from locals in the Stephenville area.

CAPE CANAVERAL, Fla. _ NASA says a survey of astronauts and flight surgeons has found no evidence of launch day drinking by crew members, despite a report last year of two cases of drunkenness.

The anonymous survey uncovered a single case of "perceived impairment" by someone just a day or more from blasting into space. That turned out to be a reaction between prescription medicine and alcohol.

NASA officials won't say when or where the episode happened, only that it was on one of the final days leading up to launch but not on launch day. The crew member ultimately was cleared for flight.

LOS ANGELES (AP) _ Some parts of Southern California are recovering from record rainfall, while others have had to deal with heavy snow. More than four inches of rain fell along the coast in Santa Barbara yesterday, shattering the record for the date set back in 1943.

Heavy snow halted traffic in both directions on a major interstate in the mountains north of Los Angeles. California Highway Patrol officers escorted vehicles caught in a pass to safety.

Intense rain prompted flash flood watches and warnings in the Los Angeles area, including Malibu, still reeling from recent wildfires.

RELIGIOUS NEWS

TULSA, Okla. (AP) _ Hundreds of students and alumni turned out Wednesday on the eve of Oral Roberts' 90th birthday to pay tribute to the evangelist and the namesake university he founded in 1963.

The school's first Founder's Day celebration comes months after a lawsuit filed by three professors that accused Oral Roberts' son, former university president Richard Roberts, of using school funds to bankroll a lavish lifestyle at a time when ORU faced more than $50 million in debt.

At a chapel service, Oral Roberts delivered a prerecorded message taped at his home in California, saying he's confident the school's new board will carry on the school's mission "until Jesus comes."

Last week, school leaders voted to accept a $62 million donation from Christian businessman Mart Green. The deal is still contingent on whether the university can settle several lawsuits.

NASHVILLE, Tenn. (AP) _ Tennessee lawmakers are considering a proposal to exempt churches from a state law that requires "No Smoking" signs to be posted at their entrances.

Tennessee's indoor smoking ban went into effect in October. It applies to most indoor businesses and public places and requires that the international "No Smoking" symbol be posted at all entrances.

The church exemption is scheduled for a hearing in the state Senate next week.

VATICAN CITY (AP) _ A Vatican official says Pope Benedict doesn't want to roll back the modernizing liturgical reforms of the Second Vatican Council.

The pope last year removed restrictions on celebrating the old Latin Mass, a rite that was all but swept away by the Second Vatican Council. But Monsignor Guido Marini told Vatican radio that Benedict only wants to maintain continuity with Roman Catholic tradition.

On January 13th, the pontiff celebrated Mass in the Sistine Chapel using the original main altar, facing away from worshippers during parts of the prayer. Under the modernizing reforms, clergy generally celebrate Mass facing the congregation.

Marini said artistic conditions at some churches can make it desirable to celebrate Mass at the ancient altar."

HANOI, Vietnam (AP) _ Quietly, Vietnam's Catholic Church is challenging the nation's government more boldly than it ever has since the communists took power over five decades ago.

For several weeks, church leaders and their followers in Hanoi have been gathering daily to pray in front of the old Vatican embassy, one of many church properties taken over by the government after 1954.

The church wants the government to return the lot in central Hanoi, where such land is now worth millions of dollars.

Although the dispute could raise church-state tensions, it also offers dramatic testimony to how much church-state relations have improved in Vietnam recently. Had church leaders dared to make such a public challenge just five years ago, police would almost certainly have jailed them.

PRAGUE, Czech Republic (AP) _ The Czech Republic is considering whether to compensate religious organizations for property seized by the former Communist regime.

Under the draft law, which requires passage in parliament and approval by the president, all of the country's churches would receive one-third of their former property now held by the state. The remaining two-thirds would be compensated for financially over the next 60 years.

The Communist regime, which seized power in 1948 in what was then Czechoslovakia, confiscated all church property and persecuted clergy. Churches were then allowed to function only under state control.

Unlike Poland or Slovakia, the Czech Republic is among the least religious Eastern European nations.

BERLIN (AP) _ Jewish groups in Germany are protesting the city of Munich's plans to hold a Carnival parade this Sunday – the same day the U.N. has established as an annual day of Holocaust remembrance.

The International Auschwitz Committee says holding the jovial parade on such a day "shows the thoughtlessness and ignorance" of city officials.

A Munich city spokesman responded that it's too late to cancel the parade and argued that the city had no authority to do so, since January 27th is not an official holiday.

The Holocaust remembrance day commemorates the liberation of the Auschwitz death camp in Poland by the Red Army on January 27th, 1945.

PARIS (AP) _ A Paris court has heard an appeal brought by Muslim
groups against a French newspaper. The satirical newspaper Charlie-Hebdo was acquitted last year of defamation charges following its publication of caricatures of Muhammad. The Muslim groups had sought more than $43,000 in damages.

Public prosecutor Antoine Bartoli has asked the appeals court to uphold the lower court's decision, saying that in France, "freedom of expression trumps all other rights."

During the 2007 proceedings, the newspaper and its director had stood accused of "publicly abusing a group of people because of their religion."It was not immediately clear when the appeals court's decision was expected.

SPORTS

Update on the latest in sports:

UNDATED (AP) _ The Cleveland Cavaliers were without their second-leading rebounder last night. It certainly showed.

The Houston Rockets outrebounded the visiting Cavs 55-35 while cruising to a 92-77 victory. Yao Ming led the way with 22 points and 12 rebounds to lead the Rockets to their ninth victory in 10 games.

Houston pulled away in the second half despite Tracy McGrady, who scored just eight points on 3-for-11 shooting. McGrady arrived at the arena less than an hour before tipoff after being hospitalized earlier in the day with an upper respiratory infection and strep throat.

LeBron James scored 32 points for the Cavs, who played without Drew Gooden because of an injured groin.

Also in the NBA last night, Chris Duhon (DOO'-hahn) scored a career-high 34 points and Joe Smith added 17 to lead Chicago past the Warriors 114-108 at Golden State. The Bulls spoiled the return of Chris Webber, who had four points and two rebounds in 12 minutes of his first game back with the Warriors.

Andre Iguodala (ig-ah-DAH'-lah) scored 25 points and Andre Miller added 21 to send the Philadelphia 76ers to their fourth victory in six games, 101-84 over Miami. Dwyane Wade scored 19 points but shot just 5-for-17 in the Heat's 21st loss in 22 games.

PHOENIX (AP) _ Newly acquired Phoenix Suns center Shaquille O'Neal promises to bring experience and leadership to help his new team "get over the hump" and win an NBA title.

O'Neal met the media yesterday, a day after the Suns acquired him from the Miami Heat for Shawn Marion and Marcus Banks.

The 14-time All Star says he's "very upset" by talk that he's washed up, and when he's upset he's "known to do certain things – like win championships."

LOS ANGELES (AP) _ Sam Cassell is denying that he wants to buy out his contract with the Los Angeles Clippers so he can play with the Boston Celtics. The 38-year old guard says there is no truth to the report in the Boston Globe, adding that he never indicated a desire to buy out his contract and that neither he nor the team has brought up the subject.

The Globe responded by saying all its quotes were accurate.

UNDATED (AP) _ The Detroit Red Wings were just 20 minutes away from a team record-tying ninth straight win last night before the Los Angeles Kings ended the streak.

The Kings scored four unanswered goals in the third period to beat the Red Wings 5-3. Brad Stuart and Alexander Frolov (FROH'-lahv) each had a goal and two assists in the final period after Henrik Zetterberg scored two straight goals to put the Wings ahead 3-1 midway through the game.

The Kings have won three straight and are 8-3-and-1 in their last 12.

Last night's NHL schedule included Pittsburgh's 4-3 win over the New York Islanders. Ryan Whitney scored twice before Kris Letang notched the game-winner with 3:39 remaining, putting the Penguins in a tie with Philadelphia for the Atlantic Division lead. Mike Comrie scored twice in the Islanders' sixth straight loss.

Dany Heatley returned to the Ottawa lineup, collecting two goals and an assist in a 5-4 victory against Florida. He scored the game-winner in the third period for the Senators, who were 3-and-8 while Heatley sat out with a separated shoulder.

Montreal is three points behind the East-leading Senators after Darcy Tucker scored twice and Kyle Wellwood provided the eventual game-winner in Toronto's 4-2 win over the Canadiens. Vesa Toskala (VEH'-sah TAHS'-kah-lah) stopped 34 shots to help the Maple Leafs win for only the second time in six games.

Mike Smith picked up his second shutout of the season by stopping 25 shots in the Dallas Stars' fifth straight win, 1-0 at Minnesota. Niklas Hagman scored early in the third period to send the Stars to their fifth consecutive road win.

Corey Perry and Chris Kunitz scored 87 seconds apart in the second period as Anaheim knocked off the Rangers 4-1 at New York. Mathieu Schneider and Todd Bertuzzi also scored as the Ducks dropped the Rangers to 0-7-and-2 against the Western Conference this season.

Third-period goals by Vancouver's Daniel Sedin (seh-DEEN') and Alex Burrows turned a 1-0 deficit into a 2-1 triumph in Atlanta. The Canucks had been 1-19-and-1 when trailing after two periods.

Tampa Bay pulled out a 2-1 win at Nashville on Vinny Prospal's goal at 58 of overtime. Brad Richards had a goal and an assist in the Lightning's sixth consecutive road victory.

Jason Chimera and Alexei Zherdev (ZHUR'-dehv) scored to give Columbus a 2-0 lead just over nine minutes into a 2-1 triumph at Phoenix. Fredrik Norrena made 26 saves and helped the Blue Jackets kill off a penalty over the final 92 seconds.

And Nikolai Khabibulin (hah-bee-BOO'-lihn) turned back 26 shots in Chicago's 3-1 victory at Calgary. Patrick Sharp's 25th goal of the season snapped a 1-1 tie late in the second period.

PEBBLE BEACH, Calif. (AP) _ Kent Jones fired a bogey-free 6-under-par 66 to grab a one-shot lead after one round of the Pebble Beach National Pro-Am. Nationwide Tour grad Roland Thatcher, Q-school grad Brad Adamonis and John Mallinger share second.

VIENNA, Austria (AP) _ The pairings are set for the Davis Cup matchup between the U.S. and Austria in Vienna.

Andy Roddick is getting set to face Jurgen Melzer in today's opening match, and James Blake will take on Stefan Koubek.

SHORT REPORTS
AP-10th NewsMinute
Stocks higher...Gains in Europe...Ledger family speaks

NEW YORK (AP) _ Stocks are showing some modest gains in early trading today. This, a day after they staged an extraordinary reversal, going from about 300 points down to 300 points in positive territory. Weekly figures on workers seeking unemployment benefits suggest the job market is holding up. But it remains to be seen whether yesterday's late-day comeback is partly because of technical reasons, or if it represents a shift in sentiment.

LONDON (AP) _ European stocks are rising following yesterday's strong showing from the U.S. market. Earlier today, most Asian markets finished trading up for the day following steep slides earlier in the week on fears of an American recession.

WASHINGTON (AP) _ A deal could be reached soon on an emergency stimulus package for the economy. Bipartisan congressional leaders met late last night with Treasury Secretary Henry Paulson in an effort to hammer out a proposal. Democratic House Speaker Nancy Pelosi says the sides are "moving toward" an agreement but "all the issues are not resolved."

BAGHDAD (AP) _ An Iraqi police chief and two other officers are dead following a suicide attack at the site of yesterday's blast that killed at least 34 people in Mosul. The U.S. military is blaming al-Qaida in Iraq for today's blast. Yesterday's bombing is Still under investigation.

NEW YORK (AP) _ Heath Ledger's family is speaking about the actor's possible mental state in the months leading up to his death. One of Ledger's uncles tells CBS' "The Early Show" that his nephew wouldn't have done anything rash. The medical examiner's office says it could be about 10 days before tests come back that could give clues to the cause of death.

AP-Morning BusinessMinute
After the rebound, data due, crude supplies seen growing

NEW YORK (AP) _ Wall Street will be hard-pressed for an encore after yesterday's strong rebound. The Dow stands at 12,270 after a rise of nearly 299 points. The S&P is at 13,338, having surged 28 points and the Nasdaq is at 2,316 after rising 24 points.

TOKYO (AP) _ Wednesday's rebound on Wall Street is fueling a trading surge in Asia for a second day. Stock markets in Asia have recovered more of the losses suffered Monday and Tuesday amid fears of a recession in the vital U.S. export market.

SINGAPORE (AP) _ Oil prices rose in Asian trading Thursday after slipping more than $2 a barrel in the previous session amid concerns that crude inventories in the United States are growing even as the economy and fuel demand are cooling. Light, sweet crude for March delivery rose 61 cents to $87.60 a barrel in Asian electronic trading on the New York Mercantile Exchange by midmorning in Singapore.

WASHINGTON (AP) _ Investors will have some data to digest in the hours ahead. The National Association of Realtors releases December's existing home sales, while the Labor Department reports on new claims for unemployment benefits.

WASHINGTON (AP) _ Supplies of crude oil are seen rising in the weekly update due from the Energy Department later today. Analysts estimate crude inventories grew by 2.1 million barrels, up for a second straight week.

KICKERS

STARBUCKS-FREE REFILLS
SEATTLE (AP) _ Starbucks for a buck? The coffee chain is going head-to-head with low-cost rivals by offering a cheaper cup of joe. But don't expect a Grande latte for a dollar. A statement from Starbucks says the low-cost java will be a small cup of drip coffee with free refills. Test marketing will be done in Starbucks' hometown of Seattle. No word though on when the buck-a-cup test will begin, or how many Starbucks coffee shops will be involved.

CUMBERLAND, Md. (AP) _ A trip to the museum could have been a blast. Authorities in Cumberland, Maryland, report a rocket on display at a veterans' museum was the real thing. It turns out the Vietnam-era Mark 1 rocket was a live round. The rocket had been in the museum for two years. It's the type fired by helicopter gunships. Bomb experts removed the rocket yesterday. Officials say it was donated to the museum by a local veteran. Authorities are now investigating how the man got the live military rocket.

GRAND RAPIDS, Mich. (AP) _ A Michigan family's black cat turned out to be good luck. The cat started making a racket and awoke sleeping family members to a fire in the garage. According to fire officials in Allendale, Diane Busscher was awakened to hear the family's cat howling and screeching. The cat was in the smoke-filled garage. Busscher grabbed the feline and got the rest of the family of five out to safety. Firefighters are investigating the cause.

SHREVEPORT, La. (AP) _ Don't offer Vicki Armstrong a penny for her thoughts. She's already got 55,000 of them. Armstrong has says she'll soon take her $550 dollars worth of pennies to a bank in Shreveport, Louisiana. She's been saving her pennies for 19 years and says it symbolizes her frugal ways. She stashed the coins in vases, bowls and shoeboxes. Armstrong is getting ready to retire from a hospital where she's a maternity technician.

INDIANAPOLIS (AP) _ College basketball coach Ron Hunter better watch where he steps tonight. He'll be on the hardwood in bare feet. Hunter is the coach of IUPUI: Indiana University-Purdue University Indianapolis. He says he'll be barefoot for tonight's game against Oakland University to raise awareness about shoeless children in Africa. He's working with a charitable organization called Samaritan's Feet, and hopes to send 40,000 pairs of shoes to Africa. Hunter says he got a firsthand look at the problem during a recruiting trip to Nigeria four years ago. Hunter adds he's already collected 30,000 pairs of shoes and filled his campus office.

WASHINGTON (AP) _ Surfing porn while on the clock will cost some Washington D.C. workers their jobs. Mayor Adrian Fenty says an audit of D.C.'s computers found dozens of employees looking at porno Web sites on the city's dime. As many as nine workers will be fired. An additional 32 will face disciplinary action. The probe of 10,000 city computers was launched after a complaint from an employee about co-workers downloading X-rated content.

by Jamie Friar

GLOSSARY

abdomen   Area immediately above and below the waist that shows proper breathing technique by movement; moves out as the diaphragm pushes down for air intake, and in as the diaphragm pushes up to expel air.

acronym   Word made from first initials of phrase that identifies a group or object, such as AC (adult contemporary) or AFTRA (American Federation of Radio and Television Artists).

AC   See adult contemporary.

action news   High-energy television news format that promotes involvement of station news reporters on the scene of news events.

active live   A newer style of field news reporting in which the reporter seeks to become more involved in the story without changing or disrupting it.

actuality   The recorded sound of a news event, either audio or video, voice or sound.

AD   Common shorthand for "assistant director." Frequently has responsibility for timing a show.

additions   An articulation problem in which extra sounds are added to words, such as saying "warsh" instead of "wash"; also, news segments or stories included at the last minute.

ad-lib   Speaking in an "off-the-cuff" manner not using a script; literally means "at pleasure."

adult contemporary (AC)   Radio format also known as soft rock or lite rock; plays current pop hits with oldies mixture.

affiliation   Agreement between an individual broadcast station and a network wherein the station carries the network's programming and advertising in exchange for compensation in some form.

AFTRA   Union for radio/television performers; American Federation of Radio and Television Artists (www.aftra. org).

agent   Person who represents talent to an employer; usually receives a percentage of the talent fee.

aircheck   Audio or video recording of a performer while on-air; used to critique work or for an audition tape.

album-oriented rock   Radio format known as AOR, which often features laid-back DJs and an eclectic mix of rock album cuts.

all-news   Describes the format of a radio station that does not play music but broadcasts only news.

all-talk   Describes the format of a radio station that features call-in or conversation-oriented programming.

alternative   Radio format that is also known as modern; features newer rock music and DJs with a brash, hip attitude.

ambient noise   Naturally occurring sounds recorded on the scene, such as crowds cheering; may detract from or enhance a field report.

American Meteorological Society (AMS)   A professional weather organization that gives its Seal of Approval to qualified broadcast weather people.

amplify   To increase the signal strength of audio or video; results in a louder sound.

analog   Technical description for sound reproduction based on imitation of sound waves by electrical impulses.

anchor   The news person in the studio who reads the news and introduces the reporters in the field.

announcer   Term used in radio to describe the person who reads copy, commercials, or performs other on-air duties.

AOR   See album-oriented rock.

AP   Associated Press, a wire service used by radio and television stations for a wide range of stories, especially national and international news.

Arbitron   A program ratings service that primarily surveys markets to obtain radio ratings.

articles The words "a," "an," and "the"; also, newspaper stories used as the basis for radio or television news.

articulation Use of the mouth, tongue, jaw, and teeth to clearly emphasize vowels and consonants in words.

assignment editor Newsroom person who decides what stories will be covered and which reporter will cover which story.

attenuator Reduces the amplitude or loudness of an audio signal.

attribution Reference to source of a story or a quote used in a story.

audio console Equipment that controls all the individual sources of audio that may be found in a studio, such as microphones, recorders, and CD players; also known as a board.

audiotape cartridge Known as a "cart," older format in which short segments of audio tape that form a continuous loop are enclosed in a plastic housing.

audition To try out for a job in broadcasting; includes actual performance, not just an interview.

audition tape Audio- or videotape that demonstrates a performer's ability to do the job; used as part of job-hunting package along with a resume.

automation Equipment that can be programmed to function without the need for an operator.

back-announce Radio technique in which announcer identifies song title and artist information after the music has been played.

back light A light cast on a subject from behind to separate it from the background and illuminate the hair.

back timing Timing a program, segment by segment, from the end to the beginning, so adjustments can be made to end the program at an exact time.

BEA Broadcast Education Association, an organization of educators who teach media classes; affiliated with the National Association of Broadcasters (NAB) (www.beaweb. org).

beat News assignment in which reporter has a specific area, such as education or health, to cover for possible stories.

beautiful music See easy listening.

bed Sound that is the background to a voice-over.

beeper Recorded telephone conversation during which an electronic beep sounds periodically to indicate the conversation is being recorded; also, a wireless paging device used to contact news reporters.

bidirectional Pickup pattern of a microphone that picks up sound from two directions, usually directly opposite each other.

billboard Listing of upcoming events on a broadcast station.

blocking Rehearsing movement of actors and cameras prior to a television production; also, program strategy in which similar programs are placed next to each other to attract a similar audience.

board The control panel for all audio sources; another term for audio console.

board announcer Also known as staff announcer; person hired to do general announcing not related to a specific program.

board operator The person who physically controls the audio sources using the audio console.

boom Apparatus with an extension arm used to hang the microphone overhead and out of the view of the television cameras or suspended over an audio console.

breathy voice Speech style in which excess air escapes while the person is speaking; a voice similar to actress Marilyn Monroe's.

Broadcast Education Association See BEA.

broadcast journalist Term associated with newscaster who not only reads the news, but also gathers, writes, and constructs the newscast.

bulk eraser Electrically powered magnetic coil that erases an entire audio or video tape when it is placed over the mechanism.

bumper Short bit or musical interlude that goes between segments of a show.

calling the game Primary duty of certain sports announcers, which is to inform the audience of the progress of a broadcast athletic event.

call-in talk show Program format in which the primary purpose is talk and includes telephone calls from viewers or listeners.

camera panic Inability to perform effectively when in front of the television camera caused by anxiety about being on the air.

cardioid Describes the heart-shaped pickup pattern of a microphone with a larger area of pickup in front of the mic and lobes of pickup on both sides.

cart See audiotape cartridge.

cart machine audiotape player that plays only carts.

cart with live tag Announcer in studio adds information after a cart has been played, such as the location of a seller of a product that has just been advertised.

carted commercials Commercials placed on carts.

carting The process of placing audio information on a cart.

cassette Audio or video tape that has been placed inside a plastic casing; when placed in a player, the tape is pulled from the box and positioned next to the audio tape heads.

catch-all question Technique used by interviewers to allow the guest a chance to say anything he or she did not get to say during an interview.

CD See compact disc.

CG See character generator

chain Group of broadcast stations owned by one company; early broadcast term for a network.

channel Section of an audio console and its associated switches that allows the operator to control a piece of equipment.

character generator Type of computer used in a television studio to place names, titles, and other graphics on the screen; also known as a CG.

cheating to the camera Placing yourself in a position that is advantageous to show your movement or action on a television camera

checkbook journalism Paying sources for news.

choppy A vocal delivery style where pauses are added too frequently, disrupting the flow of speech.

CHR See contemporary hit radio.

chroma-key Electronic effect often used by newscasters and weathercasters. Two video sources are merged into one picture; one source includes a color background, usually blue or green, and another picture is placed electronically in the color area.

classical music Radio format that features classical music of the master composers.

clearance Permission to use copyrighted material.

cliches Overused, trite expressions that have become artificial in their usage.

clip-on mic Microphone that is attached to the performer's clothing, usually a coat or blouse.

closed-ended questions Questions that result in one-word "yes" or "no" answers.

cluster Group of commercials or songs played together.

CNN Cable News Network; begun by Ted Turner in the 1980s as the first 24-hour cable all-news service; after initial struggles, its growth and popularity forced other broadcasters to expand their news operations (www.cnn.com).

co-anchors The two people in a newscast who share reading the stories and introducing field reports.

cold copy Script the announcer has not yet seen and must still perform.

color Commentator/sports announcer who adds analysis and insight to the play-by-play announcer's calling of the game or event.

commercial Advertisement on radio, television, or cable

commercial cluster A grouping of advertisements played during a break in the programming; also known as a commercial sweep, spot set, or stop set.

community billboard Announcements made by a radio, television, or cable station about upcoming community activities; also known as a community calendar or community bulletin board.

compact disc CD; audio information is digitally formatted on a small (5"), silver-coated plastic disc and played back by an optical system that incorporates a laser.

computer editing Use of computers to put together various parts of audio or video presentations.

computerized news room Television or radio newsroom that uses computerized equipment.

condenser microphone Type of microphone that uses an electric capacitor circuit to reproduce sound.

console Entire desk-like structure that holds the audio board and other audio or video equipment.

contact list   A list of friends and acquaintances in the broadcast industry who may provide a lead for a job position.

contemporary hit radio   Radio format, also known as Top 40, that features modern popular artists; songs are usually presented in a rotation and heard every 90 minutes.

continuity writers   Station employees responsible for writing commercials and transition material to move from one program segment to another; also called "creatives."

contractions   Abbreviated words that are useful to sound conversational, such as "don't" for "do not" and "I'll" for "I will."

control room   Area of a broadcast facility that houses the equipment (audio console, television switcher, camera monitors, etc.) necessary to put together a production; the nerve center.

copy   Another term for a broadcast script.

copy book   List of all the announcements or commercials that need to be read during the broadcast day.

copy marking   A system of symbols to help the announcer interpret a script.

copyright   The ownership of a creative piece of material, including music.

correspondent   News reporter assigned to a beat; often assigned to a foreign location, such as the Mideast, but also domestic locations, such as the White House.

country   Popular radio format that features country artists in a very controlled format with friendly and well-informed announcers.

cover shot   Television picture that shows the entire set.

crank up the gain   Reference to bringing the fader up on the audio console so that there is more signal strength.

creatives   Writers of commercials and other original copy for stations.

cross-fade   Transition used in radio when changing from one song to another; the board operator slowly brings down the volume on one song and at the same time brings the volume up on the other song so that for a brief period of time the listeners hear both songs.

crossover   Describes an artist or a song that is acceptable in more than one format.

C-SPAN   Cable Satellite Public Affairs Network; cable television network that broadcasts sessions of Congress, political talk, and interviews.

CU   Close-up; television term that refers to camera shot that shows a very "tight" frame, such as a person from the chest up.

cue   Physical indication to the broadcast performer to begin.

cue cards   Notes written in large print on pieces of cardboard and held next to the camera so the talent can refer to them during a performance.

cue tone   Audio signal that indicates the beginning of a tape.

cutaway shots   Reaction shots used in editing a videotape to avoid jump cuts; often of an interviewer or reporter listening to a response.

cut in   Inclusion of video from another source during a news broadcast.

DAT   See digital audio tape.

dayparts   Segments of the broadcast day, such as morning drive time, and 6:00 a.m. to 10:00 a.m.

dead air   Silence.

decibel   Unit used to show relative difference in acoustic power; measures volume of sound.

de-emphasize   Less energy in delivery.

de-essing   Elimination of high frequencies often associated with s sound.

defamation   False statement that damages the reputation of a person or group.

demographics   Characteristics of an audience, such as age, sex, or income.

dialect   Regional variation of a language with a particular accent.

diaphragm   Muscle used in breathing; separates the chest cavity from the abdominal cavity.

digital   System in which reproduction of sound or video is made by conversion of the analog source into electronic bits represented by binary numbers.

digital audiotape   Equipment in which sound is recorded and played back using a digital system.

digital cart machine   Equipment in which sound is recorded and played back using a digital system on a disc.

digital video effects   DVE; manipulation of the video picture to produce special effects, such as tumbling or flipping the video.

director   The production team person responsible for selecting and organizing the audio and visual contents of a television program.

disc jockey   DJ; the person who announces and plays the music at a radio station

dissolve   Audio or video technique in which one source slowly changes to another source; a simultaneous fade-in of one source and fade-out of another.

distortion   The warping or inappropriate changing of an audio or video signal.

DJ   See disc jockey.

dolly   To move a television camera forward and back.

donut commercial   Commercial that already has recorded copy at the beginning and end, leaving a hole in the middle for the local announcer to fill.

dramatic pause   To stop reading the copy momentarily to create anticipation or tension.

dramatization commercial   Known as a "slice-of-life" spot; announcers use dialogue, sound effects, and music to act out the selling message.

drive time   Period of the day, morning or afternoon, when people are going to work or coming home; most important times of day to reach the radio audience.

dub   To make a copy of an audio recording or video.

duration   Refers to varying the length of key words or phrases when interpreting a script.

DVE   See digital video effects.

dynamic microphone   Also known as a moving coil; a diaphragm vibrates in sympathy with the sound, moving an attached wire coil through a magnetic field and creating an electrical signal.

EAS   See Emergency Alert System.

easy listening   Radio format in which popular songs are presented in heavily orchestrated versions; also known as beautiful music.

EBS   See Emergency Broadcast System.

edit   To put together an audio or video piece by combining, cutting, or splicing.

editing booth   Small room or studio designed to house equipment necessary for editing video recordings

effect   Television term for the complex visual changes between camera shots that are generated by computers. Also, the transition itself.

EFP   See electronic field production.

egg-on-face look   Forced facial expression when performer tries to hold a smile too long; often occurs at end of production on last camera shot before video fades to black.

electronic field production   EFP; videotaping done on-location using portable equipment.

electronic news gathering   ENG; television news done on-location.

ellipsis   Three dots (…) indicating omission of a word or phrase, usually from a quotation, but also often used to indicate a pause in a broadcast script.

Emergency Alert System   EAS; national warning system using radio, television, and cable stations for disaster notification or weather alerts.

Emergency Broadcast System   EBS; the predecessor of the EAS.

ENG   See electronic news gathering.

equal time   Phrase from Section 315 of the Communications Act; refers to station obligation to provide equal air time to qualified political candidates.

ESPN   Entertainment and Sports Programming Network; sports cable network.

fact sheet commercial   List of important information about a product or service used by an announcer to ad-lib a commercial.

fade-in   Gradual increase of audio (silence to sound) or video (black to picture) signal.

fade-out   Gradual decrease of audio (sound to silence) or video (picture to black) signal.

fader   Sliding-type mechanism that controls audio or video signal level.

fairness doctrine   FCC policy that required stations to present all sides of a controversial issue; no longer in effect, but a concept still practiced by stations.

fair use   Exception to copyright law that permits minimal use of copyrighted material without payment of a fee.

FCC   See Federal Communications Commission.

feature interviews   Style of interview that is designed to entertain or to explain in depth an interesting person or issue.

Federal Communications Commission   FCC; governmental agency created in 1934 to supervise all forms of broadcasting and cable (www.fcc.gov).

feedback   A loud, piercing whistle or howl that occurs when an activated microphone is too close to a speaker.

fidelity   The accuracy of signal reproduction, especially audio.

file footage   Archival videotape of historic events (such as a presidential visit) or often used locations (such as city hall) that may be reused in news stories.

fill light   A secondary front light for lighting a subject. Placed to soften shadows created by the key light.

flaring   When a spotlight strikes a camera lens and causes a bright flash.

follow-up question   Additional question asked during an interview to gain more information based on answer to previous question

floor manager   Television studio crew person who acts as extension of director; gives cues to talent.

format   Program plan and style of radio or television station.

format clock   Radio program plan that describes what type of music or announcing should be done based on the part of the hour.

Freelancer   Individual working in broadcast on an as-needed basis without permanent job assignment.

future file   Collection of ideas for possible stories to be used in news.

gain   An increase in signal power through amplification; another term for volume.

gain control   Potentiometer that adjusts level of amplification.

general-assignment reporter   News reporter given a variety of stories to cover as needed.

graveyard shift   Working at a broadcast station between midnight and 6:00 a.m.

hand signals   Communication with gestures; used in radio and television when voice communication is not possible.

hard copy   Printed version of any script.

hard news   News of a serious nature that needs to be presented immediately.

hard rock   Intense rock-and-roll music that makes extensive use of electric guitars.

hard sell commercial   Commercial that attempts to be persuasive through fast talking and loud vocal style.

headline   Brief announcement of upcoming news stories.

headphones   Earmuff-like device worn over the ears so listeners or talent can hear program audio; also known as a headset.

hitting your mark   Television and film production term referring to actors moving to exactly the right place on the set.

hook   Beginning of a commercial, designed to capture listener or viewer attention.

homers   Sportscasters who promote and cheer for the home team during their broadcasts.

hot clock   A chart of music, sports, weather, traffic, and news to be played during an hour sequence on radio, including the point in the hour and approximate length to be devoted to each; format clock.

husky voice   Lower-pitched vocal style that displays a harsh, raspy quality; also known as a gravelly voice.

ID   Station identification given during broadcast.

IFB   See interruptible foldback.

impromptu   Speaking without rehearsal or notes.

industrial media   Audio, video, and film produced for use by corporations.

inflection   Raising and lowering of pitch of the voice for emphasis.

infomercial   Program-length commercial produced to look like a talk or interview show.

informational interview   A conversation conducted by a reporter to discover facts about a story from source; can also refer to a job-search-related interview in which only information is sought from the employer.

input selector switch   Device designed to route one of several signals to the next stage of an electronic system; determines which piece of equipment is assigned to a channel of an audio console.

international phonetic alphabet IPA; spelling system that aids in pronunciation; more useful for linguists than for broadcasters.

interruptible foldback IFB; intercom system from control room to on-air talent, who wears a small, transparent earpiece to hear director's instructions.

in the mud Audio signal that is too low, as indicated on VU meter.

in the red Audio signal that is too high, as indicated on VU meter.

intro Introduction; beginning section of a record or program.

IPA See International Phonetic Alphabet.

jargon Words used by a specific profession or social group.

jock Another term for disc jockey; individual who plays music on radio.

jump cut A video technique in which the picture is interrupted so that movement is not continuous; caused by editing videotape.

key Video technique in which a portion of one picture is electronically eliminated and another picture is substituted in that space; also known as a "super."

key light The primary light for illuminating a subject. Usually a spotlight.

kicker story Humorous or human interest story often used to end a newscast.

larynx Voice box; where vocal cords are located.

lapel microphone Small microphone attached to clothing of a performer.

lavaliere microphone Small microphone worn on a cord around the neck of a performer.

lead Opening sentence of a news story.

lead-in One show that precedes another; also an introduction to a song.

leading question Question that is worded to elicit a specific answer.

LED See light-emitting diode.

level indicator Meter that indicates volume units or video strength.

libel A written public statement that damages a person's reputation or character; also can be used in reference to broadcast statements.

light-emitting diode LED; a row of low-intensity lights used in studio to indicate audio level.

light (lite) rock Radio format also known as adult contemporary (AC).

line level Standard amount of electrical energy at which audio circuitry normally operates.

liner notes Descriptions of music and talent found in record jackets and CD cases.

live coverage Live audio or video report.

live tag Additional material given at the end of a commercial by local announcer; often used to add information such as sponsor location or sale dates.

logo Symbol of a company or product.

looping Repetition of a portion of a video or film segment for the purposes of correcting audio.

malapropism Misuse of words or expressions with usually humorous results.

market A division of the U.S. population by geography that is considered an audience for a particular radio, television, or cable facility.

major market One of the largest markets in the country, as measured by population.

marking copy Symbols used by announcers to help with interpretation and pronunciation of scripts/copy.

media event A public activity put on by a radio or television station for publicity.

mic fright Fear of performance in front of a mic in a radio or television situation.

mic level Energy output associated with microphone; this is so small that it must be amplified before it can be used in the audio system. See also line level.

microphone Device used to turn sound into electrical energy so that it can travel through the broadcasting system.

minicam Small camera used for on-location reports; can be mounted on a variety of equipment, including helicopters.

minidoc Mini-documentary; a long news report broken into segments and shown on successive nights.

mixer Equipment that allows board operator to combine various audio or video sources.

mixing The process of combining various audio sources; requires ability to balance audio sources.

mobile unit   Generally refers to a portable audio or video system that is used for on-location reports.

moire effect   Television term that refers to the apparent movement of patterns on television.

monaural   Sound that is reproduced in one channel.

monitor pot   Potentiometer that controls the volume of the monitor speakers.

monitor speaker   Audio speaker in the control room used to hear output of board.

monotone   Vocal style in which person speaks without varying pitch, volume, and rate.

moonlighting   Working at an additional job, often without your main employer being aware of it.

morgue   Storage area for program materials.

moving coil   Another term for the dynamic microphone.

music bed   Music played underneath announcing.

music sweep   A group of songs played without commercial interruption.

muting relays   Devices on audio boards that cut off studio and control room speakers when the microphone is activated to prevent feedback.

NAB   See National Association of Broadcasters.

NABET   See National Association of Broadcast Engineers and Technicians.\

nasality   Vocal problem caused when the back of the tongue touches the soft palate and closes off the resonance in the sinus cavities.

National Association of Broadcast Engineers and Technicians   NABET; union for the technical staff of broadcast and cable stations (www.nabet.org).

National Association of Broadcasters   NAB; professional association of broadcasters that represents and advises them in congressional, FCC, and technological matters (www.nab.org).

nat sound   Natural background sound often included in news video footage.

National Public Radio   NPR; national, noncommercial radio network established as part of the 1967 Public Broadcasting Act.

network   An association of local stations who affiliate with the program supplier, such as ABC, CBS.

network feed   Video or audio story that is sent from the network to the local station.

newscaster   On-air performer specifically employed to deliver the news.

news director   Individual in charge of the overall news operation.

news interview   Style of interview specifically designed to gather information about a news event, a person in the news, or a current issue.

news producer   Individual responsible for the on-air style of a newscast; second-in-charge for many news operations.

news script   Copy used by the anchors for the news program.

news/talk   Radio format, usually AM, that features straight news, interview, discussion, and listener call-in segments.

nondirectional mic   Microphone that picks up sound from all directions.

NPR   See National Public Radio.

O&O   Station owned and operated by a network.

off-mic   When announcer is out of the range or pickup pattern of the microphone; results in a hollow sound.

oldies   Radio format that plays music from the past, usually from the late 50s to the late 60s.

Omissions   Speaking problem in which sounds are omitted, such as "jog-er-fee" (geography) or "can-i-date" (candidate).

omnidirectional   Microphone pickup pattern that gathers sound from all directions.

on-air studio   Audio booth that is used for broadcast.

on-air talent   Performers who are broadcasting.

opening up to the camera   Standing so your body is facing more to the camera than to the person to whom you are talking.

open-ended question   Question that elicits a longer response and reflects the ideas of the guest.

optimum pitch   The frequency at which the voice is most comfortable in speaking.

outcue   Last four or five words of a recorded program, used to alert the announcer that the segment is over.

output   The audio or video signals sent by the board to be broadcast or recorded.

output selector switch   Device designed to route audio signals to the next stage of an audio system; most common outputs are program, audition, and auxiliary.

outro   The ending of a song, program, or script.

overmodulation   Distortion of sound caused by too much volume.

over-the-shoulder shot   Two-person camera scene in which one person is facing the camera in the background, and the other person's back and shoulder are in the foreground to frame the picture.

pacing   Changes in speed in the delivery of copy.

package   Television news story made up of edited segments.

pad   Additional copy to be used if time permits; often extra news stories that might be used at the end of a newscast.

pan pot   Potentiometer that can adjust the right/left balance of a stereo channel.

patter   Informal talk.

pattern   The direction(s) that a particular microphone will pick up a signal well.

payola   The payment by a record company of money or other goods to a DJ in return for playing a record.

PC   See politically correct.

peripheral vision   The area that we see out the sides of each eye without looking directly in that direction; used for taking cues in television without losing eye contact with the camera.

personal attack rule   FCC rule in which it is the responsibility of the local station to notify a person who is verbally attacked on-air and to give them the opportunity to reply.

personality   Refers to the star of a radio, television, or cable program.

phantom power supply   Means of powering microphones utilizing the audio lines and an external amp built into an audio console.

pharynx   Area between the nasal cavities and the larynx.

phonation   Making of speech sounds.

phone screener   Person who answers phone calls for a call-in show before they are given to the host of the show.

phrasing   Performance technique in which words are grouped together to enhance meaning and ensure smooth delivery style.

pickup pattern   Describes area in which a microphone will best detect sound.

pitch   The relative highness or lowness of the tone of a sound.

play analyst   Member of the sports announcing team whose job it is to explain the performance of the teams on the field

play-by-play announcer   Sportscaster who announces and describes each team's activity on the field during a game.

playlist   List of songs that the DJ must play.

plosive   Sudden burst of air produced when pronouncing letters such as p, b, or t.

plugola   Illegal activity in which a DJ receives money or other gifts for promoting a business or product in his or her ad-lib announcing

polar response pattern   Two-dimensional diagram that describes, using angles from a fixed reference point, the area in which a microphone can pick up sound.

politically correct   PC; refers to the way in which language is to be used so that no one person or group is offended or excluded by what is said.

popping   Burst of air produced when speaking some letters, such as p, b, or t.

post-production   Refers to the editing, manipulating, or enhancing of a program once the recording of the basic production is complete.

pot   Short for potentiometer.

potentiometer   A round knob that controls the volume on a board.

press kit   Information packet provided to reporters by anyone interested in promoting a person, product, or company

prime time   Time during which the audience is the largest and the advertisers are charged the most money; for radio, morning and afternoon drive times; for television, 8:00 to 11:00 p.m.

production studio   Area in which a recorded performance takes place; not an on-air studio designed for live broadcasts.

production value   The investment in making a show complex and polished. A very simple show would probably have a low production value.

profanity   Irreverent use of the name of God; also, vulgar language

profile shot   Camera shot that frames the talent or performer from the side rather than straight on.

program   A scheduled radio, television, or cable show.

program log   Listing with times of all programs to be aired in a specific broadcast day.

promo   Advertisement that promotes an individual program on a broadcast station.

prompter   See teleprompter.

pronunciation   How words are spoken.

prop   Property; refers to any item used during a television program, such as a telephone or wine bottle.

prop room   Part of the television facility in which props are stored.

proximity effect   Indicates the way in which some mics tend to emphasize the bass frequencies when one speaks very close to the mic.

PSA   See public service announcements.

public domain   Materials no longer protected by copyright are referred to as being in the public domain.

public figures   Readily recognized individuals, such as famous entertainers, sports stars, politicians, or community leaders.

public service announcements   PSAs; announcements for nonprofit organizations that are aired free of charge.

Q & A session   Question-and-answer session in which a performer or other noteworthy person is available to answer questions from the media.

Radio-Television News Directors Association   RTNDA; professional association for broadcast news directors (www.rtnda.org).

rate   Overall speed of speaking.

ratings   Statistical measurements of the size of the viewing or listening audience done by companies who specialize in this research; reported as a percentage of the number of people watching or listening to the station compared to the total possible number of listeners or viewers in the market.

raw footage   Video that has not been edited.

raw sound   Sound recorded on location.

real time   Actual elapsed time of a program.

redundant expression   Use of words that mean the same thing to convey an idea, such as "true fact."

reel-to-reel   Type of tape recorder in which the tape is wound on open wheels that are referred to as reels; most common tape is 1/4-inch wide; large reels permit several hours of programs.

reporter   Person responsible for investigating, writing, and often announcing the news.

resonance   Vibration of sound to produce a distinctive quality.

resonant cavities   Parts of the body in which resonance develops; includes the sinus cavities, the chest, the throat, and oral cavity.

resume   Summary of your education and work experience used in obtaining a job.

ribbon microphone   Microphone that uses a thin metallic element, suspended between magnets, which vibrates in response to sound waves and converts them to electrical energy.

riding gain   Constant adjustment of volume levels during a program in response to variations in sound levels.

rip and read   Taking copy directly from a news wire and, without practice, announcing it on-air.

robotics   Refers to common practice of having a single person in the control room operate all the studio cameras through an automated system.

roll   Cue to begin operating, such as a camera or a program; also refers to moving the credits from the bottom to the top of the screen at the end of a show.

rotating spots   Commercials that are played in a pattern during various times and dayparts.

routing   Causing an audio and/or video signal to travel over particular wires to selected parts of the electronic system.

RTNDA   See Radio–Television News Directors Association.

run-down sheet   A timed listing of all that is to be done during a program.

safe harbor   Time when airing of "adult" programming is allowed; midnight to 6 a.m.

SAG   See Screen Actors Guild. Screen Actors Guild SAG; union for film actors and some broadcast performers (www.sag.org).

segue   Transition from one song to another in which one song ends and the next song begins with no silence between and no overlap of the songs.

selecting   Choosing which of the available audio and/or video signals will be sent forward in the electronic system.

SFX   Abbreviation used in a script for sound effects

shield laws   Laws to protect sources of information for newspeople.

shift   Part of the workday the announcer is on-air; usually three- to four-hour block.

shock jock   Disc jockey who uses outlandish material to entertain the audience.

sibilance   Over-articulation of the s sound that is heard in s, sh, and z.

signal processing   Altering sound characteristics to make sound more to our liking, such as adding reverb, equalizing, and using noise reduction.

signature   A distinctive sound, musical phrase, or characteristic used to identify a person or station.

simulcast   A program broadcast on two or more stations at the same time; often a radio and television broadcast.

sing-song   A delivery style in which the speaker causes the voice to rise and fall in pitch in a predictable pattern.

slander   Oral defamation; spoken words that harm someone's reputation.

slang   Street language or words used by a specific social group.

slate   Information placed at beginning of videotape prior to the program to identify the director, program, and date.

slip start   When a DJ would place the needle where the record was to begin and hold the disc with his or her hand as turntable moved, then release it so intros could be tight.

slug line   Title for news copy placed at the top of the page; usually two or three words.

soft news   News that includes features and human interest stories; not immediate or fast breaking. The opposite of hard news.

soft rock   Radio format known today as adult contemporary that features current pop hits with oldies mixed in.

soft-sell commercial   A low-key approach to selling.

solecism   Words or phrases that are grammatically incorrect.

SOT   Sound on tape; abbreviation used in a television news script to indicate source of sound for a video clip that is recorded on the tape.

sound bite   A recorded piece of audio and video of a news event; like a radio actuality.

sounder   Oral report of a news story.

special assignment reporter   News person who is assigned to cover special events as they occur.

speech personality   Style of speaking unique to each individual announcer.

spin doctors   People hired to present politicians and others in the best possible light.

spokesperson commercial   Commercial in which a well-known individual delivers the selling message; often a music or sports celebrity or the owner of the business.

spoonerisms   Speech mistake in which certain letters of words are transposed, causing a humorous effect, such as "tee many martoonies."

sportscaster   Announcer who delivers sports news.

spot   Commercial.

spot set   Group of commercials.

spotting board   A device used by sportscasters to keep track of which players are in action. Usually also carries some basic facts about them.

Standard American English   Pronunciation of American English with little or no regional accent; the broadcast standard.

stand by   Cue given to talent just before a production begins.

stand-up   Part of an on-location news report when the reporter stands at the location and tells the story.

station ID   Announcement or visual indication of call letters and location of local station.

station logo   Symbol that identifies the station.

status-conferral function   Refers to giving extra importance to people or things that appear on radio, television, or cable.

stereo   Audio system that uses two channels, left and right.

still storer   Equipment in television studio used to capture a single frame of video, stored in digital format, and retrievable immediately.

stinger   The end of a commercial; usually a demand for action or the sponsor's name, location, and slogan. Also a musical note or two or sound effect that concludes a broadcast.

straight-read commercial   Announcer reads broadcast script only; words with no additional audio or video clips.

studio   Facility equipped for transmitting or recording a radio or television performance.

studio cards   See cue cards.

stylus   The needle on the tone arm of a turntable.

substitution   To replace a correct speech sound with an improper sound, such as "wabbit" for "rabbit."

sunshine laws   Laws governing access to government information.

super   Special video effect in which a name or graphic is placed over the picture.

sweep   Usually refers to a period of time during which ratings are done.

sweetening   Correction of audio in post-production.

switcher   Video device that chooses which video source will be seen on the air; also refers to person who operates this equipment; technical director.

tag   A sentence at the end of a commercial that usually indicates the address of the local client.

take a level   Check the VU meters for the proper audio level.

take   Television term for the instantaneous change from one camera to another.

takes   The number of times a performance is done in order to do it properly.

taking camera   Video term that means to choose a camera to go on the air by using the switcher.

talent   An on-air broadcast performer.

talking head   Video picture that shows a person announcing who is seen from only the shoulders up; considered a boring shot because there is no movement.

talk-up   Announcing material over the instrumental beginning of a song; speaking right up to the point when the vocal part of the song starts.

tally light   Red light on camera to indicate if it is on-air.

tape cart players   Audio device that plays carts.

tape delay system   Used for call-in shows; the taping of phone calls on live programs that are replayed some seconds later to allow for elimination of unwanted words by callers.

tape room   Part of the television facility where production is recorded.

target audience   The primary audience that the station wants as its viewers or listeners.

tease   Announcement about an upcoming news story, usually with some interesting facts so that viewers will tune in to see the show.

technical center   Part of the television facility where all the electronic devices that support the rest of the studio are housed.

technical director   Person who operates the switcher.

telegraphing a movement   Indicating on-camera that you will move before you actually move.

teleprompter device   mounted on a camera that rolls the script on a television screen so the talent can read the script while looking directly at a camera.

tempo   Speed of speech.

testimonial commercial   A variation of the spokesperson commercial in which the person speaking on behalf of the product is doing so based on his or her actual use of the product.

theater of the mind   Imagination; radio broadcasters use music and sound effects to create images in the minds of the audience.

thin voice   Voice that lacks resonance; sounds weak and colorless.

thoracic cavity   The upper part of the body, the area enclosed by the chest.

three-point lighting   A common lighting pattern with a major (key) light and a minor (fill) light in front of a subject and a back light behind.

throwaway   A delivery technique in which the speaker de-emphasizes the last word or two of a sentence, making it sound unimportant.

tight board   Ability to operate an audio board so that numerous program elements are played one after the other with no dead air.

tight shot   Television term for a close-up.

time code   Electronic identification of each frame of video that indicates hours, minutes, seconds, and frames; used for editing.

time cues   Hand signals that indicate to talent the amount of time remaining in a program.

tone   The quality of sound; also a steady tone on the audio board used to check levels.

tone arm   The arm on a turntable that holds the cartridge and stylus.

tone quality   Quality of sound that is made, the timbre of the voice; affected by resonance.

top 40 Radio   format that is now referred to as contemporary hit radio (CHR).

toss   A program transition where one talent indicates to another to begin speaking. An anchor "tosses" to a field reporter.

trachea   The windpipe; tube in throat that directs the air from mouth to lungs.

track   One song on a record or CD.

traffic department   Responsible for scheduling and keeping track that all commercials have been played.

transducer   Device that converts one form of energy to another; for example, the microphone changes sound waves to electrical energy.

trash television   Local television programs that feature sex, violence, and other sensational topics; often used to boost ratings.

tripod   A three-legged stand that a television camera can be placed on.

turntable   The rotating disc of a record player on which the record is placed; a record player in a radio studio.

UC   See urban contemporary.

unidirectional   Microphone that picks up the sound in one direction only.

United Press International   UPI; former wire service that provided news and informational copy.

uplink   Term that indicates the ability of a broadcast station to send information to a satellite for distribution.

urban contemporary   Radio format that plays mostly music by black artists and other programming elements of interest to the black community.

VCR   Video cassette recorder; a type of videotape recorder that utilizes a plastic container that holds the videotape.

verbal tic   Annoying vocal habit, such as repeated use of "ya know" or "like."

video jockey   VJ; announcer who introduces music videos.

video news release (VNR)   Public relations vehicle given to news organizations in hopes of getting a news story based on information provided.

videotape recorder   Electronic device that is designed to magnetically record video and audio.

VJ   See video jockey.

vocal cords   Vocal folds located in the larynx that vibrate when air passes over them to produce sound.

vocal elements   The techniques for making a voice interesting and effective, including inflection, emphasis, pausing, rate, and phrasing.

vocal folds   Another term for vocal cords.

voice quality   Characteristic of the voice usually affected by resonance.

voice-over   Narration placed over video; announcer is not seen.

voicer   Oral report of a news story.

volume   The loudness or softness of a voice or other sound.

vowel   Speech sounds of "a," "e," "i," "o," and "u."

VTR   Video tape recorder; used as an abbreviation on television news scripts to indicate that the story has a video element.

VU   meter Volume units meter; the indicators on an audio board that show audio levels.

wild sound   Sound recorded in the field.

windpipe   Trachea.

windscreen   Covering over a microphone to eliminate unwanted noises.

wipe   Video special effect in which one picture "pushes" the other picture off the air, usually delineated by a hard line that moves across the screen.

wire service   Company that provides news and information from a central source to all subscribers or clients.

wireless mic   A microphone that sends its signal to the audio console by a small radio transmitter that is either worn or built into the microphone.

working combo   Describes a DJ who both announces and runs the board.

wowing   Distortion of sound in which pitch is varied, usually caused by irregular movement of an equipment part.

wrap   The end of a production.

zoom lens   Variable focal-length lens that can be adjusted from wide angle to telephoto on the air without interruption.

INDEX